SOUTHERN CONCERNS

ISBN: 9798869307309
E-Book ISBN: 9798869307606
This edition was formatted and prepared for Tall Men Books by George Bagby in 2024.
Cover graphics by Dora.
This book was edited in Louisiana.
tallmenbooks@gmail.com

Walter Lynwood Fleming

Southern Concerns

SHORTER WRITINGS OF WALTER LYNWOOD FLEMING

Walter Lynwood Fleming

George Bagby

Tall Men Books

Contents

Editor's Forward

Walter Lynwood Fleming of Alabama (1874-1932) was a Southern historian of merit and influence. His life's work was in the thorny fields of Southern Reconstruction, in which his *Documents Related to Reconstruction,* published several times under slightly different titles, remains the indispensable and now rare edition of the primary sources from the time. As the master of the eyewitness accounts, government reports, and Congressional testimony of Reconstruction, he was also the author of two authoritative studies of the period: *The Civil War and Reconstruction in Alabama* and *The Sequel to Appomattox,* the latter being a general history of the period. A full bibliography of Fleming's books, reviews, and contributions to other works can be found in Fletcher Green's "Walter Lynwood Fleming: Historian of Reconstruction," published in the *Journal of Southern History* in 1936.

In the hundred years of active scholarship since his death, Fleming remains unsurpassed in his familiarity with his region and period. His work paved the way for a generation of historians to write regional histories of Reconstruction. Amidst his main labors, he wrote on other themes for a variety of journals, and the African-American experience remained a lifelong interest.

Fleming was forthright in his opinions on American race relations and Washington's policies. As any reader of Lincoln's speeches understands, the Great Emancipator did not posture as an abolitionist until the final years of the War, and took every opportunity before the War to distance himself from the anti-slavery radicals of his day. Lincoln ran pledging to end the westward movement of legal slavery while also pledging to execute the law, including the fugitive slave act. Lincoln, who had consolidated the support of the Whigs, Free Soilers, Anti-Masons, and Know Nothings under his new Republican Party was an advocate of protectionism, a foe of immigration, and an ethno-nationalist who said of the Western lands, "We want them for the homes of free white people." In spite of the disordered vengeance and pillage of Reconstruction, the fringe advocacy for racial egalitarianism was never the goal of the powers of the day. Fleming's record exposes the cynical exploitation of black Americans through the rhetoric and programs of the North. It was certainly always Fleming's contention, however shocking, that white Southerners were the best possible friends and advocates of black Americans. Fleming did not assume that all group differences were due to environment, and believed that the durable social differences between white and black were a residue of nature. As George Fitzhugh foresaw, these durable inequalities, beyond the reach of social reforms, made paternalism inevitable, and would take either a personal or a bureaucratic and penal form.

Fleming's serious and considered exposition of 19th century racial liberalism is built on his clear preference of experience over theory, the latter being a frequent mask for lower motives during Reconstruction. Fleming's insistence on a realistic assessment on racial differences reveals him as a dissenter. He does not permit his interlocutors to escape the critical question of the "race problem," a phrase which both terrifies and captivates, but about which conversation was possible in that day. Once grounded in experience, the tangible made a mockery of the liberal dogma that no racial differences should exist. For the formative and successful years of the Lincolnian Empire in which the mighty planners, financiers, and dreamers of Washington, D. C. and New York City crafted the League of Nations and the so-called "Nuremburg Regime," the legal segregation of the races was the norm in the United States and the normative, European character of American law, culture, religion, and even music was assumed and assured. This was a distinct dispensation of the American regime that has been swept away with recent reforms.

Identifying the "race problem" and the legacy of cynical or hopelessly corrupt policies in the desperate years after the War, Fleming leaves his readers with the poignant question of how the races cope with the record. Fleming notes in his review of Rhodes that "the southerners were not fighting altogether for the privilege of owning negroes:" an opinion shared by the Nationalist Rhodes, specifically in the exposition of the famous Hampton Roads Conference of 1864. There, Lincoln offered Confederate Vice President A. H. Stevens terms of reunification with guarantees for slavery in spite of the Emancipation Proclamation. Lincoln and Republican moderates had appealed to Southern conservatives on similar grounds with the Crittenden Amendment before violence began. The Confederate delegation rejected Lincoln at Hampton Roads and were still resolved on independence. Fleming is always quick to defend the motives of the Southerners from allegations of the radicals who ascribed all racial tensions to them. As he says in his contention with a partisan, "Slavery is the scapegoat, and to it and to the failure of the South to hold proper views about it most complications are due." In his later reviews of the 1920's and 30's, Fleming is clear with his rejection of the egalitarians, noting that the extreme policies and corruption of the Grant era were not characteristic of American norms. In Biden's America, the establishment has rehabilitated Grant as a fore-runner of the radicalism of our own era. Fleming refers to his stable, nationalist period: what Dr. Donald Livingston terms "Lincolnian America," which was revolutionized or supplanted by the Civil Rights Regime and the new national pantheon of the 1960's.

Fleming's bete noire is not just the pretense that the Southern cause was the exclusive defense of the same institution Lincoln had pledged to preserve in his first inaugural, but the equalitarian dogmas his liberal colleagues insisted on reading into Civil War and Reconstruction policies. Fleming's contributions in his "Deportation and Colonization," "Forty Acres and a Mule," and his substan-tial "Freedman's Saving's Bank," are focused on the mainstream idea, both North and South, that racial separatism and the building of parallel institutions was the policy and goal. This dovetails with the well-known proposals and attempts of the Grant Administration to purchase Santo Domingo for the Freedmen and the more radical proposal, partially realized in the Sea Islands, of the relocation of white and black populations to "Africanize" the coastal South. Population removal and resettlement for ethnically exclusive "reservations" with a partial legal independence was literally established, not for black Americans in the South, but for the American Indians in the West, and also during the Grant Administration. Ironically, it is men like Jefferson Davis who are revealed to be more liberal by our standards, for his proximity to black Americans had made him, like most of the Southern elite, the least racially antagonistic and fearful, while also the most paternalist and hierarchical. The destruction in war of this critical and conservative American elite class meant the sudden aboli-tion of slavery, but also insured the utter collapse of the Southern industrial system and the advent of the famous systems of peonage examined in the "Re-organization of the Industrial System in Alabama." The punitive intervention of radical Republicans, ostensibly to secure the rights of the Freedmen, was a cynical cover for some for vengeance on the ex-Confederates. Fleming notes, in his *Introduction* to Lester and Wilson's work, that the resulting secret defen-sive societies and vigilante violence is a common historical phenomenon in the Western world, and "as old as history." Fleming was of the opinion that the Klan and the other vigilante organizations would not have formed without the catastrophic choice to deprive white Southerners of citizenship and to place the section under martial law during Reconstruction. He often opines that white men of low character incited racial violence through cynical and irresponsible promises to the Freedman, and this resulted in the infamous vigilantism of the period.

Fleming's sentiments were clear to his critics and colleagues. William Scroggs wrote that Fleming's "sympathies are decidedly with the South, but the work is free from bitterness or prejudice, and is on the whole as impartial an account as one can expect from any writer on this subject." Always conscious of class differences and capabilities, Fleming was particular to note the political and economic consequences of what H. L. Menken called the "vast blood-letting of the Civil War, [that] half exterminated and wholly paralyzed the old aristocracy."

This volume is a selection of Fleming's many monographs and other shorter writings of interest. One element of Fleming's bibliography has been neglected entirely in this volume, and that is his many contributions to edited volumes and encyclopedias on topics historical and biographical. Depending on interest, these essays may be collected in a second volume sometime in the future. Citation footnotes have not been included. Footnotes containing additional information have been adapted into endnotes. All of these texts are complete except Fleming's Introduction to Lester and Wilson's *Ku Klux Klan,* which included a review of two Klan documents not included in this volume.

George Bagby,
Louisiana, Spring of 2024

1

Deportation and Colonization: An Attempted Solution to the Race Problem

Deportation and colonization of the negroes as a solution of the race problem of the United States is not a modern plan. It is as old as the feeling against slavery and the prejudice against the negro race. Had the slaves been of the same race as their masters, there would have been no suggestion of deportation and colonization ; the history of the unfree white classes in medieval Europe and in colonial America shows what the solution would have been. But in regard to black slaves there was another problem besides that of status — it was that of race. Was it possible for two free races, unlike in many respects, to inhabit the same territory without racial conflict? After the emancipation of the negro race, this was the problem that had to be solved.

A majority of the people of the later colonial period and the early nineteenth century who opposed slavery believed that deportation must follow emancipation. The plan for the colonization of free negroes in tropical countries had its origin in New England. It was first publicly advocated in 1770 by the Rev. Samuel Hopkins of Newport, Rhode Island, who for several years carried on an agitation on a small scale. Considerable interest in the project was aroused, and numerous individuals who were opposed to slavery and to the presence of negroes in the American population regarded it as the proper solution of the difficulties arising from emancipation. Thomas Jefferson was, in his time, the leading advocate of foreign colonization. He believed that slavery was not a permanent institution and that the negroes when emancipated could not live in the same country with their former masters on terms of equality. In 1784 in his "Notes on Virginia" he suggested foreign colonization as a possible solution of the problem. In 1801 the Virginia legislature requested Governor Monroe to correspond with President Jefferson in regard to the purchase of lands abroad "whither persons obnoxious to the laws and dangerous to the peace of society may be removed." In reply Jefferson indorsed the plan of colonization and suggested as possible colonies the West Indies, especially San Domingo. A year later he endeavored to obtain the consent of the English authorities to receive American free negroes into the colony of Sierra Leone, and, failing in this, he tried, again also without success, to obtain from Portugal lands in Brazil. In his correspondence Jefferson took the view that the blacks must be drawn off gradually to some foreign land and there protected for a time. In 1804 the Virginia legislature suggested that he set apart a portion of Louisiana as a territory for negroes, but with this plan he was not impressed.

Out of this feeling on the part of thoughtful men grew the American Colonization Society which was developed between 1803 and 1817. The actual organization of the Society was probably hastened by the renewed demand of the Virginia legislature in 1816 that the United States should acquire land outside the United States to which free negroes could be transported. Several Southern states indorsed the objects of the Society, the principal one of which was to encourage emancipation by providing a way for the removal of the freed negroes from the country. Prominent men, among whom were Jefferson, Adams, Madison, Marshall, and Clay, supported the work of the society. Most of the members, however, were from the North and from the border slave states, few residing in the plantation states; and branches of the organization were established in all the states that had large numbers of free negroes. The senti-ment that resulted in the formation of the Colonization Society also caused Congress to provide for the return to Africa of certain classes of free negroes and slaves captured from slave traders. The Society was used by Congress as its agent, $50 being appropriated to it for each negro carried back to Africa and maintained there for one year. Under this arrangement Liberia was organized as a colony for blacks, and by 1860 about 18,000 negroes had been transported thereto. During and after the Civil War about 2000 more were carried over.

Some opposition to the Society arose in the lower South when the Northern opponents of slavery demanded that the United States government accept emancipation and deportation as a principle to be worked out as soon as possible. In 1824 the Ohio legislature suggested to the other states that the national government develop a plan of foreign colonization with a view to the emancipation and removal of all negroes, and that freedom should be given to all who at the age of twenty-one would consent to go to Liberia. This plan was indorsed by one slave state, Delaware, and six free states, Pennsylvania, Vermont, New Jersey, Indiana, Connecticut, and Massachusetts, but was disapproved by Georgia, South Carolina, Alabama, Missouri, Mississippi, and Louisiana. A few years later (1827) when the Colonization Society was asking for national aid on a large scale, the house of representatives seemed favorably inclined, and the legislature of ten states, including Missouri,

Kentucky, Delaware, and Tennessee, indorsed the request of the Society, but the states of the lower South strongly objected. In general the South was quite willing for the free negroes to be removed from the country, but objected to the use of the Society as an active anti-slavery agency.

The small numbers transported to Africa show that the Society did not and could not solve the free negro problem. For this failure there were several reasons: first, free negroes, hard as was their condition in America, seldom desired to go to Africa, and none except negroes captured from slavers could legally be forced to go; second, the work of the Society was hindered by the growth of radical abolition sentiment in the North during the second quarter of the nineteenth century. The abolitionists, to a certain extent, denied the principle upon which the Colonization Society was founded, namely, that the black race was inferior to the white and that in American society there was no place for the free blacks. Those who advocated deportation were accused of encouraging race prejudice and thus strengthening the bonds of slavery. In the lower South, on the other hand, the Society was regarded as an abolition agency. The active efforts of the abolitionists, and the introduction of the slavery question into partisan politics, weakened the Society and caused greater regard for the rights of the blacks. However, until the Civil War contracts were regularly made between the Colonization Society and the Department of the Interior for the return to Africa of negroes captured from slavers.

Few other efforts were made to colonize free negroes. Small numbers of them were sent to the Island of Trinidad, where the English employers were extremely anxious to get better trained labor than could be obtained from the natives, and a colony was also located in Hayti. In 1862, when the question of acquiring territory for negro colonies came up, Senator Doolittle asserted that President

Jackson had once proposed in a cabinet meeting to purchase land in Mexico for colonizing free negroes.

The free negroes were not content with the position offered them in the Northern states before the Civil War. A national emigration convention of colored people held in Cleveland, Ohio, in 1854 issued an address giving the views of the blacks in regard to the situation in America and stating that there was hope for the race only in a new country. "No people can be free," they said, "who themselves do not constitute an essential part of the ruling element of the country in which they live. ... A people to be free must be their own rulers"; in America the blacks, slave and free alike, would always be subject to the white man, and "the white race will only respect those who oppose their usurpation and acknowledge as equals those who will not submit to their rule." The position of the free negro in the North, the address stated, was precarious; often they were kidnapped and sold as slaves to the South. Some friends of the blacks wanted to see them absorbed into the white race, on terms of equality, but this was impossible. Were master and slave of the same race, laws might easily destroy class differences, but such was not the case ; the negro was set apart by his color, which the law could not change, and this marked him for the prejudice of the whites. Besides, the race should not be destroyed; it had a mission, for "in the true principles of morals, correctness of thought, religion, and law or civil government, there is no doubt but that the black race will yet instruct the world."

The Cleveland convention declared that sooner or later a struggle would arise between the colored and white races for control of the world; the colored races were twice as numerous as their overlording whites and would not much longer submit to the rule of the minority; there was no hope of justice from the white race, which for 2000 years had been encroaching upon the colored races. In order to attain national existence and to be ready for the great conflict, the convention declared that a proper home for the race must be found, a center for organization. And such a place could be found only where the black race was in the majority and constituted the ruling element. The part of the world best suited to this purpose was tropical America, — the West Indies, Central America, and part of South America, — where, it was said, the whites were weak and worthless, where a negro was regarded as their equal, and where as a citizen he was often preferred by the authorities, owing to the jealousy of outside interference in Latin-American affairs and the consequent desire of the natives "to put a check to European presumption and insufferable Yankee intrusion and impudence." The members of the convention were certain that the blacks could organize and maintain a national existence in tropical America. They had their own racial merits and in addition much of the civilization of the whites ; and they had never failed to thrive whether in freedom or slavery. In conclusion the Address declared: "This is a fixed fact in the zodiac of the political heavens, that the black and colored people are the stars which must ever most conspicuously twinkle in the firmament of this division of the western hemisphere."

The Address is interesting as showing the opinions of many of the free negro leaders, and of the whites who advised them; it also shows that, perhaps because of the notoriety caused by the filibustering attempts of the time, tropical America, rather than Liberia, was being considered as the future refuge of free blacks.

Before the Civil War it is doubtful if any considerable number of Northern anti-slavery people, except the radical abolitionists, would have advocated emancipation without deportation. To the Southern non-slave holder, who had little sympathy with slavery, the free negro was nevertheless a bugbear, slavery only an attempted solution of the race problem, and if slavery were done away with, the negro must go. As evidence of the non-slave holder's dislike of the negroes, Senator Doolittle, during the debates of 1862 on deportation, declared, apparently upon authority, that Andrew Johnson, when governor of Tennessee in 1856, was called upon by the non-slaveholders in a certain district for arms with which to repress a threatened rising of the slaves. Investigation disclosed the fact that they really hoped to exterminate the slaves, and to protect the latter Johnson had to call out the militia.

In his opinions Lincoln was representative of both Northern and Southern anti-slavery sentiment. Born in Kentucky and living in a border state of the North, he understood better than most Northerners the feelings of the non-slaveholders of the South. While opposing the extension of slavery to new territories, lie did not, until forced to it as a war measure, favor abolition in the slave states. It was the opinion that the physical differences of black and white were so great that the two races could never live together in harmony on terms of equality. During the debates with Douglas he said that his first impulse, if the negro should be freed, would be to send them to Liberia. "Let us be brought to believe it is morally right and at the same time favorable to or at least not against our interest to transfer the African to his native clime, and we shall find a way to do it however great the task may be." Lincoln never abandoned these views.

The advocates of gradual emancipation realized that in order to meet the objection to free negroes, some practical plan of procedure must be offered. Deportation and colonization outside of the United States was the usual plan suggested. During the '50's another argument was offered in support of this measure: it was that American free negro colonies in the tropics would serve to extend American civilization and American commerce. In 1857 Horace Greeley in the *Tribune* said: "It is obvious that in this great body of civilized negroes we have ... a most powerful and essential instrument toward extending ourselves, our ideas, our civilization, our commerce, industry, and political institutions through all the torrid zone." A correspondent in the New York *Courier and Inquirer*, July 23, 1857, voiced a like sentiment when he wrote:

"But the great consideration is that which men appear resolved to conceal from themselves. It shows us that this negro race must necessarily take possession of the tropical regions ... to which they may be transported. They

will expel the whites by the same law of nature which has given the blacks exclusive possession of corresponding latitudes in Africa. [We may hope that the South will want to give up slavery. If so the West Indies and South America are the places for the negroes] ... It is therefore of the highest importance that those regions be kept open for that contingency."

The Republicans of the border states and the West were, before 1860, strongly in favor of deportation. The most prominent advocates of this plan were Montgomery Blair, F. P. Blair, and J. R. Doolittle. Their letters contain many references to the colonization scheme. For example, in 1859 F. P. Blair wrote to Doolittle:

"I am delighted that you are pressing the colonization scheme in your campaign speeches. I touched upon it three or four times in my ad- dresses in Minnesota and if I am any judge of effect it is the finest theme with which to get at the hearts of the people and [it] can be defended with success at all points. ... I made it the culminating point and inevitable result of Republican doctrine."

Montgomery Blair wrote to Doolittle about the same date that the North should demand that the emancipated negroes who had been sent to the North by their former owners should be colonized by the general government

"Where they can have political rights and where their manhood would have the stimulant of high objects to develop it, ... it would rally the North as one man to our ranks. It would do more than ten thousand speeches to define accurately our objects and disabuse the minds of the great body of the Southern people of the issue South that the Republicans wish to set negroes free among them to be their equals and consequently their rulers when they are numerous. This is the only point needing elucidation and comprehension by the Southern people to make us as strong at the South as

at the North. If we can commit our party distinctly to this I will undertake for Maryland in 1860."

But this phase of the anti-slavery attack had too short a time in which to develop. The Civil War began and the "contrabands " at once became a burden upon the government and a problem for the rulers. The deportation solution was again proposed by such men as President Lincoln and Senators Blair, Doolittle, and Pomeroy, by anti-slavery unionists of the border states, and numerous other individuals. In his first message, December 8, 1861, Lincoln suggested that provision be made for the colonization of freed negroes in a congenial climate. In order to do this he stated that territory would have to be acquired. And in regard to colonization and the purchase of territory lie asked "does not the expediency amount to absolute necessity?" A week later Senator Harlan of Iowa introduced a bill in the senate authorizing the President to acquire the necessary territory. It was referred to the committee on territories, but at the time nothing was done.

Early in 1862 the matter of deportation was again brought up in connection with the abolition of slavery in the District of Columbia. By the act of April 16, 1861, which abolished slavery in the Federal District, an appropriation of $100,000 was made to be expended under President Lincoln's direction in colonizing such negroes of the District of Columbia as might wish to go to Liberia, Hayti, and other black men's countries. The expense was not to exceed $100 each. Lincoln did not think this a sufficient sum, and he had another bill introduced which became law on July 16, 1862. By this law $500,000 was appropriated for colonization purposes in addition to the $100,000 previously voted. The next day, July 17, 1862, another act was approved which authorized the President to colonize abroad the negroes made free by the confiscation acts. The proceeds from confiscated property were to be turned into the Treasury to replace the appropriations made for colonization.

Lincoln and many of his advisers believed that the proposal to separate the races would make many who had been hesitating willing to accept an emancipation policy; even the Confederate nonslave holders would be impressed by it, they thought. This feeling is reflected in the law of June 7, 1862, providing for the sale of lands in the South by the direct tax commissioners and the setting aside of one-fourth of the proceeds raised in each state to be paid after the war to that state to aid in colonizing the blacks.

Lincoln was not content with these slight inducements to emancipation, and he had another bill introduced by Representative White of Indiana, who explained that the purpose was to assist emancipation of slaves and the colonization of the freedmen. By this measure it was proposed to appropriate $180,000,000 to purchase the 600,000 slaves belonging to unionist owners in the border states and $20,000,000 to be used in colonizing the negroes thus made free, "beyond the limits of the United States." White declared that $20,000,000 thus expended would repay the nation "a hundred fold in commerce." Evidently he had in mind a negro colonial system in the American tropics. The bill was favorably reported from the committee, but did not become a law, probably because of other colonization measures enacted about the same time.

THE COLONIZATION OF PEOPLE OF AFRICAN DESCENT.

Interview With President Lincoln.

SPEECH OF THE PRESIDENT.

He Holds that the White and Black Races Cannot Dwell Together.

He Urges Intelligent Colored Men to Exert Themselves for Colonization.

He Suggests Central America as the Colony.

WASHINGTON, Thursday, July 14, 1862.

White also made, on July 16, 1862, an elaborate report as chairman of the committee on emancipation and colonization. This committee had been appointed pursuant to a resolution of the house, April 7, 1862, which is said to have been framed by Mr. Lincoln. The committee was directed to report upon three matters: (1)

emancipation in the border states and Tennessee, (2) the practicability of colonizing freed negroes, and (3) whether the United States should aid emancipation and colonization. The committee reported that of the 1,200,000 slaves in the border states about half had been confiscated, or removed to the South, or were in refugee camps, while the other half belonged to "loyal" owners and should be paid for by the government, emancipated and colonized. The committee explained at length the position of the border and Southern states in regard to emancipation; stated that much of the opposition to emancipation was clue to a fear of too close association of races and consequent possible intermixture and to the feeling of the whites, especially in the border and free states, and declared that emancipation would result in economic competition of the races. It was the committee's opinion that

"Apart from the antipathy which nature has ordained, the presence of a race among us who cannot and ought not to be admitted to our social and political privileges will be a perpetual source of injury and inquietude to both. This is a question of color and is unaffected by the relation of master and slave. The introduction of the negro, whether bound or free, into the same field of labor with the white man is the opprobrium of the latter; and we cannot believe that thousands of non-slaveholding citizens in the rebellious states are fighting to continue the negro within our limits in a state of vassalage, but more probably from a vague apprehension that he is to become their competitor in his own right. [We believe that the white man can furnish all our labor and that] the highest interest of the white races . . . requires that the whole country be held and occupied by those races alone. . . . The most formidable difficulty which lies in the way of emancipation in most if not in all the slave states is the belief which obtains especially among those who own no slaves, that if the negroes shall become free they must still continue in our midst, and ... in some measure be made equal

to the Anglo-Saxon race. . . . The belief [in the inferiority of the negro race] ... is indelibly fixed upon the public mind. The differences of the races separate them as with a wall of fire; there is no instance in history where liberated slaves have _ lived in harmony with their former masters when denied equal rights — but the Anglo-Saxon will never give his consent to negro equality, and the recollections of the former relation of master and slave will be perpetuated by the changeless color of the Ethiop's skin. [Emancipation therefore without colonization could offer little to the negro race. A revolution of the blacks might result, but only to their undoing.] To appreciate and understand this difficulty it is only necessary for one to observe that in proportion as the legal barriers established by slavery have been removed by emancipation the prejudice of caste becomes stronger and public opinion more intolerant to the negro race."

To avoid these difficulties, to convince the poor whites that emancipation would not harm them and to give the negro an opportunity, the committee recommended colonization of freedmen in Central and South America and on the Islands of the Gulf of Mexico — a policy which would "restore to the tropics its own children." In those lands, it was declared, the whites had degenerated but the negroes had thrived. Moreover, the North American negroes had become civilized; they had learned to work ; they had our language, our religion, and many of our habits and customs, so that "no one should doubt their capacity to maintain a free and independent government under the guidance and patronage of our Republic." The sections of Central and South America considered by the committee were Yucatan, Cozumel, Venezuela, and Chiriqui (now Panama), a province in New Granada (Colombia) near Costa Rica. In New Granada large tracts of land had been granted to the Chiriqui Improvement Company, an American corporation, for colonization purposes.

Besides solving the problem of emancipation and establishing the future of the negro race, the committee believed that other benefits would result from tropical colonization. First, the governments of the Latin-American states would be more stable if under the supervision of the United States. Second, into the former slave states white immigrants would come, and free labor would thus be substituted for slave-labor, the evil economic effects of which might be observed by comparing Kentucky and Ohio, Massachusetts and South Carolina. Third, a considerable commerce would be carried on with these black colonies, populated by 4,000,000 negroes desirous of obtaining the manufactured goods of the United States, thus giving an advantage to American trade similar to that given to England by her colonics. And this commerce would be needed after the war, for many military industries would then cease and for years the trade with the ruined Southern states would be worth but little.

The views as to race relations exhibited in the above report were, and still are to a certain extent, the views of the average white man living in contact with Negroes; they were not the views of the radical abolitionists nor of the great slaveholders. Had the Republican party openly advocated such a policy from 1850 to 1860, the non-slaveholding whites of the South would never have supported and forced the secession movement. The committee was composed of men from the border states. Besides White of Indiana, the chairman, Blair of Missouri, Lehman of Pennsylvania, Fisher of Delaware, Whaley of West Virginia, Casey of Kentucky, Clemens of Tennessee, and Leary of Maryland were members. These were types of the border state men who supported the war, disliked the radical abolitionists, and who during the Reconstruction controversy sometimes became radical Democrats.

To the Interior Department was intrusted the execution of the colonization laws referred to above. Secretary Smith employed a Rev James Mitchell, who later proved to be very troublesome as an agent of emigration," and he set up an "emigration office."' The public printer prepared for the use of the department 5000 copies of a publication called "The White and African Races," no copy of which can now be found. As soon as the appropriations for colonization were passed, numerous offers were made to the government by individuals and companies desirous of obtaining grants of money for transporting negroes, or by those who wanted to obtain laborers. The President of Guatemala offered several thousand acres of his own land for an experiment in colonization. To F. P. Blair, Jr., he sent the following proposition each negro family should have free of rent a town lot of two to six acres and timber for fences and houses; farm lands would be rented to the negroes at reasonable rates or they would be hired for $12 to $14 a month; supplies would be furnished until they could produce their own.

EMANCIPATION.

The American Colonization Society offered to transport the freedmen to Liberia and support them for six months for $100 each. Lincoln asked the authorities of this Society to submit a plan for carrying the blacks to Africa, and through them agents were sent to Liberia to investigate conditions with a view to settling a large colony on the St. John River. Lincoln and Secretary Smith finally accepted the proposition of the Society to transport negroes at $100 per head, but only a few hundred could be persuaded to go. Officers of the Society were authorized by the Secretary of the Interior to go to Fortress Monroe to procure negroes, but Secretary Stanton, who did not approve the deportation plan, refused to allow the officers to go within the military lines, so that their operations were confined to the District of Columbia.

Numerous other propositions were made to the Interior Department. A New York association offered to transport negroes to San Domingo for $20 apiece, give to each fifty acres of land, and guarantee regular employment. Another New York company desired to sell its land in Costa Rica to the United States government. A Mr. Burr offered fifteen square miles in British Honduras for $75,000. Several offers also came from South America. The President of Hayti, thinking that some money could be made out of the business, sent an agent to the District of Columbia, who found sixty negroes willing to go. The Haytian government promised fifteen acres of land to each head of a family and six acres to each unmarried man, with guarantee of political rights. From 1861 to 1864 several independent colonies went to Hayti, but they were not assisted by the United States government.

The Dutch minister offered to make a contract with the United States government to carry laborers to Surinam, but his proposition was refused. The officers of tramp steamers going to Australia wanted to take negroes from Hilton Head in South Carolina and Fernandina in Florida, but they were not allowed to do so. Both the Maryland and the Pennsylvania Colonization Societies applied for assistance, which was refused on the ground that only District of Columbia negroes and those freed by the confiscation acts could be transported at public expense. Eli Thayer, of Kansas emigration fame, planned to settle a negro colony in Florida, but it did not materialize. Hiram Ketchum, of the American West India Company of New York, was permitted to take negroes to San Domingo to raise cotton, and a like privilege was granted to the British Honduras Company.

To the Danish government permission seems to have granted to take volunteer laborers to the sugar plantations of St. Croix on the following terms: contracts to be made for one year, at the end of which time the laborers might change employers; nine hours of work a day was to be given ; laborers were to have garden "patches"; and no whipping was to be allowed except upon sentence of an officer. Charles W. Kimbell, formerly United States consul to Guadaloupe, desired similar privileges and asked to be sent to Martinique and Guadaloupe to "make the necessary arrangements for the reception of sixty or eighty thousand emigrants free of all charges of transportation." In commenting upon these propositions, Secretary Smith said : "The act of April 16 [1862] may be regarded but as the commencement of a great national scheme which may ultimately relieve the United States of the surplus colored population." None of the parties above mentioned except the American Colonization Society had the direct financial support of the United States government. They carried out some negroes — how many it is impossible to say, for no records were kept, but certainly not many hundred.

The United States government, on its own account, made two distinct efforts to settle negroes outside of the United States — one colony was to be planted in Central America and another on Isle a Vache, or Cow Island, near the southwest coast of Hayti. President

Lincoln was most interested in the proposed Central American settlement and used his influence with Congress and with the leading free negroes to secure a colony there. He brought the matter up frequently in cabinet meetings, but most of the members were opposed. On August 14, 1862, a delegation of negroes was invited to see Lincoln in regard to the proposed Central American settlement. Colonization was necessary, he told them plainly, because the blacks and whites were so different that each suffered from contact with the other; in this country the negroes were nowhere given equal rights, so let them go where they would have equality; except for slavery there would have been no war, and further trouble might be expected if the races remained together; for a few leading negroes, living in comfort, to oppose colonization was selfish; they ought to sacrifice their own comfort for the good of the race; if the free negroes would go away, the whites would be willing to emancipate all; the more capable negroes ought to go first, not the newly freed; and Liberia was a good place, though at present he (Lincoln) was thinking of Central America, where the white people had no objection to the blacks and where the blacks could hope for equality.

The border state Congressmen were assured by the President that if their states would emancipate the negroes, plenty of room could be found for them in Central America. Doolittle and Pomeroy began active efforts to find negroes for a colony, and Pomeroy issued an address to the negroes of the United States advising them to accept the President's suggestions. In a letter to Doolittle, to whom he gave credit for the passage of the colonization laws, Pomeroy gave his views on the matter. Others, he said, wanted only freedom for the blacks; he himself wanted "rights and enjoyments for them." "Can he secure them with the white man ? — what are the teachings of two hundred and fifty years of history! Only this, that the free colored men of the free states are doomed to a life of servile labor ... no hope of elevation. ... I am for the negro's securing his rights and his nationality in the clime of his nativity on the soil of the tropics. . . . Nothing will restore this Union but a probable solution of the problem — what shall be the destiny of the colored race on this continent?"

At first Lincoln was anxious to purchase territory for settlement in order that the United States government might exercise control over the negro colonies. But he was prevented from doing this in Central America by the Clayton-Bulwer treaty, which prohibited the United States from exercising control over any part of Central America. When A. W. Thompson of the Chiriqui Improvement Company, indorsed by Pomeroy, offered to colonize negroes in Chiriqui province, New Granada, Lincoln wished to accept the offer. Thompson claimed to have control of 2,000,000 acres on the Isthmus beyond the boundary of Central America, i.e. below Costa Rica, and thus not subject to the terms of the Clayton-Bulwer treaty. The land contained some coal deposits, and Thompson was anxious to secure a contract to supply the navy with coal.

Gideon Welles, Secretary of the Navy, wrote in his diary that on September 11, 1862, Senator Pomeroy's scheme for deporting negroes to Chiriqui came up for discussion in the President's cabinet. Welles was opposed to Thompson's project and he believed that Pomeroy had a financial interest in it. Under date of September 26, 1862, Welles recorded that at several recent cabinet meetings the subject of deportation had been discussed. In fact, he stated that it had been under discussion almost from the beginning of the administration. "The President was in earnest about the matter, wished to send the negroes out of the country. Smith, with the Thompsons, urged and stimulated him and they were as importunate with me as the President." Lincoln, Blair, and Smith favored the Chiriqui scheme, while Welles, who pronounced it "a fraud and a cheat," with Chase, Stanton, and Bates, opposed it, the latter only because Thompson's title to the land was disputed. On September 23, Lincoln asked each member of his cabinet to consider seriously the subject of acquiring territory to which the negroes might be deported. He "thought it essential to provide an asylum for a race which we had emancipated, but which could never be recognized or admitted to be our equals." Blair and Bates were in favor of compulsory deportation, while the other members of the cabinet believed that voluntary emigration would solve the problem.

Lincoln, however, had accepted the offer of Senator Pomeroy to supervise the work of colonization without charge, and a contract was made with Thompson on September 12, 1862, so framed as to safeguard the rights of the negroes. It contained the following provisions: Pomeroy or some other agent of the President was to investigate conditions and supervise the settlement; Thompson was to be responsible for the conduct of the colonists, and the United States was not to be compromised with New Granada; equality of citizenship was to be secured for the blacks; Thompson was to give land with good titles to the negroes — twenty acres to each adult male, forty acres to the head of a family with five children, and eighty acres to each head of family with more than five children; the United States would pay the costs of surveying the lands, and as fast as the land should be settled the government would pay $1 per acre for not more than 100,000 acres, thirty per cent of the payments to go to Thompson and seventy per cent to be used in making roads and wharves; furthermore, when Pomeroy should report that one settlement had been made, then the United States would advance Thompson $50,000 to aid in the development of coal mines, this sum to be repaid in coal for the use of the United States navy.

To Pomeroy was given control of the expedition and its finances. Secretary Smith instructed him that his expenses, but no salary, would be paid, that he was authorized to organize the colony and supervise it, and that if he found Chiriqui unsuited, he might take the negroes elsewhere, though not to Guatemala or Salvador, which had raised vigorous objections to negro colonization. The Treasury Department immediately placed $25,000 at the disposal of Pomeroy. During the month of September, 1862, he paid $14,000 of this amount to Thompson, and on April 4, 1864, he paid Thompson and W. E. Gaylord $8732.37, this being the remainder of the $25,000. He himself had expended about $2300. Secretary Seward sent circulars to the Central American states and to England, France, Denmark, and the Netherlands, — countries which had tropical colonies, - inviting negotiations and suggestions with respect to colonization. From the Central American governments came prompt responses: they wanted no negro colonies which would be under any sort of control by the United States, and most of them objected to any kind of negro colonization. In October Pomeroy wrote to Doolittle: "I have 13,700 applicants. I have selected of them 500 for a pioneer party," but Seward, he said, had stopped the colonization on account of the attitude of the governments in Central America.

Professor Joseph Henry of the Smithsonian Institution helped to put an end to the Chiriqui scheme by declaring that the coal on Thompson's property was worthless, and the Central American states not only protested against colonization, but denied the legality of Thompson's title to the land. So ended the attempt to settle negroes in Central America. What became of the $25,000 is not known. Pomeroy 's accounts had not been settled in 1870. He seems to have lost Lincoln's confidence, and there is no evidence that many negroes were sent to Chiriqui.

The colonization on Isle a Vache promised to be more successful than the Central American attempt. Of several propositions to carry negroes to Hayti, Lincoln preferred that of Bernard Kock (or Koch), who had leased Isle a Vache from the Haytian government for twenty years. The island was about twelve miles from Aux Cayes on the mainland, contained about one hundred square miles, had good soil for cotton culture, and was not subject to epidemics. On December 31, 1862, Lincoln, anxious to get the colonization experiment started, made a contract with Kock to carry 5000 negroes to his island for $50 per head. Kock was to secure from the Haytian government a guarantee of equal rights for the blacks, furnish them houses, gardens, and food, build churches and schools, and give them employment under white superintendents at wages ranging from $4 to $10 a month. Kock took this contract to New York and Boston capitalists and asked for financial support. He proposed to carry 500 negroes out at once, and to raise in 1863 a thousand bales of sea island cotton which would be worth at the prices then prevailing nearly a million dollars. The outlay, he thought, need not be more than $70,000. The capital was promised, several hundred negroes were ready to go, a ship was chartered, and supplies collected at Fortress Monroe. But the opponents of negro colonization now asserted that Kock was in league with Admiral Semmes to abduct and reenslave the negroes and that he was of doubtful character, consequently Lincoln canceled the contract.

Certain New York capitalists, Jerome, Forbes, and Tuckerman, who had subscribed to the Kock company, were so impressed with the scheme that they purchased the Haytian lease and then sought to obtain a contract from the government similar to that made with Kock. Usher, who had succeeded Smith as Secretary of the Interior, was assured that the contractors were reliable men, and the contract was made by him with Forbes and Tuckerman on April 6, 1863. By this agreement the negroes were to be looked after for five years by the contractors, and upon proof of successful settlement the United States was to pay $50 per head for each negro colonist. The contractors intended to send Kock out as governor, and the money was furnished by Jerome, who, for some reason, was in bad repute with the government. But of the connection between the two men and the contractors the government authorities knew nothing at the time. Tuckerman, in 1886, asserted that Lincoln pressed the contract upon Forbes and himself, urged that they "as a personal favor" accept it and help him carry out the plan which he had so much at heart. Unwillingly, he says, they agreed to ship the first 500 negroes, for whom pro- vision had already been made.

An expedition was started at once for Isle a Vache. The *Ocean Ranger* left Fortress Monroe with about 500 negroes, "the poor refugees," according to Tuckerman, "flocking on board, shouting hallelujahs and in some instances falling on their knees in thanksgiving for the promised blessings in store for them." Kock, the governor or manager, with several white superintendents, accompanied the negroes to the island. On the voyage the negroes were not well cared for, smallpox broke out, and twenty or thirty persons died, among them several of the whites ; the blacks had to purchase drinking water from the ship's steward, and the food was bad. They were landed during the rainy season, but found no houses and but little lumber out of which to construct them, and were forced to build rude huts for shelter. Kock brought no supplies, no seeds, and no implements, but, being charged with the discipline of the colony, he brought handcuffs, leg chains, and stocks. He proved to be despotic and incompetent, and some of the negroes were maimed for life by his harsh discipline. He managed to get all the coin money that the negroes had, and paid them for their work only in paper money which he had printed. The exasperated blacks finally drove him off. When his employers, who cared only for the promised one thousand bales of cotton, heard of this, they stopped the meager supplies which they had been sending, and left the negroes to shift for themselves. Tuckerman's account (1886) does not agree with the above, which is based on the records of the Interior Department. He says that "no sooner were the survivors landed and the necessity for manual labor on their part apparent than the lowest characteristics of the negro — indolence, discontent, insubordination, and finally revolt — prevailed. Mistaking liberty for license, they refused to work and raised preposterous demands for luxuries to which they were wholly unaccustomed during servitude." He further states that discontent was fostered by the natives, who wished the colonists to desert and become Haytian subjects. This" we refused to allow the freedmen to do."

To Lincoln the failure of this enterprise was a bitter disappointment. Soon after the *Ocean Ranger* had sailed for Hayti the State Department learned that Bernard Kock was the prime mover in the expedition; and that Leonard Jerome had furnished the capital. Secretary Usher at once informed Tuckerman and Forbes that they might count upon no more contracts, for the connection of Kock and Jerome with the undertaking was regarded as an act of bad faith to the United States. From Confederate newspapers Lincoln learned that the negroes had been neglected, and he caused remonstrances to be made to the contractors. Jerome now came forward and avowed his intention to expend no more money for the negroes. Usher tried to hold Tuckerman and Forbes to their contract, but soon found that they were acting only for Jerome. He charged Tuckerman and Forbes with acting in bad faith throughout the transaction and informed them that no money would be paid until the contract was carried out. To Jerome he wrote: "Candor induces me to inform you that when your name was proposed as one of the contracting parties by Mr. Tuckerman I declined to have it inserted [in the contract] because I did not think that your avocation and habits of life would induce you to persevere in the enterprise if it should prove disastrous and unprofitable."

Reports of bad conditions in the colony continued to come in, and Lincoln was troubled by the accounts of the sufferings of the negroes. Finally D. C. Donahue of Greencastle, Indiana, was sent in October, 1863, to investigate conditions on the island. In his report to the Secretary of the Interior, he described the situation of the blacks as deplorable and their treatment by Kock and his men as inhuman. Instead of preparing to care for the negroes for five years, as they had agreed, the contractors had already ceased to furnish supplies.[2] Donahue found 378 negroes out of about 500 who had been carried from Fortress Monroe, and for several months supplied them at the expense of the United States government. He thought that the principal cause of the failure was mismanagement, for the soil was good and cotton could be profitably raised. Then, too, the Haytians were opposed to the colony. Kock had not received permission to colonize the island, nor had anything been done to secure citizenship for the colonists. Another difficulty in the way of successful colonization lay in the fact that the American blacks were quite different from the Haytians in language, customs, religion, and ideas of government. The negroes wanted to return to the United States, and the Haytians were anxious for them to go. It was Donahue's opinion that a successful colony could not then be developed in Hayti.

Reluctantly Lincoln abandoned his second serious attempt at colonizing the blacks, and on February 8, 1864, he requested Stanton to send a ship to bring the Cow Island colonists back to the refugee camps in the District of Columbia. For some reason practically all of the colonization work had been done more or less in secrecy. When the Ocean Ranger took the five hundred negroes from Fortress Monroe to Hayti there were few who knew what was being done, and hence there arose the widespread rumor that the negroes were simply kidnapped and turned over to the Confederates. Even more secret was the bringing back of the colonists. The ship *Maria L. Day* was chartered at New York and provisioned as for a voyage to Aspinwall to take on five hundred United States troops returning from California. Captain Edward L. Hartz was placed in charge, with directions to proceed toward Aspinwall and with sealed orders which he was to open when he reached 20° north latitude. He found 293 negroes on the island under Donahue's care; the others had died or wandered away. Clothes were distributed to the destitute, and on March 4, 1864, the return trip was begun. On March 20 the colonists were landed at Alexandria, Virginia, and the venture was at an end. For several years the contractors made efforts to collect their expenses from the United States government but did not succeed.

Though Lincoln still believed in the necessity for colonization, the failure of the Cow Island colony prejudiced the blacks against such attempts and strengthened the efforts of those whites who now opposed colonization and favored the incorporation of the negroes into the American population. In December, 1862, Lincoln had stated in his message that the failure of the Central American scheme had disappointed many negroes who wanted to leave the United States, and that only two places were left to which they might go — Liberia and Hayti — but that they were unwilling to go to these places. Now, after the failure of the Kock expedition, Hayti was out of the question.

The Secretary of the Interior, in December, 1863, reported that the negroes were no longer willing to leave the United States, and that they were needed in the army. For these reasons he thought that they should not be forcibly deported. Referring to some attempts to settle negroes in the North, he declared that "much prejudice has been manifested throughout most of the free states in regard to the introduction of colored persons," yet he thought it might be possible to use them in constructing the Pacific railways, where labor was needed and where there would be no objection to them.

In Congress opinion was turning against colonization, and in March, 1864, Senator Wilkinson introduced a bill to repeal all measures making appropriations for deportation of negroes. He declared that these attempts had been "extremest folly" and that the results had been "hazardous and disgraceful." On July 2, 1864, Lincoln signed an act repealing all the laws relating to negro colonization.

The Interior Department gradually discontinued its "emigration office." In May, 1863, Usher attempted to get rid of Rev. James Mitchell, whom Lincoln had appointed as "agent of emigration," but Mitchell continued in office for a year longer. Usher complained that Mitchell, without permission, corresponded in the name of the department on emigration matters. He was forbidden to do this, and the records of his office were called for. These he refused to give up, and he was discharged at the end of June, 1864. For months he besieged the Secretary of the Interior for an extra year's salary, but finally dropped out of the records in 1865. When, in 1870, the House called for the accounts of the emigration agents, it was found that $38,329.93 had been expended by them. Of this $25,000 had been paid to Senator Pomeroy, and the remainder had been expended by other agents. The American Colonization Society returned in 1864 the $25,000 that it had received in 1863.

After the failure of foreign colonization the advocates of separation of the races suggested that sections of the South be set apart for the negroes. Some thought that South Carolina and Georgia should be given them; others that the lower Mississippi valley should be cleared of whites and divided among the ex-slaves; a third proposition was that in each Southern state a section should be set apart for the blacks. Senator Lane of Kansas strongly advocated a bill to set apart for the blacks that part of Texas bounded by the Rio Grande, the Gulf, the Colorado River of Texas, and the Llano Estacado. Lane thought that the negroes should be forced to go to this region at their own expense. The United States might use, he said, the $600,000 already appropriated to purchase titles, might carry colored troops out there and discharge them, and then send their families to them. Thus would be formed the nucleus of a negro state. He stated the following reasons for favoring colonization: the North was opposed to the negro as a laborer and wanted no mixture of races; in the South the whites would hate the ex-slaves whom they had so mistreated; the sentiment in favor of negro rights, now so strong, would in time die out and the negro would be left with no chance for social or political equality; at the end of the war there would be a surplus of labor, due to the discontinuance of war industries and to the discharge of soldiers; it would be impossible to give to the negroes the lands of their masters and to secure quiet titles, for even if the Southern men were killed, the women and children would remain, and, after amnesty, would hold the lands. "I had hoped," he said, "the time should come when the foot prints of the white man should not be found on the soil of South Carolina," but in this matter the best interest of the blacks must be considered. Lane's bill was favorably reported but did not become a law.

President Lincoln continued to believe that deportation was the only permanent solution of the problem. General B. F. Butler, who had had considerable experience in dealing with negroes in Virginia and Louisiana, was called into consultation by Lincoln soon after the Hampton Roads Conference. Butler says that Lincoln asked him to report upon the feasibility of using the United States navy, which would soon be free from war service, to deport the negroes. The President told Butler that he feared more trouble between the North and the South "unless we can get rid of the negroes," especially the negro soldiers, who, he thought, were certain to give trouble; that the Southern whites would be disarmed at the end of the war while the negroes either had arms or could easily get them from the North ; and that a race war might result. The question of the colored troops, Lincoln said, troubled him exceedingly. He believed that all of them should be deported to some fertile country of the tropics. Butler, a few days afterward, made an oral report in which he made the famous assertion which is still quoted: that all the vessels in America could not carry away the blacks as fast as negro babies were born. However, in order to dispose of the negro troops, Butler proposed that he take them to Panama and use them in digging the canal. One-third of them could labor on the canal, one-third could raise food, and the other one- third could provide shelter, etc. The wives and children of the soldiers could be sent to them. Butler states that Lincoln was impressed by this proposition and asked him to confer with Seward to see if foreign complications were to be feared. Butler wrote out a report which he carried to Seward, who, knowing Lincoln's interest in the problem of the negro troops, promised to examine the matter carefully. But the murder of Lincoln and the wounding of Seward put an end to this plan.

While few practical attempts were made to separate the races, yet much opinion in the North was in favor of it, until the end of the war. Especially was this true of the army, which to the last cared little for the negro per se. This feeling that the blacks should be set apart is shown in the regulations made from 1862 to 1865 by officials controlling the blacks in the Mississippi valley and on the Atlantic coast, which almost invariably prohibited whites from entering the black communities. Sherman in his famous Field Order No. 15, setting aside the coasts of Georgia and South Carolina for the negroes, directed that no whites were to be allowed to live in the negro districts.

Since the close of the war there has been much discussion of deportation and colonization, but very little effort has been made to colonize. The American Colonization Society kept up its work after the war, but could get only a few hundred negroes a year. Bishop Turner of the African Methodist Episcopal Church was for years the leading exponent of the colonization idea, and while his views have been indorsed in theory by many of his race, relatively few of them have gone back to Africa. After the failure of the "Exodus" movement of 1879-1882 to Kansas there was strong sentiment among the negroes in favor of "separate national existence." The "United Transatlantic Society," organized during the '80's by one of the "Exodus" leaders, reflected this feeling but had slight results. One thing that has prejudiced the negroes against going to Liberia or to other proposed places of settlement is the fact that many swindlers have taken advantage of the various colonization schemes to defraud the negroes by collecting passage money from them and giving them fraudulent tickets. Negroes who went to Liberia have come back with bad reports of the country. The negro and the Southern white, each in a way, favor colonization. Some negroes would be glad to go if they were sure of doing as well in Africa as in the United States, while every white man would be glad to have the entire black race deported — except his own laborers. Any organized emigration scheme invariably meets more or less forcible resistance from the employers of black labor.

Note:

1. Lincoln in December, 1862, in proposing compensated emancipation, stated, first, that he strongly favored colonization and, second, that free negro labor would not displace white labor or lower wages. The American Freedmen's Inquiry Commission felt it necessary in 1863-1864 to declare that emancipation would not flood the North with negroes, but that those already in the North would go South. This is the tone of much of the emancipation literature in 1862-1865.

2. On the other hand, Tuckerman stated in 1886: "Shiploads of provisions and other necessities were forwarded and instructions of the most concise and liberal nature were given for the maintenance and support of the families until they could be returned to the

United States under proper protection. All this involved great delay and . . . eight months of anxiety and expense on our part." The loss, he said, was about $90,000, which Congress refused to pay.

2

Immigration to the Southern States

At the present time a paper on immigration to the South must be a study of conditions and tendencies rather than of definite results.

Until the early 80's the southern people desired no immigration either from the North or from foreign countries. There were many reasons for this sentiment. Before the Civil war the agitation of the slavery question served to unite the south- ern people in a general dislike of outsiders; the war left be- hind it bitter feelings which made the immigration of desirable persons impossible; and the rule of the carpetbagger during Reconstruction increased the prejudice of the average southerner against men from the North. The former slaveholders — the old planting class — preferred negro labor to white; railroad companies and other employers of gang labor feared strikes and other complications if white workmen were brought in; and back of these concrete considerations there was a general desire to keep the southern white stock pure, with no admixture of foreign blood, and to hold fast to the old southern philosophy of living, which would have been disturbed by the advent of numbers of foreigners, strangers to the traditions and customs of the South.

On the other hand, northerners and foreigners had as little desire to go South as had the South to receive them. Foreign immigrants and northerners in search of homes passed the South by and went to the West, where they were welcomed. On the part of many home-seekers there was a dislike and fear of the black population, as constituting a social and economic danger; on the part of others there was a dislike of the whites as former slaveholders. The troubles of the Civil War and Reconstruction caused the better class of home-seekers to prefer the West. Land was cheaper in the West, or at least the immigrants thought so. Those persons from the North who went South from 1865 to 1870 expecting to make fortunes by planting cotton invariably failed, and their failure made capital distrustful and business opinion hostile. Laborers and artisans were in demand in the mills and factories and on the railroads of the North. The main lines of the railways ran to the West, and each road had a very efficient immigration service. From the agents of these roads and from northern opinion the immigrants learned much about the advantages of the West and a good deal about the disadvantages of the South. When the South first began to invite immigration it was found that the southern states were regarded very unfavorably by immigrants. They had heard from unfriendly critics of the South that the climate was too hot for white men ; that the water was bad and malarial fever common ; that the southern whites were lazy and proud, living upon the toil of the black and believing that it was not honorable to engage in manual labor; and that both races were so lawless that it was not safe to live among them. There was a notion that negroes abounded everywhere in the South, that no place was free from them, and that any one who worked at manual labor, especially if he worked with a negro, would be socially ostracized.

The schools and churches were said to be very poor; and some were afraid of mixed schools. The general opinion was that cotton was the only crop that could be grown. Accordingly foreign immigrants were hurried West, as soon as they arrived, by the immigration agents of the railroads, and later comers preferred to go where others of their kindred and nationality had gone before them.

The result was that the foreign element remained insignificant in the South. The census statistics for 1900 show that the entire South, including the old border states, had only about 620,000 inhabitants of foreign birth — six per cent of the foreign-born population of the United States. Michigan had as many foreign-born, New York three times as many. In five of the great producing states — Georgia, Alabama, Mississippi, North Carolina and South Carolina — out of a total population of 8,830,424, of whom 4,122,540 were negroes, the foreign-born element numbered 44,996, or about as many as in Vermont, which had a total population of only 343,641.

If the exchange of population among the states be taken into account, the disadvantageous results for the South are equally striking. Since the Civil war the South has sent to the North and West about 2,500,000 whites, and has received from all parts in return less than half as many. Georgia alone sent out to other states 412,000 and received 190,000, a net loss of 220,000. In 1900, 307,132 people born in Massachusetts were living in other states, but the loss was more than made up by the immigration of 1,262,257, of whom 415,933 were from other states and 846,324 from abroad. In the same year South Carolina had 234,062 of her sons and daughters living elsewhere, and had received in return only 60,744, of whom 5528 were foreign-born, a net loss of 173,328.

The lack of immigration has left the southern states thinly populated. Alabama has but 35 persons to the square mile; Arkansas, 24; Louisiana, 30; North Carolina, 39; South Carolina, 41; Florida, 9; Texas, 11. On the other hand, New York has 152; Illinois, 86;

Ohio, 102; Pennsylvania, 140, and Massachusetts, 349. If South Carolina were as densely populated as Massachusetts, it would have 10,500,000 people.

Such statistics as those above, showing that the southern people are almost entirely native-born and that future generations have unlimited resources still to develop, have been until lately a source of pride. But in recent years, especially within the last ten years, there has been a gradual but marked change of sentiment in the South in regard to the desirability of immigration. The South now wants it and is working hard to get it. Many influences have operated to cause this change. The passions aroused by the Civil war and Reconstruction have somewhat subsided, and the whites feel free to attend to the development of their section. Eastern capital is now sympathetic, and the capitalists who have invested money in the South desire immigration in order to develop the country and make their investments pay. The resources of the South have scarcely been touched, and under the most favorable circum- stances it will require many generations to develop them. There are millions of acres of cotton, cane, rice and tobacco lands that have never been cultivated. Louisiana alone has 19,000,000 acres of vacant land, out of a total of 26,000,000; and it is estimated that not more than one-eighth of the cotton lands of the South are in cultivation. The mineral resources of the South are almost unlimited; it has more timber than any other section of the United States; in every southern state there is water-power never yet used, and there are ideal situations for market-gardening on the largest scale. All these re- sources are undeveloped and will long remain so unless the population is increased by immigration.

The negro cannot furnish either in quality or in quantity the labor necessary to develop the South. By its lack of initiative and inventive genius the black race has acted as a hindrance to progress. Free negro agricultural labor has in most places, except the Yazoo

Delta, proven to be a failure; the fertile lands of the black belt have never again reached the production of 1860; the better wages paid to the negro have simply enabled him to work less — three days a week instead of four. Yet the most fertile land of the South is still in the hands of the negroes, who do not equal in production the white farmers on the poorest land. In 1876 the whites of the cotton states, forming 55.8 per cent of the population, produced 40 per cent of the cotton; the blacks, forming 44.2 per cent of the population, made 60 per cent of the crop. In. 1899 the whites, now constituting 59.1 per cent of the population, produced 60 per cent of the crop; the negroes, constituting 40.9 per cent, produced only 40 per cent. Every year the negro produces less, proportionately as well as actually, in agriculture. The educated blacks leave the farms, where they might do well, and turn to other occupations. Many of the best negro laborers have been carried north as strike breakers; others have deserted the fields for work in the mines and lumber camps or on the railroads ; many have gone to the cities to earn a precarious living. Agricultural development in the black belt is at a standstill because of the worthlessness of the black and the difficulty of getting more white labor.

The progress of the South since the war has been almost wholly in the white districts. During the twenty years from 1880 to 1900 the white population of the South increased 57.3 per cent and the negro population 37.5 per cent. During the same period the total value of southern products increased 61.7 per cent, almost all in white counties. Since 1860 the total southern population has increased 60 per cent, while the value of products has increased 250 per cent, the increase being mainly in industries operated by whites. Great numbers of whites have been drawn from the farms into the mills and factories that have lately sprung up. Mr. D. A. Tompkins estimates that in North Carolina 100,000 whites have left the fields for other industries. In South Carolina a similar movement has taken place; and yet for a portion of the year 1904, one- third of the spindles in the state were idle on account of the lack of labor. Every branch of industry is calling for efficient labor which only whites can furnish, and the native whites are not numerous enough to supply the demand. The development of industry in the South has far outrun the increase of population. For example: in 1895, in southern mills, 862,838 bales of cotton were manufactured as against 2,083,839 bales in northern mills ; in 1903, southern mills used 2,000,729 bales while northern mills used 1,967,635 bales. Commerce, business, manufacturing and railways have more than absorbed the increase of white population.

After its experience with negro labor the South now turns to the northern and foreign whites to assist in the development of the country. The younger southerner knows of the latent wealth of his country; he wants the profit from it. The negro has failed to assist him, and now he, unlike his father, the ex- slaveholder, is anxious to find a substitute for the negro. Many southerners have visited the North and observed the superiority of white labor. Northern men who have capital invested in the South have no patience with the negro. The railroad authorities know that satisfactory dividends cannot be expected until the country is more thickly settled and is developed by the varied industries which the white immigrant and the northern capitalist will bring. Some manufacturers have mills in New England and also in South Carolina. The future seems to be with South Carolina, and therefore they are friendly to immigration. With the present labor supply the South has about reached the limit of cotton production though the demand for cotton is increasing. Consequently makers of cotton goods encourage immigration, be- cause it means to them a more certain supply of cotton at a reason- able price. Likewise the cotton planters are interested in averting any danger of a cotton famine, for this would force Europe to grow cotton in Asia and Africa with peons and coolies as laborers, and such development would destroy the Southern monopoly of cotton growing. Improved methods among white farmers have resulted in a constantly increasing quantity of cotton produced per capita. To gather future large crops additional labor must be had, unless a cotton picker be invented. White immigration is looked forward to by some as a solution of the race problem. In parts of the country thousands of white farmers have moved away from their farms to villages and towns, be- cause they do not feel safe with their wives and daughters in the midst of the black population. For these many reasons the South now wants white immigration.

And within the last few years northerners and foreigners have shown an increasing willingness to settle in the South. There are several influences back of this change of opinion in regard to the desirability of the South as a place in which to live. The Northwest is filling up with people and the cheap land is nearly all taken. This is shown by the rush of settlers to each Indian reservation thrown open to settlement, and by the fact that thousands of persons have had to cross over into Canada to find the cheap farms that they expected to find in the West. Prices of farm lands are high in the North and West and rents are in proportion, so that it is practically impossible for the average poor man to look forward to owning his home. Thanks to the efforts of the various southern immigration agencies, more is known about the South, and the unfriendly tales still told find some sceptical listeners. Into each southern state a few northerners have gone and have achieved success; and their example attracts kindred and friends. It is now be- coming known that the climate is better in the South than in the Northwest; that lands are cheap and rents are low; that wherever a negro can work white men can do the same; that work is deemed honorable; that those who do not like to live near negroes can find great stretches of country where there are only whites; that cotton, rice and to- bacco are not the only crops that can be raised; and that there are openings for all kinds of new industries. In consequence the South has begun to attract from the North and West, and even from abroad, an immigration which, as compared with the movement or lack of movement in the past, is very respectable.

This immigration is solicited and encouraged by various agencies in the South: by the state governments, by the rail- roads, by real estate agents, and by numerous immigration societies, boards of trade and industrial associations. Each southern state has now a bureau of immigration, which in some cases is separately organized, in other cases is connected with the department of agriculture and industries. The efforts of the state authorities are directed not so much toward inducing immigration of laborers as toward securing a class of independent farmers who will do their own work, dispensing with the negro. The state immigration bureaus print and distribute throughout the North and West information of interest to prospective immigrants. Much of this literature is printed in German or in other foreign languages. At the St. Louis Exposition there were numerous state agents to call attention to the advantages of the undeveloped southern states. Speeches by southern members of Congress, welcoming immigration, published as extracts from the Congressional Record, are scattered broadcast over the North and West and are sent abroad. Florida sends out lists of state lands, maps of the attractive portions of the state, and beautifully illustrated pamphlets relating to cattle raising, lumbering, fruit and truck growing, fish and game, and winter resorts. Louisiana publishes free information concerning the climate, soil, resources, industries, schools and churches, and sends out lists, with descriptions and prices, of 6,000,000 acres of land for sale. The other southern states follow much the same methods. South Carolina officially encourages immigration of "white citizens of the United States, citizens of Ireland, Scotland, Switzerland and France, and all other foreigners of Saxon origin." This state does not yet officially encourage immigration from southern Europe, although between the cotton growers and the rice planters there is a severe competition for labor. Most of the states have representatives in New York and in the West, whose business it is to disseminate information and secure immigration.

The state immigration bureaus have had fair success, though they have been hampered by insufficient appropriations. Louisiana has probably secured the best results. The authorities confine their work principally to the middle West, aiming to attract substantial farmers rather than laborers. Since 1900 many northern farmers have settled in northern Louisiana. In New Orleans, however, the work of the negro roustabouts who loaded and unloaded the steamers at the wharves became so unsatisfactory that whites from the West were brought in to supplant them. South Carolina has secured several settlements of Scotch, Canadians and Germans, and is now trying to secure Scandinavians. Several hundred of the latter have arranged to settle on one tract of land. Captain Lindberg, former Swedish consul at St. Louis and a veteran promoter of immigration, has undertaken to bring 1000 Scandinavian families to South Carolina. In Greenville, South Carolina, where mill labor has been very scarce since the high price of cotton drew native help back to the farms, the problem has been partially solved by the introduction of foreign labor into the mills. A number of factories have secured newly arrived Germans and Poles — three factories as many as twenty-five families each. These immigrants have proved to be satisfactory, both as work-men and as citizens. During the year 1904, the state bureau of South Carolina also settled 204 families of farmers. The authorities estimate that each good farmer is worth $1000 to the state. In North Carolina the desire is to obtain farmers from England and Scotland, and a few families are now arriving each month. In Wilmington, where the negro laborers have proven so unreliable, the preference for north Europeans has given way before necessity, and Italians are being brought in to furnish more efficient labor. Texas has secured colonies of northerners, of Germans and of Italians, and smaller numbers of Japanese rice farmers. Mississippi reports an encouraging influx of substantial northern farmers (principally from Illinois, Nebraska, Iowa and Kansas) and of Italian cotton farmers. Alabama has received many northerners, especially in the industries, many Italians also, and enough Germans to Germanize four of the sixty-six counties. In north Alabama whites are displacing negro miners. To Virginia have come some Swedes and Germans, and many farmers from the Northwest. Several counties in the state are gradually passing into the hands of the immigrants. To Hanover county have come 200 families from the West; and in that county industry has been revolutionized, and the native tenants have now learned to "hustle." Maryland secured 4000 very desirable immigrants in one year at an expense of only $15,000. Other southern states have had more or less success in turning toward the South streamlets from the great tide of immigration.

The state authorities have been greatly aided by hundreds of immigration and development societies. Every commercial and industrial body acts also as an immigration society. In Louisiana alone there are. more than one hundred; one of them has 700,000 acres of land for sale. The southern industrial associations have recently been planning to bring about a visit from the British Cotton Spinners' Association, believing that a view of the South by the people who are interested in cotton production would tend to make sentiment favorable to immigration. The Shreveport Progressive League secured several factories last year and sold to twenty families of newcomers more than 10,000 acres of land. The Memphis Industrial League was instrumental in founding, during 1904, twenty new industrial establishments, the value of which to the city is estimated at $65,745,000. Cities offer special inducements to newcomers. An Oklahoma town advertises as one of its attractions that its population of 14,000 includes only 150 negroes, and that separate schools are provided for the latter. Other towns state that immigration of blacks is not encouraged, and many of them emphasize the separate school feature. Newspapers issue special homeseeker's editions for distribution by state authorities, real estate agents and railroads. Trade magazines have been useful in calling the attention of business men to the opportunities afforded by the undeveloped resources of the South. The most influential journal of this kind in the United States, The Manufacturers' Record, has for many years been urging immigration as a partial solution of the economic troubles of the South. The real estate agents of the West are coming to the South as a new field of labor and are bringing with them western methods and experience. They usually work in connection with the railroads. Some real estate agents bring periodically, at their own expense, responsible men from the West who will report to their neighbors upon the desirability of the country. One Tennessee firm has made money by bringing a party down from the Northwest every two weeks. Many of these excursionists have returned to stay in Tennessee.

The "colony " plan has also brought desirable immigrants to the South. Every few days the newspapers publish ac- counts of the location of colonies of farmers from the North or from abroad. Land companies in the middle West buy large tracts of land in the South and induce colonies to settle upon these purchases. Dunkards sell their high-priced little farms in the West and go south to purchase larger ones. Other religious and socialistic organizations have found homes in the southern states. Some of the best known colonies are: Fitzgerald, Georgia, settled from Indiana; Dudley, Georgia, from Indiana and Ohio; Fairhope, Alabama, from Iowa; Cullman and adjoining colonies in Alabama, by Germans; Independence, Louisiana, by Italians. A branch colony from Fitzgerald is being founded on St. Mary's River near the Florida line, and several thousand northern people expect to follow Mr. Fitzgerald to this new Mecca of homeseekers. In Florida there are many small towns in which the majority of the in- habitants are from the North. The Japanese government recently sent an agent to investigate conditions in the South and to report upon the availability of that section for settlement. A colony of Japanese agricultural students has been established in Florida and another in Texas. The object is to experiment with silk, cotton, rice, tobacco and fruits. A colony of fifty families has secured 67,000 acres of land in Dade county, Florida. If results are favorable, more Japanese are to be expected. A colony of Scandinavians has been located at Thorsby, Alabama. In Lauderdale county, Alabama, a German colony purchased land at $10 to $15 per acre; their land now commands $50 to $60 per acre. Three colonies of Dunkards from Indiana, numbering 800 families, settled during 1904 upon 100,000 acres of land in northern Texas. Around nearly every southern city are growing up colonies of northern, German or Italian market gardeners. They come only after they have carefully investigated conditions. Reports sent or brought to other sections by successful colonists are gradually removing baseless prejudices. A Swede who strayed South several years ago returned to the West on a visit. He states that he was welcomed as if he had been lost. His friends had an idea, he said, that the South was beyond the limits of civilization.

But the most potent factors in the immigration movement are the railroads. Each important railroad company has hundreds of thousands of acres of land for sale and wishes to see industries developed along its lines. Until within the last few years the north and south lines have not offered special rates to homeseekers except in colonies. Now, on the first and third Tuesdays in each month, special homeseekers' rates are offered on every railroad east of the Rocky Mountains that runs into the South or Southwest. A twenty-day ticket, sold for one-half the regular price of a round-trip ticket, allows the holder to stop off at every station and gives the prospective immigrant opportunities to look about for a location. These excursions have proved a great success. The Union Station at St. Louis is crowded every other Tuesday with men from the Northwest bound to the South and Southwest. On the night of September 15, 1903, the Iron Mountain road carried out of St. Louis within two hours six special trains with three thousand homeseekers. Hundreds of immigration agents are employed in the West and Northwest by southern railroads. For example: The Missouri Pacific and Iron Mountain system has three hundred such agents; the Southern Pacific has six hundred agents in the middle West; the Nashville, Chattanooga and St. Louis has one thousand agents in Illinois, Indiana, Iowa, Michigan, Minnesota, Nebraska, North and South Dakota, Ohio and Wisconsin. Some of these agents are veterans who helped to fill up the West and are now using the same arts to people the South. As inducements to immigrants they offer cheap land, low rents, several crops a year, mild climate, fertile soil, plenty of timber, separate schools for the races and light taxes. The railroads cannot afford to deceive new comers; they are working for the future, for permanent settlements and for increasing settlements. When possible, several representative westerners are sent on passes over the lines to see the land and report to their neighbors. When drought or flood injures the crops in the Northwest, the immigration agent sees to it that the disgusted farmers learn of the advantages of the country along his road in the South. Perhaps he finds a former northwesterner and sends him to his old home on a visit to tell of the country where he lives. Settlers who are already in the South write back and urge their friends to come. The railroads do not expect great returns at first. They proceed on the principle that their best course is to do so well for the first comers that these will send for their relatives and friends.

Believing that the North and West must be educated as to the possibilities of the South, the railroads send out all kinds of literature, including their own, that of the state, and that of immigration societies and real estate agents. Each road has its immigration newspaper, which is widely distributed in the United States, in Canada and in Europe.[1]

On the whole, the roads of the Southeast have had more difficulties to contend with than those of the Southwest. However, the Southern Railway settled 1,000 families along its line in 1902, and in 1903 about 2000 families were located on 2,270,018 acres. This road is now reaping the benefits of an intelligent campaign for immigration from the West. Its many small bodies of immigrants at widely separated points have been serviceable in quieting opposition and in causing others to come. In January, 1905, this railway was in correspondence with 35,000 persons who desired to purchase from one acre to several thousand. The Alabama Great Southern road has found that many westerners like to lease land and experiment for a year or two before purchasing. For several years it has been making an average of a 1000 leases a year. Lately, however, the number of leases is decreasing and the number of sales increasing. The Norfolk and Western, which recently began to offer inducements to immigration, now settles from ten to fifty families a month along its lines. Old plantations and improvements are sold to them at cheap rates. The Atlantic Coast Line, in 1903, settled 650 families of fruit growers in Florida and 500 families in Alabama, Georgia and the Carolinas, besides placing several important industries. The Louisville and Nashville reports the sale, in 1903, of 95,702 acres of farm lands and 255,048 acres of mineral and timber lands. Along this road eighty-seven new industrial establishments were set up by newcomers from thirty-one states — principally from Illinois, Wisconsin and Indiana. The other roads of the Southeast have made similar records.

In the Southwest a dozen colonies have been settled on the lands of the Illinois Central, and several other colonies are in process of establishment. Several million acres of land have been sold to homeseekers along this road. In 1904 it settled 1200 Italians, forty per cent of whom became farmers. In Mississippi a colony of Danes was established in the business of dairying. In Louisiana sixty-four Hungarian families were located as market gardeners. Each family bought from twenty to sixty acres of land. A German colony was established in Mississippi and a Swedish colony in Louisiana. In 1904 the Nashville, Chattanooga and St. Louis road reported three times as many immigrants as in 1903, and twenty-five times as many requests for information. The Missouri, Kansas and Texas reported 1300 homeseekers per month, thirty-five per cent of whom located. Along this line the truck farms increased in size and value sixty-three per cent in 1904. In addition there was an influx of capital and a notable development of industries. The Kansas City Southern reports that on a select ten- mile strip along its line the population in 1904 was 504,962 as against 304,326 in 1900. Of this increase 116,061 was in the urban population and 84,575 in the rural. The effectiveness of homeseekers' excursions is well illustrated by the results attained in 1904 by the Frisco system. Out of a body of homeseekers numbering 8132, the system located 1508 on the first trip, selling them 164,008 acres of land. A farmer on this line is estimated to be worth $300 a year to the railroad company. The foreign representatives at the St. Louis Exposition were taken by the Frisco system on an observation tour through the Southwest for the purpose of showing the resources of that section. The Japanese were particularly interested in Texas as a rice-growing country. Colonies from Illinois, Iowa and Nebraska have settled along the lines of the Rock Island system. On the lines of the Missouri Pacific and Iron Mountain system 10,000 newcomers have recently found homes, 2000 within the state of Arkansas. The price of land along this road advanced ten to twenty per cent in one year. One small station in the homeseekers' country in Arkansas shipped $75,000 worth of eggs last season, besides vegetables, fruits and poultry. The six hundred agents of the Southern Pacific sold, in a few months in 1903, 2,000,000 acres of land, and have been selling to Westerners since that date at the rate of 100,000 acres per month. Since 1894 this road has sold between Corpus Christi and New Orleans 3,000,000 acres of land, of which 800,000 acres were rice land, to 75,000 settlers from the Northwest. Col. S. F. B. Morse, the head of the immigration department, a veteran of western immigration, has carried more than 25,000 farmers to Texas. This road has also established colonies of Italians, Japanese and "Bohemians" along its line as rice farmers.

Before the Russian war broke out it had an agent at Kobe, Japan. As an index to the development of this section of the Southwest may be mentioned Crowley in southwest Louisiana. Twenty years ago the place was considered barren and worthless. Land sold for twenty-five cents an acre. A station was established which did not pay expenses. Westerners were persuaded to come, and now there are 7000 people in the town, a dozen rice mills, and 25,000 western farmers, besides the southerners in the country around. In 1902, 13,000 car-loads of rice were shipped from Crowley. Land is now worth $30 to $50 per acre. At another Louisiana station the total receipts in 1883 were $875; after immigration, in 1903, the receipts for milk tickets alone in one month amounted to $987. In connection with the efforts of the railroads to attract immigration from abroad should be mentioned the plan of Commissioner-General Sargent for distributing newly-arrived immigrants. In November, 1904, at a meeting in Birmingham of the immigration agents of the southern railways, a committee was appointed to confer with Mr. Sargent in regard to securing better facilities for receiving immigrants at southern ports. Sargent, however, proposed to establish at Ellis Island, New York city, an information bureau where immigrants might get impartial accounts of the attractions of every section of the country. For several reasons, the southerners interested in immigration have not favored Mr. Sargent's plan. It would involve a discontinuance of advertising abroad and would make necessary a certain amount of government control over the distribution of immigrants. It was feared that the proposed bureau of information would be employed primarily for the purpose of relieving the congested cities of the North with slight regard for the needs of the South. The South has trouble enough in its present race problem, and it decidedly objects to being made the government dumping-ground for undesirable immigrants. It does not want the lower-class foreigners who have swarmed into the northern cities; it wants the same sort of people who settled so much of the West. It is safe to say that no plan involving federal regulation of the distribution of immigrants will be acceptable to the southern states.

The newcomers from the western states and from western Europe are not mere laborers. They work for themselves on their own holdings. In those parts of the South where un- skilled labor is wanted to supplement the work of the blacks, such immigration will not solve the problem. The black belt planter cannot rely upon the labor of the negroes; there are plenty of them, but each year they become less efficient. Two years ago there was a significant demand from many quarters of the black belt for Chinese laborers. One planter complained that he had land sufficient to produce 1000 bales of cotton, but labor enough for only 300. He thought that the exclusion laws could be repealed if the southern states should advocate this policy. It is certain, however, that the South will not tolerate the introduction of large numbers of Chinese or Japanese for fear of possible race complications. The solution seems to be to induce Italians to come in as farm laborers, with the prospect of becoming landowners on a small scale. They have come in larger numbers than other foreigners, and, much to the surprise of all, they have proved successful as laborers on cotton and sugar plantations. The great lumbering companies also are employing them. The north Italian is preferred, but the principal immigration is from southern Italy, Sicily, and the old Papal states. The numbers are constantly increasing. In Louisiana, in 1900, there were 17,000 Italians; in 1904, there were 30,000. In 1904, it was estimated that more than 100,000 Italian farm laborers were working in the southern states of the Mississippi valley. Numbers come from Sicily or from the North to work during the cane-cutting season, and then return to the North or to Sicily. Between New Orleans and Baton Rouge the Italian laborer has largely displaced the negro, and the same is true of many other localities. In Arkansas, Tennessee, Texas and Mississippi there are numbers of Italian farmers and truckers also, notably in the vicinity of Bryan, Houston, Dallas, Galveston, San Antonio, Memphis, Greenville and Friars Point. In Texas they produce rice and cotton; in Mississippi, cotton; in other states they produce various crops. The Italian authorities have investigated conditions in the South, and so has the Society for the Protection of Italian Immigrants. Some Italian newspapers in America, such as *Il Vesuvio* in Philadelphia, favor the settling of Italians in the South, where they have opportunities to become independent small farmers. The southern planters fear no troubles from agricultural immigrants. A line of steamers has recently been put in operation between New Orleans and Italy. In late years, Italians have frequently arrived in New Orleans by ship- loads — 2134 in one week in 1903. The demand from planters for labor on cane and cotton plantations remained, however, in excess of the supply. In 1904 an agent of the White Star line was sent to Naples to arrange for the colonization of 10,000 families along a new railroad controlled by the Rock Island system, between Corpus Christi and Brownsville.

Side by side with negroes, the Italians have proved their superiority as farm laborers. Mr. Dougherty, a planter of Baton Rouge who employs about forty Italian families, states that they are peaceable and more industrious than the negro ; that they quickly learn to do unfamiliar work, treat stock better and cultivate their crops more intelligently; that they are more economical and do not rush into debt nor spend their earnings extravagantly. Other planters report that they are good farmers ; that they have model farms and well-kept houses and premises; and that they raise everything at home. Near Greenville, Mississippi, is an Italian colony engaged in cotton farming. Each family on twenty acres usually clears on each crop $200 to $300 above expenses. In 1903 twenty families returned to Italy, each family with $400 to $800. Some of them have purchased good homes, intending to remain.[2]

One of the earliest experiments with Italian agricultural labor was in Chicot county, Arkansas, on the Austin Corbin plantation. In 1895, Corbin, a New Yorker, sent an agent to Italy and secured from the former Papal states 500 Italian families who were located on an island in the Mississippi river. The colony was called Sunnyside. The colonists were well treated, the soil was fertile, a school and a church were provided; but the death of Corbin put an end to the sanitary improvements that were being made, and disease appeared. The colony nearly broke up; some of the people formed three other small colonies in Missouri and Arkansas; others went to Louisiana, Mississippi or Alabama, or back to Italy. In 1897, only forty families were left. Since then conditions have improved. About 2000 acres are in cultivation by Italians, whose numbers are increased every year by immigration. The manager states that they are better cotton growers than the negro, but that they have not yet developed the land-owning instinct ; they expect to return to Italy. There is no friction between Italian and black; but there is no race mixture. In 1903, the owners of the Corbin plantation advanced to their tenants $4000 to $5000 to send for relatives and friends. The entire loan was repaid out of the fall crop. One man returned to Italy with $8000 in cash, never having worked over thirty acres. He left his family, with supplies for a year, to work his land while he was gone. It was hoped that the thrifty example of the Italians would be an incentive to effort by the negro, but no such result was observed.

At Independence, Louisiana, in 1904, 275 carloads of strawberries, valued at $500,000, were produced by Italian laborers. These colonists have begun to purchase little farms, have good homes and some money in the banks. The younger ones do not expect to return to Italy. A tract of 1600 acres of land in this community sold in 1879 for $1600; in 1904, 200 acres of the same tract sold for $10,400. In the same community other pieces of land have risen in value from $1 to $50 per acre within two years. Many planters have substituted Italians for negroes as tenants. The former are not criminal, are prompt to pay debts, and have improved morally as well as materially since they arrived in America. The Italians are mainly from Venice. The community was developed under the supervision of the Illinois Central railroad.

In spite of the inducements offered the number of immigrants is still relatively small. It will be of interest to examine into the causes of the prejudice against the South as a place to live in. In the first place, public opinion in the North is still unfavorable to the South, and this affects the views of homeseekers. Immigration is thought by some to lessen the opportunities for the negro, which is true. The advice given to southerners against the immigration of whites is somewhat curious: the South is warned against such dangers as "the scum of Europe," the tendency of the whites to form labor combinations, a "congested city" problem caused by crowding negroes off the farms, a negro-Latin race conflict, and so on. The South is advised to hold fast to the docile, tractable negro, who works for low wages, never organizes, never strikes, seldom buys land, and who is so well suited to the climate. In short, all the slavery arguments in favor of negro labor are repeated. The prediction is made that the South will be dissatisfied with white labor.

The Manufacturers' Record asserts that any strong effort to induce immigration to the South causes a great deal of misrepresentation in northern and foreign journals. The so-called " Ogden movement" has undoubtedly, though unintentionally, done much to misrepresent actual conditions by exaggerating the poverty, illiteracy, intolerance and crime of the South. Unfortunate, also, in this movement is the fact that it is sup- ported most loudly by a few newspapers and individuals in the North that have never been noted for friendly feelings toward things southern. Another manifestation of northern interest in southern problems is found in the agitation against child labor in southern mills. Here manufacturers, philanthropists and labor agitators can meet on common ground. There is really no reliable information in regard to the numbers and ages of children employed in southern mills, but it is assumed that there is more child labor than in the northern mills. An outcome of the agitation has been a demand, pushed by a limited number of northern manufacturers, that Congress pass uniform hour and age laws and thus prevent unfair southern competition. Coincident with this demand were the publication of unfavorable accounts of conditions in Carolina mines, written by Marie Van Vorst, and assistance given by Irene Ashby McFadyen, an English agitator, in a crusade in the South against child labor. Miss McFadyen was well received, and something might have resulted from the movement had it not been discovered that she represented the American Federation of Labor. It is feared in some quarters that an extensive immigration to North and South Carolina would make these states formidable competitors to New England in cotton manufacturing. In the matter of immigration, therefore, as in the question of child labor and in that of education, southern manufacturing interests are extremely suspicious of outside interest. Of the serious effect of this agitation on immigration there can be no doubt. The state agent of South Carolina in England and Scotland found that the Van Vorst and McFadyen literature had been widely circulated in order to induce labor not to migrate to the southern mills. The labor organizations there generally opposed emigration to the South. The agent states that he tried to get the newspapers to publish favorable articles about the South, but was sometimes told that " the South had such a bad reputation that they were afraid to publish anything which would tend to induce emigrants to go there." The editors said that they had read many articles about the bad condition of labor in the South, and that never having heard them denied, they supposed them to be true.

The lynching of Italians at New Orleans some years ago has been constantly used since then as an argument against every kind of migration southwards. In particular it has checked the coming of Italians, and prominent Italian newspapers in America have fostered the prejudice against the South. On June 7, 1904, *Die Gartenlaube* of Berlin printed a typical warning to German immigrants who were thinking of going to Arkansas, Tennessee, Mississippi or Louisiana, states that have been trying to secure German settlers. This warning was based on information sent from the United States with regard to the swamps, malaria, bad water, excessive heat and bad climate of those states. An old method of condemning the South is still sometimes used: a map is shown which has the entire South printed black and labelled "black belt." The advice accompanying is designed to cause the homeseekers to avoid that section, which is described as a "plague-infested district." There is no doubt that the negro is a bugbear to prospective white settlers. Labor organizations have not been friendly to southern immigration, because of the presence of cheap negro labor and because labor organizations have not yet thriven among the southern whites. There is a widespread belief that the new constitutions of some of the southern states are used to get whites as well as blacks out of politics. It is certain that many people in the North and West who are Re- publicans in politics (and most of those who come South are Republicans) feel uncertain about the treatment which they are likely to receive in the South. During the presidential campaign of 1904 immigration fell off considerably; after the election it again increased. The New York *Journal of Commerce* recently declared, in discussing the slow migration to the South, that the " stories about the treatment of negroes, the condition of poor whites, the uncertainty of legal protection, social prejudice, political intolerance and the lack of adequate school facilities are not without effect in diverting immigration from the South." Behind all this is, of course, the fundamental fact of the presence of the negro.

There is still some sentiment in the South itself that deters immigration. Some fear cheap labor in the mills, others fear that behind the immigration movement are the foreign manufacturing interests desiring to keep down the price of cotton. A Georgia " mossback " opposed a state bureau of immigration because, he said, it would benefit the railroads; and a Texan objected that "the people now flocking to Texas do not agree with the old settlers, morally, religiously and politically."

There is no doubt that heavy immigration will result in political changes and re- alignments. The experience of West Virginia during the past ten years proves this point.

In conclusion, it may be said that immigration to the South seldom reaches the black belt. There seems to be a dislike of contact with the negro. Where new comers enter the black belt they go in colonies, settle near the railroad and dispense with the negro.

Much of the immigration does not increase the population of a community; it simply displaces the negro. The new settlers, not at first knowing how to cultivate cotton, fortunately never become wholly addicted to the cotton-raising habit, but produce a variety of crops. They send to market vegetables, fruit, poultry, eggs and dairy products. Large farms are not common. Improved implements and up-to-date methods are employed, and the native whites profit by the example.

Compared with the great volume of immigration to the West and North, the numbers that go South are insignificant; but compared with the numbers that went South ten years and more ago, the recent movement is very important. There is plenty of vacant land; and the southerners say that if a million settlers have come and are satisfied, there is no reason why other millions may not come.

Notes:

1. The Rock Island system publishes The Western Trail; the Louisville and Nashville, North and South ; the Iron Mountain, The Arkansas Homestead; the Southern Railway, The Southern Field; the Seaboard Air Line, The Seaboard Magazine ; the Florida East Coast Line, The Homeseeker, etc. Occasionally the railroad literature takes the form of verse, sent out by the bushel. For the following specimen the Iron Mountain is responsible: "Forests with game, rivers with fish abound, Rich vegetation covers all the ground Spontaneously. A land of plenty, liberty and law, Such is the matchless stale of Arkansas, Go there and see."

2. Since this article was written, Mr. A. H. Stone, a planter of Greenville, Mississippi, has published a paper on the " Italian Cotton Grower " in the South Atlantic Quarterly, January, 1905. He states that "the matter has long since passed the experimental stage," and that the " white man has become the negro's problem." In regard to negro and Italian labor, he says : " It is always difficult

to get a negro to plant and properly cultivate the outer edges of his field — the extreme ends of his rows, his ditch banks, etc. The Italian is so jealous of the use of every foot for which he pays rent that he will cultivate with a hoe places too small to be worked with a plough, and derive a revenue from spots to which a negro would not give a moment's thought. I have seen them cultivate right down to the water's edge the banks of bayous that had never before been touched by the plough. I have seen them walk through their fields and search out every skipped place in every row and carefully put in seed, to secure a perfect stand. I have seen them make more cotton per acre than the negro on the adjoining cut, gather it from two to four weeks earlier, and then put in the extra time earning money by picking in the negro's field." Compare this with " the spectacle of broken-down fences, patchwork outhouses, half-cultivated fields and garden-spots rank with weeds," where the negro works.

3

—

The Buford Expedition
to Kansas

By the Kansas-Nebraska Act passed by Congress in 1854, the Territories of Kansas and Nebraska were organized and thrown open to settlement with the proviso that all questions relating to slavery were to be decided by the people of each territory when it should be ready for admission into the Union as a state. The South conceded and the North was sure of the admission of Nebraska as a free state. In the case of Kansas it was doubtful if the anti-slavery party would ever be strong enough to control the elections, but the leaders at the North intended to make a fight to secure Kansas. Consequently there was great excitement in different sections of the country, especially at the North, where, almost before the bill became a law, Emigrant Aid Societies were formed whose object was to assist emigrants opposed to the institution of slavery to go to the territory and settle in order to be ready to vote at the proper time. In this movement of importing men the North had nearly two years the start, the South being confident that no exertion would be necessary in order to secure Kansas as a slave state. So there was very little pro-slavery emigration into this "debatable land" before late in 1855 except from the neighboring state of Missouri.

The first territorial elections were in favor of the Southern party, but the Emigrant Aid Societies in the Northern states kept pouring men and arms into the territory until late in 1855 the outlook was gloomy for the pro-slavery cause.

Pro-slavery Emigrant Aid Societies were now organized in Missouri, and soon other similar societies were formed in the remaining Southern states. Missouri appealed to her sister states in the South to come to her assistance. For two years she had borne the burden alone and would still do her utmost for the integrity of the South.

' ' But the time has come when she [Missouri] can no longer stand up single-handed, the lone champion of the South, against the myrmidons of the North. It requires no foresight to perceive that if the ' higher law ' men succeed in this crusade, it will be but the beginning of a war upon the institutions of the South, which will continue until slavery shall cease to exist in any of the states, or the Union is dissolved.

"The great struggle will come off at the next election in October, 1856, and unless at that time the South can maintain her ground all will be lost. We repeat it, the Crisis has arrived. The time has come for action — bold, determined action. Words will no longer do any good; we must have men in Kansas, and that by tens of thousands. A few will not answer. If we should need ten thousand men and lack one of that number, all will count nothing. Let all then who can come do so at once. Those who cannot come must give their money to help others to come. . . . We tell you now, and tell you frankly, that unless you come quickly, and come by thousands, we are gone. The elections once lost are lost forever. ' '

With Kansas a free state, Missouri and the states west of the Mississippi would soon be abolitionized, then Tennessee, Kentucky, and Virginia, until finally slavery would be shut up in a few states on the Gulf and South Atlantic.

In all sections of the country, during the fall and winter of 1855, there was excitement and agitation over the Kansas question. The South was now thoroughly canvassed by agents of the pro-slavery Emigrant Aid Societies. Bands of men were made ready to start for the territory in the early spring. Alabama, South Carolina, and Georgia took the lead among the slave states in the work of sending men to Kansas to settle and vote for the interests of the South.

In Alabama the first body of pioneers for Kansas was enrolled by Thomas J. Orme, who on November 18, 1855, made this proposition : " If the people of Alabama will raise $100,000.00, I will land in Kansas 500 settlers. I have over one hundred volunteers now." Nothing resulted from Orme's proposition, but on November 26, 1855, Major Jefferson Buford, a lawyer of Eufaula, who had served with distinction in the Indian War of 1836, published the following call:

Aid to Kansas. Col. Buford' s Propositions.

' ' To Kansas Emigrants —

Who will go to Kansas? I wish to raise three hundred industrious, sober, discreet, reliable men capable of bearing arms, not prone to use them wickedly or unnecessarily, but willing to protect their sections in every real emergency. I desire to start with them for Kansas by the 20th of February next. To such I will guaranty the donation of a homestead of forty acres of first rate land, a free passage to Kansas and the means of support for one year. To ministers of the gospel, mechanics, and those with good military or agricultural outfits, I will offer greater inducements. Besides devoting twenty thousand dollars of my own means to this enterprise I expect all those who know and have confidence in me and who feel an interest in the cause, to contribute as much as they are able. I will give to each contributor my obligation that for every fifty dollars contributed I will within six months thereafter place in Kansas one bona fide settler, able and willing to vote and fight if need be for our section, or in default of doing so, that I will on demand refund the donation with interest from the day of its receipt. I will keep an account of the obligations so issued, and each successive one shall specify one emigrant more than its immediate predecessor, — thus: No. 1 shall pledge me to take one emigrant; No. 2, two; No. 3, three, etc., and if the state makes a contribution it shall be divided into sums of fifty dollars each and numbered accordingly. Here is your cheapest and surest chance to do something for Kansas, — something toward holding against the free-soil hordes that great Thermopylae of Southern institutions. In this their great day of darkness, nay, of extreme peril, there ought to be, there needs must be great individual self sacrifice, or they cannot be maintained. If we cannot find many who are willing to incur great individual loss in the common cause, if we cannot find some crazy enough to peril even life in the deadly breach, then it is not because individuals have grown more prudent and wise, but because public virtue has decayed and we have thereby already become unequal to the successful defense of our rights."

H J- Buford.

November 26, 1855.

In a letter written near the close of December, 2 Major Buford describes the prospective settlers whom he had already enrolled as " honest, clever, poor young men from the country, used to agricultural labor, with a few merchants, mechanics, printers, and carpenters."

The organization of the party was to be military, with officers corresponding to those of the regular service, the officers below the rank of captain to be elected by the emigrants. By a majority vote a company could expel a member. Four places of rendezvous were appointed: Eufaula, Silver Run (now Seale), Columbus, Ga., and Montgomery. A date was set for assembling at each of these places, and the issue of rations began on that day.

On his return Buford was to make a report giving the name and place of enrollment of each settler, and showing where in Kansas he was left. Contributions were asked for and those who could not contribute in cash were asked to do so in notes, thus:

Cross Road P. O., Barbour Co., Ala., January 1, 1856.

One year after date I promise to pay to Jefferson Buford per

----

head for every emigrant he may take to Kansas within that time, provided

that I shall in no event be liable to pay over dollars.

(Signed) --------

January 7, 1856, forty plantation slaves were sold by Major Buford in Montgomery (at the average price of seven hundred dollars), and the proceeds put into the fund for defraying the expenses of the expedition. Donations were coming in, and Wm. L. Yancey was appointed to receive contributions. The state was thoroughly canvassed by Buford and others during the month oi February. 1 Alpheus Baker made some of his wonderfully persuasive speeches in Georgia and South Carolina in the interest of the crusade. William L. Yancey, Henry D. Clayton, LeRoy Pope Walker and Henry W. Hilliard delivered addresses to the people of Alabama, calling for good and true men to protect Southern rights on the Kansas battleground. Representative F. K. Beck of Wilcox County introduced a bill in the state legislature to appropriate $25,000 for the purpose of aiding emigrants to settle in Kansas. The bill was referred to the Committee on Federal Relations, and was never reported upon.

Early in January Major Buford made a speech in Montgomery before the state legislature in which he explained his plans for securing Kansas to the South. A citizen of Worcester, Massachusetts,

Wm. T. Merrifield, was in Montgomery at the time and heard of the designs of Buford. He at once returned to Massachusetts, told Eli Thayer, the originator of the Emigrant Aid Societies, about Buford's plans, and arranged with him to send men to oppose this Southern force. One hundred and sixty-five men well armed with Sharp's rifles (Beecher's Bibles) 3 were sent to Kansas for this purpose.

It was intended that the Buford party should go armed, but in March Major Buford announced that in deference to the President's proclamation, and in consonance with the true designs of the expedition, it would go unarmed.

The Eufaula contingent left that place on March 31, accompanied by Alpheus Baker, who at all resting-points made addresses of encouragement to the men. Passing through Columbus, Ga., and taking with him a company of fifty men from that town, Major Buford reached Montgomery on April 4. There were now collected here about four hundred men, of whom one hundred were from South Carolina, fifty were Georgians, one was from Illinois, one from Boston, and the rest were Alabamians. The *Alabama Journal* of this date characterizes the emigrants collected in Montgomery as a superior class of young men, quiet, gentlemanly, temperate. Later some members of the party seem not to have deserved this praise.

On Saturday, April 5, Major Buford formed his men in line in front of the Madison House, and made a speech to them urging that they abstain from intoxicating liquors, and conduct themselves as gentlemen and good citizens. They were then marched to the Agricultural Fair Grounds and organized into a battalion of four companies under temporary officers, and Buford was elected General of the force. Saturday night a meeting of the citizens of Montgomery was held in Estelle Hall, and addresses were made by prominent gentlemen. Major Buford explained that he had undertaken this mission in order to settle Kansas with good and true Southern men who would uphold the right of their native land in the new country which was to be their future home. He was followed by other prominent speakers who declared that the fate of the South depended on the success or failure of the efforts now being made to save the new territory for the South. Resolutions were passed thanking the men who had so nobly responded to the call upon them for the defence of Southern rights against Northern aggression.

The battalion attended divine service on Sunday at the Baptist church. After the sermon the pastor, Rev. I. T. Tichenor, proposed that since some ministers at the North had been raising money to equip emigrants with Sharp's rifles, they present each man of Buford's battalion with a more powerful weapon — the Bible. The necessary amount was subscribed at once; it being found that there was not a sufficient number of Bibles in Montgomery, the money was turned over to Major Buford, who was to purchase them at some point on his route.

The next day the emigrants were marched again to the Baptist church where Rev. Mr. Tichenor on behalf of his congregation presented a handsome Bible to Major Buford, a song written by a lady of Montgomery was sung by the crusaders, and then the Rev. Mr. Dorman of the Methodist Episcopal Church, South, offered up a prayer asking the blessings of heaven for Buford and his men. It was noticed that the battalion carried two banners with inscription on them. One had in large letters upon it: "*The Supremacy of the White Race,*" and on the reverse side was : "*Kansas, The Outpost.*" The second banner had the simple legend: "*Kansas.*" The Montgomery company wore silk badges with the inscription: "*Alabama for Kansas — North of 36° 30 . Bibles — not Rifles.*" From the church the battalion marched to the wharf and after speeches from Alpheus Baker and Henry W. Hilliard the emigrants boarded the steamer Messenger and departed for Mobile, followed by the cheers of five thousand people and the booming of cannon.

A stop of two days was made in Mobile and an election of officers was held. In Montgomery the party had been divided into four companies and Buford made General. The officers elected now were : B. F. Treadwell, Colonel; Major L. F. Johnston, Quartermaster-General; Captain E. R. Bell (of S. C), Adjutant-General; John W. Jones (Auburn, Ala.), Surgeon; Gordon, Brown, Andrews, Jernigan (of Ga.), Captains. 1 On April 11, the command was marched to the bookstore of the Messrs. McIlvaine, where each man was supplied with a Bible, and then to the wharf to embark on the steamer *Florida* for New Orleans. At New Orleans a few additional emigrants were picked up and the battalion was divided for making the trip up the Mississippi in the steamers *America* and *Oceana.*

St. Louis was reached on April 23 and a stop was made for one day. The people of St. Louis rated Buford's enterprise very highly, and regarded him as the best friend of Kansas in the whole South. As the party was leaving St. Louis on the steamer Keystone for Kansas City, a thief broke into a trunk belonging to Major Buford and stole from it $5,000. It was believed that one of the emigrants was the thief, but the money was not recovered. The next stop was made at Westport, where the men were equipped for settlement in Kansas, and on May 2 they passed over the line and scattered about the country seeking desirable locations for homesteads.[1]

The arrival of Buford with settlers from the South greatly encouraged the pro-slavery leaders and alarmed the free-state men.

"Our hearts have been made glad," wrote one of the Southerners, "by the late arrival of large companies from South Carolina and Alabama. They have responded nobly to our call for help. The noble Buford is already endeared to our hearts; we love him; we will fight for him and die for him and his noble companions." On the free-state side, ex-Governor Reeder writes in his diary: "There have come to the territory this spring three or four hundred young men, including Buford's party, who evidently came here to fight, and whose leaders probably understood the whole program before they left home." Before the party left Westport there was a meeting of the citizens to make the presentation to Major Buford of a fine horse, with fine saddle and bridle. Nearly half a century later an old citizen of Westport writes: "The people of Westport were glad to see Buford's men come. They were doubly glad when they went away finally."

By May 7 the colonists had scattered over different portions of the territory with the intention of locating permanently as citizens, and Buford was seeking some central location for himself in order that he might maintain communication with the members of his colony. Blue Jacket on the Wakarusa was suggested to him as a desirable place in which to settle.

The emigrants had not yet settled permanently, or at least few of them had done so, but were seeking favorable locations for claims on the government lands before pre-empting their quarter-sections. Most of them were destined never to make their homes in Kansas, for at the very time when they came over the border there was trouble again between the territorial government and the free-state settlers at Lawrence. Indictments had been found by the Douglas County grand jury against a number of free-state men living at Lawrence, and the United States marshal feared to undertake their arrest without a strong posse. So on May 11 he summoned the citizens of Kansas to appear in Lecompton in force sufficient to execute the laws.

In response to this call for men, Buford gathered his colonists, some of them at Lecompton, but the greater part of them at Franklin, where they were enrolled and armed by Governor Shannon as territorial militia. Buford's force at Franklin numbered four hundred men, and was under the direction of United States Marshal I. B. Donelson.

Captain E. R. Bell of South Carolina, one of Buford's officers (Adjutant-General), was sent with a company of men to intercept arms and armed men and prevent them from getting into Lawrence, which was preparing to withstand a siege. May 16, he captured a wagon loaded with guns and sabres. Three days later he was notified that three wagons loaded with arms would attempt to cross a bridge near where he was stationed. Taking volunteers from the companies at Franklin, Bell went with thirty-six foot-soldiers and five mounted men to catch the wagons. The mounted men reached the bridge first and drove off a sentinel party of free-state men stationed there. These men warned the drivers of the wagons and they escaped. Shortly after the mounted men reached the bridge a free-state man came up and attempted to cross. He was halted "by order of the United States Marshal." "I do not recognize that authority," he said, and tried to force his way across, presenting a pistol at the guards. He was "halted" three times and was then fired upon and wounded. The next day ten of Buford's men carried G. W. Brown, editor of the Herald of Freedom, as a federal prisoner to Lecompton. Two of these men on their return to Franklin were fired upon by a party of free-state men and one of the Southerners was shot through the arm. The other Southerner killed the man who had shot his comrade, and then, followed by a volley, assisted the wounded man to escape.

On May 20, the marshal began gathering his forces, to assemble before Lawrence. On the morning of May 21, early risers in Lawrence were astonished to see a force of soldiery drawn up on Mount Oread, a high hill near the town. Buford did not arrive until eleven o'clock. His men carried the banners that had been brought from Alabama. These banners seem to have offended some good citizens of Lawrence worse than the sack of the town and the destruction of property. The force investing Lawrence was Kansas territorial militia under the command of United States Marshal I. B. Donelson and Deputy-Marshal Fain. The latter with a small party entered the town and made several arrests, meeting with no resistance. He then returned to the militia assembled outside of the town and declared the posse disbanded. Samuel J. Jones, Sheriff of Douglas county, immediately summoned the entire body to assist him in serving some writs.

The Free State Hotel in Lawrence had been used during the Wakarusa War as a place of armed rendezvous, and each of the newspapers had published articles of an inflammatory and seditious nature denying the legality of the territorial government. Consequently the grand jury of Douglas County had declared them " nuisances," and as such had recommended their abatement. To "abate" them was the intention of Sheriff Jones. He marched his posse to the foot of the hill and formed a hollow square. Ex-Senator Atchison and others addressed the party, declaring their intention to destroy the hotel and the two printing-presses. Major Buford and many others of the sheriff's posse protested against this outrage, and endeavored to dissuade the sheriff from carrying out his designs. In a "Memorial to the President from the Inhabitants of Kansas " dated May 22, the prominent citizens of Lawrence state that "Col. Buford of Alabama also disclaimed having come to Kansas to destroy property, and condemned the course which had been taken;" that he used his influence to restrain the sheriff, and expressed his disapproval of the outrage in the strongest terms.

After the destruction of Lawrence the Alabamians again separated, some going back to Lecompton with Buford ; others camped on Bull Creek near Paola, not far from the scene of the John Brown murders, and a third party camped near Dutch Henry's Crossing, where they were visited by John Brown, who passed for a federal surveyor. He mingled with the men, heard their plans to catch him, and made his arrangements accordingly.

Civil war broke out in Kansas after the murder of the pro-slavery settlers by John Brown. Col. Sumner in command of United States troops took the field and dispersed or drove out of Kansas all armed bodies of men. All of Buford's men who were in arms were forced to go back into Missouri, most of them returning to Westport. At this time Buford bought twenty-five horses for the use of his men at Westport. These horses were used in their trips to Kansas afterward, and became well known as " Buford's Cavalry."[2]

The events leading up to and following the raid on Lawrence and the murders by John Brown had greatly demoralized the Buford settlers. Unable on account of the hostility of the anti-slavery party to make homes for themselves in Kansas, they were forced to live on the country by contributions made by sympathizers with their cause or forced from their enemies. On the night of June 4 a number of Alabamians at Franklin were attacked by a free-state company, who broke into the stores Buford had provided for the settlers and carried away provisions, arms, ammunition, etc. Four of Buford's men were wounded in this fight. Two of the Montgomery company (Powell and Vickers) with three Georgians were sent by Buford for a wagon and returning were captured by the free-state men, robbed of their arms, and tortured several hours before being released.

The first week in June a large part of Buford's men accompanied General Whitfield into Kansas to protect pro-slavery settlers who were being driven from their homes. The governor however ordered all armed parties to disband, and Col. Sumner again sent the Alabamians back to Missouri. On this expedition into Kansas Captain Jernigan was captured by free-state guerrillas, but was released by United States troops.

Buford himself spent the first part of June in Westport and Kansas City consulting with the pro-slavery leaders, and endeavoring to devise some plan to support the failing cause of the South in Kansas. Alpheus Baker and Major L. F. Johnston had returned to Alabama soon after reaching the territory, for more men and more money. Now, on June 21, Buford and others sent an appeal to the South for more emigrants to check the abolitionists in their efforts to drive the pro-slavery party from Kansas.

June 26, Buford left the territory on a mission to the South in the interest of Kansas. He visited Washington and the principal cities of the slave states. In Washington he remained several weeks endeavoring to interest the Southern leaders in his scheme for the colonization of Kansas. Robert Toombs, R. M. T. Hunter, J. B. DeBow and other prominent Southerners gave him valuable aid in forwarding his projects. After an absence of several months spent in trying to arouse the South to a sense of her danger, Buford returned to Kansas late in 1856.

Meanwhile all had not gone well with the colonists he had left behind. Numbers had returned to Alabama after the first troubles in the territory in May. A state of civil war existed for months after the Brown murders and the raid upon Lawrence. The proslavery settlers lived in constant fear for their lives. Under such unfavorable conditions the Buford party disbanded. A good number enlisted in the United States troops stationed in Kansas, some of them went over to the other side and became free-state partisans, others made their way south again, while one party remained during the fall at Westport. They were encamped near the home of Col. McGee, an ardent states-rights man, who, however, reports himself as having suffered much from disorderly pro-slavery friends. In December Buford was at Westport and made preparations to return to Alabama in the spring. He published an account of the receipts and expenditures of his expedition in the Westport *Star of Empire*. The figures were as follows:

Cost of enterprise... $24,625.06
Contributions 13,967.90
Leaving a loss of..$10,657.16

These figures show the expenditures and losses of the Buford enterprise only. None of the expenses of the Clayton and other colonies or his own expenses and losses from theft are reckoned in this account. The loss was borne by Major Buford.

January 12, 1857, Buford with others signed an address to the South in behalf of the National Democratic Party of Kansas. This is the last appearance he makes in the affairs of the territory.

More clearly than any other man Buford had foreseen the results that must follow the admission of Kansas as a free state. He gave his fortune to the cause, and worked long and faithfully to arouse the South to the impending danger, but his prophetic voice was not fully heeded. His colonization plan was a failure financially and politically. The institutions of the South could not be transplanted to Kansas. The question that he hoped to have settled by votes in Kansas was finally decided by bayonets on a hundred bloody battle-fields in the South. [3]

Notes:

1. While at St. Louis Buford addressed a communication to Col. Wm. Walker, provisional governor of "Kansas Territory," an organization attempted by Wyandotte Indians previous to the white settlement, asking permission to settle a portion of his men, who should be carefully selected from the party, on the Wyandotte Reservation. The writer has a certified copy of this letter made by G. W. Martin, Secretary of the Kansas Historical Society.

2. Letter to *Alabama Journal* of July 2, dated Westport, June 15, from Wilson, a former printer on that paper. He writes: " Very nearly the last man of us is flat broke. Impossible to get work in the

territory. Clothes are giving out, and some of the boys are returning home. Some are going to stay and see it out. Major Buford is preparing a statement of expenditures to show to the South. He has spent his fortune on this enterprise and will not have a cent left for his children. However, he relies on the sympathy of friends at home to assist him out, and take care of us poor devils until the question is settled and Kansas becomes a State."

3. After his return from Kansas Buford lived at Clayton, Alabama, where on August 28, 1861, he died suddenly of heart disease. "At the time of his death not one scrap of the history of the expedition, of the number of men enlisted in it, or their names, places of residence, or anything pertaining to it could be found he had deposited them all in some bank or other place of security in Washington City of which he told no one. No trace of his papers could be found after his death. He was a very secretive man, and seldom informed any one of his plans or purposes." — J. M. Buford.

4

Jefferson Davis' First Marriage

Legend deals freely with the early lives of most men who attain fame. Traditions cluster about every real happening in those years when records are few or are lacking, and it is frequently difficult even after careful research, to sift from the legendary chaff the grain of truth. About the early years of Jefferson Davis there are many conflicting stories , most of which have no foundation, though a few have some slight basis of fact. About his first marriage we find a mass of tradition, reminiscence and record that is almost hopelessly confused. In this paper an attempt is made to extract from the numerous contradictory accounts which have appeared during the last half century the true story of the marriage of Jefferson Davis and Sarah Knox Taylor. There were few events connected with that wedding of seventy- seven years ago so unusual that in the case of ordinary people they would long be remembered by any except intimate friends and the persons concerned, but Jefferson Davis became famous and tradition began its work.

At the beginning of the second quarter of the nineteenth century, when Jefferson Davis served in the United States army on the northwestern frontier, life at the military posts was monotonous in the extreme. The army career of the future statesman was spent on the outer edge of civilization , on the farthest frontier of white settlements and among unfriendly and often hostile Indians. The forts were merely rough places of safety for troops, and the officers, when ordered to such distant posts as Fort Crawford, Fort Winnebago, or Fort Snelling, usually left their families in the more settled States. The coming of a woman to one of these northwestern stations was an event to be celebrated. At Fort Winnebago, where Davis served for two years, there was, for a time, no white woman; later there was one, and then a second, but both were married. When the one officer's wife at Fort Winnebago brought an unmarried lady from the East to visit her, the young officers passed resolutions of thanks. When an unmarried officer who had been away from civilization for several years had the good fortune to be transferred to a post where there were young women, he was usually in a susceptible mood. So it was with Jefferson Davis, who in 1831 , after a three years' tour of arduous duty in the woods and on the plains of Wisconsin and Iowa, was ordered to Fort Crawford at Prairie du Chien. Fort Crawford had been made headquarters of the First United States Infantry, and here several of the garrison officers and some of the leading civilians of the frontier had brought their families.

Traditions about the early love affairs of Davis are remarkably few. The only one of interest is that he first became attached to Mary Dodge, daughter of Henry Dodge who was afterwards colonel of the First Dragoons, later Governor of Wisconsin Territory and, when the territory became a State, one of its United. States Senators. Davis became acquainted with Miss Dodge in 1831 and saw much of her in 1832, and after the Black Hawk War. He and a Colonel Dement, it is said, were rivals for her favor. Colonel Dodge, with a predilection for people who had or could get good positions, favored the suit of Dement because the latter had enough influence with Andrew Jackson to secure a good federal office. It is to be inferred that the daughter's inclination coincided with her father's for she married Dement. But she always remembered kindly the other man. For a while Davis, it is said, was much disappointed, and later Dodge complained of Davis's opposition to his (Dodge's) candidacy for the governorship of Wisconsin. However, Davis was soon consoled elsewhere and retained only pleasant memories of the Dodges. A little note of his to the lady has been preserved, written just fifty years after he saw her for the last time, in which he says:

*"Widely and long we have been separated but your image has not been dimmed by time and distance. *** If you have preserved enough of the pleasant memories of one springtime to care for one who flitted with you over the flowers of youth's happy garden, it will give me sincere gratification to hear from you and to learn of the welfare of yourself and children."*

The center of social life at Fort Crawford while Davis was stationed there was the home of Colonel Zachary Taylor, who in 1832 succeeded Colonel Willoughby Morgan in command of the First Infantry. The buildings were unfinished and some families had to live in tents, but Taylor's wife and daughters came to the frontier and other army wives and daughters came with them. Mrs. Taylor was a motherly, domestic woman, who, after long and rough frontier experience, had learned to make a home anywhere. There were three daughters in the Taylor family-Anne, Sarah Knox, and Betty. Anne, the eldest, married Dr. Robert Wood, later surgeon- general of the United States army. Her son, John Taylor Wood, who died recently in Nova Scotia, was a daring Confederate naval officer, and the last man to leave Jefferson Davis before his capture in 1865. Sarah Knox, the second daughter, eighteen years old when Davis first knew her, was her father's favorite. He called her Knox in honor of Washington's Secretary of War. Elizabeth, "Miss Betty," as she was known after she grew up, was then six years old. Richard, the only son, who thirty years later was famed as a brilliant and eccentric Confederate general, was at this time "a lubberly sort of a boy." A close friend of Sarah's was Mary Street, daughter of General J. M. Street, the Indian agent for that part of the western country.

Life at Fort Crawford was often monotonous to the young people. The arrival of a steamboat from St. Louis was an event, while in the winter the nearest settled parts of the States were a two weeks' journey away. Social relations on the frontier were free and easy and the older Taylor girls were noted for their love of mischief which frequently took the form of practical jokes. Once while on a fishing excursion they persuaded a young officer, named George Wilson, to climb a small sapling that overhung the river. They then took axes and hacked at the roots until it fell, carrying the lieutenant into the river. Since Davis, who was of the party, had some difficulty in seeing the point of a practical joke it is fortunate that he was not the victim. To while away the time the women and girls at the fort occupied themselves at Indian bead work, and some of them became quite expert. The only souvenir of Sarah Knox Taylor in existence is a small silk reticule worked with colored beads which she gave to Mary Street whose granddaughter now possesses it. The young people made the most of their few opportunities for amusement, and Davis, though he spent much of his time quietly reading law, was often thrown with the young daughters of the colonel and soon formed an attachment for Knox.

The mutual regard of the two young people quickly ripened into an engagement of marriage, subject to the approval of Colonel Taylor. By most people it would have been considered a proper match. Davis had the reputation of being one of the best of those young officers, sent out from West Point under the Thayer regime, who were now making their influence felt in army affairs. Personally he was attractive, though by some he was considered too reserved, almost austere. Probably the only person now (1907) living who ever saw Davis when he was an officer of the United States Army, said of him as he was the year of his engagement to Sarah Knox Taylor:

"I shall never forget him as I saw him first, a young lieutenant in the United States army, straight as an arrow, handsome and elegant. It was at the governor's mansion at Detroit; my brother was governor of Michigan, the State's first executive; Lieutenant Davis was our guest; the Black Hawk War in which he had greatly distinguished himself was just ended and he was bringing Black Hawk through the country. I was much impressed with the young lieutenant."

But Colonel Taylor, with slight regard for the feelings of the young people, had other plans. He wanted his favorite daughter to marry a business man, return to civilization, and have a comfortable home. He did not intend that his daughters should be obliged to undergo the hardships that his mother and his wife had experienced, and the wife of a poor army lieutenant would, he knew, live a rough life. Besides it was evident that the army in time of peace offered slight opportunities to an officer for a career. His daughter had been educated in the East and had lived in comfort among relatives in Kentucky; she knew little of the conditions of frontier life. Mrs. Taylor, having experienced the hardships of army life, agreed with her husband that her daughter ought not to marry in the army. So the marriage was forbidden.

But Knox Taylor had much of her father's decision of character, and neither she nor Davis would accept Colonel Taylor's answer as final. Some of the senior officers of the post, friends of Davis, endeavored to persuade Taylor to consent to the marriage. To one of these, Captain Kearney, Taylor answered:

"I will be d-d if another daughter of mine shall marry into the army. I know enough of the family life of officers. I scarcely know my own children or they me. I have no personal objections to Lieutenant Davis."

Probably he would have relented ; for one of his daughters was already an officer's wife and "Betty" was later permitted to marry into the army, but for an unfortunate and absurd quarrel that arose between Davis and himself. The circumstances were these: Four officers, Taylor, Davis, "Tom" Smith, and another whose name is not known, were detailed as a court martial. Taylor and Smith disliked each other exceedingly. The fourth officer had been ordered up to Fort Crawford from Jefferson Barracks and had lost or left behind his full dress uniform which it was the custom to wear when serving on court martial duty. So he asked the other members to excuse him from wearing uniform. Taylor voted not to excuse him, Smith voted, therefore, to excuse him, and Davis voted with Smith. This enraged "Old Rough and Ready" who after further irritation swore, it is said, that no man who voted with "Tom" Smith should ever marry his daughter.

Davis was ordered to cease his attentions to Miss Taylor and to come no more to her father's quarters. Davis had considerable temper himself and the quarrel grew hotter and hotter until finally Davis asked Captain McRee, later paymaster-general of the army in Mexico, to serve him as second and take a challenge to Colonel Taylor. The " code" was the accepted mode of settling difficulties in those days, and duels in the army were common, but McRee refused to serve as second or to take a challenge to Taylor unless Davis would first agree to give up the daughter. Davis would not consent, so McRee refused "to help him shoot. his own father-in-law."

This account of the disagreement between Taylor and Davis is somewhat discredited by records preserved by the family of Lieutenant George Wilson, one of Davis's intimate friends, which indicate that the stories of the quarrel are exaggerated . The Wilson records prove that officially Taylor never discriminated against Davis, but that on the contrary he often chose him for important details, such as looking after the lead mines in Illinois and commanding the escort that carried Black Hawk to Jefferson Barracks . Wilson reports also that other young officers thought Davis was favored by Colonel Taylor, for, in 1833, when a lieutenant was to be promoted and transferred to the new Dragoon Regiment Davis was selected . Another opinion was that Taylor was very willing for the handsome and impecunious young lieutenant to leave the regiment in order that his daughter might forget him.

It is certain that Taylor continued to oppose the marriage. Miss Taylor refused to break the engagement unless her father would give her what she considered "a good reason" for so doing. She told her father that she would never marry without his consent and that she would never marry any one but Davis. "The time will come, " she said, "when you will see as I do all his rare qualities. " The young people had some difficulty in their love making after Davis was forbidden the house, but friends assisted them. Mrs. McRee, who lived in a tent frequently invited Miss Taylor to visit her, and Davis would make it convenient to call at the same time. There in the midst of crowded housekeeping, romping children and other things superfluous, they managed to keep the spark alive. After a time the mother relented and consented to the meetings. Colonel Taylor, according to family accounts written down in later years, knew of them but did not withdraw his opposition.

Miss Mary Street, Knox Taylor's devoted friend, and her admirer, Lieutenant George Wilson, were in a like situation. General Street objected, as Colonel Taylor had done, to his daughter's marriage to an army officer. The young people finally made an arrangement satisfactory to the four. Davis and Wilson each called at the home where he had no intentions, and when Davis called at General Street's he found Miss Taylor there also; and Wilson would find Miss Street at Colonel Taylor's. When Davis escorted Black Hawk to Jefferson Barracks in 1832, Miss Street was sent down on the same boat on her way to school to get her away from the attentions of Wilson. One of the last recorded reminiscences of Davis was that on the way down to St. Louis he delivered a letter from Wilson to Miss Street by bribing the chambermaid on the boat. She and Wilson were married before Davis and Miss Taylor. At the wedding on March 26, 1835, the attendants were Miss Taylor and Major E. A. Hitchcock, Davis's West Point friend and instructor. A few years before Davis died he saw Mrs. Wilson again in St. Louis and recognizing her at once with "Well, well, Mary! How do you do?" saluted her with a kiss.

Mrs. Phillip Pendleton Dandridge, who was "Betty" Taylor, the youngest of the Taylor sisters, said that after parental opposition ceased somewhat the lovers had little difficulty in meeting. Miss Taylor would take Betty and Dick out for a walk. Davis would soon appear and the children would be told by their sister that they might play a little. Mrs. Dandridge described them a "ideal lovers." And so the lovers contrived until 1833 when Davis left Fort Crawford to join the new Dragoon Regiment at Fort Gibson in the Indian Territory.

During the next two years when Davis was in the Far West with the Dragoons he and Miss Taylor kept up a correspondence, and finally decided to marry during the summer of 1835 even if Colonel Taylor should continue to withhold his consent. There is no evidence that they saw each other during Davis's service with the Dragoons. During the Civil War all of the papers of Jefferson Davis left at his Mississippi home were confiscated by the Federals.

Among the papers a Federal soldier, named Spillman Willis, of the Thirty-third Illinois Regiment, found the following letter from Davis to General Taylor's daughter:

FORT GIBSON, December 16, 1834.

TO MISS SARAH K. TAYLOR,

Prairie du Chien:

'Tis strange how superstitions sometimes affect us, but stranger still what aids chance sometimes bring to support our superstitions. Dreams, my dear Sarah, we will agree, are our weakest thoughts, and yet by my dreams I have been lately almost crazed, for they were of you, and the sleeping imagination painted you, not as I felt you, not such as I could live and see you, for you seemed a sacrifice to your parents' desire, the bride of a wretch that your pride and sense equally compelled you to despise. A creature here, telling the news of the day in St. Louis, said you were about to be married to a Doctor McLarin, a poor devil, who served with the battalion of rangers. Possibly you may have seen him. But last night the vision was changed. You were at the house of an uncle in Kentucky. Captain McCree was walking with you. When I met you he left you and you told me of your father and of yourself, almost the same that I have read in your letter to- night. Kind, dear letter; I have kissed it often and it has driven away mad notions from my brain.

Sarah, whatever I may be hereafter, neglected by you I should have been worse than nothing, and if the few good qualities I possess shall, under your smiles yield fruit, it shall be yours, as the grain is the husbandman's. It has been a source productive of regret with me that our union must separate you from your earliest and best friends. I am prepared to expect all that intellect and dignified pride brings. The question, as it has occurred to you, is truly startling. Your own answer is the most gratifying to me; is that

which I should have expected from
you, for you are the first with whom I ever sought to cast my
fortune, so you are the last from whom I would expect desertion .
When I wrote to you I supposed you did not intend soon to return
to Kentucky. I approve entirely of your preference to a meeting
elsewhere than at Prairie du Chien, and your desire to avoid any
embarrassments which might widen the breach made already cannot be greater than my own. Did I know when you would be at St.
Louis I could meet you there. At all events, we will meet in
Kentucky. Shall we not meet soon, Sarah, to part no more? Oh I
long to lay my head upon that breast which beats in unison with
my own, to turn from the sickening sights of worldly duplicity and
look in those eyes, so eloquent of purity and love.

Do you remember the heart's- ease you gave me? It is as bright
as ever. How very gravely you ask leave to ask me a question. My
dear girl, I have no secrets from you. You have a right to ask me
any question without apology. Miss Bullitt did not give me a guard
for a watch, but if she had do you suppose I would have given it to
Captain McCree? But I'll tell you what she did give me a most
beautiful and lengthy lecture on my and your dreams once upon an
evening at a fair in Louisville. You can, and I have left you to guess
what, besides a resistibility to your charms, constituted my offense.

Pray, what manner of message could La Belle Florine have sent
you concerning me? I hope no attempt to destroy harmony. I
laughed at her demonstration against the attachment of dragoons,
but that, between you and I, is not fair gains ; it is robbing to make
another poor. But, no, she is too discerning to attempt a thing so
difficult and in which success would be valueless. Miss Elizabeth,
one very handsome lady- Oh Knox, what did you put that semi-
colon between ' handsome' and 'lady' for. I hope you find in the
society of the Prairie enough to amuse, if not to please. The griefs
over which we weep are not those to be dreaded; it is the little

pains, the constant falling of the drops of care, which wear away the heart. Since I wrote you we abandoned the position in the Creek nation and are constructing quarters at Fort Gibson. My lines, like the beggar's day, are dwindling to the shortest span.

Write to me immediately, my dear Sarah, my bethrothed; no formality between us. *Adieu ma chere, tres chere amie.*

JEFF

Davis sent his resignation to take effect June 30, 1835, and during the month of June he was granted leave of absence from his regiment which was stationed at Fort Gibson, a frontier post then in Arkansas, now in the Indian Territory part of Oklahoma. He went to St. Louis and from there completed the arrangements for the marriage. Miss Taylor now asked her father to give good reasons why she should not marry Davis and she would give him up. He would only say that he did not want his daughter to marry into the army, and she prepared to go to her relatives in Kentucky, near Louisville, to be married.

At this point the stories of the elopement begin. There are various versions and all have had persistent existence since the Civil War; one has it that the young people eloped during the winter of 1834-1835, going in a sleigh to Galena where they were married; another is that Davis stole his bride from the upper window of her father's house and they went across the river to Iowa and were married on the boat by a Catholic priest ; and yet another is that they were married in St. Louis in a house that is still pointed out, at the corner of Monroe and Hall Streets. A fourth story was that they fled by night from Prairie du Chien taking four horses from Taylor's stables and that along with them eloped their friends, George Wilson and Miss Mary Street. At Fort Gibson, Indian Territory, the tradition is handed down that Davis and

"Betty" Taylor eloped from that post. There is no foundation for any of these stories and most of them are of comparatively late origin. The story of the runaway marriage angered Davis very much, especially after it appeared in Appleton's *Cyclopedia of American Biography* in 1888. He then denounced the story of the "romantic elopement" as a "baseless scandal." A detailed statement of Davis would have settled the whole matter but he would never discuss it , for, as a friend said, "The dead whom in life he has loved, he shrinks from bringing up; for the pain and sense of their loss never grows old; and so he has held his early marriage sacred from the gossip of the curious."

Even the second Mrs. Davis knew little about the first wife, as her account shows. The only known facts about Miss Taylor's departure from Prairie du Chien are these: Captain McRee, at Fort Crawford, engaged passage to Louisville on a St. Louis steamboat for Miss Taylor who had prepared her trousseau at home. Her father frequently came on board the boat on business after his daughter had gone to her stateroom. Captain McRee tried to arrange a reconciliation between them, and Miss Taylor "on bended knee begged his forgiveness and consent to the marriage, but in vain," and she went on to her relatives in Kentucky where Davis was to join her, and the marriage was to take place in the early fall.

At this point we again have conflicting accounts as to Colonel Taylor's conduct. The usual story is that Taylor never forgave his daughter; that he said, "No truly honorable man would thus defy the wishes of parents and no truly affectionate daughter be so regardless of her duty. " But Mrs. Dandridge and the other Taylor relatives have insisted that Taylor was never estranged from his daughter, though he opposed the marriage. While it is certain that Taylor did not approve the marriage there are facts to indicate that he was relenting. His daughter was in Kentucky for some time before her marriage and her father wrote to his sister, Mrs. John Gibson Taylor, that "if Knox was still determined to marry Lieutenant Davis he would no longer withhold his consent, but wished her to marry at her aunt's house." Though it was first decided that the wedding should take place in the fall, after some delay an earlier date, June 17th, was fixed and Davis came to Louisville. Mrs. Dandridge has declared that Colonel Taylor would have attended the wedding but for the fact that he was ordered to the Falls of St. Anthony, now Fort Snelling, Minnesota, to keep hostile Indians in check.

On the morning of the wedding day the bride-to- be wrote to her mother of the approaching marriage. This letter which follows, is one of the few written by the first Mrs. Davis that have been preserved:

LOUISVILLE, June 17, 1835.

You will be surprised, no doubt, my dear mother, to hear of my being married so soon. When I wrote to you last I had no idea of leaving here before fall ; but hearing the part of the country to which I am going is quite healthy I have concluded to go down this summer and will leave here this afternoon at 4 o'clock; will be married as you advised in my bonnet and traveling dress. I am very much gratified that sister Ann is here. At this time having one member of the family present, I shall not feel so entirely destitute of friends. But you, my dearest mother, I know will still retain some feelings of affection for a child who has been so unfortunate as to form a connection without the sanction of her parents, but who will always feel the deepest affection for them whatever may be their feelings toward her. Say to my dear father I have received his kind and affectionate letter, and thank him for the liberal supply of money sent me. Sister will tell you all that you wish to know about me. I will write as soon as I get down and as often as my mother may wish to hear from me, and do, my kind ma, write. I shall feel so much disappointed and mortified if you do not. I send a bonnet by sister, the best I could get. I tried to get you some cherries to preserve, but could not. Sally has kindly offered to make your preserves this summer. Farewell, my dear mother; give my best love to pa and Dick.

Believe me always, your affectionate daughter,

KNOX.

The wedding took place at Beechland, the home of John Gibson Taylor, near Louisville. Davis's own statement about it is this:

"In 1835 I resigned from the army and Miss Taylor being then in Kentucky with her aunt-the oldest sister of General Taylor-I went thither and we were married in the presence of General Taylor's two sisters, of his oldest brother, of his son- in- law, and many other members of the family."

This statement omits some interesting details which have been handed down in the Taylor family. Mrs. Anna Magill Robinson, who was one of the Taylor children present at the wedding says:

"My Cousin Knox Taylor was very beautiful, slight, and not very tall, with brown wavy hair and clear gray eyes, very lovely and lovable and a young woman of decided spirit. She was dressed in a dark traveling dress with a small hat to match. Lieutenant Davis was dressed, in a long-tail cutaway coat, brocaded waistcoat, breeches tight- fitting and held under the instep with a strap, and a high stovepipe hat. He was of slender build, had polished manners, and was of a quiet, intellectual countenance."

Just before the ceremony Davis arrived in a disturbed state of mind. The clerk of the court had refused to grant the license "upon the plea that the bride-elect was under age." Her uncle, Hancock

Taylor, went back with Davis to the city and upon his oath that Sarah Knox Taylor, was of lawful age the license was procured.[1]

Those present were Hancock Taylor and wife, Mrs. John Gibson Taylor; Doctor and Mrs. Wood, the older sister of Knox Taylor, and the children of the two families. The attendants were Sally and Nicholas Lewis Taylor, cousins of the bride. One witness of the ceremony is still living in Louisville, Kentucky— Mrs. Anna Magill Robinson, the daughter of Hancock Taylor. She was eleven years of age at the time. She remembers that "after the service everybody cried but Davis, and the Taylor children thought this most peculiar. "

After the ceremony the bride and groom left for Mississippi to visit Joseph E. Davis at his plantation called "Hurricane." Joseph E. Davis was the oldest of the Davis brothers, and it was he who persuaded Jefferson to resign from the army, and after his marriage come back to Mississippi to plant cotton and enter politics. To establish the young people Joseph E. Davis gave to his brother a tract of land known as "The Brierfield" and sold him fourteen slaves on credit. From Warrenton, Mississippi, on August 11 , 1835, Mrs. Jefferson Davis wrote her last letter to her mother. In this, after referring to the news contained in a letter just received from home, she says:

*"Mr. Davis sends his best respects to you. Did you receive the letter he wrote from St. Louis? * * * Write to me, my dear mother, as often as you can find time, and tell me all concerning you. Do not you make yourself uneasy about me, the country is quite healthy."*

Jefferson Davis worked with his negroes at opening the place until the fever season arrived when he and his wife, being unacclimated, went to visit his sister, Mrs. Luther Smith, of Locust Grove plantation, in West Feliciana Parish, Louisiana. But they had remained too late in Mississippi, and after their arrival in Louisiana both fell ill with malarial fever. Davis was too ill himself to be told of his wife's danger, but, after she became delirious, he heard her voice singing a favorite song, "Fairy Bells," and rising from his bed he reached her side in time to see her die unconscious. She had always expected to die early. She was buried in the Locust Grove Cemetery and there in a dark grove her neglected tomb is to-day. Five years later her father removed the family home to Baton Rouge, a few miles away, and there it remained until he was in inaugurated as President.

The first Mrs. Davis was a handsome woman, refined, well educated, and intellectual, with great strength of character inherited from both her father and her mother. No likeness of her exists, but we have several descriptions of her. "Betty," her sister, remembered her as "extremely pretty, small, with dark eyes, with great vivacity and charm of manner, winning every one who knew her." Anna Taylor, her cousin, who was at the wedding, said that she "was very handsome, as graceful as a nymph and the best dancer in the State of Kentucky. She was witty, fascinating and clever." Posey Wilson, the son of George Wilson and Mary Street, who wrote down his mother's recollections of young Mrs. Davis, said:

"She had an exquisitely beautiful figure, but was not a pretty woman. She was dark, small, and much like her father, particularly as to her forehead which though indicating strength and courage, moral and physical in a man, was not particularly becoming to a woman. She had her father's splendid hazel eye and strong even teeth, and her mother's domestic traits and amiability."

It is related that once, long after her death, Davis in looking through the contents of an old trunk came upon one of her slippers and was so overcome by emotion that he lost consciousness. For ten years after her death he lived in seclusion at Brierfield.

Of the so-called reconciliation between Davis and Colonel Taylor the accounts are conflicting. The Wilsons maintain that there was no violent estrangement to heal ; the second Mrs. Davis, who, however, had no details from her husband, remarks that the trouble was not smoothed over "during the life of Mrs. Davis," but states that the two met again as friends in February, 1845, on a Mississippi River steamboat, when Davis was on his way to Natchez to marry Miss Varina Howell. So there was no dramatic reconciliation at Monterey nor at Buena Vista, as is often asserted. In the Boston Public Library is a letter written by Colonel Taylor from Matamoras on August 3, 1846, to Colonel Davis, the tone of which makes it certain that at that time there was no ill feeling on the part of Taylor, and hence no reconciliation was necessary. The Taylor letters recently published by Mr. W. K. Bixby, of St. Louis, show that during 1846-1847 Davis and Taylor were good friends. In the newspapers and in Congress Davis defended Taylor's course during the Mexican War. At the White House when Taylor was President, Davis was a frequent visitor and in after life the members of the Taylor family were his firm friends.

Beechland, the house in which the marriage took place still stands near Louisville in a dilapidated condition . It is now owned by German gardeners. The upper story has been removed and negro tenants use the rest, while round the yard are farm implements, and pigs, and chickens. Nothing but a crumbling chimney remains of the Mississippi home to which Davis brought his bride in the morning of the century . Half a hundred years later a gray old man whose deeds will rank him with the immortals and whose ambitions all lay behind him, made his last visit to Brierfield, there contracted the same fever that had killed his young wife, and went down the river to die at New Orleans.

Note:

1. The most circumstantial account of this incident is related in the *Confederate Veteran* of August, 1909: "The wedding was set for the afternoon of the 17th, and as the happy bridegroom was riding in his buggy through the shady roads he was hailed by Patrick (Pendleton) Pope, the County Court Clerk, who had issued the license, who said: 'Lieutenant, will you let me see that license ? I want to look at it again.' When he took the license in his hands, he deliberately tore it into bits and threw them in the road. Dumfounded, the bridegroom, whose wedding was not three hours off, stared at the man and demanded an explanation of what seemed the act of a madman. The clerk said he had been informed that Miss Taylor was under age and that her father was intensely antagonistic to the marriage.

"There was not time for arguments. So Lieutenant Davis drove quickly to the house of the bride's relatives and told the story. Hancock Taylor was very indignant, and called his sister, Mrs. Gibson Taylor, to the conference. She said she had lately receive a letter from her brother Zachary, in which he stated that he still opposed the marriage for old reasons, but that his daughter was of age; and if she persisted in her intention, the wedding had best take place in the family home. This was enough for Hancock Taylor, who with his nephew- elect drove rapidly to the courthouse. Here he swore to the bride's age, twenty-two, and demanded of Clerk Pope a reissuance of the license. With this they returned, the horse covered with foam from the swift drive."

5

The Religious Life of Jefferson Davis

That Robert E. Lee, the military leader of the Confederacy, was a very religious man, every one knows. His religion was a part of his life; his letters, even his military orders, show that his character and conduct were influenced by the teachings of the New Testament. Lee's great lieutenant, Stonewall Jackson, who taught a Sunday-school class of little negroes and prayed for his foes before going into battle, was a Christian of the Covenanter type. But few people ever think of Jefferson Davis, the civil leader of the South, as a religious man, or believe that to any important degree religion influenced his life. He is thought of by some people as a great criminal, a plotter, a traitor, an advocate of hopeless human slavery; by others, more friendly, he is remembered mainly as one who upheld certain abstract political principles which finally came to a practical test and failure in the Civil War. The purpose of this paper is to show that there is another side to the character of the great advocate of Southern rights that he held decided views on religion and, in later life at least, was a devoted Christian.

The religious life of Jefferson Davis reflects the religious development of the South of which he was so important a part. The South of Davis's youth was not, strictly speaking, a religious section; the South of his prime and his old age was a very religious land. In the Eastern South until about 1830 the Episcopal Church, though weak in numbers, was perhaps the most influential; while the Southwest was a land of few churches. Before 1860 the great missionary, democratic Churches-the Baptist, Methodist, and, to a slight extent, the Presbyterian- spread over the turbulent new South and the old, bringing the strongest of civilizing influences to bear upon the rude builders of the new commonwealths and upon the savage and half- savage black slaves, until at the outbreak of the Civil War the South was a land of church members, where not being attached to some church organization was regarded as a state of doubtful respectability.

The parents of Jefferson Davis were members of the Baptist Church. They lived for a while in the newer part of Georgia, then for several years in frontier Kentucky, finally settling in an older region, Southwest Mississippi. They were of the sound average American stock which filled and soon made powerful the two great Southern Churches-the Baptist and the Methodist. Samuel Davis, Jefferson Davis's father, and his wife ruled their large household strictly according to the religious views of the times; both were Bible students, and from the Bible they took the names of all but one of their sons. Most of the children did not unite with the Church of their parents, but remained churchless or gravitated toward some of the other organizations. In the early days religious conditions on the Southwestern frontier were not very promising. Angry disputes among the various denominations were the rule, and this caused many, through disgust, to become indifferent.

When young Davis was seven years of age, he was sent to St. Thomas College, a Roman Catholic school at Springfield, Ky., for the purpose of getting him into a quiet moral atmosphere. Few Protestants attended the school, and Davis decided that he ought to become a Catholic. He went to Father Wilson, who was in charge of the school, and informed him of his desire. "Father Wilson," he said, "received me kindly, handed me a biscuit and a bit of cheese, and told me that for the present I had better take some Catholic food" ; and that was the end of the matter. Davis liked the kind priests, and always afterwards had the greatest respect for the Catholics; he believed that above all others they sympathized with the weak and oppressed, but he never knew much about their doctrines. Fifty years after he left St. Thomas College, a Virginia priest wrote, after a visit to Mr. Davis in prison, that he was very fond of individual Catholics, but was quite ignorant of the truths of "our Holy Church." To his friend L. B. Northrop, a Catholic, who was Commissary General of the Confederate Army, Davis wrote late in life: "I dare not attempt to discuss a doctrinal question with you, and will only say, if we do not meet in Paradise, I join you in the hope that we shall meet in Purgatory, lest we go further and fare worse."

For several years after leaving St. Thomas College, Davis remained in Mississippi among the usual nonreligious surroundings. When thirteen years of age, he went to Transylvania University at Lexington, Kentucky. The religious influences here were not favorable. There was in Kentucky at that time a strong "freethinking" spirit, and the mass of the people were disgusted at the quarrels among the Churches. Some of the denominations had been fighting for control of the university, and when in 1818 Horace Holley, a Unitarian, was elected president, the sectarians turned their batteries against him and the institution. Davis spent three years here in the midst of the struggle, which was not conducive to orthodoxy.

His sympathies were with the liberals who supported Holley, though he liked best of all Professor Bishop, his teacher of Bible history and a very orthodox Presbyterian. Of Professor Bishop, Davis afterwards said: "His faith was that of a child, not doubting nor questioning but believing literally." Of religious conditions at Transylvania, Bishop wrote: "The majority of the students were at all times from families which made no religious profession, and at times the influences both within and without the college were very unfavorable to religion and morals."

When Davis left Transylvania in 1824 to go to West Point, he was sixteen years of age. His religious environment, which had been unusual for a Southern youth-Baptist at home, Catholic, Presbyterian, and Unitarian at school-and the skepticism prevalent in Mississippi and Kentucky, probably resulted in a certain liberal but slightly indifferent attitude toward theological doctrines.

At West Point he remained four years. Among many good people West Point had borne a doubtful reputation; it was a place, one mother declared, where young men "were trained to vice and the army." In Davis's time it was better; the cadets were trained to rigid truth and honor, but few of them and few of the instructors were in any way religious; some were openly skeptical. The chaplains, until 1825, were inferior men and had no influence. The cadets slept or read through their long and dull sermons. But in 1825 a chaplain came who was of a different type. This was Rev. C. P. McIlvaine, later Protestant Episcopal Bishop of Ohio. He soon interested the young men and secured the respect of all. For him Davis, during his West Point life and always afterwards, had a reverential regard. It was a year after McIlvaine came to West Point before a cadet had the courage to kneel in chapel. The first to do so was Leonidas Polk, of North Carolina, later the Bishop- General of the Confederacy. Jefferson Davis, Albert Sidney Johnston, who was killed at Shiloh, and others soon followed. Polk left the Military

Academy to become a clergyman, but Davis was less influenced and did not formally unite with a Church until 1863. At West Point he was a high-spirited, mischievous boy, who thought little of serious things.

After leaving West Point, in 1828, Davis served in the army for seven years, all of the time on the extreme Western frontier, where there were few or no priests or preachers, and church buildings did not exist. In the scanty records of the time we find that he showed considerable interest in religious work. He was, it is said, a young officer of rather serious temper, given to reading and reflection. He and his friend, Captain Harney, were the only officers at Fort Winnebago who neither drank nor gambled. Mrs. Kinsey in her book, "Wau Bun," which describes the frontier life of those days, says that it was mainly through the efforts of Lieutenant Davis that a missionary preacher was sent to Fort Winnebago in far-off Wisconsin, where Davis was stationed for two years. In the diary of the Rev. Cutting Marsh, an early missionary to the Indians of the Northwest, occurs the following
passage relating to Davis:

Wrote [July 25, 1831] to Lieutenant Davis, Fort Winnebago. Contents of letter: First, the bill of the Bibles, etc. Second, urged the importance of his inquiry whether he could not do something for the moral renovation of the soldiers at the Fort. Love and gratitude to the Saviour should induce it immediately. Although alone, he should not feel that a sufficient excuse for declining to make an effort. David went alone against his foe and the defier of the armies of Israel, but in the name of the Lord of hosts, and he conquered. God has without doubt something for you to do in thus bringing you, as you hope, to the knowledge and to the acknowledgment of the truth as it is in Jesus.

Afterwards, when stationed at Fort Crawford, he with his commanding officer, Colonel Zachary Taylor, was instrumental in organizing mission schools among the Indians of Iowa. No other glimpses of Davis's attitude toward religion during his army service can be had. At Fort Gibson, Oklahoma, there is still pointed out an old church which, it is said, Davis attended when in the dragoon regiment, 1833 to 1835.

Davis loved above all others the soldier's profession ; among soldiers could be found, he believed, the finest characters of the world's history. Napoleon's sayings in regard to religion were, in his opinion, wonderful expressions. In his daughter's estimate of her father's character is an anecdote which shows his high regard for the profession of arms:

A quaint expression of his professional pride was the interpretation which he put upon that incident in the crucifixion mentioned in three of the Gospels, and especially by St. Luke:"And the soldiers also mocked him, coming to him and offering him vinegar." My father contended that the testimony of St. John as an eyewitness was much more credible than that of his fellow evangelists who were obliged to rely upon hearsay evidence. St. John refers to the presentation of vinegar and hyssop as an act of mercy to a man suffering under a death thirst. Said my father: "The guard around the cross were Roman soldiers, and no brave men would ever torment a dying person wantonly. It is much more likely that the legionaries, touched with compassion by the heroic endurance and suffering of the Saviour, ran and brought him their own portions of sour wine, the acidity of which was corrected with hyssop, and presented it on a sponge as the only way of reaching his lips. It is not like a soldier at any period of the world's history to taunt or revile a helpless person, least of all one who suffers silently." He always dwelt upon the superb courage of our Lord's character, a quality that is too often, overlooked in the pulpit.

When Davis, in 1835, returned to Mississippi to live, he found a more effective organization of Church forces than had existed in his boyhood days. The Episcopal Church had the more cultured membership, but the great democratic Churches were growing rapidly in numbers and in influence. From this time Davis seems to have been thrown mainly with Episcopalians, though for several years he lived a retired life. There is a tradition in Natchez that when a young man he joined the Episcopal Church of that place, and that he never withdrew his membership. It is the opinion of the writer that before 1863 Davis was not a member of any Church. His first wife, Sarah Knox Taylor, was an Episcopalian, as was also his second wife, Varina Howell; and he attended the Episcopal Church as a rule, though frequently he went to the Methodist Episcopal Church, South, for which he had great respect. "The Methodist Episcopal Church, South," he once said, "has been to me the object of admiration and grateful affection, because of its fidelity to principle, and because of the unselfish devotion of its underpaid ministers, who have gone along the highways to penetrate unfrequented regions and there preach the gospel to the poor. "

Mr. Davis believed that slavery was an institution based on fundamentally right principles. He sometimes defended it by the use of biblical texts. The following extract from one of his speeches will illustrate his views:

Its origin was divine decree—the curse upon the graceless son of Noah. Slavery was regulated by the law given through Moses to the Jews. It was foretold of the sons of Noah that Japheth should be greatly extended, that he should dwell in the tents of Shem, and Canaan should be his servant. Wonderfully has this prophecy been fulfilled; and here in our own country is the most striking example.

Believing that slavery was the best agency for elevating an inferior race, he made provision for the religious training of his slaves. He and his brother Joseph sometimes paid the salary of a white Methodist preacher, who was sent out by the Southern Methodist Church to work among the negroes. "Uncle Bob," a resident black preacher at Brierfield, Davis's plantation, was supported by Mr. Davis, who said of him: "He was as free from guile and as truthful a man as I ever knew." Davis once expressed the opinion that in religious work the South "has been a greater practical missionary than all the Society missionaries in the world. "

During that period of his life between his second marriage and the outbreak of the Civil War, we know nothing in detail about the religious life of Mr. Davis. His wife being an Episcopalian and his own inclinations being toward her Church, he usually attended it. When Secretary of War he took steps to secure at West Point a chaplain who was able to command the respect of the cadets and thus exert a good influence. When he became President of the Confederacy it was with the conviction that the Southern cause was a losing one, unless Providence should support it. He believed that the right would be so sustained, and to the end was not daunted by misfortunes, for "his faith in God's interposition to protect the right never faltered. " This feeling is expressed in his official papers and in his letters. At Montgomery, in 1861, when inaugurated Provisional President, he closed his address with the following words:

Reverently let us invoke the God of our fathers to guide and protect us in our efforts to perpetuate the principles which by his blessing they were able to vindicate, establish, and transmit to their posterity. With a continuation of his favor, ever gratefully acknowledged, we may hopefully look forward to success, to peace, and to prosperity.

A year later he closed his inaugural address with a formal prayer, a circumstance which the newspapers North and South seem to have considered remarkable. The last paragraph of the address, as the papers gave it, is as follows:

With humble gratitude and adoration, acknowledging the Providence which has so visibly protected the Confederacy during its brief but eventful career, to thee, O God, I trustfully commit myself, and prayerfully invoke thy blessing on my country and its cause.

Soon after his inauguration in Richmond he joined St. Paul's Episcopal Church in that place. With him were confirmed General and Mrs. Gorgas. Rev. Charles Minnegerode, rector of the church, gave the following account of this event in Davis's religious life:

It was soon after his inauguration that he united himself with the Church. Our intercourse had become more frequent, and turned more and more on the subject of religion ; and by his wife's advice I went to see him on the subject of confessing Christ. He met me more than halfway, and expressed his desire to do so, and to unite himself with the Church ; that he must be a Christian he felt in his inmost soul. He spoke very earnestly and most humbly of needing the cleansing blood of Jesus and the power of the Holy Spirit; but in the consciousness of his insufficiency he felt some doubt whether he had the right to come.

All that was natural and right ; but soon it settled this question with a man so resolute in doing what he thought his duty. I baptized him hypothetically, for he was not certain if he had ever been baptized. When the day of confirmation came, it was quite in keeping with his resolute character, that when the Bishop called the candidates to the chancel he was the first to rise and, as it were, lead the others on, among whom were General Gorgas and several other officers.

From that day, so far as I can know and judge, "he never looked back." He never ceased trying to come up to his baptismal vow and lead a Christian life. And so he went on bravely and perseveringly, even when it became clear that hope of success was failing. He could not leave his post. He did not lose heart. The cause lost-defeated for a time-he felt sure would yet bring forth blessings upon the country.

He favored strongly and assisted to the best of his ability the work of the chaplains and religious organizations in the army. It will be remembered that during the latter part of the war a religious revival swept the Southern armies when thousands upon thousands made profession of faith and joined the army churches. To Rev. Z. E. Dickinson, who was pushing the work of colportage, Mr. Davis wrote: " I most cordially sympathize with this movement. We have but little to hope for if we do not realize our dependence upon Heaven's blessing and seek the guidance of God's truth."

One action of Davis's was criticised at the time by some extreme Protestants in the Confederacy and ridiculed by some Northern people. This was his correspondence with Pope Pius IX. Davis's early training and later friendships had caused him to admire greatly the Roman Catholics. In 1863 he wrote to the Pope expressing his appreciation of the letters relating to the war which the latter had written to the bishops of New York and New Orleans. The Pope sent a courteous response. The criticism caused by this episode assumed that Davis was simply seeking for Catholic indorsement of the Confederacy. Later, when Davis was in prison, Pius IX. sent a portrait of himself with this inscription: "Come unto me, all ye who are weary and heavy laden, and I will give you rest."

More and more, as time wore on and the lines were closely drawn about the Confederacy, did Mr. Davis look for providential interposition in its behalf. So also had believed Stonewall Jackson, the stern Presbyterian who had "passed over the river"; and so wrote in every letter the great General who led the armies of the Confederacy. When Stuart lay wounded and dying, Mr. Davis knelt and prayed that "this precious life might be spared to our needy country."

"Little Joe," the favorite son of the President, always insisted upon saying his prayers at his father's knee. No matter what the business in hand, when bedtime came, Joe always came to his father. Mrs. Gorgas relates one incident:

We were calling at the Davis house one evening, when through the half open door I saw descending the steps a little figure, barefooted and in his night robe. He came into the room, walked up to his father and kneeling said his evening prayer. Mr. Davis laid his hand affectionately and reverently on the child's head, and bending his head whispered the prayer along with the child.

In prison for two years, after the fall of the Confederacy, much of the time excluded from intercourse with the outside world, Mr. Davis exhibited a deeply religious character. At first no reading matter was allowed to state prisoner Davis. After a few days the Secretary of War permitted a Bible to be given to him, and later, after considerable hesitation, a prayer book. For several weeks he was permitted to have no other reading matter," and not until the late fall was he allowed to write to Mrs. Davis. These letters were closely censored by General Miles, his jailer, and many of them never reached their destination. In the first letter he wrote:

The confidence in the shield of innocence with which I tried to quiet your apprehensions sustains me still. "Tarry thou the Lord's leisure, be strong and he will comfort thy heart." Every day, twice or oftener, I repeat the prayer of St. Chrysostom . Be not alarmed by speculative reports concerning my condition. You can rely on my fortitude, and God has given me much resignation to his blessed will. Remember how good the Lord has always been to me, how often he has wonderfully preserved me, and put your trust in him.

As soon as the war was ended, some Southern leaders made of Davis a scapegoat-the cause of the Confederacy's failure. In regard to their criticisms and the demand of Northern people that he be executed, he said:

An unseen hand has sustained me, and a peace the world could not give and has not been able to destroy will, I trust, uphold me to meet with resignation whatever may befall me. If one is to answer for all, upon him [me] it most naturally and properly falls. If I alone could bear all the suffering of the country, and relieve it from further calamity, I trust our heavenly Father would give me strength to be a willing sacrifice.

Mr. Davis's little daughter was told by her mother that she might write to her father, but that she must write nothing to which General Miles would object. She copied after days of labor the Twenty-third Psalm and signed her name. General Miles suppressed it. In some way Mr. Davis heard of it, and wrote:

Our injuries cease to be grievous in proportion as Christian charity enables us to forgive those who trespass against us, and to pray for our enemies. I rejoice in the sweet sensitive nature of our little Maggie, but I would she could have been spared the knowledge which inspired her "grace," and the tears which followed its utterance. As none could share my suffering, and as those who loved me were powerless to diminish it, I greatly preferred that they should not know of it. Separated from my friends of this world, my heavenly Father has drawn nearer to me. His goodness and my unworthiness are more sensibly felt, but this does not press me back, for the atoning Mediator is the way, and his hand upholds me.

When affairs seemed to be at the darkest, the prisoner of state wrote to his wife:

I am sustained by a Power I know not of. The Protector of the fatherless and the widow, I am permitted to hope, hears my prayer. Your trust that the son of the righteous will not be forsaken has also been to me the suggestion of comfort. When Franklin was brought before the privy council of George III., and a time- serving courtier heaped the grossest indignities upon him, he bore them with composure, and afterwards attributed his ability to do so to the consciousness of innocence in the acts for which he was reviled.

What under Providence may be in store for us I have no ability to foresee. I have tried to do my duty to my fellow-men, and while my penitent prayers are offered to our heavenly Father for forgiveness of the sins committed against him, I have the sustaining belief that he is full of mercy, and knowing my inmost heart, will acquit me where man, blind man, seeks to condemn. From our mediating Saviour I humbly trust to receive support, and whatever may befall me in this world, to have justice, dictated by Divine wisdom and tempered with Divine mercy, in the next.

Besides Davis's own Church, the Catholic Church was the only other religious organization in the North that pursued a policy of conciliation after the war. Its priests and bishops showed sympathy with the South and with the South's imprisoned leader. After hearing of their good work for the afflicted Southern people, Mr. Davis wrote:

I am deeply impressed by the kindness of the Bishop, and that of the priests who have so nobly shown their readiness to do their Master's work in relieving the afflicted and protecting the fatherless. They have sent thus the sweetest solace to one in the condition of him who went down from Jerusalem to Jericho. I feel with you, that God has been very good to us. In the time when nations were ruled by arbitrary power, the Catholic priests stood between the despots and their victims, sublimely defying the rage of one, and divinely bending to raise the other. From time to time the heroic spirit of that ancient line has been called forth, and in plague, pestilence, and famine, in the wilderness and on fields of blood, in the prison, on the scaffold, and among the deserted mourners, nobly have they maintained the glory of their order.

After the authorities began to better the treatment of Mr. Davis, he was permitted to read books printed before the war or those of a devotional nature. Since he was allowed to see no one except his guards and to write to no one except Mrs. Davis, this was a great privilege. Extracts from his letters will show the nature of his reading and the reflections aroused by it:

I have lately read the "Suffering Saviour," by the Reverend Dr. Krummacher, and was deeply impressed with the dignity, the sublime patience of the model of Christianity, as contrasted with the brutal vindictiveness of unregenerate man. Misfortune should not depress. Beyond this world there is a sure retreat for the oppressed; and posterity justifies the memory of those who fall unjustly. To our own purblind view there is much that is wrong, but to deny what is right is to question the wisdom of Providence. I have been reading "Thoughts on Personal Religion," by Dr. Goulburn. His instructions as to prayer have impressed me particularly. How like is the experience of men! It is no small encouragement to a sinner, striving for a better state, to find that those who have, at least in the world's estimation, won the crown of glory had passed through such tribulation as he is beset with. Did it never occur to you how much evil is done by the use of a text startling in its terms, and so iterated and reiterated that any explanation of its meaning by reference to other texts bearing on the same subject is lost? It occurred to me, after last writing to you, that something of that kind might have happened to you in regard to forgiveness; and I regretted not having pointed out the illustration of his meaning which our Saviour gave in the parable of the King who took an account of his servants.

When we shall pass into the future state of pure intelligence, so as to judge not by external signs but by the inner motives, how different men will appear to each other from the estimates of their carnal life! May it not be that we shall then find our most earnest efforts at self- examination brought us but to a poor knowledge of ourselves? Though my prison life does not give me the quiet of solitude, its isolation as to intercourse affords abundant opportunity for turning the thoughts inward; and, if my self-love, not to say sense of justice, would have resisted the reckless abuse of my enemies, I am humbled by your unmerited praise. It teaches me what I ought to be, and lifts my eyes to Him whose all sufficient grace alone can raise me to your ideal standard. With the communion of the Church, I am not alone, nor without remembrance that the burden is not permitted to exceed the strength. I live and hope.

The ways of Him who doeth all things well are inscrutable to man. Let us learn to say, "Not mine but Thy will be done." The bitterness which caused me to be so persistently slandered has created a sentiment which will probably find vent in Congressional speeches, and test all your Christian fortitude. Remember that the end is not yet. A fair inquiry will show how "false witnesses have risen up against me and laid to my charge things that I knew not of."

A small worn copy of the "Imitation of Christ" used by Davis while in prison is still preserved. The marginal notes and marks made by the prisoner indicate his appreciation of certain passages.

For example, on Chapter 48, "Of the Day of Eternity and the Miseries of this Life, " the following note is made : "November, 1865. Great comfort in this"; and the following passages in the chapter are marked:

The citizens of heaven know how joyful that day is; but the banished children of Eve lament that this day is bitter and tedious. The days of this life are short and evil, full of sorrow and miseries, where man is defiled with many sins, is insnared with many passions, attacked with many fears, disquieted with many cares, distracted with many curiosities, entangled with many vanities, encompassed with many errors, broken with many labors, troubled with temptations, weakened with delights, tormented with want. When shall I enjoy a solid peace, a peace never to be disturbed and always secure, a peace both within and without, a peace everywhere firm? I desire to cleave to heavenly things, but the things of this life and my unmortified passions bear me down. I am willing in mind to be above all things, but by the flesh am obliged against my will to be subject to them. Thus, unhappy man that I am, I fight with myself, and am become burdensome to myself, whilst the spirit seeks to tend upward and the flesh downward. O, my God! remove not thyself from me, and depart not in thy wrath from thy servant. Dart forth thy lightning and disperse them; shoot thy arrows, and let all the phantoms of the enemy be put to flight. Come to my aid, O eternal truth, that no vanity may move me. Come, heavenly sweetness, and let all impurity fly from my face.

For five months after Mr. Davis was imprisoned, his pastor, Rev. Charles Minnegerode, tried unsuccessfully to obtain permission from Secretary Stanton to visit him. At last, through the influence of Stanton's pastor in Washington, permission was secured. Dr. Minnegerode had to promise to talk only of spiritual matters, and General Miles refused to leave them alone together. The meeting has been described by the minister as follows:

I was his pastor, and of course our conversation was influenced by that, and there could be no holding back between us. I had come to sympathize and comfort and pray with him. At last the question of the holy communion came up. I really do not remember whether he or I first mentioned it. He was very anxious to take it. He was a pure and pious man, and felt the need and value of the means of grace. But there was one difficulty. Could he take it in the proper spirit in the frame of a forgiving mind, after all the ill-treatment he had been subjected to? He was too upright and conscientious a Christian man "to eat and drink unworthily," i. e., not in the proper spirit, and, as far as lay in him, in peace with God and man. I left him to settle the question between himself and his own conscience and what he understood God's law to be. In the afternoon General Miles took me to him again. I had spoken to him about the communion, and he promised to make preparation for me. I found Mr. Davis with his mind made up. Knowing the honesty of the man, and that there would be, could be, "no shamming," no mere superstitious belief in the ordinance, I was delighted when I found him ready to commune. He had laid the bridle upon his very natural feeling and was ready to pray, "Father, forgive them." Then came the communion-he and I alone, no one but God with us. It was one of those cases where the Rubric cannot be binding. It was night. The Fortress was so still that you could hear a pin fall. General Miles, with his back to us, leaning against the fireplace in the anteroom, his head on his hands, not moving; the sentinels ordered to stand still, and they stood like statues. I cannot conceive of a more solemn communion scene. But it was telling upon both of us, I trust, for lasting good.

From this time forward the treatment of the prisoner was constantly bettered. In spite of the uncertainty of the future, his spirits rose. The discipline of adversity had its full effect. Patience had never until now been a virtue of Jefferson Davis. The following passages from letters written early in 1866 show this changed spirit:

The gifts with which men are divinely endowed are various, and the requirements of the Lord are never beyond the range of possibility; for he knows our infirmities and judges of our motives. These man cannot know, and is therefore forbidden to judge. We hope and pray for God's forgiveness on the ground of true repentance; and as we cannot tell, in the case of those who trespass against us, whether the repentance is true or feigned, we are bound to accept the seeming. This is possible, but is not easy. I am supported by the conscious rectitude of my course, and humbly acknowledging my many and grievous sins against God, can confidently look to his righteous judgment for vindication in the matters whereof I am accused by man.

Dr. Craven, the sympathetic surgeon who was Mr. Davis's medical adviser for six months, has left an estimate of the religious character of his patient. He said:

There was no affectation of devoutness in my patient; but every opportunity I had of seeing him convinced me more deeply of his sincere religious convictions. He was fond of referring to passages of Scripture, comparing text with text, dwelling on the divine beauty of the imagery and the wonderful adaptation of the whole to every conceivable phase and stage of human life. The Psalms were his favorite portion of the Word, and had always been. Evidence of their divine origin was inherent in their text. Only an intelligence that held the life threads of the entire human family could thus have called forth every wish, joy, fear, exultation, hope, passion, and sorrow of the human heart. There were moments, while speaking on religious subjects, in which Mr. Davis impressed me more than any professor of Christianity I have ever heard. There was a vital earnestness in his discourse, a clear, almost passionate grasp in his faith ; and the thought would frequently recur that a belief capable of consoling such sorrows as his, possessed, and thereby evidenced, a reality, a substance, which no sophistry of the infidel could discredit. In my judgment no more devout exemplar of Christian faith now lives, whatever may have been his political crimes. Errors like other men he had committed ; but stretched now on a bed from which he might never rise, and looking with the eyes of faith, which no walls could bar, up to the throne of Divine mercy, it was his comfort that no such crimes as men laid to his charge reproached him in the whispers of his conscience.

After a year, Mrs. Davis was permitted to visit her husband, and the letters ceased. The last one, written in the early spring when it was supposed that Davis was slowly sinking, contains this passage:

The weather is quite warm, the earth is clothed in her bright robes of promise, and birds sing joyously, and I will not, like the "Bard of Ayr," complain that they are so tuneful while "I so weary fu' o' care." I draw from it the pleasure it was designed to give by the bounteous Creator, who did not mean that man's happiness should be at the mercy of man, and therefore formed him for companionship with nature, and endowed his soul with capacity to feed on hopes which live beyond this fleeting life.

After two years in prison, Mr. Davis was released on bail. Amid the rejoicings of his people, white and black, he walked forth a free man. Of the first hour of this freedom his pastor tells us:

But Mr. Davis turned to me: "Mr. Minnegerode, you who have been with me in my sufferings, and comforted and strengthened me with your prayers, is it not right that we should now once more kneel down together and return thanks?" There was not a dry eye in the room. Mrs. Davis led the way into the adjoining room, more private; and there, in deep-felt prayer and thanksgiving, closed Jefferson Davis's prison life.

Mr. Davis had hoped, he once said, that the concentration of hate upon him would relieve the South somewhat. But with the progress of radical reconstruction he began to fear the worst. From Montreal, where he was living after release from prison, he wrote to a friend in Richmond:

My trust in earthly powers is lost; but my sorrow is not without hope, for God is just and omnipotent. His ways are inscrutable, and history is full of examples of the greatest good being conferred upon a people by events which seemed to be unmitigated evil. Nations are not immortal, and their wickedness will surely be punished in this world.

General Robert Ransom, of North Carolina, who visited Mr. Davis in Memphis during the 70's, when he was trying to mend his fallen fortunes in the insurance business, was struck by his pleasant temper and unaffected piety. Of this he wrote:

At his table he "said grace," or "asked a blessing," first seating himself, and then with bowed head, making the invocation. When he lived in Memphis, I sometimes met at Mr. Davis's residence the venerable and Reverend Dr. Wheat, between whom and Mr. Davis there existed the sweetest relations. As together, on one occasion, we left his residence, Dr. Wheat said to me: "If that man were a member of a Romish Church, he would be canonized as a saint, and his sufferings for ours and the South's sake should forever enshrine him in our hearts as our vicarious sacrifice."

At his home at Beauvoir, Mississippi, he had more time for reading and reflection. In his library was a collection of devotional works, with the best of which he was quite familiar. But as his daughter wrote:

Of all the books that he referred to, the Bible and Shakespeare had the foremost place. His knowledge of the Divine Book was not exceeded by that of any clergyman I ever met, and he contended that in Shakespeare and Solomon one might find a symposium of all human wisdom. The Book of Job was especially loved by him, and I have often heard him say that it contained much of the finest poetry in the language.

In 1886 Mr. Davis made a trip to his birthplace, Fairview, Kentucky, to make a deed of gift, to the new Baptist Church, of the ground upon which the Davis house had formerly stood. During his address he said : "It has been asked why I, who am not a Baptist, give this lot to the Baptist Church ? I am not a Baptist, but my father, who was a better man than I, was a Baptist.'

Every year the Methodists held a seashore camp meeting near Beauvoir, and Mr. Davis always attended for one day at least, exhibiting great interest in the services. Bishop Keener, in a funeral sermon at the death of Mr. Davis, said in part:

It was my good fortune to know Mr. Davis intimately. He attended our seashore camp meetings and ate at my tent. He was a sincere believer in the Christian religion. He listened to the Word and to the experiences of the people of God with reverent interest. I remember on one occasion he met me as I came out of the pulpit and thanked me heartily for the sermon, and said: "You have removed difficulties from my mind in respect to the atonement, and I shall be a better man for it from this time to the end of my life." The sermon was on the sinner who anointed the feet of Jesus, and of the debtors: "When they had nothing to pay, he frankly forgave them both." He did not say this merely as a compliment to the preacher. I was somewhat surprised at the earnestness with which he spoke, and his manner made a great impression on me. My last interview with him was on the cars, on the subject of experimental religion and the wonderful expressions of Napoleon the Great in respect to the Saviour and the gospel.

Of his daily life at Beauvoir his religious duties formed a part. He was an early riser. After private religious devotions, his custom was to call together the family and servants and conduct religious exercises himself. One of his servants said of him: "Mr. Davis was a perfect Christian gentleman in his home. " With Roman fortitude and Christian resignation he met the misfortunes of his declining years. The hatred of enemies still marked him for hostile attack ; some of his own people denounced him; his great ambition had failed of fulfillment; his fortune was lost; one after another his young sons had died,—never did any man suffer more than he did, but never now was he bitter and impatient. One by one the friends of his time of power died. General Gorgas, with whom he was confirmed, died in 1883, and he then wrote to Mrs. Gorgas:

Together we three knelt before the altar to receive confirmation. In the order of nature I, the oldest, should have been first called away; but it has pleased Him who doeth all things well that my friend should go before. If, as I believe, we shall know each other in the future state, it will, I pray, be permitted me to join him in the blessed abode vouchsafed to him by the pure and faithful use of the talents committed to his care.

His favorite hymn was "How Firm a Foundation," every line of which he could repeat from memory:

> *How firm a foundation, ye saints of the Lord,*
> *Is laid for your faith in his excellent word!*
> *What more can he say than to you he hath said,*
> *You who unto Jesus for refuge have fled?*
>
> *When through the deep waters I call thee to go,*
> *The rivers of woe shall not thee overflow;*

For I will be with thee, thy troubles to bless,
And sanctify to thee thy deepest distress.

The soul that on Jesus hath leaned for repose,
I will not, I will not desert to its foes;
That soul, though all hell should endeavor to shake,
I'll never, no never, no never forsake!

Though a member of the Episcopal Church, Mr. Davis cared little for denominational creeds. He was a religious cosmopolitan at home in any religious assembly. His faith was less emotional than intellectual and practical. Impatience and intolerance-temperamental faults-of early life disappeared in later life. "With age I have gained wisdom and lost hauteur," he wrote to a friend. The iron discipline of prison and of later misfortunes strengthened and deepened his spiritual nature. The old warrior and statesman passed through a long and stormy life to a serene and happy ending.

6

Jefferson Davis, the Negroes, and the Negro Problem

If the question were asked, What were the views of Jefferson Davis concerning the negroes? Many people would now as in 1861 unhesitatingly answer that he, like the most extreme of the slaveholders, looked upon the negro as nothing but a form of property somewhat more valuable than horseflesh, and that he considered the race hopelessly inferior and incapable of progress and therefore doomed to the permanent status of slavery. Some of his speeches in Congress would seem to commit him to this view. Yet such an impression would be almost wholly incorrect. His dealings with the race and his private utterances show that he regarded the negro as quite capable of reaching a higher civilization, that he believed slavery to be a more or less temporary status and that he was a most considerate master. In his opinion, slavery was not only a temporary solution of the labor problem in the newly settled South, but it was also a partial solution of what we now call the race problem — the problem of how to make two distinct races live together without friction. That the negro race was fundamentally inferior to the white was his firm conviction. That there was any moral wrong in holding slaves, he, in company with most of the slave-holders, would never admit. By him, as by most men of his class, then as now, slavery was considered a benefit to the negro and a recognition of that law of nature which subjected the weaker to the stronger for the good of both. Slavery took idle, unmoral, barbarous blacks and gradually rooted out their savage traits, giving to them instead the white man's superior civilization — his religion, his language, his customs, his industry. The negro was a child race and slavery was its training school. These convictions shaped his attitude toward the individuals of the race. And never were there more intimate friendships between whites and blacks than between Davis and his servants, as he always called his slaves.

Davis was always popular with young people, dependents and inferiors. When serving in the army among the Indians of the West he was so well liked that in one tribe he was adopted and known as "The Little Chief." As Mrs. Davis said, "he never had with soldiers, children or negroes any difficulty to impress himself upon their hearts." 1 In his intercourse with them he always assumed that they were reasonable beings, able and willing to follow a proper line of conduct, and capable of under- standing mistakes when pointed out to them. Blind obedience was never exacted. To children and to negroes he carefully explained the reasons for doing or not doing a thing and was not satisfied until the understanding was complete. Like his oldest brother, Joseph, he was so careful to regard the rights of the weak that others found it difficult to keep order with his children and servants. From him the black skin never hid the man or woman. He was as polite to a negro as to a white person. Of this trait of Davis's character Major R. W. Milsaps, founder of the

Mississippi college that bears his name, recently related the following incident: "I got a lesson in the treatment of negroes when I was a young man returning South from Harvard. I stopped in Washington and called on Jefferson Davis, then United States Senator from Mississippi. We walked down Pennsylvania Avenue. Many negroes bowed to Mr. Davis and he returned the bow. He was a very polite man. I finally said to him that I thought he must have a good many friends among the negroes. He replied, 'I cannot allow any negro to outdo me in courtesy.' "

In his youth Davis saw less of slavery than is supposed. He did not grow up on a typical Black Belt plantation; the South-west of his youthful days was a new country in which institutions, social and economic, were only forming, and even here, up to the age of twenty-eight, he had lived less than eleven years. Perhaps the first negro who came into close relations with Mr. Davis was James Pemberton. Pemberton was given to him by his mother as a body-servant when he entered the army and remained with him during his entire service — from 1828 to 1835. Though stationed much of the time in free States or in free territory, Pemberton devoted himself with perfect faith to Davis. He carried the purse, took care of his master's arms, accompanied him on dangerous scouting expeditions, foraged and cooked for him and nursed him when sick. In 1831 Davis was ill of pneumonia for several months in the forests of Wisconsin and had no other nurse or physician than James Pemberton. During the illness that followed the death of Davis's wife in 1835 he was again devotedly nursed by Pemberton. After his master returned to Brierfield, James was made manager of the plantation, and held that position until his death in 1852. Davis and his negro manager in their constant intercourse treated one another as gentlemen. When Pemberton came to report he would not take a seat until asked, but Davis always asked him to do so and frequently brought a chair for him. At parting Davis always offered cigars, and Pemberton would accept with grave thanks. Mr. Davis never called him "Jim" but always James, and objected when anyone shortened the name. And so it was with the other negroes; no nicknames or fancy names were allowed, and the negroes had to be called, as they wished, by their full names; no classical names were forced upon them.

The practical acquaintance of Jefferson Davis with the conditions of negro slavery was made during the '30'sand '40'son the Mississippi plantation belonging to his brother and himself. In a bend of the Mississippi River known then as Palmyra Bend, twenty miles below Vicksburg, Joseph Davis, during the twenties, gradually acquired several thousand acres of fine cotton lands by entering government lands, by buying out small frontier farmers who held from 25 to 160 acres each, and who as the slave system grew desired to go farther west. This was the typical development of the plantation system. As an inducement to leave the army Jefferson Davis was offered by his brother Joseph the use of several hundred acres of land and the loan of money for the purchase of slaves. The offer was accepted by the younger brother, who with "his friend and servant James Pemberton" and fourteen negroes began to clear up the plantation which was known as "The Brierfield" on account of the thick growth of briers which covered the fertile land. Davis could not afford to employ an overseer, and except for the assistance given by Pemberton, he was in direct control of all the work. The first house at Brierfield, a log house chinked with clay, was built by the two — master and slave manager. For eight years Davis scarcely left the Bend, and frequently during his brother's annual absences during the hot season he was in charge of both plantations — Brierfield and Hurricane.

Briarfield Plantation, photographed while occupied by Federal troops

One of the most interesting experiments ever made with negro slaves was that initiated by Joseph Davis and carried out by the two brothers on the Hurricane and Brierfield plantations in Warren County, Mississippi. In the management of his own slaves Jefferson Davis was influenced to a considerable extent by the opinions and example of his brother Joseph. It was the theory of the latter that the less the negroes were disciplined by force the better they would conduct themselves. So he tried to train them into habits of self-government. If one could make money for himself he was allowed to do so, paying to his master the wages of an unskilled laborer. Some of Joseph Davis's slaves set up in business for themselves. Notable among these was Ben T. Montgomery, who, with his sons, later purchased both the Davis plantations. Other planters and overseers laughingly spoke of "Joe Davis's free negroes," and when hoopskirts came in assumed that the Davis negroes were to get them and predicted that "Joe Davis will have to widen his cotton rows so that the negro women can work between them." From his brother Joseph, Jefferson Davis adopted the negro self-government plan. No negro was ever punished except after conviction by a jury of blacks. This jury was composed of "settled" men; an old negro presided as judge; there were black sheriffs or constables; witnesses were examined as in white courts, and the punishments were inflicted by negroes. The negroes took great delight in the workings of the court and showed no disposition to be too lenient with criminals. Davis retained the right to modify the sentence or to grant pardon. Mrs. Davis relates an incident which illustrates the workings of the system:

A fine hog had been killed and it was traced to the house of a negro who was a great glutton. Several of the witnesses swore to a number of accessories to the theft. At last the first man asked for a private interview with his master, and in a confidential tone said; "The fact of the matter is, master, they are all tellin' lies. I had nobody at all to hope me. I killed the shote myself and eat pretty near the whole of it, and dat's why I was so sick last week." . . . Davis pardoned the thief but the jury were much scandalized at master's breaking up "dat Cote, for fore God, we'd a cotch de whole tuckin' of 'em, if he had let we alone."

After the death of Pemberton in 1852 Davis employed white overseers, some of whom did not approve of his system of managing negroes. They were not allowed to inflict punishment — only to report offenses. One of them left because of his objection to the negro court. The Davis system which was practiced until 1862 had vitality enough to survive for a while after the Federals had occupied the plantations, and a year later a Northern officer who saw what remained of the self-governing community and knowing nothing of its origin took it for a new development, and an evidence of how one year of freedom would elevate the blacks.

The Library of Hurricane Plantation, photographed under occupation by Federal troops

It is quite likely that Davis could not have understood the mental make-up of such a negro as Frederick Douglass, but he did understand the ins and outs of the average negro's nature. Instinctively the negroes knew this and since he used his understanding for their good his servants were devoted to him. When one was charged by a white person with misconduct Davis always insisted on hearing the negro's side of the story. To him the slaves would appeal from decisions of the overseer and the latter often found it difficult to exact any kind of obedience, so accustomed were the negroes to take all their disputes to their master. One negro girl refused to wait on the overseer's wife because, contrary to her master's rule, she had been called "out'en her name" — Rose instead of Rosina. A man who was disobedient and had threatened the overseer asked Mrs. Davis, "How does you speck us ter b'lieve in them poor white trash when we people has a master that fit and whipped everybody?"

The negroes were allowed the usual plantation privileges. Each family had its "patch" for vegetables and fruits, pigs and chickens, which were raised for their own use and for sale to the master's family. At the birth of a negro child an outfit was given, and at death the burial clothes and food for those who "set up." When a negro was ill the master was expected to furnish or to pay for delicacies, and for a wedding he provided the dinner and the finery. A dentist came regularly to Hurricane and Brierfield to keep the negroes' teeth in order. So careful was Davis of the comfort and health of his negroes that when he was absent in Washington his income from the plantation greatly decreased. The negroes would work well for him but not for his overseers who were not authorized to force them to work.

Some of the negroes did not always appreciate their master's rather gentle methods. Especially did some of them chafe under his attempts to reason with them and thus to make them see their mistakes. Like a small white boy a negro sometimes perferred a thrashing or a round scolding to a serious temperate talk. One negro woman who pretended to cook for him after the death of his first wife was much troubled by the joking way in which he disposed of her failures. As she told the second Mrs. Davis, "Master did me mighty mean dat time; he orter cussed me, but it was mean to make fun of me." Davis, however, never was familiar with his servants in that way peculiar to many Southern masters — a sort of sublime condescending as to a very small child or to a pet animal. To him they were men and women and were treated accordingly.

Provision was made for the religious training of the slaves. Sometimes Davis and his brother paid the salary of a white Methodist preacher who was sent out by the Southern Methodist Church to work among the negroes. "Uncle Bob" was the resident black preacher at Brierfield. Davis said of him: "He was as free from guile and as truthful a man as I ever knew." He had long passed the age for active labor, but still kept up his spiritual supervision of the Brierfield flock. He had a comfortable house and a horse and buggy in which he drove every day to the plantation. It was Davis's conviction that in religious work for the negroes the South "has been a greater practical missionary than all the Society missionaries in the world."

In many ways the plantation negroes showed their appreciation of his mastership. When his first son was born the women and children came to see the newcomer, bringing gifts of chickens, eggs and fruit, and all of them brought boisterous good wishes. When the master would go through the quarters the little negroes would swarm out of the houses to greet him, shake hands with him and catch him around the legs. Upon his departure for a long stay all came to bid him good-bye and to say what they wanted him to bring back for them. When he came home again all duties were suspended until the servants could see and welcome him. In a letter written by his niece, is an account of a home-coming that she witnessed:

"On one occasion when I was a child he arrived at Hurricane, my grandfather's plantation, after a protracted absence, and took me with him to Brierfield, a distance of a mile and a half. It was at once known that he had arrived and .... [the slaves] came running to the house and without ceremony made their way to the room where we were and to my surprise threw themselves before him and embraced his knees at the risk of pulling him down. He must have been accustomed to such demonstrations for he very gently extricated himself and patiently answered their questions and asked kindly for their families."

Whether Davis looked forward to early emancipation it is impossible to say. At times it would seem that he and his brother were training their negroes for freedom soon to come. After the war when in prison Davis spoke of the hopeful emancipation movement of the twenties and thirties which in his opinion was killed by the reaction following the growth of radical abolition sentiment in the North.' But before the civil war neither brother ever made a more definite declaration about negroes in the South than that the exceptional negroes would emerge from slavery. And it is well known that Davis believed slavery a better state for negroes than any sort of freedom offered them in the North or in the South. For the free negro there was then nowhere a place, and Davis believed that it would be difficult to make a place for him. In this conviction he was not so fixed as was Lincoln, for he had a higher opinion of the negro than his great rival had.

While demanding the theoretical right to carry slaves to all territories Davis did not really expect slavery to extend into the far West and Northwest. In fact he thought that the slight expansion that would result would ultimately weaken slavery. In a speech in 1860 he said: "There is a relation belonging to this species of property, unlike that of the apprentice or the hired man, which awakens whatever there is of kindness or of nobility of soul in the heart of him who owns it; this can only be alienated, obscured, or destroyed, by collecting this species of property into such masses that the owner is not personally acquainted with the individuals who compose it. In the relation, however, which can exist in the northern territories, the mere domestic association of one, two, or at most half a dozen servants in a family, associating with the children as they grow up, attending upon age as it declines, there can be nothing against which either philanthropy or humanity can make an appeal. Not even the emancipationist can raise his voice; for this is the high road and open gate to the condition in which the masters would, from interest, in a few years, desire the emancipation of every one who may thus be taken to the north- western frontier."

To rule negroes by laws made for whites was, Davis thought, barbarous. Once before the war he visited a reformatory in the North. Most of the inmates were whites but there was one negro boy who caught Davis by the coat, with the plea "Please buy me, sir, and take me home wid you." "I tried to procure the little fellow's liberty," said Mr. Davis, "and offered to take him and guarantee his freedom, but he was in a free State and I could not get him. It was bad enough to keep white children there, but it was inhuman to incarcerate that irresponsible negro child."

During the Civil War the Confederate President saw nothing of his Brierfield servants. When summoned to Montgomery to lead the Confederates he went to Brierfield, assembled the negroes and made a farewell talk. They expressed devotion to him and he left them never to see them again as slaves and never to live again at Brierfield. He understood that slavery as an economic system had a precarious existence and it was his belief that no matter how the war might end slavery would be destroyed. Before leaving Brierfield he gave to the negroes all the supplies that he could command. To "Uncle Bob," who was rheumatic, he gave so many blankets and supplies that when the Federals came they confiscated them because they said that Davis could never have given him so much, that he must have stolen them or he must be trying to save them for his master. Mr. Davis said, "Nothing ever done to me made me so indignant as the treatment of this old colored man."

After the fall of Vicksburg some of the Davis negroes were carried into the interior to keep them from falling into the hands of the Federals. When Sherman's army captured them the Federals were surprised to find that they would not follow the army. Finally the soldiers set fire to the houses occupied by them in order to make them leave. Some never left the plundered plantation at Davis Bend, others returned, and the self-government system was for a while continued. Grant planned "a negro paradise" on the Davis plantation and many other negroes were brought to the Bend and everything turned over to them. The land was "consecrated as a home for the emancipated .... a suitable place to furnish means and security for the unfortunate race which he [Davis] was so instrumental in oppressing," so that "the nest in which the rebellion was hatched has become the Mecca of freedom." In the crowding that resulted many of the Davis negroes lost their homes, among them "Uncle Bob."

Toward the close of the Civil War, Davis and Robert E. Lee advocated the enlistment of negroes as Confederate soldiers, freedom to be the reward for military service. This plan met much opposition, though Davis used all his influence in favor of it. To members of Congress he declared that the negroes would, in his opinion, make good soldiers if well led, that he himself in Mississippi had led negroes against lawless white men. Finally becoming impatient at the bringing forward of technical objections by the opposition, Davis said: "If the Confederacy falls there should be written on its tombstone, 'Died of a theory. '"

So far as known only two slaves went with Davis to Richmond. These were the son of James Pemberton, who soon ran away to the Federals, and Robert Brown, who remained faithful. The other servants were whites and free negroes. It was found difficult to keep the white servants; it was said that some of them took service with the Davis family for the purpose of acting as spies. One free black girl also went to the Federals. Two other free blacks were connected with the Davis establishment — James H. Jones and James Henry Brooks. The latter was a little negro boy rescued by Mrs. Davis from a drunken mother who was beating him. Mr. Davis went to the mayor of Richmond, had free papers made out for the boy and took him home as a playmate for the children who spoiled him completely. He took part in their games and fights also, and once got a broken head in a clash between the "Hill Cats," or wealthy children, and the "Butcher Cats," or working men's children. He was fighting as a "Hill Cat." President Davis, seeing his injury went down the hill and endeavored to persuade the "Butcher

Cats" to make friends, but though they expressed respect for him they refused to make peace with the "Hill Cats." After the collapse of the Confederacy, the Brooks boy went with the Davis family in their flight toward the Southwest and was captured with them in Georgia. He saw the soldiers forcibly separate Mr. and Mrs. Davis, and long after he declared to some Northern teachers that when grown he intended to kill the officer who took hold of Mrs. Davis. One of the captors named Hudson, who Mrs. Davis thought was a bad character, threatened to adopt the boy. So, when on the way to prison at Fortress Monroe a stop was made at Port Royal, South Carolina, Mrs. Davis sent the boy to General Saxton, an old friend, who was stationed there. The boy fought furiously to keep from going. General Saxton turned him over to a New England school marm then teaching the Sea Island blacks. She reported that he was constantly fighting other negro children who made slighting refer- ences to Davis or sang "We'll hang Jeff Davis on a sour apple tree." He was later sent North to school where he had other fights. A few years before Mr. Davis's death some one sent him a Massachusetts paper containing an account of young Brooks in which it was stated that the man would bear to the grave the marks of beatings inflicted by the Davises. "

Two trusted servants were James H. Jones, a free negro, and Robert Brown. Jones was Davis's valet and coachman; Brown was Mrs. Davis's servant. Both gave faithful service during the war, and in 1865, just before the collapse of the Confederacy, they were sent South with Mrs. Davis. On May 10, 1865, Mr. Davis overtook his wife in the pine woods of Georgia and that night was captured. It was Jones who had the President's horse saddled and ready, and hearing the coming of the enemy waked Mr. Davis and threw over his shoulders the famous rain- coat which Mr. Stanton's imagina- tion and ingenuity magnified into a female costume. After accom- panying the Davis family to Fortress Monroe, Jones went to live in

Raleigh, North Carolina. Some years later when Mr. Davis was in North Carolina Jones called and his old master excused himself to a distinguished company in order to see "my friend, James Jones." Jones, now employed in the Stationery Room of the United States Senate, is full of reminiscences of his master and nothing makes him more indignant than to hear the story about Mr. Davis's disguise when captured. Among his treasures are letters and pictures from the Davis family and a stick that Mr. Davis once used. Jones claims that on the retreat through the Carolinas Mr. Davis gave him the Great Seal of the Confederacy to hide and that for a while he had charge of the coin of the Confederacy treasury. While it is certain that Davis gave him something to hide it is doubtful whether it was the seal. Jones says that his master was a fine "every day man" who "didn't take nobody into his bosom too soon."

Robert Brown spent his whole life in the service of the Davis family. He went with Mrs. Davis and her children from Fortress Monroe to their captivity in Savannah and was nurse and protector to the family. On the vessel that brought Mrs. Davis to Savannah, a sailor was very abusive of Davis and seemed anxious to teach Brown that he was now his master's equal. Brown asked "Am I your equal?" "Yes, certainly," the sailor replied; "Then take this from your equal," said Brown, and knocked him down. On several occasions Brown stood between the helpless family and insult or outrage. Mrs. Davis was not permitted to leave Savannah, so Brown took the children to relatives in Canada. When Mr. Davis was released from prison Brown went to him and as soon as possible re- entered his service. After Davis's death in 1889 Brown went to Colorado to live with his master's daughter, Mrs. Hayes, and there he died.

While in captivity Davis showed intense interest not only in the welfare of his own servants but in the prospects of the race. And he was not left without evidence that the negroes did not hate him as was supposed at the North. When his captors stopped for dinner at

Macon, Georgia, a strange negro servant, of his own accord and at the risk of offending the rather relent- less captors, secretly brought flowers to Davis and messages from Confederate friends in the city. A year later, Mrs. Davis was again in Macon and wrote to Mr. Davis of the friendly inquiries made by negroes. He replied: "The kind manifestations mentioned by you as made by the negro servants are not less touching than those of more cultivated people. I liked them and am gratified by their friendly remembrance. Whatever may be the result of the present experiment the former relation of the races was one which could incite to harshness only a very brutal nature!"

As soon as he was allowed to write and receive letters and to read, Davis's first inquiries were for the Brierfield negroes, and in his letters he expresses apprehension lest the crowding of strange negroes on the place by the Freedmen's Bureau might cause the home negroes to suffer. Later he was much angered when he learned that "Uncle Bob" had been robbed and turned out of his home, and frequently asked about him "with painful anxiety." The imprisoned Confederate ex-President did not endorse the methods adopted by the "Johnson" State governments, which endeavored to fix the place of the negro in the social order. He believed that complete civil rights should be given to the blacks. In one of his letters, dated October 11, 1865, occurs the following passage which illustrates his views:

"I hope the negroes' fidelity will be duly rewarded, and regret that we are not in a position to aid and protect them. There is, I observe, a controversy, which I regret, as to allowing negroes to testify in court. From brother Joe, many years ago, I derived the opinion that they should then [as slaves] be made competent witnesses, the jury judging of their credibility; out of my opinion on that point arose my difficulty with Mr. C--- [an overseer who left the employ of Davis because slaves were allowed to testify in the plantation courts], and any doubt which might have existed in my mind was removed at that time. The change of relation diminishing protection must increase the necessity. Truth alone is inconsistent, and they must be acute and well trained who can so combine as to make falsehood appear like truth when closely examined."

In 1866 Mrs. Davis was allowed to go to Fortress Monroe and live near her husband. Frederick Maginnis, a former free servant, then came and insisted upon re-entering the service of the family. He stoutly resented all unfriendly conduct toward or criticism of Mr. Davis and saved him from much annoyance by sightseers and others. In spite of the fact that General Burton, who succeeded General Miles, was liked by the Davises, Frederick refused to invite the General to his wedding when he married Mrs. Davis's maid. No one, he explained, who held his master in prison should come to his wedding. Of his kindly devotion Mrs. Davis wrote: "What this judicious, capable, delicate-minded man did for us could not be computed in money or told in words ; he and his gentle wife took the sting out of many indignities offered to us in our hours of misfortune. They were both objects of affection and esteem to Mr. Davis as long as he lived."

During this period of enforced seclusion Mr. Davis talked and wrote more about the negro problem than about any other topic. The disturbed condition of the race excited his pity; he did not believe that a million had perished during and just after the war, as some asserted, but thought that the negroes who had left the plantations had suffered greatly; for as slaves they had been cared for, now no one looked after them and they were not yet competent to care for themselves. Most of the immorality exhibited was due, he said, to the removal of the restraints of slavery; the state of freedom was more than the negro could comprehend and he was aimlessly drifting. Of amalgamation of races, that bugbear of many whites, he said that nature had erected barriers against it; no normal white or black desired it; the few cases of intermarriage in the North had no significance; "there could be no problem of the negro at the North for they were too few to be of consequence." The disturbed condition of the race was, in his opinion, due less to the mere fact of freedom than to the evil teachings of the Bureau officers and such people who had excited the ex-slaves with talk of lands, houses, equal rights, etc. He believed that the South- ern States should be left to deal with the negroes. They could do it better than the Bureau. Were its officers soldiers it might be different, but camp followers were a most unsafe class to entrust with the care of a helpless race. He compared them to the Indian agent of the West who so mistreated the red wards of the nation. In this connection he told the following ancedote to Doctor Craven, his physician:

Driving to church one Sunday, a pious but avaricious old gentleman of Mississippi saw a sheep foundered in a quagmire on the side of the road and called John, his coachman, to halt and extricate the animal. John endeavored to pull out the sheep but found that fright and exposure had so sickened the poor brute that its wool came out in fist-fulls whenever pulled. With this news John returned to the carriage.

"Indeed, John, is it good wool?"

"First-class. Right smart good, Massa. Couldn't be better. "

"It's a pity to lose the wool, John. You'd better go see if it is loose everywhere? Perhaps his sickness only makes it loose in parts." John pulled out all the wool and carried it to the carriage.

"It be's all done gone off, Massa. Every hair on him was just fallin' when I picked 'em up."

"Well, throw it in here, John, and now drive to church as fast as you can; I am afraid we shall be late."

"But the poor sheep, Massa! Shan't dis chile go fotch him?"

"Oh, never mind him," returned the philanthropist, measuring the wool with his eye, "even if you dragged him out he could never recover and his flesh would be good for nothing to the butchers."

President Jefferson Davis

So the sheep, stripped of his only covering, was left to die in the swamp, concluded Mr. Davis; and such will be the fate of the poor negroes entrusted to the philanthropic but avaricious Pharisees who now propose to hold them in special care.

The views of Mr. Davis on the economic situation are also interesting. "There is no question," he said, "but that the whites are better off for the abolition of slavery ; it is an equally potent fact that the colored people are not." The planter would no longer be obliged to purchase his labor at high prices, nor care for laborers and their families in sickness and when idle. If a free negro died his master would lose nothing; when a slave died he lost $1,000 or more. True, all the wealth invested in slaves was swept away, but the labor itself remained, and it was possible that the negro race might develop into an efficient tenantry that would make the South again prosperous. For the immediate future the operation of the laws of supply and demand would, he thought, serve to adjust economic relations between whites and blacks, but if theorists continued to interfere the result would be bad.

Davis had the usual mistaken Black Belt belief that only blacks could be efficient laborers in producing the staple crops of the lower South; that Germans, Irish and other immigrants might produce tobacco, and might, for a few years, do some- thing with the other Southern staples, rice, cotton and sugar; but that, in the end, the climate would overcome them, for only negroes could successfully cultivate, year after year, those crops. How mistaken he was, forty years of opportunity' for the whites have shown — -the whites now make nearly all the rice, half the cotton and are beginning to go into the sugar industry. It is now known that a white man can work anywhere in the United States that a negro can and can usually do better work.

Davis foresaw, however, the development of other industries in the South. He believed that the industrial revolution would come early, for he did not foresee the destruction of Reconstruction. The high price of cotton would attract immigrants from the North and from Europe, the great water power of the South would be utilized, factories would spring up and "the happy agricultural state of the

South will become a tradition, and with New England wealth, New England grasping avarice and evil passions will be brought along."

But of the ultimate independence, economic and social, of the negro race he was doubtful. Wherever the races were thrown into political and economic competition, there the negro would finally suffer. Doctor Craven has reported his views on this point, and time has shown the correctness of many of them:

"The papers bore evidence from all sections of increasing hostility between the races, and this was but part of the penalty the poor negro had to pay for freedom. The more political equality was given or approached, the greater must be the social antagonism of the races. In the South, under slavery, there was no such feeling because there could be no such rivalry. Children of the white master were often suckled by negroes, and spoiled during infancy with black playmates .... it was under black huntsmen the young whites took their first lesson in field sports. They fished, shot and hunted together, eating the same bread, drinking from the same cup, sleeping under the same tree with their negro guide. In public conveyances there was no exclusion of the blacks, nor any dislike engendered by competition be- tween white and negro labor. In the bed-chamber of the planter's daughter it was common for a negro girl to sleep, as half attendant, half companion; and while there might be, as in all countries and amongst all races, individual instances of cruel treatment, he was well satisfied that between no master and laboring classes on earth had so kindly and regardful a feeling subsisted. To suppose 'otherwise required a violation of the known laws of human nature. Early associations of service, affection and support were powerful. To these self-interest joined ....

"The attainment of political equality by the negro will revolutionize all this. It will be as if our horses were given the right of intruding into our parlors, or brought directly into competition with human labor, no longer aiding it but as rivals. Put large gangs of white laborers belonging to different nationalities at working beside each other and feuds will probably break out. . . . Emancipation does this upon a gigantic scale, and in the most aggravated form. It throws the whole black race into direct and aggressive competition with the laboring classes of the whites, and the ignorance of the blacks, presuming on their freedom, will embitter every difference. The principle of compensation prevails everywhere through nature, and the negroes will have to pay, in harsher social restrictions and treatment for the attempt to invest them with political equality."

In 1865 the Davis negroes drifted back to Hurricane and Brierfield which were soon restored to Joseph E. Davis, and there they tried to begin the new life. Both plantations were sold in 1866 by Joseph E. Davis to three of his former slaves, Ben Montgomery and his two sons, Thornton and Isaiah, for $300,000. Jefferson Davis was then in prison and Joseph E. Davis was too old to manage the plantations. He believed that his former slaves could, under the Montgomery supervision, gradually attain self-control and economic independence. Jefferson Davis was not so sanguine as was his older brother; he believed that white supervision of the blacks was still necessary. The plan failed mainly because of the general business depression in the South during the seventies. The Montgomery negroes later achieved success as farmers in Kansas, North Dakota and Canada and more recently as the founders of Mound Bayou, a negro town in Mississippi. Isaiah was the only negro member of the Mississippi Convention of 1890; he supported the movement to restrict the suffrage.

For several years after regaining his freedom Mr. Davis had little direct connection with the ex-slaves ; but he never lost interest in their welfare nor did they lose their regard for him. In 1867, after being released from Fortress Monroe, he went to Mississippi on a short visit. Many of the negroes came up to see him at Vicksburg and others went to New Orleans, while to see the remaining ones he made a trip to Brierfield and Hurricane.

In spite of Mr. Davis's Confederate pro-slavery record no instance is known of his having been insulted by an ex-slave, though the negroes at times during Reconstruction became exceedingly impudent to the whites. But as the carpet-bag scalawag regime wore on, the white leaders of the blacks began to consolidate their negro following by arguing that if the white party should come into power the Confederacy would be re- organized, Jefferson Davis would come to Montgomery and slavery would again be established. Thousands upon thousands of negroes over the South came to believe that Jefferson Davis represented all that was hostile to their freedom, and even after the downfall of the reconstruction governments some negroes were afraid of Davis. When in the late seventies and eighties he began to travel about the South many a negro was frightened by his visits and the accompanying demonstrations of the whites. The negroes often avoided the railway stations when his train would stop for him to speak. Before he died most of the blacks lost their fear of him. Proof of this changed feeling was shown by the behavior of the colored school children, who, when Davis visited Atlanta in 1886, attracted general attention by their extravagant welcome.

Among the negroes who knew him Davis was always popular. When he was living at Memphis as the president of an insurance company he was often surrounded by the negroes at the steamboat landing or on the streets and made the object of ovations that surprised strangers. After he again took charge of Brierfield he was, on account of his lenient ways with the tenants, unable to secure as much income from the estate as the Montgomery brothers had paid him in rent. In this connection a relative wrote: "His managers complained that it was impossible to maintain discipline on the plantation, for his former slaves were continually appealing to him and he would write re- proving them [the managers] for being too exacting with the old servants."

After the death of Mr. Davis a Florida newspaper published some letters written to an old negro, Milo Cooper, who then lived in Orlando, but who is now in the Miami, Florida, poor house. Cooper had formerly belonged to some member of the Davis family. He frequently sent little gifts of fruit to Mr. Davis who always returned a courteous acknowledgment. The last letters to Milo were written less than a year before Davis's death.

The following extracts from letters written in 1885 will illustrate his appreciation of the friendship of this humble man:

My Good Friend Milo: The plants did not arrive until the day before your letter came. They have been planted and are much valued by me, and Mrs. Davis unites with me in thanking you for them. . . . Mrs. and Miss Davis unite in kindest regards to you and with best wishes, I am, with thanks,

Yours sincerely,

Jefferson Davis.

. . . We are indebted to you for kind attentions. ... I shall always be glad to hear of your welfare. . . .

Both Mr. and Mrs. Davis are thankful to their friend, Milo Cooper, for the lemons and for his congratulations. Mr. Davis passed his eightieth birthday in good health and spirits for one of his age, and is cheered by the kind spirit evinced by so many friends.

Your Friends,

Jefferson and V. H. Davis.

The cane arrived safely. Please receive my thanks and the assurance that it is a valued testimonial which I shall keep. The peaches were very fine and I have ordered the seed planted in the orchard and hope to raise some from them of better quality than those I have. . . . Always remembering you with friendly interest, my family and self have thankfully to acknowledge your kind attention in sending to us the choice fruits of the season. With renewed assurance of our cordial good wishes, I am,

Very truly yours,

Jefferson Davis.

At the funeral of the great Southern leader his humble friends were there to pay the last tribute of love and respect. Among them was Robert Brown, now an aged man, who had spent his life in Mr. Davis's service, and from Mississippi came his former slaves and their children. "He was a good, kind master," they said "everybody that he ever owned loved him." An old negro of eighty, who could not walk alone, came because he "wanted to see him once more. " One division of the funeral procession was made up of New Orleans negroes. From North Carolina came a telegram from James Jones who had learned of the death too late to reach New Orleans in time for the funeral. From South Florida, Milo Cooper came. He had heard that Mr. Davis was very ill and had started at once to New Orleans hoping to see him in life once more. Old and un- used to travelling Cooper was often delayed and reached New Orleans after the death of his master. His distress upon learning this was pitiable. Mrs. Davis received letters from Thornton Montgomery then living in North Dakota, and the negroes at Brierfield united in sending the following:

We, the old servants and tenants of our beloved master, Honorable Jefferson Davis, have cause to mingle our tears over his death, who was always so kind and thoughtful of our peace and happiness. We extend to you our humble sympathy.

Respectfully,

Your Old Tenants and Servants.

Since all who served Mr. Davis loved him it will not be out of place here to quote what Betty, a white maid in the employ of the Davis family, said to a New Orleans reporter:

"You are writing a good deal about Mr. Davis but he deserved it all. He was good to me and the best friend I ever had. After my mother died and I went to live with Mr. and Mrs. Davis at Beauvoir, he treated me like one of his own family. He would not allow any one to say anything to wound the feelings of a servant."

His servants always said of him that he was "a very fine gentleman."

Jefferson Davis in Retirement at Beauvoir

7

Jefferson Davis's Camel Experiment

When Jefferson Davis was secretary of war he inaugurated an interesting and important experiment for the purpose of determining whether camels could be used for transportation purposes in the United States. Never before or since that decade preceding the Civil War has the government been confronted with such serious problems as were caused by the territorial expansion of the late forties, and of these not the least serious were the difficulties of communication and of transportation on the far western frontiers. Even before the annexation of Texas, New Mexico and California it had been a difficult task to administer government on the outer frontier; after the Mexican war the troubles were multiplied. Immense territories had been added, the frontier was more than doubled in length and was more exposed and dangerous; much of the unsettled region was mountainous, or was dry and without grass and water for pack animals and cavalry horses. The settlements on the Pacific coast also had a frontier-an eastern frontier which had to be guarded as well as the western frontier on the other side of the mountains. And for political and military reasons it was necessary that communications between California and the rest of the United States be made shorter and safer. The experiences of the army officers, especially those of the Quartermaster's Department, during the Mexican war caused them to turn serious attention to the question of transportation. On account of the rough or desert character of much of the country it was not possible to make much use of horses and packmules. Railroads, it was thought, would not for years traverse any of this country, and would never open up all of it. A formidable danger to frontier settlements, to small army garrisons and camps, and to communication of any kind, lay in the attacks of the hostile Indians of this region who, on their swift ponies, could make sudden raids and escape capture by the foot soldiers or the small bodies of cavalry.

That the camel would suit such conditions was the belief of several army officers and particularly of Jefferson Davis, who when a young man had served in the army on the western frontier and later had commanded a regiment in the war with Mexico. The camel could travel faster than a horse and carry heavier loads over rougher ground, could go without water for days at a time and could live upon the poorest forage. It could also endure better than the horse or mule the extremes of heat and cold in this western region. The experience of other peoples had proved the value of the camel. In northern Africa and over the greater part of Asia the animal had always been the beast of burden the most important agent of transportation. In climate and physical geography our western frontiers were similar to the regions which were the home of the camel.

Camels had been used in America, but not in large numbers. The Spaniards had imported them into Cuba and South America for use in transporting ore from the mines to the coast, but this experiment had not been a success. In 1701 some camels were brought to Virginia but nothing more is known of them. In Jamaica, where the English tried them, the "chigger" or "chiqua," an insect which infested the feet of the negroes, got into the feet of the camels, rendering them unserviceable.

The proposal to substitute camels for mules, horses and oxen ir transporting supplies for the army was first made by Major George Hampton Crossman, a graduate of West Point, who was Zachary Taylor's quartermaster in the Seminole war. The difficulty of transporting supplies in Florida caused him to suggest that camels be introduced and used for that purpose. He made a study of the subject, and twenty years later was considered one of the authorities concerning camels.

Prominent among the officers who took an interest in the matter was Major Henry Constantine Wayne, a Georgian, who during and after the Mexican war, served in the Quartermaster's Department. He, with Senator Jefferson Davis, late colonel of the Mississippi Rifles, made extensive studies in regard to the different breeds of the animal, its habitat, the proper care of it, and its adaptability to the arid plains of Texas, New Mexico and California. Wayne, in 1848, made a formal recommendation to the War Department that camels be imported for experimental purposes, and Davis, who was on the military affairs committee, undertook to get an appropriation. In March, 1851, he proposed to insert in the army appropriation bill an amendment providing the sum of $30,000 for the purchase of fifty camels, the hire of ten Arabs, and other expenses. In support of his measure he made a speech reviewing the history of the camel as a servant of man and explaining the need for the animals in the west. There they would be valuable, he said, not only because of their burden-bearing capacity and their ability to live long without water and to eat scraggy bushes, but because of their greater speed. The dromedaries, or swift camels, could be used to mount cavalry and could carry small cannon, as had been done in Persia and in Egypt. Senator Ewing at first objected that the climate in the mountainous parts of the west was too cold for the animal, but Davis convinced him that camels were useful in parts of Asia where the extremes of heat and cold were greater than in the west. Senator Rantoul objected that the proposition was extravagant and others that it was ludicrous. The appropriation was not made.

A year later, when Davis had returned to Mississippi, Bissell, of Illinois, introduced into the House a bill carrying a $20,000 appropriation for the purchase of camels. Both Evans, of Maine, and Shields, of Ohio, who supported the measure, spoke of it as originating with Davis. The remarks made show that the War Department had considered the matter carefully and favored the measure. The house passed the camel bill but it was lost in the senate.

By this time the public was becoming familiar with the proposal to import camels and numerous suggestions were made to the government. John Russell Bartlett, the author and ethnologist, who for three years (1850-1853) had worked on the southwestern boundary, was of the opinion that camels should be used in that region. George Robins Gliddon, the archeologist, who had lived in Egypt for twenty- three years, wrote a memorial to congress declaring that the project was feasible. Another eminent person, who was exerting himself to get the government to make the experiment, was George Perkins Marsh, the philologist and diplomat, who had lived in the Levant and who was acquainted with the camel in Turkey and Italy. To help the cause he delivered a lecture in 1854 at the Smithsonian Institution and also wrote a little book which was published in 1856: "The Camel, his Organization, Habits and Uses, considered with reference to his Intro- duction into the United States." The general interest in the camel project caused the organization of "The American Camel Company," of New York, which proposed to import burden camels for use in the west. About 1857 the company landed one shipment in Texas, but nothing is known of further activities.

In 1853 Jefferson Davis returned to Washington as secretary of war and at once took up the question of importing and experimenting with camels. He had already made extensive researches into the his- tory and habits of the camel when a member of the senate committee on military affairs. Now Major Wayne, of the Quartermaster's Department, and Lieutenant Beale and Captain Adams, of the Fort Yuma post, were directed to prepare information with reference to the use of camels on the western deserts. In his report at the end of the year Davis made a strong recommendation to Congress in favor of an experiment. He went into details about the great extent of newly acquired territory, its lack of navigable streams and of good roads, and the absence of grass and water for long distances. With horses, mules and oxen long circuitous routes had to be followed; the cost of transportation alone in this region was for one year nearly half a million dollars; and Indians made attacks and escaped because they could not be followed into the deserts and mountains; moreover, the Pacific coast, 120 days distant, was defenseless and for that reason quicker and better transportation must be provided.

Congress refused to make the desired appropriation and in December, 1854, Davis renewed his request for money to make the experiment. When the army appropriation bill was reported it carried no appropriation for the purchase of camels, but Senator Shields of Illinois and some western representative secured the amount of $30,000 for this purpose. The bill became a law on March 3, 1855, and Davis at once proceeded to send for the animals. The camels could be procured only from the Levant. The mission to the Orient was first offered to Major Crossman, who nearly twenty years before had first suggested the use of camels. He declined, and Davis sent Major Wayne and Lieutenant David D. Porter of the Navy. Wayne was to go to England and France to secure further information about the camel, and Porter was to take the storeship Supply to the Mediterranean and meet Wayne at Spezzia. Davis furnished Wayne with a digest of all that was known about the camel and his letters of instruction show that the secretary possessed full knowledge of the subject.

Wayne visited first the Zoological Gardens in England and reported that camels had been reared there under such conditions that he was certain of success in the United States. Next he went to Paris to consult with the French officers who had made use of camels in Algeria. From the information secured he decided that the African camel would not succeed in America as well as the Asiatic. He adopted the following classification: The Bactrian was the large two-humped animal, the Arabian the one-humped, and the "dromedary" was merely a swift Arabian, not a burden camel. These were points then confused by naturalists. Meanwhile Lieutenant Porter had gone ahead and inspected at Pisa the camel herd of the Duke of Tuscany. These were descendants from Egyptian stock and had been used in Italy for two hundred years. There were 250 of them, Porter wrote, and they performed the work of 1,000 horses-some of them carrying as much as 1,200 pounds at a load; but he considered them overworked and badly cared for.

After Wayne and Porter met at Spezzia they decided to get a camel at once in order to study its habits and to learn the proper treatment. They went in the Supply to Tunis, where Mohammed Bey gave them two animals which they hoisted on board, and proceeded to the Asiatic coasts, studying on the way the habits, ailments and care of the animals. Their observations were carefully reduced to writing and sent to Davis. The first stop after leaving Tunis was made at Smyrna, where they found fine burden camels, but no dromedaries such as Davis was anxious to get for chasing the Indians; at Salonica, the next stop, there were no camels-from both places the dromedaries had been taken for use in the Crimean war then going on. Davis had instructed Wayne and Porter to go to Persia to see about the Bactrians of that region, but at Salonica they found that the roads were closed by snow- it was now December-and that the country was in an unsettled condition. So after sending circulars to the English-speaking missionaries, consuls and business men in the Levant requesting information, the two officers sailed to Constantinople and thence went to the Crimea to see what was being done there with the camels. Wayne reported that the Bactrians seemed to be of little use because they were slow and because of their two humps, which made it difficult to fasten on the loads. But the one-humped Arabians were valuable; 3,000 were already in the Crimea and more were to be imported for the next campaign. The English officers who had used them in India were enthusiastic.

At Constantinople Wayne was disappointed in not getting a supply of both kinds of animals. All there were worthless or had the "itch." The Sultan sent far into the interior for good ones to give them, but Wayne, anxious to go to Egypt, did not wait for them to be brought to Constantinople. The Supply sailed to Egypt and while Wayne went to Cairo to get permission to export dromedaries Porter remained at Alexandria looking over the market and making a lengthy report to Secretary Davis. He was now an enthusiast on the subject of camels. "I hope to see the day," he wrote, "when every Southern planter will be using the animal extensively." The education of Wayne and Porter progressed rapidly. They were soon expert camel traders. Animals at first palmed off on them as good they were now able to pronounce worth- less. These they got rid of-two, for instance, they sold to a butcher in Constantinople for $44. Porter said "the good condition of these camels recommended them to a butcher of Constantinople, who bought them for pur- poses known only to himself." The natives now could not impose upon the ignorance of the American officers. An amusing incident happened in Egypt. Wayne found it difficult to get permission to carry camels out of the country. He wanted twenty dromedaries; but could get permission to carry out only two. After protest this number was increased to four and later to five. Some what dis- gusted, Wayne started to leave Egypt, but the viceroy notified him that he would present six camels to the United States government. After delay the animals came. Porter after looking at them wrote an indignant letter refusing to accept the gift. They were worthless and diseased," he said, and "I can not conscientiously receive them? The attempt of the Egyptian officials, he said "fraudulently to force a present on us" was a "discourtesy" to the United States which he would not tolerate. The viceroy laid the blame upon his servants and finally six good dromedaries were secured. Only three others were taken on board here, and the Supply sailed for Smyrna to complete the cargo.

The loading of the camels was done under Porter's supervision. Before leaving the United States he had prepared a "camel deck" or stable on the lower deck and had cut through the upper deck to secure a constant supply of fresh air for the animals. To get them on board he constructed a long flat-bottomed boat which could be run ashore. On this was a strong car with wheels which could be pulled out on land to receive the camels who often had to be dragged into it, and then the car was rolled back on the boat. From the boat the car holding the camel was hoisted into the ship and let down to the "camel deck "

While in Alexandria waiting for the viceroy to act, Mr. G. H. Heap, an American who had lived in Tunis and who accompanied the expedition, was sent on ahead to purchase other camels and equipments. When the Supply reached Smyrna, on January 30, 1856, Heap had the camels, saddles and other supplies ready. They were taken on board and on February 15 the Supply was turned toward America. The cargo consisted of thirty-three camels: nine dromedaries (Arabians) from Egypt; twenty Arabian burden camels; one young Arabian camel; two Bactrian (two humped) males; one Booghdee or Tuilu, the offspring of a Bactrian male and an Arabian female, having one hump.

Before leaving Smyrna the females that were not already with young were covered by the males, since it was the rutting season, and it was desired to increase the herd as fast as possible. To take care of them four Americans, two Turks and three Arabs were brought along-all under the supervision of Albert Ray, an army wagon master During the return trip, which lasted three months, the weather was rough. Wayne and Porter had been requested by Davis to stop at the Canaries to see the camels there, but they were prevented by heavy winds. Wayne occupied himself in writing a long report to the secretary of war and in translating French works relating to camels. He wrote Davis that the information furnished by the letter had been generally accurate. The report gave a detailed history of the camel, an account of the different breeds, their habits and usefulness, the nature of their diseases, the location of the best stock, the cost, the proper food and the methods of transportation. One of the papers translated was by Linant Bey, a French engineer in the Egyptian service, on "The Egyptian Dromedary"; one by General J. L. Carbuccia on "The Use of the Camel in Algiers." A paper by Colonel F. Columbari entitled "The Zemboureks, or the Dromedary Field Artillery of the Persian Army," had been translated and illustrated by Wayne in 1854.

During the voyage the animals were under the direct supervision of Lieutenant Porter, who interested himself in the minutest details. On the camel deck he posted detailed regulations to be followed in the care of the camels. A "journal of the camel deck" was kept, and in it every day wagon master Ray made note of every item of interest concerning the animals, their ailments, feed, appetites, when they were rubbed, curried, oiled, salted, etc. Some of the names are given: Said, Ayesha, Gourmal, Ibrim, etc. The first young camel born on board the ship was dubbed "Uncle Sam" and was trained by one of the Turks as a Pehlevan, or wrestler. Four of the grown camels were Pehlevans. Camel fighting was as much an oriental amusement as horse racing was a Kentucky sport, and Porter thought that the Americans might in time come to like camel contests.

When the weather was stormy and the ship unsteady there was danger of the animals falling on the smooth deck and injuring themselves. To prevent this Porter fashioned a sort of harness for each one and in rough weather made them kneel and strapped them to the deck. Once they were so strapped down for seventy-two hours.

During the voyage six calves were born. Of these only two lived; the others were probably killed by the ministrations of a quack Turkish camel doctor on board. Porter took care of the young camels as if they had been children, and gravely wrote to Davis about their diet, appetite, health, etc. Soon he was a better camel doctor than the Turk and the latter was superseded. To the secretary of war Porter sent some of the Turk's prescriptions: For a cold give the camel a piece of cheese; for swollen legs, tea and gunpowder; cauterize frequently for skin diseases; and for other complaints tickle the camel's nose with a chameleon's tail, or boil a young sheep in molasses and administer half of the mixture while hot. No wonder Porter was certain that Americans could manage camels better than the Asiatics.

At Kingston, Jamaica, a stop was made and great numbers of visitors came on board to see the camels-in one day 4,000 came. But here the camels suffered so much from heat that departure was hastened. On April 29, 1856, the store ship reached Pass Cavallo, off Indianola, where, it was planned, the camels were to be landed. But the sea was so rough that the transfer to lighters could not be made. Porter then sailed to the Balize, the southwestern mouth of the Mississippi River, and there on May 10 he transferred his cargo to the steamer Fashion under Major Wayne. Four days later Wayne landed the cargo at Powder Point, three miles below Indianola. The animals were in good condition notwithstanding the long confine-ment-one of them had been on board nine months. "On being landed, and feeling once again the solid earth beneath them," Porter wrote, "they became excited to an almost uncontrollable degree, rearing, kicking, crying out, breaking halters, tearing up pickets, and by other fantastic tricks demonstrating their enjoyment of the 'liberty of the soil.' Some of the males becoming even pugnacious in their excitement, were with difficulty restrained from attacking each other." The Texans were greatly interested in the camels and

Porter wrote later to Davis that "perhaps the love of amusements may render the importation of camels in Texas popular if their utility does not recommend them." He meant that the Texans might possibly take to camel fighting.

Less than one third of the appropriation had been expended and Davis determined to send at once for a second cargo of camels. Wayne was again offered command of the vessel, but he preferred to remain in Texas to conduct the experiment. Major Crossman also declined to go, Finally Porter and Heap were sent. Before leaving Porter carried to Davis the "Camel Deck Journal," his letters rejecting the camels offered by the viceroy of Egypt, and some drawings of camels in harness made by Mr. Heap. Porter arrived at Smyrna in November, 1856, where he found that Heap, who had gone on ahead, had collected a number of young camels. The six dromedaries presented by the Sultan had been sent to Smyrna and these with the others were taken on board, On November 14 the Supply again set sail for Texas. On board were forty-four animals: Two Bactrian males; three Arabian males; one Tuilu, cross-bred, male; one Tuilu, cross-bred, female; thirty-seven Arabian females.

The second voyage homeward lasted eighty-eight days and was rougher than the first. For thirteen days at one time the camels were strapped to the deck. But only three died during this voyage and Porter turned over to Captain Van Bockelen, quartermaster at Indianola, forty-one animals in good condition. There were now seventy in the herd, five of the first number having died since reaching Texas.

Meanwhile, during the summer of 1856, Wayne had been testing the value of the camel as a burden bearer. Certain of success, he wanted to breed camels until the herd was large, but Davis wanted to ascertain first whether they would be useful. For a few days the animals rested at Indianola. The Texans refused to believe in their burden bearing capacity, so one day Major Wayne had two bales of hay, weighing 314 pounds each, loaded on one of the males; the spectators were sure that he could not rise; Wayne then put two more bales on, making 1,256 pounds in all. The camel rose easily and walked off. Wayne wrote to Davis that it quite convinced the skeptical and that it caused a Texan poet to break into verse in the *Indianola Bulletin.* Later Miss Mary A. Shirkey, of Victoria, Texas, knitted from camel's hair a pair of socks for President Pierce. Major Wayne forwarded them through the secretary of war.

During the latter part of May the camels were marched by easy stages to San Antonio where they were kept nearly a month and then removed to Val Verde (Green Valley)—a military post sixty miles southwest of San Antonio. Here at Camp Verde, as it was called, the permanent camel post was located. In September Wayne sent camels and horses to San Antonio for supplies. The camels easily brought 600 pounds each; six of them carrying as much as twelve horses could haul in wagons and in forty-two hours less time; the camels made the sixty miles in two days and six hours, while the horses required over four days. Later tests, made in November and December, 1856, showed that camels could easily climb mountain trails where wagons could not go, and that on muddy roads over which horses could not draw wagons, the camels traveled without fatigue. Only on slippery slopes were they troubled, and at the crossing of streams. Not being accustomed to fording, they had to be driven in by throwing water in their faces. At the end of 1856 Davis reported that in his opinion the experiment was a success.

Davis left the War Department in March, 1857, and was succeeded by John B. Floyd. Wayne was transferred to Washington and the camels were left under the supervision of Captain J. N. Palmer, at Campe Verde. In 1858 the "Société imperiale Zoologique d'acclimatation" of Paris, awarded to Major Wayne a first class gold medal for the successful introduction and acclimation of the camel in the United States. Secretary Floyd was convinced of the usefulness of camels on the western plains, and in his second report, December, 1858, he recommended that 1,000 be purchased. This recommendation was repeated in 1859 and in 1860, but Congress paid no attention to the matter.

After 1857 some of the camels were sent to the army posts at El Paso and Bowie. They were disliked by the army hostlers; the Arabian and Turkish caretakers were regarded with contempt, and it was difficult to get the American hostlers and wagon masters to help in the experiments. The horses objected to the smell of the camels when stabled or picketed near them and the hostlers sometimes turned the camels loose to get rid of them. However, during the four years before the outbreak of the civil war some interesting and successful attempts were made to use the "ship of the desert" for military transportation purposes. The first lengthy expedition was made by Lieutenant Edward F. Beale, who on September 1 set out to make a wagon road from Fort Defiance, New Mexico, to California. Camels, as well as mules, were used by the road-making party. The work lasted forty- eight days. Beale reported that the camels had been subjected to the severest tests and had failed in no instance; that they even learned to swim rivers. Beale considered that one of them was worth four good mules. From 1857 to 1861 Beale with twenty camels was occupied in exploring the unknown regions of the southwest. He found that the camels could do successfully all that was required of them. By 1861 his herd of twenty had increased to twenty-eight.

Other trials of the camels were made in 1859 by Major D. H. Vinton, who used twenty-four of them in carrying burdens for a surveying party. From May to August, 1859, Lieutenant Edward L. Hartz was in charge of the camel herd. Hartz sent to the War Department a full journal of an exploring expedition in which camels and mules were used. His verdict was not quite so enthusiastic as those of Wayne and Beale, but he pronounced the experiment a success. The camels were inferior to mules, he said, on slippery surfaces; they were not as good climbers as mules, but they were much swifter on level, rocky or sandy ground; it was difficult to keep the loads on the camels and frequent stops had to be made to replace the saddles, which could not be properly fastened by inexperienced packers. It was his belief that the female camel was better than the male; that the camels really preferred bushes, dry shrubs and grasses to grazing grasses; that they could go without water for more than two days and not suffer. All in all, he concluded, the camel was much superior to the mule.

The success of the War Department tests caused other importations. In 1858 a British vessel brought over two cargoes of camels for a Mrs. Watson, who lived near Houston, Texas. Arab caretakers were employed and F. R. Lubbock, later governor of Texas, was put in charge of them. He says that they were healthy, and useful, but that they created too much sensation when they went into Houston or traveled about the country.

There is a tradition that ten animals were brought to New York in 1857; of these two survived and were sent to Nevada, where by 1875 their offspring numbered ninety-five.

In 1861 a San Francisco company imported twenty Bactrians (two-umped) camels from the highlands of Asia for use in transporting alt from Esmeralda County, Nevada, to the Washoe Silver Mill, a istance of two hundred miles. The discovery of a nearer supply of alt left the camels without regular occupation. Some were used near Virginia City as late as 1876 to carry cord-wood.

When the civil war began the government camels were scattered. Some were at Camp Verde, Lieutenant Beale's herd of twenty-eight was in California, and others at various posts in Texas. Beale, whom in 1861 Lincoln had appointed surveyor-general of California, proposed to Stanton that the government animals, which were scattered about in California doing nothing, should be turned over to him for use in carrying supplies and in making explorations. His request was not granted. In 1863 an attempt was made to use the camels in carrying the mails between New Mexico and California, but the officers in charge of the mails, knowing nothing of camels, objected and they were not used. In 1864 the herd, now numbering thirty-five, was sold to Samuel McLaughlin, who disposed of them later to circuses and zoological gardens.

The herds at Camp Verde and other places in Texas were constantly used by the army quartermasters up to 1861. The ugly animals were well known sights in the towns near Camp Verde and between San Antonio and the gulf coast. But horses were often frightened by them and people began to regard them as a nuisance; Brownsville had an ordinance forbidding them on the streets. When the United States forces were withdrawn from Texas in 1861, the camels fell into the hands of the Confederates who made little use of them and spent little care upon them. They were turned loose to graze and some wandered away. Three of them were caught in Arkansas by union forces and in 1863 they were sold in Iowa at auction. Others found their way into Mexico. A few were used by the Confederate Post Office Department. At the close of the civil war the animals at the Camp Verde station, numbering sixty-six, were advertised for sale. Only three bids were received, one for $5 each, one for $10 each, and one for $31 each. So on March 8, 1866, the quartermaster in New Orleans sold to Colonel Bethel Coop-wood the camels then in Texas. Colonel Coopwood carried them to Mexico and disposed of them to traveling circuses.

The stray camels were heard from occasionally-stampeding horses and ravaging fields. The Indians killed and ate some. The Navajos, it is said, once tied a Mexican shepherd to a camel's back and turned the animal loose. During the seventies soldiers in the southwest reported seeing strange camels. Colonel Philip Reade writes that in July, 1875, he saw a herd of wild camels near Oatman's Flat, on the Gila River. One of the government camels was living a few years ag in the public parks of the City of Mexico.

The attempt to make use of camels might have succeeded under different conditions. Davis, the strongest advocate of the use of the camel, went out of the war office just as the experiment promised. success. Major Wayne, who alone of army officers had full theoretical and practical knowledge of camels, was transferred to office work at Washington, and Beale, who later accumulated considerable experience, was not encouraged by the War Department officials. The army' teamsters and most of the officers outside of the Quartermaster's Department, took no interest in the matter and some opposed the experiment; the members of Congress were too deeply engaged in sectional controversies to care much about transportation problems in New Mexico. The Civil War afterward occupied the attention of those in authority while the herds were neglected, and the fact that Jefferson Davis had inaugurated the experiment was, in the opinion of many, enough to condemn it. After the war the rapid development of railroads solved many of the problems that seemed so serious in the fifties.

And yet had Wayne, Beale and Hartz been given ten years of favorable conditions, it is probable that camels would now be used as beasts of burden in some parts of the south and west, for conditions still exist in that section under which the camel would be useful.

8

William Tecumseh Sherman as College President

The Louisiana State Seminary (now the Louisiana State University,) began its first session on January 2, 1860, with William Tecumseh Sherman as superintendent or president. The University, a few months ago, celebrated with brilliant exercises its semi-centennial, and upon that occasion there came from New York to speak for the family of its first executive P. Tecumseh Sherman, the youngest son of the general. During the first years of its existence the institution has passed through many vicissitudes and has developed from a small military seminary into a modern University, but it has never lost the impress of its first organization , perfected from 1859 to 1861 by Sherman. During the war Sherman's expressed wishes preserved the institution from total destruction by the Federal armies, and after the war the University, struggling under the weight of carpetbaggism, continued to receive assistance from him in his position of authority. Finally, it was due mainly to him that the Federal government gave to the University its present beautiful site -the old military post of Baton Rouge.

LOUISIANA STATE SEMINARY IN 1860
Sherman's office was the room to the left of the entrance

The Louisiana State Seminary, to the presidency of which Sherman was elected on August 2, 1859, was in origin and organization similar to the state universities of other states. Its endowment was derived from the sale of public lands donated in 1806 and 1811 for educational purposes to the state of Louisiana. For the location of the school many towns fought before the legislature until 1852 when that body chose a site out in the pine woods four miles from Alexandria, in Rapides Parish, on the north bank of Red River. Here during the next six years a fine building was erected, and meanwhile the legislature enacted several laws providing for the academic organization.

The first faculty was elected in August, 1859. Sherman was made superintendent and professor of engineering; Dr. Anthony Vallas, a noted Hungarian scholar, exiled on account of his connection with the Revolution of 1848, was professor of mathematics; Francis W. Smith and David French Boyd, both young Virginians and graduates of the University of Virginia, were professors respectively of chemistry and ancient languages; E. Berte St. Ange, a graduate of the Lycée Charlemagne, Paris, and formerly an officer of the French navy and a noted duellist, was professor of modern languages. The surgeon and adjutant was Dr. John Sevier of Tennessee who had served with distinction in Nicaragua under William Walker, the filibuster; later Dr. Sevier gave place to Dr. Powhatan Clarke, a Virginian, trained in Paris, who now is the president of the Retired Baltimore College of Physicians and Surgeons and is the only surviving colleague of Sherman.

The appointment of Sherman was somewhat of a surprise to him. After resigning from the army he had tried banking and law in California, New York, and Kansas, and, being disgusted with both professions, had applied for the Louisiana position. His attention had been called to this place by Major Don Carlos Buell of the War Department, and his election was brought about mainly through the influence of General G. Mason Graham, of Louisiana, half brother of General R. B. Mason, who had been Sherman's commanding officer in California. Graham, then a resident of Rapides parish and vice-president of the Board of Supervisors, had formed a favorable opinion of Sherman. In connection with the election an interesting incident is related. Before coming to Sherman's application the board examined voluminous papers relating to the merits of several other candidates. Sherman's application consisted of a half page note making application for the place and referring to Braxton Bragg, P. G. T. Beauregard, and Richard Taylor, all then living in Louisiana. "No sooner was this letter read, " so the story goes, "than Sam Henarie, a plain business man and a member of the board, exclaimed; ' By God, he's my man. He's a man of sense. I'm ready for the vote.' 'But,' said Governor Wickliffe, ' we have a number more of applications. We must read them all . ' 'Well, you can read them, but let me out of here while you are reading. When you get through, call me and I'll come back and vote for Sherman.'"

Sherman was in Leavenworth, Kansas, practicing law when notified of his election. He went at once to Lancaster, Ohio, where his family was staying and there remained during the rest of the summer. In preparation for the opening of the Seminary he carried on an extensive correspondence with army officers, notable among them Captain George B. McClellan, in regard to the plans and policies best suited to military schools. In November he came south to arrange for the beginning of the first session.

Sherman's first work in Louisiana was the preparation of a body of rules for the government of officers and students of the Seminary. For some of these he drew upon the regulations of the Virginia Military Institute, already famed as a military school, and upon his own experience at West Point. Some of the more interesting rules are as follows:

No Cadet shall keep a waiter, horse, or dog.

No Cadet shall in any way use tobacco, nor have it in his room or in his possession.

No Cadet shall cook or prepare food in the Seminary building, or have cooked provisions in his room, without permission.

No Cadet shall visit the room of any other Cadet during the hours allotted to study and sleep.

No Cadet shall send or accept a challenge to fight a duel, or shall be the bearer of such a challenge, written or verbal.

Any Cadet who shall abuse another Cadet, by playing unjustifiable tricks on him, shall be punished according to the nature of the offense.

No Cadet shall throw stones or other missiles in the vicinity of the building.

No Cadet shall play cards, or have them in his possession. Games of Chess and Backgammon will be allowed, but only in recreation hours; and in no case will betting of money or other things be permitted.

All unnecessary talking at the table is prohibited. The Carvers alone shall call for the waiters.

Wasting, or taking from the Mess Hall, provisions, or mess furniture of any kind, is strictly forbidden.

A minority of the Board of Supervisors was opposed to the military feature of the organization, and one of these secured the manuscript of the regulations prepared by the superintendent and for several months refused to return it. Consequently it was not printed until the summer of 1860. The original manuscript of the regulations in Sherman's handwriting was taken from the Seminary during Bank's Red River expedition in 1864 by General T. Kirby Smith and was returned to the Louisiana State University by his son in 1909.

A circular of information was next prepared and sent out over the state. This circular emphasized the fact that the school would be a military and scientific institution, and not a classical school similar to the numerous other colleges which the state of Louisiana had tried to establish but had failed.

Early in November, 1859, Sherman moved to the Seminary building in order to push to completion the work which still had to be done. In his memoirs he says of this work:

"A carpenter named James resided there and had the general charge of the property; but, as there was not a table, chair, blackboard, or anything on hand, necessary for the beginning, I concluded to quarter myself in one of the rooms of the Seminary, and board with an old black woman who cooked for James, so that I might personally push forward the necessary preparations. There was an old rail fence about the place and a large pile

of boards in front. I immediately engaged four carpenters, and set them to work to make out of these boards mess-tables, benches, black- boards, etc. I also opened a correspondence with the professors-elect, and with all parties of influence in the State, who were interested in our work."

The fact that Sherman boarded with the carpenters gave the foundation to the story of later days that the state of Louisiana, gathering all its resources for war, refused to pay Sherman's salary and thus reduced him to such straits that he was forced to live on servant's fare. He, at the time, complained that the negroes thought him "as rich as Croesus himself. " He wrote to Mrs. Sherman "that the old cook Amy always hid away for me the best pieces of butter and made my breakfast and dinner better than the carpenters', always saying she knowed I wasn't used to such kind of living. She don't know what I have passed through. "

In December as soon as he had cleared the building of rubbish Sherman went to New Orleans and there purchased furniture and the texts and reference books necessary for the beginning of academic work.

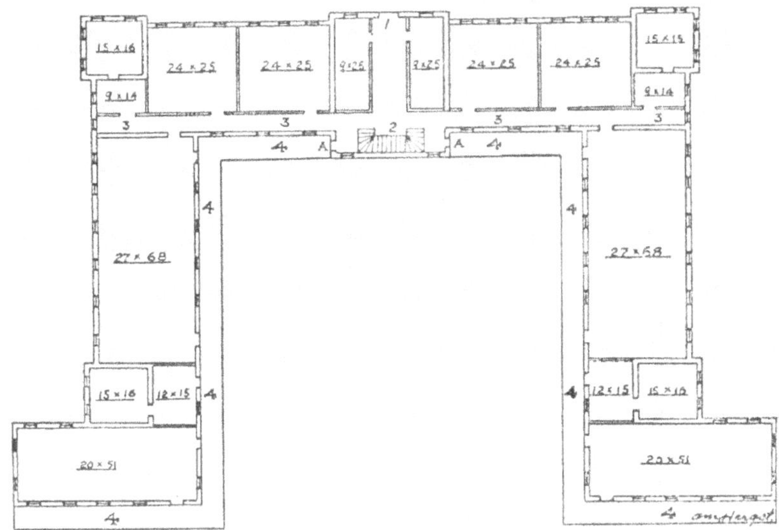

The First Floor of the Seminary Building

During November and December he conducted an extensive correspondence with those who were interested in his work. To former army acquaintances he wrote for advice as to organization and administration. From Chicago George B. McClellan sent information as to text-books, uniforms, athletics, and the course of study. Braxton Bragg, formerly Sherman's commanding officer in the Third Artillery, wrote from his plantation at Thibodeaux, Louisiana, that he was urging the merits of the Seminary, and P. G. T. Beauregard, then stationed in New Orleans, sent greetings and offers of support to the institution.

In December the professors gathered at Alexandria and at the Seminary in readiness for the opening. Sherman's estimates of his colleagues are found in his letters to his wife. Of Dr. Vallas he wrote, "he is an Episcopal clergyman but his religion don't hurt him much. He seems a pleasant enough man, fifty years old, fat, easy and comfortable. " Of the others he said: "Professor Boyd is a young man a very clever gentleman .. Mr. Smith is one of the real Virginia F. F. V's a very handsome young man of twenty-two who will doubtless be good company-(Vallas and St. Ange are very clever gentlemen-but these are foreigners with their peculiarities.) We have also a Dr. Sevier here of Tennessee, a rough sort of fellow but a pretty fair sort of man-indeed, on the whole, the professors are above the mediocrity. "

Of his first meeting with Sherman, Professor Boyd, who succeeded him as president, wrote in later years: "Late in the afternoon of the day before the school was to open, I reported at the office of the superintendent, Colonel W. T. Sherman. He received me very kindly and in his characteristic way chatted about everything. He was then, as he ever was, the prince of talkers. I fell in love with him at first sight. His appearance was very striking. Tall, angular, with figure slightly bent, bright hazel eyes and auburn hair, with a tuft of it behind that would, when he was a little excited, stick straight out. Until I met him I had supposed him a Georgian; and, when he corrected me, and told me, that he was from Ohio, I could but ask, considering the great sectional feeling and excitement then over the country, if he was related to the then famous Republican candidate for the speakership of the House, John Sherman? 'Only a brother,' said he, 'and I don't care who knows it !' I could but admire the courage and defiance of his reply. But from that time on, he and I had it up and down, hot and heavy on politics, yet always so pleasantly. "

THE FIRST FACULTY
(1) William Tecumseh Sherman; (2) Powhatan Clarke;
(3) Anthony Vallas; (4) D. F. Boyd; (5) Francis W. Smith
Dr. Clarke's portrait is of 1910; the others are of 1860. No portrait of Professor
St. Ange can be found

To the opening of the Seminary on January 2, 1860, there came "a heterogeneous crowd of matriculates. " "The sons of wealthy planters from the rivers, and aristocratic Creoles from the South, the nimble pony-riding Cajeans from the prairies, and the diligent quiet fellows from the pine woods composed the corps of cadets and came to be known as ' Sherman's boys'. He always spoke of them as ' my boys, ' continuing to do so after he left the college. Among them were some wild subjects, impatient of control, and Sherman's life at the college was not all smooth sailing." So wrote one of those boys who for two years sat under Sherman's instruction.

The superintendent remarked upon the fact that many of the boys were accompanied by their mothers who seemed to think that going to college was a dangerous business and who parted from their sons "with tears and blessings". "The dullest boys", he said, "have the most affectionate mothers, and the most vicious boys here come recommended with all the virtues of saints. Of course I promised to be a father to them all. " Some of the parents wrote to Sherman giving minute instruction as to how their sons were to be looked after, how disciplined, fed, and clothed. The superintendent was expected to perform duties ranging from those of a nurse or mother to those of a jailor. But most of them, he states, were wholly sensible in their views of what they expected their sons to get from their college course. A curious request made by Major P. G. T. Beauregard, then living in New Orleans, was that his son begiven a room-mate "who has not seen much of city life."

The best source of information about the opening of the Seminary is the private correspondence of Sherman, who wrote frequently and without reserve to his wife and little daughter and other relatives. From letters written in January, 1860, we learn that the work was rapidly organized. He says:

"I took things in hand ala militarism, usurped full authority and began the system ab initio. We now have thirty-two cadets who attend reveille and all roll calls like soldiers, have their meals with absolute regularity and are always hard at work at mathematics, French and Latin. I am the only West Pointer, but they submit to me with the docility of lambs. A good many gentlemen have attended their sons and are much pleased with the building and all arrangements.

I have to write many letters to their fathers and mothers, who think I must take particular care of their children, but I cause all to be treated just alike. They all recite every day in algebra, French and Latin, besides which we drill them like soldiers an hour each day. At present I help the other Professors , but after a while that won't be necessary, and therefore I will have more time. We now have fifty young men, some of whom are only fifteen years old and some are men, but all of them eat, sleep, study and recite their lessons in this building.

We put three or four in a room. All have their beds, which they make on the floor; at daylight they make up their beds, roll them up and strap them. They then sweep out their own rooms, and study their lessons till breakfast at seven o'clock, then they commence to recite and continue reciting till 4 P. M. when they are drilled an hour. At sundown they get their supper and study their lessons till 10 o'clock, when all go to bed and sleep till day- light."

Engineering	300
Mathematics	300
Natural philosophy	300
Conduct (demerits)	300
English studies and literature	300
Chemistry	200
Infantry tactics	200
Mineralogy and geology	100
Artillery	100
French and Spanish	300
Latin and Greek	300
Compositions	100
Declamation	100
Drawing	100

Sherman's Plan for the Weight of Various Grades

With the students Sherman was popular in spite of the fact that by the military system he was given a peculiarly irritating control over the liberty-loving young southerners. He saw to the enforcement of the usual military regulations; he confiscated the boxes of good things sent from home to the hungry young fellows; he advised the students about their accounts at the Seminary store; he looked after their clothing, and, as much as possible, performed the duty of parent. He soon knew each student personally, and, since he frequently attended the recitations, he soon knew every man's class standing. "When occasion required," writes an old student, "he knew how to reprimand, and the words of kindness and encouragement often fell from his lips." With student and professor he was on pleasant, familiar terms and in each he took a deep interest. A colleague wrote of him:

"He made every professor and cadet at the Seminary keep his place and do his duty; at the same time, he was the intimate, social companion and confidential friend of the professor, and a kind, loving father to the cadet. All loved him. In the ' off hours' from study or drill, he encouraged the cadet to look him up and have a talk. And often have I seen his private rooms nearly full of boys, listening to his stories of army or western life, which he loved so well to tell them. Nor could he appear on the grounds in recreation hours without the cadets one by one gathering around him for a talk. Nothing seemed to delight him so much as to mingle with us freely, and the magnetism of the man riveted us all to him very closely, especially the cadets. Scarcely a day passed that he did not see each and every one of them personally, asking not only about themselves and all that concerned them at the school, but about their people at home, when they had last heard from them, how they were and about the crops, etc And if a cadet fell sick, the loving care and attention he gave him! He was at his bedside several times day and night, watching him closely, consoling and encouraging him. Such interest in his students, and such confidence and affection for him in return, and such impressing of his character upon

his student, I have never seen in any other college president. History tells that he was one of the greatest generals of this century; let history also tell that he was one of the greatest college presidents."

Military drill began a few days after the opening. Major Smith, the commandant, was in charge of this work, but during the first weeks he was assisted by Sherman, whose attention was given mainly to the "green squad", composed of those whose control of arms, hands, feet, and knees seemed to be limited. "We were an untutored set", said an ex-cadet, "and often provoked the disgust of the officers. Some of us made such slow progress that an awkward squad was formed, of which I was a prominent member, being placed there by Sherman's own direction."

The uniforms were designed by Graham and Sherman, with the suggestions and advice of Captain McClellan. The boys were delighted when the uniforms arrived . The dress coat was a dark blue military frock, with standing collar and gilt buttons bearing the coat of arms of Louisiana. The pantaloons were blue with a black welt down the outer seam. For ordinary wear there was a fatigue uniform. During the first session the professors wore uniforms similar to those of the cadets except that the coat was double breasted. Most of the professors objected to the uniform, but not so the students who were immensely pleased with the show they made. "Our uniforms were showy and uncomfortable," wrote one of them who later wore the gray, "the hat for dress occasions was a gorgeous affair-high and broad and stiff, with brazen ornaments representing the college building, and the coat of arms of the state, and waving black ostrich plumes. An African prince would have given treasures of ivory and gold dust for such a royal head piece. "

The question of discipline was of course a serious one. Young southern men of that time were not accustomed to rigid discipline. It was mainly the desire for a stricter training for their sons that caused southern fathers to establish in each southern state a military academy. However at the Louisiana State Seminary for a month after the opening all went well. There were no serious breaches of discipline, and Sherman was congratulating himself upon the situation. But about February 1, when the newness of the situation had worn off, the test of strength came. Among the students were several hard characters sent by their parents to the Seminary as a last resort. These planned a campaign of passive opposition to the authorities. But other happenings brought matters to a crisis quickly. The orderly sergeant reported one of the cadets, and out of this a fight resulted in which knives were drawn. Sherman convened a faculty court of inquiry and upon its findings summarily dismissed both belligerents. Both then apologized profusely and were readmitted only to join the passive opposition. Sherman soon disposed of this. One was expelled upon Professor Boyd's report "for singing a blackguard song". Another, W--- came to Sherman to draw money for the purpose of going into Alexandria to see a dentist. Sherman gave him an order on the dentist, but W--- complained that that was "no way to treat a gentleman" and was soon on his way home.

Then came the C--- case which Sherman reported to his wife as follows: "It is against the rules for cadets to use tobacco-(but we know that they do use it) , but this morning one did it so openly that I supposed he did it in defiance. I went to his room to see him but he was out, and in one drawer of his washstand I found plenty of tobacco. I, of course, emptied it into the fireplace. Soon after the young gentleman, named C—— came to me, evidently instigated by others, and complained of ill treatment and soon complained of my opening his drawer, intimating that it was a breach of propriety. Of course I soon advised him that his concealment and breach of regulations, as well known to him, was the breach of honor. He said he would not stay and after some preliminaries I shipped him.

Another came with a similar complaint and I sent him off and then the matter ended. These two last were dull at books and noisy, quarrelsome fellows and a good riddance. "

This "emeute", as Sherman called it, settled the question of mastery. The troubles of discipline after this were slight. One parent, P--- T--- , alarmed at Sherman's energetic methods, wrote to General Graham that the Seminary, "the last best hope of Louisiana's sons" might be endangered by this severe treatment of the young men; "Will our sons submit to the arbitrary commands of dictators?"; he "fears the effects of stringent personal command-the government which originates in the mere will of the superior. " Graham responded with his familiar argument in favor of military government and added that some "have sent chronic cases to this institution as their last hope for a cure, but we don't intend to keep this kind of a hospital. "There is no other name known unto men' whereby he can get creditably through this institution but order and industry". Upon investigation Sherman found that young T—— had been "oppressed" by Professor Boyd who ordered him out of the class-room for making a disturbance about a pig's tail which some one had tied to a fellow student's coat. These facts calmed his father.

Board at $12 per month	$120.00
Washing at $2 per month	20.00
Medical attendance and medicines	15.00
Rent of fixed furniture	5.00
Uniform suit of cloth	25.00
Fatigue suit of jeans	17.00
Summer pants, vests, and jackets	21.00

Sherman's Estimates of Student Expenses

The dry fare at the Seminary mess hall was a cause of much mischief and of violation of rules on the part of the students. To get something to eat they were accustomed to escape from the building at night and take a short cut through the woods to Pineville and Alexandria or to some house where such delicacies as ham and eggs could be had. Raids were made upon the poultry yards of the steward Jarreau and of the country people who lived from one to three miles away. Chickens, turkeys, and small pigs were cooked in negro cabins or in the rooms of the students. The superintendent was at times kept busy protecting the property of his neighbors and several times marauders were caught by him. A member of the faculty said of his activity in this direction:

"He was a natural born detective. From the least little clew he would infer what a cadet was doing. Once I remember we were strolling in the woods, and passed a group of cadets a little distance off. I had observed nothing unusual when he spoke up: "Those fellows seem a little flushed. They are up to something.' I thought no more of it. The next day he called me into the office and said.' You remember those boys we passed in the woods? They were concocting a plan to rob the hen roosts of the neighbors. They have confessed it all to me.' And by his everlasting vigilance and quick perception he prevented much petty mischief. He was well named Tecumseh. The wily old Indian was hardly superior to Sherman in reading the' signs' and divining the plans of the foe or cadet."

Some of the students organized a foraging society. Sherman discovered it and obtained "the constitution of the marauders". In order to break it up he demanded that certain innocent students who knew those guilty of stealing chickens-the "Mose Chicken Case" this was called-should disclose the names of the offenders. With much difficulty was the information obtained, the students maintaining that it would be dishonorable "to tell on" the guilty parties. In this connection Sherman issued an order from which the following extract is taken:

"The Superintendent will call upon no cadet to expose the little pecca-dillos of his fellow, but when these peccadillos amount to violence, breaking the laws of the State, and insults to superiors, the case is different, and it should be the pride of every cadet to keep in check these things, for they aim at the destruction of the Institution itself. There is a wide difference in the two classes of cases. Older and better informed cadets are now cautioned against being drawn into the custom of concealing real wrongs and outrages, because it looks like "tattling". Mischievous cadets will try to establish this rule, because it will shelter them in their mischief."

When the food was unbearable, as it was at times, the students were almost uncontrollable. On one occasion when the meat was odorous the student body threw the dishes and their contents on the floor; at another time they ran the waiters from the messhall, a few of the lawless element firing pistols at the fleeing menials as they ran. After each outbreak the leaders were dismissed, and the food was slightly improved.

The use of tobacco and whiskey was forbidden, but it was hard to break some of the boys of habits long formed. One student, who had stored whiskey in his room, threatened the superintendent with a pistol and then left without waiting to be dismissed. The most lawless were in this way soon "renvoyé, " as the records politely say, but the ones who remained were lively enough. They ducked the negro servants in the spring, polished Dr. Vallas's blackboards with bear grease hair oil, and raided the steward's stores. Finally a regular guard, as in the army, was established and the mischief was moderated.

There was some church going on Sundays, but the students had to walk three miles to service unless Dr. Vallas preached at the Seminary, which was seldom. There were rumors that the church squad visited the bar-rooms before returning to the Seminary, but Sherman declared these stories were invented by the disappointed shopkeepers of Alexandria who could not get cadet custom. Such games as chess, backgammon, etc. , were encouraged in the barracks, though gambling was forbidden. But Sunday was a hard day for the authorities; the boys were without occupation and much mischief was then concocted, especially on their long rambles in the surrounding woods or on fishing excursions.

But Sherman looked after the amusements and recreations as well as the discipline of his boys. Parties and hops were frequently given, and to these the pretty daughters of the planters came in numbers. Sherman was as anxious as the boys for the girls to see the new uniforms, but he says that on all holidays he felt nervous, always looking for some manifestation of cadet mischief.

To the young Louisianan, accustomed to outdoor life and to little restraint, the Seminary routine work, discipline, and indoor life was irksome in the extreme. That the difficulties of discipline were no greater was due largely to the administrative ability and the tact of Sherman, who, in spite of his strictness, was always popular with the students.

The fame of the Seminary spread over the state, and many visitors came to see the school at work. These were treated with the greatest consideration, were shown over the buildings, and entertained at luncheon. To encourage the cadets in habits of neatness and order, Sherman always exhibited the cadets' rooms to those visiting parties which contained young girls and ladies. This scheme, it is said, worked well and markedly reduced the amount of tobacco consumed, or at least lessened the evidences of it.

Sherman's estimates of his colleagues, formed upon brief acquaintance, have been quoted above. He modified his views but little upon further acquaintance. He held the members of the faculty rigidly to their work, believing, as he said to a member of the Board of Supervisors, that "since you pay your professors well, you have a right to expect them to work. " He had little patience with the southern habit of procrastination whether in professors or in students. When two of his professors, through neglect to order books found themselves with large classes and no texts, Sherman had the classes marched regularly to their rooms to be given oral instruction . This was kept up until the books arrived.

The superintendent made frequent visits of inspection to the class rooms, dropping in at the most unexpected times. The professors and students were thus stimulated to do their best at all times. A friendly professor wrote:

"Sherman looked well not only to the happiness and health of his charges and to the military discipline and drill, but especially to the progress of the cadets in their academic studies. He had no patience with inefficient teaching, whether from want of ability, or too much ability, rendering it difficult for the savant to come down to the plane of comprehension of beginners. Yet he himself was no scholar in the professional sense-not a man of varied and extensive literary and scientific acquirements nor even a general reader. He was rather the rough unpolished diamond, made great by nature and of deep discernment, needing little the ideas of other men. But brilliant and original as he was in thought, he had not the usual accompaniment of genius-want of practicability. Sherman was eminently practical."

The following incident is related of Sherman at the inaugural lecture of one of the professors in January, 1860: The professor "talked as he might have done to the faculty and seniors of Harvard. I noticed Sherman looking glum and biting his lips; and the lecture over, he whispered to me-' Every d-d shot went clear over their heads' . But he soon clipped the wings of our grandiloquent soaring eagle and made him a plain barnyard fowl, a practical instructor. "

Likewise he had no respect for labored explanations and reasoning. "Once I remember" said one of the professors, "he asked me my opinion about something. I gave it and then began to give my reasons when he stopped me with this remark: 'I only wanted your opinion. I did not ask for your reasons, and remember, never give your reasons for what you do until you must. Maybe after a while a better reason will pop into your head.'"

While Sherman insisted upon having firm control over the professors, as well as over the students, there was little friction on this account. Two of the professors-the foreigners-chafed a little and wanted more freedom of action, but personal relations were always pleasant. The superintendent had the respect of his colleagues and, after a few months, the affection also. When in 1860 he was about to resign in order to go to London the manifestation of good will and esteem by the professors was rather a surprise to him, though a pleasing one.

The supervisors and faculty had confidence in Sherman's judgment, fairness, and probity. He complained to his wife that the board placed too much confidence in him, allowed him too much freedom in financial matters, etc. A member of the faculty, Dr. Clarke, tells the following to illustrate the unwillingness of Sherman to be paid for certain duties.

"He was the most conscientious man I ever knew, especially in the discharge of public duty. His salary was $3,500 and in addition the Board allowed him $500 as treasurer (and he received $500 more as Superintendent of the Central Arsenal) . One day he said to me: 'It is not right for me to be at the head of this school and (at the same time) its treasure. I want you to act as treasurer and you must take the $500 too.' He patiently taught me bookkeeping and insisted upon my receiving the pay."

The Seminary was isolated from the outside world, and the professors were thus thrown much in one another's society. It was difficult to secure supplies nearer than New Orleans and New York, and servants could with difficulty be secured even by purchase.

The unmarried professors and Sherman lived in the main building and messed together. The poor commissary arrangements worried the professors as much as the students. While in Ohio during the vacation of 1860, Sherman wrote to one of the professors:

"I wish we had Cincinnati near us at the Seminary. We should then not be troubled to get provisions, books, or furniture. . Though no gourmand I will return with regret from the apples, pears, vegetables, meats, and luxuries of Ohio to the poor bread and poorer meat of the pine woods. It does seem to me that our lot is cast in the remotest part of the present civilized world."

WILLIAM TECUMSEH SHERMAN, 1860
From a painting by Colonel S. H. Lockett, owned by
Louisiana State University

He says he lost fifteen pounds while in Louisiana and that his
wife, thinking that he had been starved down there, was preparing

dainties for him to take back with him. The old accounts show that wine was frequently brought on to offset the poor bread, bacon, and greens. Sherman at first opposed the use of wine at the faculty table. He wrote to General Graham: "Governor Moore sent a fine lot of cake for the cadets and a basket of wine for the professors. The former was added to their stock and enabled them to set a nice table for the ladies (on July 4). The wine is untouched and I hardly know what to do with it. I think it prudent that we should exhibit as little wine as possible in our rooms or on our tables. I have always paid, and advised the professors to pay, largely toward the general hospitality, and thus far we have done so without wine except claret."

But the fare was so poor that the rule about wine was relaxed. General Graham and other friends of the school frequently sent to the Seminary delicacies from their plantations. To supply the needs of the school Sherman kept a store or commissary at the institution, much to the irritation of the Alexandria shopkeepers. Sherman's accounts show that he sometimes had to restrain the professors, especially St. Ange, to keep them from spending all their salaries at the store.

The young professors admired Sherman and looked upon him somewhat as an elder brother. He was fond of relating his experiences in the army and the west, and they were fond of listening. Many of the long winter evenings were spent by them in Sherman's rooms, the young Virginians smoking and listening and Sherman roasting apples and talking. "What a charming and instructive companion he was to those of us who were thrown
with him constantly at the Seminary, " said Professor Boyd. "To me certainly was it a treat to listen to his clean cut and original views on nearly every subject that came up. And young as I was intimate association with so strong and fertile a mind, along with his sterling honesty and warm heart, was a rare benefit then, and a pleasing memory now. When the world knew but little of him, I looked

up to Sherman as a singularly gifted man, his mind so strong, bright, clear, original and quick, as to stamp him a genius; and his heart under his stern, brusque, soldierly exterior, the warmest and tenderest. Of a happy nature himself, he strove to make all around him happy; and his integrity and scorn for a mean act were as firm as the rock. Such was Sherman as I knew him most intimately for two years in the pine woods of Louisiana, before he became a great figure in American history. I respected and loved him then as I did ever after, though I became a southern soldier, and I revere his memory now. "

Shut off from the world as they were, the young professors welcomed every opportunity of getting out and mingling in the society of the community. When work was ended for the week Smith, Clarke, St. Ange, and sometimes Sherman went visiting the neighboring plantations where they were always welcome. Vallas seldom left home, and Boyd, who was not socially inclined, took charge of the school. St. Ange went to horse races and once bought, with a large part of his quarter's salary, a worthless horse and buggy much to the amusement of his colleagues. General Graham, so Professor Smith said, "was down on him (Smith) for gallanting". Sherman assured Graham that Smith was criticised mainly because he was attentive to a lady who was not of Rapides parish and added that " if we must conform to every rumor we will lead a devil of a life here. " Professor Boyd, who preferred reading to "gallanting" wrote:

"Sherman studied the amusements and recreations of his charges. Fond himself of young society and dancing, he gave the cadets frequent hops, the planters and their pretty daughters coming in swarms. They soon got to be as fond of Sherman as his cadets were. They delighted to have him at their homes on the river and bayous, and many an evening did he spend with them, usually accompanied by his handsome young commandant of Cadets, Major Frank Smith, (killed in Lee's army the night before the surrender at Appomattox), and his accomplished surgeon, Dr. Powhatan Clarke, now living in Baltimore, while not so much of a lady's man remained behind to run the school."

Rapides Parish in which the Seminary was located was noted in the Southwest for its refined and intelligent population-Creole and Anglo-American. The latter element was mainly from the upper South-Virginia, Maryland, the Carolinas, and Kentucky; the former was native to the soil-for more than a hundred years they had preserved in Central Louisiana the best qualities of the Louisiana French. It was a community of planters; hospitality was unbounded; social intercourse was free and pleasant. In Rapides Sherman was a social favorite, and was much in demand for week end visits at the planters' homes on the river. He was generally well-liked, a fact remarked upon by the Federal generals who passed through this region during the Civil War. The politicians would have called him "a good mixer." Says one of his colleagues:

"He loved to mingle with all classes of people, the lowly as well as the high. He understood them all, and he made all understand him. He would drop in on business men in their offices, or stores, and say a pleasant, encouraging word to the common laborer or negro slave. He was fond of children, would pet them, and they would play with him. No one ever lived in Louisiana so short a time, and commanded so thoroughly the respect, confidence and love of the people as did Sherman. He was popular with all classes, easily adapting himself to all conditions and to any circumstances. As a case in point, one evening in Alexandria, he and I had taken tea with Judge Manning, of the Supreme Court, afterwards United States Minister to Belgium and to Mexico. We were there till late. Sherman was to take the early stage next morning for the mouth of Red River, there to take a boat for Ohio to spend the vacation. When he went to the hotel it was crowded-not a room, not a bed. 'But,' said he to the clerk, ' we must have a bed.

I am to take the stage in the morning; nor could we go over the river to the Academy, even if we wished ; the ferry boat isn't running at this time of night.' 'Indeed, Colonel Sherman, ' said the clerk, 'I am mighty sorry; but I have no place to put you.' ' But', replied Sherman, 'you must make a place ; we'll not take no for an answer.' After studying a while the clerk said.' Well, if you will stay, the best I can do is to turn out the boot-black and give you his bed; but I dislike to offer you such matter about that', said Sherman; 'it will do first rate. If the boot-black can stand it every night, we surely can stand it one night.' And the boot-black turned out, and we turned in; and the bootblack was a darkey."

Before the close of the first session the Seminary and its students and professors had the good will of the people of Central Louisiana. To a Fourth of July celebration the Seminary authorities invited many people, and so successful was the occasion that hundreds flocked to the final examinations a month later. Sherman announced in the newspapers that all visitors would be entertained at dinner and supper, and, of course, the attendance was large.

Of the closing days of the first session Professor Boyd wrote years afterward:

"Our session of 1859 closed successfully and most pleasantly with the usual examinations, drills, speeches, and great ball. Sherman made an address, and though he had not then acquired that facility which afterwards made him one of the best public speakers in the land, he acquitted himself most creditably , even in the opinion of the large number of able and eloquent men who heard him . At the ball Sherman was at his best and in his glory. He loved company, gay, happy company -and to feel that he was making all have a happy time. Both fathers and mothers of the gay young dancers were there too; also the Governor of the State, the Supervisors, and other distinguished guests. None was neglected. Sherman personally

welcomed all, saw all, chatted pleasantly with all— made all feel at home, and have a royal good time. It was a treat to his guests, young and old, to see him enjoy their presence so heartily. Wonderful social man was he! prince of entertainers —a warm, generous spirit all aglow, and a bright, facile mind all devoted to making those around him happy. The ball lasted till broad daylight; and the beauty and chivalry of Louisiana went away with admiration and love for Sherman.

"But I must tell rather a funny thing that happened at the examinations. I had an English class; and among other bits of ungrammatical language to be corrected , I had put on the board an expression taken from General John C. Breckinridge's good "democracy" but bad "Lindley Murray". Well, old Jesse Bynum, the famous fire-eating Congressman in the days of General Jackson and one of the Supervisors of the Academy, spied it. Turning to Sherman he said:"We can forgive you for being born in Ohio, and even for being the brother of John Sherman, the Black Republican , but d--d if I like your poking fun at our candidate ." Sherman thought it a good joke; told him it was put there by the only Breckinridge man in the faculty . Old Jesse excused Sherman, but don't think he ever quite forgave me, though I voted along with him for Breckinridge. Sherman favored Bell for President, but thought Douglass would be elected . He didn't think Lincoln could be. He was farthest from an Abolitionist-not even a Republican then."

There was much to be done to perfect the organization of the Seminary , and during the two years of his stay in Louisiana Sherman made frequent visits to the capitol at Baton Rouge and to New Orleans to secure needed legislation, etc. He had intimate friends among the Louisiana leaders -Braxton Bragg, Beauregard , Dick Taylor , Governor Wickliffe and Moore and many others . He was , he said "in the land of clover as well as molasses" all the time when traveling about the state.

During the whole of Sherman's stay at the Seminary there was some controversy among the authorities as to the degree of military discipline which should be enforced. General Graham and the majority of the board wanted a second West Point-a scientific school with strict military discipline, the superintendent to have full authority over faculty and students . Sherman stood between the extremes. His friends Braxton Bragg and Dick Taylor were ardent advocates of the strict military régime. Bragg wrote to Sherman: "The more you see of our society, especially our young men, the more you will be impressed with the importance of a change in our system of education if we expect the next generation to be anything more than a mere aggregation of loafers charged with the duty of squandering their fathers ' legacies and disgracing their mothers."

The question was carried before the legislature in March, 1860, and Sherman went to Baton Rouge to represent the Seminary. The legislature compromised by pursuing a middle course. The military system was sanctioned , and the institution was renamed "The Louisiana State Seminary and Military Academy," while the question of discipline was left to the judgment of the board. Against strong opposition the legislature voted to maintain fifty four beneficiaries at the Seminary. Dick Taylor objected to "pauperising " the school. All of Sherman's requests for appropriations were granted.

For a time it looked as if the controversy would injure the Seminary, and Sherman began to think of leaving. An offer of a business position in London paying $7,500 a year led him to send in his resignation, but so strong was the wish of both factions that he stay at the head of the school that he agreed to go North to investigate the position before deciding.

When General Graham learned that Sherman was about to leave, he at once called upon the board to meet the increase of salary offered. He offered to guarantee from his own funds an increase of $1000, (making $4,500 a year). To Governor Moore Graham wrote that the danger of losing "our irreplaceable Superintendent" had kept him awake half the night ; "that a man competent to govern , control, and instruct a large institution is of rare occurrence and if we throw away this one there is little likelihood that we can replace him . . I have seen enough to satisfy me that we could not hope to get again exactly such a man for the position , one of so clear, quick and decided a mind, such practical administrative and executive qualities, such experience and varied knowledge of men ,the world and its business, combined with such kindliness of heart and parental care and watchfulness. I have found fully realized in him all which General Gibson, Colonel J. P. Taylor (brother of the late President) and other gentlemen told me in Washington last September, when they said in the words of Colonel Taylor, 'if you had hunted the whole army from one end to the other you could not have found a man in it more admirably suited for the position in every respect than Sherman.'"

So attractive were the inducements offered that Sherman withdrew his resignation and remained in Louisiana. A few months later the board rather unexpectedly curtailed his authority, and he then expressed his regrets that he did not go to London. Sherman wished the professors to wear uniforms on formal occasions; some of the professors disliked uniforms, and the board was divided on the matter but finally excused the faculty, and the students became more turbulent after the strict régime was relaxed. In a letter to Mrs. Sherman the superintendent wrote on November 29, 1860: "I observe more signs of loosened discipline here. Boys are careless and last night because the supper did not please them they smashed the crockery and made a riot generally. Pistols were fired, which scared Joe, (an Ohio employee) very much,- his education has been neglected, but I think he will get used to it. I fear that the institution is in danger from causes which arose after I left last summer. The alterations made after I left were wrong in principle , causing

General Graham to resign, and since then he will take no interest in our affairs. Governor Moore is intent on politics, same of Dr. Smith, so we are left to the chances of the caprices of a parcel of wild boys."

The superintendent was also professor of engineering, but since his classes would not be formed until 1862 he had no regular instruction work. He taught Spanish when Prof. St. Ange was sick. He says that his Spanish was that of the Mexican border- "Greaser " Spanish. Once in a while a class in mathematics recited to him, and on Friday mornings he presided over the "speaking " in the assembly hall. But his most effective teaching was in history and geography . He was a firm believer in the principles upon which the republic was founded and frequently lectured upon them. He was also an expansionist and fond of talking about that aspect of American history. One of the cadets who sat under him said: "Much given to silence and the keeping of his own counsel, he was fluent and eloquent when he spoke. I have heard him lecture charmingly to the assembled students on the history of his country, selecting by preference chapters of exploration and adventure, or heroic struggle and enterprise, such as gave to the Union the territory of Texas and the great West. Upon me and others he made the impression of an ardent , powerful man, governed by duty and a sense of devotion to his country and humanity."

The students not only liked his Friday talks on geography, battles , expansion , and the far west, but they began to call at his rooms to hear more, and it is said that frequently he would be seen on the campus surrounded by an interested group to whom he was talking of the picturesque events in the nation's history. Few people have ever believed more strongly than Sherman in the political and social results of geographic conditions , and his teachings of the time were permeated with his views.

Sherman's family did not join him in Louisiana but remained at home in Lancaster, Ohio. At first there was no suitable dwelling for them, and later when a residence was available the political conditions were so threatening that Mrs. Sherman hesitated to come. From November, 1859, to March, 1861, Sherman carried on a lengthy correspondence with his wife, his little daughter and other relatives. It is mainly from these letters that we learn of Sherman's life in Louisiana and of the beginnings of the Louisiana State University. In August, 1860, he went North for a vacation period which lasted until November . After visiting Washington and New York on Seminary business he spent the rest of the time with his family in Lancaster-going to country fairs, speculating about politics, hunting chestnuts with his children, playing and romping with them, and writing of it all to friends in Louisiana.

He had hoped to have his family in Louisiana with him, the state of Louisiana had built him a fine house, and he had taken great interest in arranging for the coming of Mrs. Sherman and children in November of 1860, but the disturbed political situation caused him to leave the family in Ohio. In a letter to his nine year old daughter, written a month before the secession of Louisiana , Sherman said:

"In the back yard I have prepared for a small garden, but the soil is poor and will not produce much, except early peas, lettuce and sweet potatoes. The house itself looks beautiful. Two front porches and one back, all the windows open to the floor, like doors, so that you can walk out on the porch either upstairs or downstairs. I know you would all like the house so much. What I have been planning so long and patiently, and thought that we were all on the point of realizing, the dream and hope of my life, that we could all be together once more in a home of our own, with peace and quiet and plenty around us-all, I fear, is about to vanish, and again I fear

I must be a wanderer, leaving you all to grow up at Lancaster without your Papa. Men are blind and crazy, they think all the people of Ohio are trying to steal their slaves, and incite them to rise up and kill their masters. I know this is a delusion, they believe it harder than a real fact and these people in the South are going, for this delusion, to break up the government under which we live. You cannot understand this but Mamma will explain it to you. Our Governor here has gone so far that he cannot change, and in a month maybe you will be living under one government and I another. This cannot last long, and as I know it is best for you to stay in Lancaster, I will not bring you down here at all, unless some very great change takes place. If this were only a plain college I could stay with propriety, but it is an arsenal with guns and powder and balls, and were I to stay here I might have to fight for Louisiana and against Ohio."

Sherman's views on politics were moderate. He was an Old Line Whig and considered his brother John, the "Black Republican," as quite too radical. He deplored the sectional feeling and the resulting controversies and was overwhelmed with grief when he heard of the secession of South Carolina. No secret was ever made of his own sentiments: he would not go against the Union. So in January, 1861, when the governor of Louisiana seized the forts at New Orleans and Baton Rouge, Sherman resigned. For a few weeks longer he remained settling up his affairs, and late in February he left for the North. Of his leavetaking we have the following account by one of the professors: "The morning he left us he had his battalion formed. Stepping out in front of them he made them a short talk, and then, passing along the line, right to left, bade each and every officer and man-not a dry eye among them-an affectionate farewell. Then, approaching our sad group of professors, he silently shook our hands, attempted to speak, broke down, and, with tears trickling down his cheeks with another effort, he could only lay his hand on his heart and say: 'You are all here'. Then turning quickly on his heel, he left us, to be ever in our hearts."

He stopped in New Orleans for a short stay with Braxton Bragg who was then organizing troops for the "Independent State of Louisiana". From a letter written while in New Orleans to a friend at the Seminary the following passage is taken:

"The truth is I have socially been too much isolated from my children, and now that they are at an age when for good or ill we should be together, I must try to allay that feeling of change and venture which has made me a wanderer. If possible I will settle down-fast and positive. Of a summer eve, with little Minnie and Willy, and the rascal Tom, I can live over again my Florida life, my ventures in California, and my short sojourn in the pine woods of Louisiana; and I will teach them that there are kind, good people every where; that a great God made all the world; that he slighted no part; that to some he assigned the rock and fir, with clear, babbling brooks, but cold and bitter winters; to others the grassy plain and fertile soil, to others the rich alluvium and burning sun to ripen the orange and sugar cane, but everywhere He gave the same firmament, the same gentle moon, and to the inhabitants the same attributes for good and evil."

AUTHOR'S NOTE This paper is based mainly upon manuscript material preserved in the archives of the Louisiana State University. This material consists of the manuscript records of the old Louisiana State Seminary, the letter books and miscellaneous correspondence of W. T. Sherman, G. Mason Graham, P. G. T. Beauregard, Braxton Bragg, D. F. Boyd, Stokes A. Smith, Francis W. Smith, Governors R. C. Wickliffe and Thomas O. Moore; correspondence of students and their relatives; the reminiscences of W. S. Bring- hurst, René T. Beauregard, D. F. Boyd, and Powhatan Clarke.

9

General William T. Sherman as a History Teacher

That William Tecumseh Sherman was once a Louisiana teacher few people outside of the state know; fewer still know that he taught history in Louisiana during the critical period from 1859 to 1861.

Sherman was elected Superintendent of the Louisiana State Seminary (now the Louisiana State University) in 1859. He was to teach engineering, architecture, and drawing as soon as the students were ready to undertake the study of these subjects. When the Seminary opened it was found that the first year there would be no class except the fourth or freshman. Consequently it would be two years before students were prepared to take up work in engineering.

Sherman then announced his intention to teach history and geography; and all the instruction that he ever gave to Louisiana youth was in those subjects . Nine days before the time appointed for the promotion of students to his engineering classes he was commanding a Federal brigade at Manassas, and in the opposing Confederate army were half the students who four months before had sat in his classes.

An old list made in 1860 gives the titles of the texts used in history and geography: Mitchell's *Geography*, Long's *Ancient geography and Atlas*, Willard's *History of the United States*, Peter Parley's *Universal history*, Taylor's *Manual of ancient and modern history*, Liddell's *History of Rome*, and Smith's *History of Greece*.

During the first year it is probable that the historical library was very small, but in August, 1860, Sherman went to New York to purchase books and other supplies. He sent down to the seminary several thousand volumes, among them about four hundred volumes of history and geography. The list, in Sherman's handwriting on Van Nostrand's business paper, is before me as I write. It shows that Sherman was much interested in travel, exploration, and discovery. Marco Polo, Layard, Humboldt, Commodore Perry, and many other authors whose names are now forgotten, are on the lists. Sherman evidently tried to get at least one history of every country; and there are two of Japan-a pretty good list for 1860. The best modern biographies were chosen, from Peter the Great to Madison and Washington. In the collected works and speeches of American statesmen there were represented Washington, Jefferson, Clay, Webster, Calhoun, and Benton. The standard atlases and maps are on the list : Colton, Maury, Alison, Anthon, and Lippincott. Books on local and United States history are scarce-Gayarré, Monette, Lossing, Prescott, and Bancroft are all. Of the European works that are still known there are Grote, Gibbon, Rollin, Sismondi, Hallam, Schiller, Puffendorf, Lieber, De Tocqueville, Alison, Hume, and Macaulay.

The books were shipped by steamer to New Orleans, thence to the mouth of Red River; from there some boxes were sent by small steamboats to Pineville, a little village opposite Alexandria, and from Pineville an ox wagon hauled them to the Seminary three miles out in the pine woods north of Red River. One of the boxes by mistake was carried on up to Shreveport, where, owing to low water in the river, it remained several weeks. Low water also forced the Seminary authorities to haul overland from the mouth of Red River the rest of the boxes and supplies. Most of the books purchased in August had reached the seminary by November, when the session began, but a few old volumes were delayed. The bills for these volumes were not paid, owing to secession and civil war, until 1865, when the seminary settled Van Nostrand's bills against ex-Superintendent Sherman, then Lieutenant General of the United States Army.

Little is known of Sherman's instruction except that given in American history. It is probable that during the first session no other course was given. In addition to the formal class work Sherman once a week spoke to the assembled students on some interesting phase of United States history. Former students remember that he preferred to dwell upon battles, great leaders, explorations, American expansion, etc. One of his students said of him: "Much given to silence and the keeping of his own counsel, he was fluent and eloquent when he spoke. I have heard him lecture charmingly to the assembled students on the history of his country, selecting by preference chapters of exploration and adventure, or heroic struggle and enterprise, such as gave to the Union the territory of Texas and the Great West."

Of the Friday lectures Sherman himself wrote to General G. Mason Graham, one of the supervisors of the Seminary: "Every Friday evening all hands attend in the large section room to declaim. After they are thru I generally speak an hour or so on some interesting piece of history. They take great interest in it. Next Friday I must in connection with my last [lecture] approach and maybe recount the leading events of the conquest of California. Altho not liking a critical audience, if you happen to be here on Friday next you may be admitted."

Sherman was perhaps fondest of describing the expansion of the United States and of telling about army life on the Western frontier. And both professors and students liked to hear him talk, whether in the Friday assembly, or in his own rooms, or out on the grounds. Colonel D. F. Boyd, who succeeded Sherman as Superintendent, wrote, in after years: " In the off hours from study or drill he encouraged the cadets to look him up and have a talk. And I have often seen his private rooms nearly full of boys listening to his stories of army and Western life, which he loved so well to tell them. Nor could he appear on the grounds in recreation hours without the cadets one by one gathering around him for a talk. Nothing seemed to delight him so much as to mingle with us socially, and the magnetism of the man riveted us all to him very closely, especially the cadets."

The Friday declamations and the holiday proceedings were under the direction of Superintendent Sherman. The published speeches of some of the students clearly show his influence. A Fourth of July oration, for example, describes in a strongly national spirit the development of the colonies, the achievement of independence, the greatness of the founders of the republic, the development of the nation, and the evils of sectional rivalry. It ends with Sherman's familiar plea for a return to the original principles of the Republic.

Sherman's views as to the nature of the Union and as to the questions of controversy between North and South were well known to the students and the faculty. He hammered them in for two years and stated just before leaving in 1861 that, while few agreed with him, no one in Louisiana had ever made an unpleasant remark to him about his opinions. He declared that secession was treason and rebellion, and would result in civil war ; that it could never succeed, because physical and economic geography was against disunion. He developed the geographical argument in its strongest and most scientific form. As to slavery, he disliked it, but thought it a necessary institution, at least in the lower South. Strangely enough he thought that it was not in any sense a real cause of the sectional controversy, but merely a pretext. For both abolitionists and secessionist agitators he had a profound dislike, which he frequently voiced. His letters to his brother John, begging him to be moderate, sound queer today.

When at home in Ohio he defended the Southern people as being on the whole humane and conservative, and condemned the abolition agitator. When in the South he endeavored to convince the people that not all in Ohio were nigger stealers and lawbreakers, and intimated that the proslavery politicians were much to blame for the disturbed state of affairs. The inscription cut in marble over the main entrance of the Seminary, to which Sherman was fond of referring, exprest his views very well :—

By the liberality of the general government

The union-esto perpetua.

10

"Forty Acres and a Mule"

For several years after the close of the Civil War, the negroes of the South believed that the estates of the whites were to be confiscated by the Washington Government, and that each negro head of a family would obtain from the property thus confiscated "forty acres and a mule." Some old negroes still believe that the homestead and the mule will be given to them. This belief has often, especially in late years, been ridiculed as the childish dream of an ignorant people; for it is assumed that the negro had no reason for expecting land and stock from the Government. The purpose of this paper is to show that the expectations of the blacks were justified by the policies of the Government and the actions of its agents, and also to show that rascals took advantage of these expectations to swindle the ignorant freedmen.

The first step in the policy of confiscation was taken by Congress on August 6th, 1861, when the first Confiscation Act was passed. This law provided that property used in aid of the Confederacy should be liable to confiscation. Under this act, many slaves Were captured and declared free. The Confiscation Act of July 17th, 1862, declared that all property of Confederates was liable to confiscation. Property not subject to confiscation under the law might be seized as "abandoned" or as "captured." The Treasury Department ruled that property was "abandoned " when the owner was away in the Confederate service. Any property seized by the army was classed as "captured," and was sold at once without the formality of legal proceedings. If the owner was unknown, the property was ordered to be sold for taxes, which were made a lien upon the land. In order to dispose of confiscated property, the South was divided into nine "Agencies," each under a Treasury agent, whose duty it was to collect and dispose of confiscated property. In this work they were aided by the negroes, who acted as guides and informers. The latter, both from hearing their masters talk about the policy of the Federals and from observation after invasion, were easily convinced that, if the struggle went against the South, the property of their masters would be seized, and many whites, North and South, believed the same. The Northern armies seized everything — even church property was generally taken, and the property of well-known ""Unionists." The church property was usually turned over to some Northern denomination or given to the negroes. The Southern Methodist Publishing House at Nashville was seized and operated by the Federal army, and finally given to the Freedmen's Bureau. George S. Houston, a "Unionist," later Governor of Alabama, lost his property by confiscation. Since the war, about $30,000,000 has been paid by the Government to "Unionists" who had property confiscated; Confederate sympathizers recovered nothing. The greater part of the property taken before the end of the war consisted of movable goods, especially cotton, which was seized wherever found. The negroes gave valuable information to the Federals in the search for cotton. The debates in Congress and the speeches made in political campaigns, show that many Northern people believed that wholesale confiscation and division of property ought to follow the close of the war. Thaddeus Stevens of Pennsylvania began early to agitate the question, advocating that the land be seized to pay the expenses of the war, to punish the Confederates, and to provide for "loyalists " and for the blacks. The white people of the South, Stevens said in 1863, were entitled to no rights of person or property; the United States should treat the former Southern States as "conquered provinces, settle them with new men, and exterminate or drive out the present rebels from the country." In 1864, Stevens declared that "every inch of the guilty portion of the usurping power should be held responsible to reimburse all the cost of the war; to pay all the damage to private property of loyal men; and to create an ample fund to pay pensions to wounded soldiers and to the bereaved friends of the slain." During the same year, Andrew Johnson, then Military Governor of Tennessee, in a public speech said that "treason must be made odious, and traitors must be punished and impoverished; their great plantations must be seized and divided into small portions and sold to honest, industrious men." These declarations soon became known to the blacks, the more intelligent of whom were always well informed on the important issues, either through their masters or by "grape-vine telegraph." Often such matters were known to the negroes before the Southern whites knew them. I have been assured by old negroes that a general topic of conversation in some negro "quarters" was the intention of the Federals to confiscate the lands and divide them among the blacks. They heard about this from the " big house " and from "word that was saunt in."

The Confiscation Acts of the Federal Congress were constantly referred to by the Confederates as showing what the policy of the North would be in case the South were conquered. Through fear of confiscation and division of lands, the Southerners were rallied to fresh exertion. The several Southern Legislatures and the Confederate Congress repeatedly mentioned this matter in addresses to the people. The last address of the Confederate Congress, in March, 1865, reminded the people that the penalty for failure would probably be confiscation of estates, which would be given to their former bondsmen.

Meanwhile, what was actually being done to convince the blacks that they were to be cared for at the expense of the Southern whites? As the Northern armies invaded the South, many negroes went within the Federal lines; and, after 1861, thousands of them had to be cared for. In every Southern State where the Federals had military posts, great camps of freedmen were formed, rations were issued, and supplies taken from the captured property were given to them. As far as possible, the refugee blacks were subsisted upon the substance of their former owners. The care of these helpless persons devolved first upon the army, later upon Treasury agents, then again upon the army, and again upon the Treasury agents. Neither the War Department nor the Treasury desired the responsibility. The agents of the Treasury and the officers detailed from the army, assisted by benevolent associations in the North, endeavored to organize the negro colonies and camps so as to make them somewhat self-supporting. Little was done before 1863 except to seize plantations and houses, in territory held by the Federal army, and turn them over along with much movable property to the use of the negroes.

After the Emancipation Proclamation was issued, a more determined effort was made to settle the negroes upon their masters' lands. In March, 1868, thousands of acres of cotton-lands along the coasts, and in the sea islands of South Carolina, Georgia and Florida, were confiscated and sold at auction. The land was divided into small plots of twenty to forty acres. Many negroes were purchasers, as long credit was given, and land worth forty to sixty dollars in 1860 was sold for a dollar and a quarter per acre. The white owners had all been driven away by the negroes and the Federals; In Louisiana,

General Banks organized a little commonwealth of blacks on the community-plantation system. On the borders of Virginia and in Tennessee were similar bodies. In April, 1863, Adjutant-General Lorenzo Thomas, after consultation with Grant and Lincoln, announced that the Government had determined to locate a "loyal" population on the banks of the Mississippi from Kentucky to Grand Gulf, Mississippi, in order to protect commerce and navigation. Commissioners were appointed to seize the estates of Confederates and lease them for moderate rents to negroes, or to persons who would employ and care for negroes. The Government sold, rented, or gave to the lessees the stock, implements and supplies found on the plantations. This system worked badly ; the white lessees were of bad character and swindled the negroes, while making fortunes for themselves; the mortality in the plantation camps was fearful; the few negro lessees failed because of ignorance.

During the next year, "Superintendents of Freedmen " were employed by the Treasury Department. It was their duty to locate negro colonies called "Freedmen's Home Colonies" on the confiscated estates of prominent Confederates, to issue supplies to them and to induce them to work a little to support themselves. " Home Colonies " were established in every Southern State, the largest ones being in Tennessee, South Carolina, Alabama, Mississippi and Florida. One colony was located on Jefferson Davis's plantation, another on the estate of ex-Governor Chapman of Alabama, and another on the Destrehan plantation of Judge Host in Louisiana. The superintendents committed much fraud in their supervision of the blacks, and their regime was not successful; but, before the war closed, all negroes who had come into contact with the Federals were convinced that the Government meant to care for the blacks at the expense of the whites.[1]

The most sweeping confiscations took place and the most important colonies were located along the coast and on the sea islands of South Carolina, Georgia and Florida. In 1863, in addition to about 15,000 acres which were sold to negroes, other large tracts were confiscated in the parishes of St. Helena and St. Luke in South Carolina, and in Georgia and Florida. When Sherman reached Savannah, in December, 1864, his army was encumbered by a multitude of negroes who had followed him in his march across Georgia. After State agents from the North had enlisted many of them to fill up the quotas of their States, there were still thousands who had to be provided for. Secretary Stanton and Adjutant-General Townsend came to Savannah; and, in consultation with General Sherman and a score of negro preachers it was decided to form negro colonies on the coasts, where they could be protected by the United States forces. The negroes were unanimous in asking to be colonized away from the whites. So Sherman, with the knowledge and advice of Stanton, issued on January 16th, 1865, his famous " Special Field Order No. 15," which set aside for the settlements of negroes all the sea islands south of Charleston, the rice-fields along the rivers for thirty miles inland from the sea, and the country along the St. John River in Florida. In the territory thus set apart for negro settlements, no white persons were allowed to live; the management of affairs was to be left to the blacks. General Rufus Saxton was appointed inspector of negro settlements, and was authorized to grant, with a possessory title, forty acres of land to each family, in the possession of which the military authorities would protect them until Congress should regulate their titles.

Before the end of 1865, more than 40,000 freedmen were located on the sea islands by General Saxton, who called them together in public meetings, and encouraged emigration to the lands set apart for them. He reported that the movement was a great success. Thousands of acres were allotted to blacks; negro com- munities grew up; the government was carried on, churches and schools were established and roads made, by the negroes under the supervision of army officials. A Government steamer carried supplies to them regularly. The white owners were not allowed to set foot on the islands, and one solitary white " Unionist " who had remained on his plantation during the war was now forced to leave under the terms of Sherman's order.

During the summer and fall of 1865, numbers of the owners of the coast and island plantations were pardoned by President Johnson. One effect of the pardon was to restore property rights, and consequently the land confiscated for the blacks by General Sherman and others was now to be returned to the owners, un- less Congress should intervene. The owners at once demanded possession. The Freedmen's Bureau, now in charge of matters relating to negroes, refused to release the land, and asked Congress to confirm the titles of the blacks, who, encouraged by the Bureau agents, armed themselves and refused to allow any owner to return to his plantation. Meanwhile improvements were going to ruin, and the owners had no other homes. Repeated applications were made to Washington demanding restoration; Secretary Stanton and General Howard of the Freedmen's Bureau opposed it, asserting that the negroes had been led to expect permanent possession of the lands, and that to dispossess them would be an act of bad faith and would cause bitter disappointment. President Johnson, however, with more regard for legalities and less vindictive than in 1864, asserted that the effect of pardon was to restore all rights of property, and ordered restoration to those whom he had pardoned. But all recognized that the blacks were entitled to some consideration. So General Howard, Commissioner of the Bureau, went south to make a settlement.

Howard reached Charleston on October 19th, 1865, and two days later, accompanied by William Whaley, a representative of the planters, went to Edisto Island to explain matters to the freedmen. The latter, as well as the majority of the white people, North and South, believed that the intention of General Sher- man and the Government had been to give them the land; and now they were confident that the Government would stand by them, and that a general confiscation would soon take place. The Freedmen's Bureau Act of March 3rd, 1865, had provided for the division of confiscated and "abandoned" lands among the blacks in forty-acre lots, and there were millions of acres classed as "abandoned." Consequently, when Howard came, the blacks were confident that he would sustain them. More than two thousand met him at a church on the island, and were angry and overwhelmed at the news he brought. While their leaders were conferring with Howard and the representative of the planters, the rest of the blacks held a meeting in the church. Mournful songs were sung, prayers were offered and the preachers made touching addresses. They felt that the Government had deceived them, and a stormy outbreak was with difficulty averted. But the planters were reasonable, and Howard finally succeeded in making the negro leaders understand the situation. A compromise was patched up, and Howard decreed that no lands should be restored until the crops were gathered; no rents or damages were to be paid to the owners; " loyal " men or those who had been pardoned might then receive their lands, provided they gave homes and employment for the following year, at good wages, to all the negroes settled on their plantations, and did not oppose the establishment of schools for them; no unpardoned owners could have his land restored; and no negroes who had paid the Government for their land in 1863-1865 were to be dispossessed. Howard then went to Savannah and to Fernandina, where similar settlements were made. He then urged that Congress purchase these coast lands and give them to the freedmen.

It was not possible to carry the agreement fully into effect. The freedmen were in possession and in many localities refused to abide by the compromise and allow the whites to return. It was found that Bureau agents encouraged them in this attitude. The Act of March

3rd, 1865, had provided that the blacks should be protected in the use of their allotted lands for three years, and that meanwhile they might purchase the land at merely nominal prices. Under this law, the Bureau refused to allow the lands to be released to the owners. In the spring of 1866, efforts were made by General Tillson, of the Freedmen's Bureau in Georgia, to consolidate the grants made to the negroes and gather them together on a portion of each estate, restoring the remainder to the owner. The Freedmen's Bureau Act of July 16th, 1866, secured the negroes in the possession of lands actually purchased at the nominal rate of a dollar and a half per acre, and provided that no land settled upon by blacks under Sherman's order should be restored until the crops of 1866 were gathered.

The Bureau now declared the grants on the coasts and sea islands to be valid, and confirmed the blacks in the possession of all lands held by them in 1865. Later, when it was seen that the courts would probably restore the lands to the owners, the Bureau made it known that only those negroes who had possessory titles from the Government would be protected in possession of their twenty and forty-acre plots. It was found that very few negroes were settled on the land that their grants called for; many had no titles whatever or had lost them. Evictions then began; the Federal soldiers, late in 1866, were sent into some localities, and, having no great liking for the Bureau or for its wards, removed many of the latter in a summary fashion, causing much hardship. This was a grievous disappointment to the blacks.

In spite of the longing of the negroes to possess lands, those who retained their grants on the South Atlantic coast profited little by them. Deprived of the supervision of the whites, the negroes neglected their little crops and allowed their homes and industries to go to ruin, while they eked out a leisurely living by hunting, fishing and by killing the cattle that grazed on the salt marshes. The land has never again reached the production of 1860. The whole affair served mainly to irritate the whites and to disappoint the blacks.

So much for the plan of Sherman and its results. On a smaller scale, something similar had been done in the other Southern States. In the first flush of freedom at the close of the war, the negroes in the interior of the country, encouraged by the workings of the Freedmen's Bureau, believed that henceforth they were to be supported by the Government; that they would never be cold, or hungry or tired any more. In Alabama, General Swayne reported in 1866 that "freedmen were not uncommon who believed that work was no part of freedom." This belief lasted for months with those who lived in the vicinity of the Bureau "offices" and received the regular issues of rations and other supplies. Later, many of them were convinced that the Government would not support them, but that it contemplated a division of property among them. Most of them expected only the lands, houses and stock; and now arose in the interior country the definite expectation of " forty acres of land and a mule," or the equivalent in other property. Some few believed that, in addition, the white owner would be given as a slave.

In 1865, there was much foundation for the hopes of the negroes. The Confiscation Acts were still in force, and nearly all Southern property was by law liable to seizure. The Constitution provided that forfeiture could be made only after conviction and for the lifetime of the owner, but the negro and his friends knew or cared little about this restriction. The Bureau Act of 1865 legalized Sherman's Special Order, by providing that each negro might have forty acres at a low price on long credit; the Bureau Act of 1866 confirmed the sale of lands to negroes; General Howard, in May, 1865, ordered that no lands be restored to " dis-loyal " owners, and the military authorities were directed to receive no applications for restoration. In Virginia, a large amount of land was ready for sale under the Confiscation Acts; but, when the Bureau was established, in March,

1865, this land was turned over to that institution, and in June, the President directed that all Confederate property in possession of the military authorities be turned over to the Bureau. During the year 1865, the Bureau held 768,590 acres of land and 1,596 pieces of town property confiscated from individuals, besides an immense amount of property formerly belonging to the Confederacy. General Howard instructed his subordinate officials to scatter abroad among the negroes copies of the "homestead" law with its promise of free land, and this also aroused false hopes. The negro colonies were still held together and supported by the Government ; and the Treasury agents, guided by negroes, were searching out and seizing cotton, tobacco and other produce, under the pretence that it had been subscribed to the Confederate Produce Loan. Even those who had failed to pay the tax-in-kind to the Confederacy now had to pay it to the rapacious Treasury agent, who turned over to his Government only a small part of his confiscations. The barns, storehouses, offices, dwellings, public buildings, court-houses, hospitals, prisons, armories, arsenals, ironworks, boats, mills, factories, and all kinds of supplies used by or intended for the use of the Confederacy were seized and, for the most part, after June 2d, 1865, were given for the use of the blacks. Church and school buildings belonging to the whites were given to the missionaries for the negroes. Property in the hands of the Bureau was sold or rented, and the proceeds applied to the support of the blacks or given directly to them. Naturally, the negroes thought that they were in permanent possession, and the policy of the Bureau encouraged them in this belief. General Howard endeavored to nullify the effect of the President's pardon, by refusing to restore to the owners any land occupied by negroes ; he directed that no eviction of negroes be allowed, and generally obstructed the restoration of land. The President ordered positively that property be restored to pardoned men, whereupon Howard asked Johnson to grant pardon only on condition that the pardoned party give to each slave family formerly belonging to him five to ten acres of land, or the equivalent in cash. Though property was gradually restored, the Bureau held quantities of it for several years: 768,590 acres in 1865; 272,231 acres in 1866; 815,024 acres in 1867; and 139,634 acres in 1868, besides many pieces of town property. Restoration was grudgingly performed; General Saxton, for instance, declared (for South Carolina, Georgia and Florida) that those who did not "announce" to the freedmen the fact of their freedom and "admit" it publicly to them would have their property seized and divided.

The speeches of Stevens and other radical leaders, in pamphlet form, along with the Bureau laws and regulations, the homestead laws and the Confiscation Acts, were sown thickly over the South; and the Bureau agents, the missionaries and the teachers, taking the cue from these, encouraged the belief in the " forty acres and a mule." The negroes were told that, since their labor had produced the property of the South, they ought at least to share it. Lincoln's second inaugural message suggests the same thought in regard to the origin of Southern property. Probably this belief that the property of the South was due to uncompensated negro labor was held by many Northerners and inclined them to favor a proposition to confiscate the land.[2]

Stevens, in a speech to his constituents at Lancaster, Pennsylvania, in the summer of 1865, declared that each negro family ought to receive forty acres of land, and that sufficient land should be secured by confiscating the estates of those Confederates who had owned over two hundred acres, and by seizing the lands belonging to the Southern States. Of State lands, Texas possessed about 110,000,000 acres, and the other Southern States about 50,000,000 acres. In December, 1865, in Congress, Stevens again expressed himself in favor of giving homes to the negroes, and as time went on he was more and more strongly in favor of it. Wendell Phillips, in the

"Anti-Slavery Standard," advocated the gift to each negro family of eighty acres of land or "forty acres and a furnished cottage." Other leaders favored confiscation from the whites and provision for the blacks; but, Stevens being the foremost advocate of the policy, his part is emphasized.

At first, the blacks expected an immediate distribution of property, but, when that did not take place, they unanimously decided that the division would take place at the end of the year 1865, either at Christmas or at New- Year's. In the mean time, while awaiting the allotment, thousands crowded into the towns near the army posts and Bureau stations, where congested conditions gave rise to vice and disease. All over the South, the assistant commissioners of the Bureau reported that, in expectation of support by the Government or of distribution of land and stock, the negroes were refusing to make contracts; none would contract beyond the end of the year; few worked steadily at day work in the mean time. This belief grew stronger in the fall and early winter, and the assistant commissioners and higher officials of the Bureau and the army made earnest efforts to disabuse the minds of the freedmen of this impression, but there is no evidence that the inferior officials pursued a like policy.

Andrews, a Northern traveller in the South, stated in the fall of 1865 that the negroes believed firmly in the division of property, and that this belief was causing idleness and discontent. Northern men were besieged by the negroes who wanted information. Andrews was asked: "When is de land goin' fur to be dewided?" Some negroes in South Carolina believed that they would be colonized on the coast, thus showing the influence of Sherman's plan, and in this belief large numbers set out to go to Charleston, Savannah, and other places near the "promised land." They believed that the whites were to be driven out of the low country, which was to be given up to the negroes. In the interior, as a rule, the freedmen believed that they were to be located on the home plantations. Andrews told of one old man who refused to leave home and celebrate freedom, as others were doing, because he feared that the division might take place in his absence and "de home house might come to me, sah, in de dewision." While waiting for the distribution, the blacks who would not work, and who were not within reach of Bureau supplies, were forced to live by foraging. In the black districts, the corn, fruit, pigs, cows and poultry suffered from the "taking" propensities of the African who believed that he was using what would soon be his own anyway.

The policy of Johnson and the statements of the higher Bureau and army officers reassured most of the whites who had feared confiscation. Estates were gradually restored to the owners. The negroes clung to their old hope, but began to fear that they were being tricked. They had secured arms, and now some of the leaders threatened that, if the division did not occur, they would forcibly seize the land. Among the whites there was a wide- spread fear of insurrection when the black should be disappointed at New-Year's. Some of the Bureau officials also feared trouble. For defence, the whites organized patrols in each community, and the organizations that preceded the Ku-Klux movement were now formed — notably the "Black Cavalry." The Federal military authorities overlooked this reorganization of the white militia. In Virginia, when the blacks learned that their hopes were vain, they destroyed the fencing and other improvements. But in general they were not inclined to violence, and Christmas and New- Year's passed without the anticipated outbreak. The negroes then settled down somewhat, still hoping, however, for the " forty acres and the mule," now in the far future; ceasing to hope for immediate confiscation, they rather expected the Government to do something for them, to send them to homes in the West or to take them North, but there was now probably little thought that their masters' property would be divided among them.

But in the latter part of 1866 and early in 1867, when it was seen that Congress would probably be victorious over the President and that some form of negro suffrage would be imposed, hopes were again aroused by the activities of those who expected to use the negroes to get into office. The speeches of Stevens in regard to banishment of Confederates and confiscation for the benefit of the "loyal" and black men, and about negro suffrage for the purpose of securing perpetual ascendancy to the " party of the Union," were widely circulated. The tales of "Southern outrages" and the reported rebellious spirit of the ex-Confederates caused many Northern people to believe that some punishment ought to be inflicted. The negroes were led to believe that their friends in Congress were fighting for their rights, that is, for property and supplies for them. The Reconstruction Acts of March, 1867, which overthrew the "Johnson" State Governments, and provided for negro suffrage to be inaugurated under the superintendence of the army, was to the blacks a sign that they were coming to the long-expected confiscation. To thousands of them, the issue in the elections of 1867 and 1868 was freedom with land on one side, slavery and no property on the other. This feeling in an ignorant and helpless people was strengthened by the circulation in the South of a bill introduced in Congress by Stevens on March 19, 1867, providing for wholesale confiscation and division of lands. By the blacks this measure was considered a part of the Reconstruction, and from their leaders they had learned that Reconstruction was for their good alone. The bill provided for the confiscation of land owned by the Southern States — about 150,000,000 acres — and for the seizure of private property liable under the Confiscation Act of 1862. A commissioner was to be appointed in each Southern State to condemn property for sale or division, and from the land thus obtained each head of a negro family, male or female, and each adult male, was to get a homestead of forty acres. For ten years, this land was to be inalienable, and then an absolute title was to be granted. From the proceeds of the sales of confiscated property, each person who received a homestead was also to get fifty dollars for a building; and $500,000,000 was to be set aside to pay pensions and to pay for the losses of " loyal " persons during the war. The bill further provided that no estate worth less than $5,000 should be confiscated, unless the owner had been an "officer or employee " in the Confederate or State service during the war.

In support of this bill, Stevens said: "We have liberated the slaves. It is our duty to provide for them, and we have the right to take land for homes in order to do it." On the success of the measure depended, he declared, the happiness, respectability, and continued existence of the blacks. They were not capable of caring for themselves, he stated; the Freedmen's Bureau could not much longer protect them; the former slaveholders were hostile, and, if they were not protected, they would become extinct or there would be a civil war. Already, he said, they were murdered with impunity, and "I doubt not that hundreds of thousands would annually be deposited in secret unknown graves." But if they were rendered independent by the gift of homesteads, the danger would be removed. "They have earned for their masters this very land and more," he said, " and divisions of the plantations into small farms would be good for the South any- way." Stevens was in earnest about the distribution of property, and announced that " to this issue [to punish the Southern whites by confiscation and to provide for the negroes] I desire to devote the small remnant of my life."

As a result of the agitation of the matter of homesteads for the negroes, the latter became a prey to swindlers who traded upon their hopes. They had much faith in Northern men, and sharpers came down and made collections, representing to the negroes that they would secure that land for them. A common method of swindling the negroes was to sell them little striped pegs about the size of the stakes used in the game of croquet. The negro was told that, if he would take four of those stakes and mark off forty acres on his former owner's plantation, the part inclosed by the stakes would then belong to him. An eye-witness has described the sale of stakes that took place in Sumter County, Alabama. The negroes had a political barbecue at Gainesville, and a man appeared with a bundle of red and blue stakes. He declared that he had been to Washington to get them from the Government, which had made them for the express purpose of marking off the "forty acres of land." The instructions given by the seller were to stick a peg at one corner of the desired lot, and then walk a certain distance and stick down another peg, then turn and at a certain distance place another, and so on. The seller advised the buyers not to encroach upon one another's lots in staking out the claim, and not to take a whole lot in wood land or in cleared land, but to select about half in each. The man with the stakes explained that the nominal charge he made — about a dollar a peg — was only for his expenses. The pegs were sold for less if the negro had not a dollar. This peg-selling swindle lasted intermittently for about ten years. The same community was rarely swindled twice, but, sooner or later, every negro settlement suffered. In Georgia especially, the pegs could be seen set up all over the country. Each of Grant's elections served to stimulate the swindlers and to encourage again the blacks who believed that Grant sent the pegs out for distribution. General Howard was also credited with similar benevolent actions. The pegs were sometimes called " pre-emption rights." A pretended deed for land, given with one set of stakes, was in part as follows:

" Know all men by these presents, that a nought is a nought and a figure is a figure; all for the white man and none for the nigure. And whereas Moses lifted up the serpent in the wilderness, so also have I lifted this d— — d old nigger out of four dollars and six bits. Amen! Selah!"

Politicians informed their black constituents who complained of delay that the intention of the Government was good, but that the trouble lay in the fact that they had no one at Washington to look after their interests. One man who hailed from Skowhegan, Maine, went to Congress from Alabama in 1868, because the negroes favored him above other carpetbaggers for his promises in regard to the "forty acres." In the campaigns of 1870, in Alabama, the "forty acres" was an issue with the negroes. The speakers told the blacks: " All this property you see here, these lands were cleared by you; you made all these fences; you dug all these ditches; you are the men they belong to." When the Coburn committee was investigating the reason for Alabama's going Democratic in 1874, they were confronted at Opelika by a negro who demanded that something be done for him. In the recent campaign (1874) he had been promised an old mule, forty acres of land and some bacon, in return for voting the Republican ticket. All negroes, he said, had been promised the same. Another negro said that he had been promised " forty acres and an old gray horse." As much as possible, the Republican majorities of the committees of investigation sent South during the later years of Reconstruction endeavored to avoid this particular aspect of the negro problem.

In South Carolina, where Sherman's plan had so much influence and where the negroes were so numerous, the carpetbag State Government undertook to strengthen itself by promising lands to the homeless blacks. More than $700,000 was appropriated for the purchase of lands and homes, but as usual it profited only the rascals. The officials who purchased the land pocketed most of the money. Some tracts of swampy and worn-out lands were purchased — in all worth about $90,000 or $100,000 — on which about 100 persons, it is said, found homes. The rest of the money — more than $600,000 — was distributed among the land commissioners and their friends.

In the later years of Reconstruction, there was a variation in the tale told by the office-seeker in the black counties. The programme now announced was to place heavy taxes on property, especially in the Black Belt, so that the whites would have to leave ; and then the land would fall into the hands of the negroes and the Northerners. When the taxpayers in South Carolina in 1870 were complaining about heavy taxation, Senator Beverly Nash, a noted negro politician, said in Columbia to a crowd of several thousand blacks:

"The reformers complain of taxes being too high. I tell you that they are not high enough. I want them taxed until they put these lands back where they belong, into the hands of those who worked for them. You toiled for them, you labored for them, and were sold to pay for them, and you ought to have them."

Judge E. B. Carpenter, a Republican, testified that "that was the key-note of the whole stumping, from the seacoast to the mountains."

Such were the conditions during Reconstruction. After the carpetbag and negro rule was overthrown, the negroes were no longer led by low politicians with tales of "forty acres and a mule," but the credulous were preyed upon by a new species of sharper, one who travelled about the country with what he pre- tended were the claim papers of negroes entitled to land. From each negro on his list, he would collect a small "attorney's fee," sometimes for several years in succession, always pretending to be working for the negroes' rights. Since this was illegal, it was done in a very quiet way, and the blacks were warned it would be fatal to their prospects if the matter became public. Naturally, they would say little about such a matter to their white neighbors, who had told them that they were foolish to expect anything from the Government; and, after being convinced that they had been swindled, pride would prevent confession and exposure. Many thousands of hard-earned dollars were thus collected from the more ignorant blacks, under the pretence that it was for attorneys' fees. The collection is still to some extent being carried on, principally in remote communities; the educated negro and the city-dweller would rarely be approached by an " agent."

Another and more recent method of swindling, based on negro credulity, is the "slave-pension" scheme. A respectable member of Congress is induced to introduce a measure providing for pensions to ex-slaves. This he does " by request," and then forgets about it. But the damage has been done. Sharpers procure numerous copies of such bills, together with commendatory comments from newspapers and prominent men, and then descend upon the blacks for "attorneys' fees." The matter is made worse for the negroes, and easier for the swindlers, by the fact that a certain sentiment among Southern whites is favorable to pensioning the old negroes. One of the latest manifestations of the working of the "pension scheme" occurred in 1903, after Senator Hanna had "by request" introduced a slave-pension measure. Of course, he believed that the object of those who wanted the measure was good; just as certainly did he know that such a measure would not be seriously considered; but he introduced it and thought that the matter was ended. A camp of Confederate Veterans in Fort Worth, Texas, taking the measure in good faith, passed resolutions asking their representatives in Congress to support the bill. Other camps did the same. Here was good material for the purpose of the swindlers, and within a few weeks they were operating in the South. Arrests were made by State officials in Alabama, Mississippi, Louisiana, and North Carolina. The inference is, then, that the swindling was general.

By the methods detailed above the ignorant and helpless blacks have for forty years been victimized. Perhaps some have been swindled who were not ignorant and helpless; for the blacks had reason to expect something from the Government, and it required no more credulity to believe in the "forty acres and a mule" than to believe in the claims to " Trinity Church property," of the " fortunes in England," so extensively advertised.

Notes:

1."The Davis plantation contained about 10,000 acres of fertile land; General Dana "consecrated it as a home for the emancipated," declaring in the order setting it apart for the blacks that it was " a suitable place to furnish means and security for the unfortunate race which he {Dayis} was so instrumental in oppressing." It was now said that ." the nest in which the rebellion was hatched has become the Mecca of freedom." Here, as elsewhere, where negroes were colonized, no whites were per- mitted to live. The colony was. guarded by a regiment of negro troops. — See Garner, "Reconstruction in Mississippi," pp. 252, 253.

2. In 1871 the Republican majority of the Ku-Klux committee stated that "the negroes heard and were inclined to believe {those reports} by their sense of justice which suggested that as their labor had produced the greater part of the property, they should have a portion. Hence the idea was widespread and common among them that each head of a family would have ' forty acres and a mule.' "—Ku-Klux Report, p. 217.

11

Ex-Slave Pension Frauds

Next to the "forty acres and a mule" swindle* the slave pension schemes have drawn more hard earned dollars from the ex-slaves than any other of the numerous frauds perpetrated on them. Unlike the "fort}^ acres and a mule" swindle, which was contrary to the interests of the Southern whites and was therefore opposed by them, the pension fraud owes much of its success to the fact that influential Southern whites have favored slave pensions and have spoken or written or introduced bills in Congress to secure them, and numerous Camps of Confederate Veterans have pro- posed or endorsed the pensioning of faithful slaves. So the old negroes have felt that, after all the promises made, something surely was due them.

While the pension fraud is not one of the Reconstruction swindles, it is not of recent origin. The state of mind in black and white that made it possible dates from the returning good feeling between the races after the downfall of Reconstruction. There was some talk of it and some resulting swindling during the 80's, but the most important movement began with the early 90's and was not effectually checked for ten years. The former slaves were growing old, often too old to work, and the idea of pensions appealed strongly to them.

The immediate cause of the great swindling movement of the 90's was the activity of one man whose intentions, however mistaken, were probably sincere. This man was William R. Vaughan, a native of Alabama, a Democrat in politics, who removed to the Northwest and was at one time mayor of Council Bluffs. He was an eccentric person, probably ill-balanced men- tally, and was possessed by two ideas: that the South was being robbed by the Federal pension system, and that the negroes by slavery had been robbed of proper returns for their labor. In order to right these wrongs he originated his slave pension scheme and between 1890 and 1903 secured the introduction into Congress of nine bills in succession. These bills were introduced "by request" of Connell of Nebraska, Cullum and Thurston of Nebraska, Mason of Illinois, Curtis of Kansas, Pettus of Alabama, Blackburn of North Carolina, and Hanna of Ohio — all men of standing. The bills were identical, each one providing that ex- slaves should be made pensioners of the United States and that pensions should be granted according to the following scale: negroes 70 years old and upward to receive $500 cash and $15 a month; those 60-70 years old to receive $300 cash and $12 a month; those 50-60 years old to receive $100 cash and $8 a month; those less than 50 years old to receive $4 a month.

To push the bills in Congress several organizations were formed, the first of them by Vaughan himself, the others by tricksters who grasped the opportunity-- to gather a golden harvest. Vaughan declared that he formed his slave pension plan as early as 1870, but not until 1890 did he begin to organize his work. In 1890 he published a small book entitled "Vaughan's Freedmen's Pension Bill, A Plea for American Freedmen," which contained a sketch of prominent negroes, opinions of Vaughan and others about slave pensions, and a number of symbolic pictures, such as Justice giving reparation (pensions) to the blacks; negroes working in cotton, cane and tobacco fields, with this sentiment attached: "Southern products grown by stolen negro labor for over a hundred years;" a woman (the South) handing gold (Federal pensions) to another woman (the North); and on the inside cover a slave in chains laced on the opposite page by a picture of W. R. Vaughan of Selma, Council Bluffs, Chicago, and District of Columbia. This book was sold for one dollar to help defray expenses. The first edition of 10,000 was sold in one year, and several new editions were printed. In 1892 a large poster containing about the same matter was published. It also contained a picture of Vaughan and his five sons, all "pledged to plead that justice be done America's former slaves by the United States government and Great Britain."

The circular announced the organization of a secret order entitled "Vaughan's Ex-Slave Pension Club." The object of the club was to elevate the race, to act as a fraternal order, and to assist Vaughan in getting information about ex-slaves with a view to securing pensions for them. Any negro over sixteen years of age could join, but, the circular stated, "no white person will be allowed to join said organization except it be a member of the family of the originator of the order." The headquarters of the society were in Chicago where Vaughan lived. Should any negroes wish to organize a branch of the Society they might, Vaughan said, send one of their number to Chicago "to obtain the secret work, grip, password, etc. I will initiate such in the Chicago or Parent Lodge and give them full authority to establish such subordinate orders. For the present there are but two secret degrees. It is my purpose to increase the degrees within the next twelve months. The paraphernalia, masks, secret work, etc., for each subordinate lodge will cost $25."

Numerous branch clubs were established, and the certificates of membership state that each person paid twenty-five cents entrance fee and ten cents a month dues, the proceeds to be used in pushing the pension bill. On all these certificates appear Vaughan's picture and the member's slave record, that is, the date of his birth, name of his master, etc. In 1897 Vaughan issued a circular denouncing by name individuals who were imitating his methods in order to get money from the negroes. He warned the ex-slaves that he was the sole author of the pension bill and that it was copyrighted by him; others claiming to be his agents were swindlers.

Until 1897 Vaughan's headquarters seem to have remained in Chicago, but in that year they were removed to Nashville, Tennessee. Vaughan, whose title had been Grand National Director, delegated his authority to one P. J. Hill to whom all records and secret work were turned over. In a circular announcing the change Vaughan stated that no persons would be "considered by me" or be entitled to any benefits under Senator Thurston's bill "without they hold a certificate" from Hill. A year later the name of the order was changed to the "Ex-Slave National Pension Club Association," and local clubs were notified that unless they sent in their dues they would be dropped. Agents were urged to push the work, to induce other ex-slave organizations to unite, and thus make a strong organization that could "make old Rome howl."

For several years Vaughan continued the work of collecting fees from the negroes and agitating in a small way the matter of slave pensions. Rival societies gave him much trouble, so in 1899 to help in the work he established a newspaper called the U. S. Department News-Eagle The paper had a semi-official appearance and name to which the United States authorities objected, and publication was stopped. In 1902 Vaughan's "Justice Party" appeared. The old organization had fallen into the hands of rivals, and Vaughan invented a distinctive title for his new order which emphasized the injustice to the South of the Federal pension laws.

In 1903 Vaughan succeeded in getting his pension bill re-introduced by Senator Hanna, and since then nothing has been heard of him. He expended, he said, $20,000 in the pension work, but there is no doubt that he made more than he spent. The Commissioner of Pensions in 1899 estimated that he had collected $100,000 in dues. Such was the history of the more honest part of the slave pension movement.

The other organizations were all fraudulent, designed merely to secure money from the ignorant blacks by the most barefaced misrepresentations. The most noted were the "National Ex- Slave Mutual Relief, Bounty, and Pension Association," and the "Ex-Slave Petitioners' Assembly." Smaller organizations were the "Western Division Association," the "Ex-Slave Pension Association of Texas," and "the Ex-Slave Pension Association of Kansas." In every Southern State there were also numerous local organizations, all formed by shrewd negroes to fleece their own race, and in addition to these there were numbers of individual swindlers not connected with any organization. Of all the swindlers the worst were I. H. Dickerson and Mrs. Gallic House, two negroes who for several years conducted the "National Ex- Slave Mutual Relief, Bounty, and Pension Association." Dickerson was for a time one of Vaughan's agents but was suspended with others for embezzlement. He and the others at once organized a new society and with literature and blanks stolen from Vaughan went to work. They copied Vaughan's methods, detached his followers to themselves, and even used his name in their literature. The National Capital, later the National Industrial Advocate, published in Nashville, was their official organ. Mrs. House was the leading missionary of the order and was sent out to form branches. Unlike Vaughan, Dickerson and his agents often falsely represented that the pension bill had become law and that those who wanted pensions must join his order. Dickerson and Mrs, House were so reckless in their promises to the blacks that the Post Office Department forbade them the use of the mails, and the headquarters were then removed to Washington. Driven from there they returned to Tennessee, and then again went to Washington. So closely were they watched that they were unable to keep up their organization. At one time they claimed 600,000 members, old and young, each of whom was supposed to pay twenty-five cents entrance fee and ten cents a month dues.

The "Ex-Slave Petitioners' Assembly" of Madison, Arkansas, organized in 1897, was managed by three negroes. I. L. Walton, the secretary published a paper called the Ex-Slave Assembly, in which he published regularly the old pension bills making it appear that they were laws. He announced that he had accepted the agency for the slave pension business and authorized his agents to collect from each member twenty-five cents and to forward each name with ten cents to him. In 1899 agents were authorized to collect money on the highway without organizing clubs. At that time Walton claimed 285,000 members, and in one issue of the Assembly he published the names of 130 travelling agents. Walton would himself enroll names at twenty-five cents each; to agents and others he sold constitutions and rituals at fifteen cents each. Agents were permitted to write letters for publication in the Ex-Slave Assembly, but when they were too long the writer had to pay for printing them, Walton was driven out of business in 1899 by a "fraud order" of the Post Office Department. The smaller orders sooner or later suffered a like fate.

Various methods were used in the field by the agents of these societies and by the local swindlers. Some of the agents were honest, but most of them were dishonest; the methods used and the results were similar. Each pension organization had numerous representatives who went over the South explaining to the negroes the pension scheme. Sometimes they represented them- selves as agents of the United States Pension Office, and often without transgressing the law they managed to create the impression among the negroes that they possessed authority from the government to enroll and receive fees from claimants for pensions. The usual procedure was as follows: an agent, usually a "professor" or a "reverend," went into a negro community, made a speech in the negro church to announce his business, and then proceeded to organize the ex-slaves into a club which paid $2.50 for a charter, and each member paid twenty-five cents entrance fee and monthly dues of ten cents. A portion of the fees and dues was sent to the headquarters of the organization. In organizing the clubs the agent would show papers "with the District of Columbia seal which he said authorized him to do this work,"* would exhibit and read copies of the pension bills which he would say had "passed the White House," or had been read twice and had to be read only once more before it became a law. In Illinois an agent of the "Petitioners Assembly-" warned the members that the}' must not "rite to the white house to find out," for it was like a "society," that is, secret. An agent named Butler Harris in North Carolina gathered together the ex-slaves, read a chapter from the Bible, prayed and then made the negroes swear on the Bible to give correct information in regard to their masters, their own ages, terms of slavery, etc. One rival pension organization was denounced by the agents of another. Much emphasis was placed upon the fact that some certain man, e. g., Vaughan, was the "author" of a bill, and held a "copyright" and that his corn- pan}' was "chartered" or "incorporated." Certificates of membership were given to those entitled by the bills to pensions. In North Carolina an agent told those who held this certificate that "it must be kept in their trunk" and not exhibited until the proper time; he represented his certificate as coming direct from "the Department." Some agents, especially those representing only themselves, offered reduced rates — one certificate for fifteen cents or two for twenty-five cents.

The promises made to the blacks were numerous and attractive. A North Carolina agent offered to secure $75 within ten day's for a fifty cent fee or $100 for a one dollar fee, and for each additional dollar fee a $100 extra pension. Those who paid no fees could get no pensions. A Georgia negro agent promised a uniform pension of $12 a month for services from 1863 to 1865. The larger organizations insisted that the fees must continue to flow to headquarters until the pension "passed." One club of ex-slaves was informed that the "United States government was now ready" to pay pensions of $4 a month to ex-slaves under fifty years of age and $8 dollars a month lo those over fifty years of age. A North Carolina ex-slave wrote to President McKinley that a man had promised his "society" that for twenty-five cents each he would write a letter to the "Pension Department" which would then send them $200 dollars each and a monthly pension afterwards. A "ginger-cake nigger" in Virginia called on the sick and helpless ex-slaves and convinced them that for a fee of one dollar he could secure $200 outright for each man and $50 for his wife.

Great show was made by the swindlers of making out and carrying away full records of the ex-slaves. The local clubs also were required to keep records and to send transcripts to head- quarters along with the dues. Some of the record books were sent to Washington by United States officers. It is not a pleasant experience to look over the long lists of names, with the attached records of age, master's name, old slavery name, etc., and the pitiful accounts of the ten cents monthly dues which were often paid for years. Of three books that the writer examined one had 110 names, another 293, and a third 330. Some lists of members, it is said, ran into the thousands.

Most of the pension orders distributed printed constitutions and rules, with suggestions for exercises at the meetings of the local clubs. Poems on slavery and "ex-slave pension songs" found a place on the program of the meetings. The various pension bills were read each month and explained. To keep the clubs together the "Mutual Relief, Bounty, and Pension Association" and other similar organizations sent out quantities of literature to inform and excite the negro members. This literature consisted of circulars containing reprints of the pension bills, statistics of the amounts due the ex-slaves, pictorial histories of the pensions movers — Vaughan, Dickerson, Callie House and others — statistics of membership, and denunciation of rival organizations. In some sections, notably in Tennessee and in the District of Columbia, conventions of pension seekers were held under the supervision of the agents. At these meetings the exercises were calculated to incite those present to a firm belief in the certain t}' of slave pensions. In Tennessee posters were sent among the blacks announcing the forthcoming conventions, the programs, and speakers. Barbecues were held on convention days, and the harvest from the new members was great. The pension bills were always read, and very few negroes knew that they were not really law. One negro preacher said "I was in a meeting in New Bern, North Carolina, where there were over 400 people, and the Thurs- ton bill was read and every one in the audience except myself believed it had already passed. Those in charge of the meeting collected money and the people gave it freely — forty cents a head." The swindlers met opposition from the better class of negro preachers and teachers. Consequently in their speeches and in the advertising matter sent out the pension people warned the negroes that they must expect opposition from preachers and teachers who were in league with their enemies. One report asked for by the Dickerson-House people from the local clubs was for the names of "ministers, teachers and other prominent negro opposers." The Interior Department has in its files many pathetic letters from preachers asking the government to do something to stop the frauds which were not only making the black people poorer, but were injuring the work of the ministers and teachers. The advice given by the pension agents against the influence of the preachers and teachers often had serious results. Schools were broken up because the teachers pronounced the scheme a fraud. Negro ministers lost popularity and influence; churches were divided and sometimes ruined. One agent told the members of one church that the minister's opposition had delayed the pension, and the minister reported that as a result of this statement "a great many refuse to tend church on that account," and that "these poor people reads only one paper — the National Capital, said paper is almost run some of them crazy." A Tennessee preacher demanded that the movement "be nipted in the bud" for it was "a Robery." The letters show that the negro ministers withstood temptations, suffered persecutions, and made material sacrifices in order to check this robbery of their people. The young negroes also often opposed the movement. The old negroes were instructed to expect this attitude from those who would not profit by slave pensions. Usually it was ordered that whites be not consulted; agents only must be dealt with. Whites who denounced the movement were to be considered enemies of the race and boycotted. A circular sent out by Dickerson and House stated that opposition had been encountered from ministers, politicians and teachers which only proved that these men were "enemies to the race, fakes, and frauds" and that while education is "grand" it is "dangerous for fools to have." One minister wrote: "I got the floor to explain to the people that they were being deceived, and I got in some dispute with the parties and had to get out a warrant and have them arrested for obtaining money under false pretenses."

The pension movement resulted in a considerable correspondence directed by ex-slaves to Presidents Cleveland and McKinley and to the Pension Bureau. Many of the letters excite a reader's sympathy, for they frequently lay bare quiet tragedies and always pitiful anxiety. A Louisiana teacher wrote that he wanted a job to look after the ex-slaves who were to get pensions under "Senitor" Hanna's bill. A petition signed by 110 Alabama negroes and sent to McKinley states that "we old people are Whoring [worn] out, no good in us now... [we are] praying god to open the heart of each congressmen"... [for] "if any race need pension we do need them bader than any Race under the Sun." Another letter stated that "ther was a agent saying that the presentdent sent her around saying for them to pay 25 cents.. .and she got a good many Siners [signers]." A Kansas City negro wanted "sum idea of this great Bill now pending known as the Pettus Bill no. 1176 of Alabama." One old Georgia negro wrote that a man had gotten his "pension papers" some time before and fearing crooked dealing he instructed the President to "pleas hole them" when presented. The officers of a pension club wrote to get news of the pension bill, stating that 293 ex-slaves "have pade theare 25 cent for thear stiffacate." A Florida preacher said that "the report did cause a many pore ex-slave heart to re-joice with fals Joy for his Pension." Reuben McCoy of Woodlawn, Alabama, was disgusted with Dickerson and Vaughan. "I have got tired," he wrote, "of so much foolishness. ..of state celisiters and treasure holders," who promised pensions which never came. In 1898 a delightful letter came to Mr. McKinley from Tennessee. "I will set down to Drop you a few lines to let you here from me I am will at this time and I hope when this Reach you I hope it will find you and all of your family Doin will...I am agent for your Life and Distinguished Services and know your wife's name," and he wanted news of his pension. A letter from Sparta, Illinois, is typical of many received by McKinley from old negroes. It began with the usual polite expressions: "It is with much pleasure that I write you a few lines to inform you of my health I am well & hope you are the same." He had heard of the pension law and suggested to McKinley that "you might send me a couple of dollars" in advance. He lived "in a little old Cabin... [and] it rains in same as if there was no roof... I am eighty-four years old,— stove up with old age and rheumatism."

So great was the interest of the colored people in the proposed pensions and so wide spread were the fraudulent operations of the societies which claimed to be working for the ex-slaves that the Pension Bureau took steps to disabuse the minds of the old negroes in regard to the matter and to check the illegal activities of the pension agents. Information was given to the press generally, and especially to the colored newspapers, to the preachers, teachers, and prominent men in the districts infested by the swindlers. Beginning in 1896 circulars were sent to all negro men known to be active in the slave pension business warning them against representing themselves as agents of the government or saying that the slave pension bills had become law. Agents who pretended to have official authority would be prosecuted under a law of 1884- which made it a crime to pretend to be an officer of the United States. This action of the Pension Bureau had at once a distinctly good effect. A person like Vaughan hastened to make clear his aims which heretofore had been vague and misleading. Some of those who had been claiming official authority ceased to do so, others quit the business.

In answer to circulars some amusing letters were received. One agent of the "Ex-Slave Petitioners' Assembly" wrote in reply that his business was official and perfectly legitimate and requested the pension authorities to strike off for him a lot of circulars containing the seal an d endorsement of the Bureau. Many wrote stating that they had believed themselves to be authorized by the government. An agent of the Vaughan movement wrote: "If I have been wrong in receiving money in this way the National Convention that was held in Nashville is wrong." This agent in 1897 was still basing his work upon the Connell bill of 1890. One man wrote to McKinley that he had "Rec'd a nice letter from the law division" (of the Pension Bureau) and evidently felt flattered. A Georgia negro was alarmed and sent an urgent request: "please don't authorize an officer to accompany me to you, just send me word an I will go as strait to you, as a babe to its mother."

But the swindlers though checked were not stopped. The United States authorities in order to prevent fraud by pretended officials sent officers to the ex-slave meetings to watch the agita- tors and to arrest those who claimed to have authority from the government. The Pension Bureau has record of eight or ten convictions in United States courts, and many more were secured in state courts. This action practically stopped the illegal frauds, but the worst swindlers were now operating inside the law- collecting money under the pretense of paying the expenses of organizing the ex-slaves and pushing pension bills in Congress. The leaders in this were again Vaughan, Dickerson, Walton of Arkansas, and Callie House, with two new ones, T. Starr Murfree in Tennessee and A. A. Washington in Mississippi. To put an end to the schemes of these people the aid of the Post Office Department was asked, and "fraud orders" were issued against all of them. As a result none of them could continue his business through the mails. It was a deadly blow, and only Dickerson and House survived it for any time. They changed their ad- dresses several times and tried to work through the express companies, but finally they were, it is thought, driven out of business. As soon as a money collection scheme based on the slave pension idea was heard of, the receiver of the money was "fraud ordered" and the old negroes then kept their dimes and quarters. Much credit is due the officers of the Interior and Post Office Departments for their persistent efforts to run the swindlers out of business.

A remarkable feature of the business is the ease with which the members of Congress were unknowingly made to lend their aid to these fraudulent schemes. Between 1890 and 1903 ten bills were introduced "by request," and not until 1899 did any one call attention to the bad results of such bills. In December, 1899, when Senator Pettus introduced an ex-slave pension bill, Senator Gallinger of New Hampshire, chairman of the Senate Committee on Pensions, declared that such bills were harmful because they deluded the negroes and subjected them to fraud. Senator Alason, who had once introduced the same bill, then said that he was convinced that bad use had been made of it. An "immense correspondence" from all over the South proved to him that it had resulted in fraud. Senator Thurston made a similar statement as to the results of the bill introduced by him; he said he had received about 2,000 letters indicating that the bill had cloaked a scheme of fraud. Upon this information and upon a mass of facts presented by H. Clay Evans, Pension Commissioner, Senator Gallinger in January 1900 made a strong report exposing "the mischievous features of the movement" in order to prevent the introduction of more such bills. Senator Hoar, however, unwittingly used a few expressions which seemed to show that he favored the principle of the measure, and thus unfortunately further swindling was aided. In 1903 Senator Hanna re-introduced "by request" the same hoary bill, and with copies of its windlers at once descended upon the black South.

Since 1903 there has been little visible evidence of renewed ex-slave pension frauds. It is not illegal and cannot of course be made illegal to organize ex-slaves and advocate slave pensions and collect money to push the pension bills, but the literature and correspondence of the pension agitators cannot be carried on through the mails. Some swindling probably still goes on and will continue as long as any number of ex-slaves are alive. This, however, is done by individuals with no organization be- hind them. One of the last cases in which the United States secured a conviction will illustrate the utter meanness and the tragedy of the business. An old negro woman living near Nor- folk, Virginia, had saved her money and purchased a house, lot and well stocked chicken-yard and pig-pen.

One spring evening about dusk she was sitting in front of her house resting after the day's work. A well dressed negro man came to the front gate, fired a pistol three times, and marched up the walk to the house. "I am an officer of the United States," he told the old woman, "see my white pants, see my blue coat, see my pistol. Magnum!" All of which impressed the old colored woman, especially the frequently repeated word "Magnum," which she thought had a magic meaning. The negro then announced: As an officer of the government I am entitled to free board at your house, to have fried chicken and waffles for supper and clean sheets on the bed." So he was established as a boarder The negro woman being an ex-slave her boarder offered his services to get her a pension. She was on the records, he said, to get lands in far off Arkansas and also to receive $700 in gold, but to get the latter she had to prepay the "freight" which amounted to $90. A mortgage se- cured the $90. The pension agent lived on the best the woman could give until she became nervous about the $700 in gold. Then he discovered that a slight mistake had been made. She was due $1800 in gold without any western lands, but the "freight" was $250. A second mortgage secured this and she went with him to a public telephone, heard him drop the money in, as he said, and ring up the "Department" which would send, he told her, the $1800 as soon as the "freight" tinkled in the telephone. Since he had consumed the entire substance of the old woman, he now left. When the United States authorities caught him he was given ten years in the penitentiary.

12

The Freedman's Savings Bank

I. ORGANIZATION OF THE FREEDMEN'S BANK SYSTEM

The Freedmen's Savings Bank was one of the few sensible attempts made at the close of the Civil War to assist the recently emancipated negro; it was one of the most promising schemes ever planned to elevate a helpless people, and its failure caused serious injury to the black race, the effects of which are still felt.

The Freedmen's Savings and Trust Company, commonly known as the Freedmen's Savings Bank or the Freedmen's Bank, was an outcome of the efforts of the Northern friends of the negro to find some means of elevating the blacks by fostering habits of thrift and economy, by encouraging them to save their earnings, and thus secure a safe, economic position in society. Before the close of the war several experiments in the way of savings banks had been made among the negro soldiers for the purpose of preventing them from squandering their pay and bounty money, as it is the nature of the race to do. The first military savings bank was established in 1864 by General N. P. Banks in New Orleans, for the benefit of the negro soldiers under his command, and for the negroes generally. In the same year similar banks were established at Norfolk, Virginia, by General B. F. Butler, and at Beaufort, South Carolina, by General Rufus Saxton. The negro soldiers welcomed this provision for their welfare, and many of them placed their pay and bounties in these banks, to remain until the close of the war. It is not known exactly how large the deposits were, but the Beaufort Bank had about $200,000 on hand when the war ended. Large sums were left uncalled for when the negro troops were mustered out of service or transferred to other posts, and the military banks were unable to wind up business at once.

Two distinct efforts were being made early in 1865 to organize savings banks for the benefit of the negroes: (1) an attempt by Anson M. Sperry, an army paymaster, and others, to found an institution which would absorb and continue the military savings banks; (2) the effort of John W. Alvord, which resulted finally in the incorporation by Congress of the Freedmen's Savings and Trust Company. Alvord was a Congregational preacher from New York, an attaché of Sherman's army, who had gone to Savannah in 1864 and had there observed the condition of the blacks. Upon his return to the North he worked out a plan for a negro savings bank, and on January 27, 1865, a meeting of business men and philanthropists was held at the National Exchange Bank in New York City to listen to his explanation of the plan. At this meeting measures were adopted to organize the bank, and have it incorporated by Congress. At the request of Alvord and others interested, Senator Wilson of Massachusetts introduced in the Senate on February 13, 1865, a bill to incorporate the Freedmen's Savings and Trust Company. The bill was referred to the Committee on

Slavery and Freedmen, of which Charles Sumner was chairman. The latter reported back the bill with some minor changes on February 18, and on March 2d moved its consideration. He stated that it conferred no extraordinary privileges, that it was an ordinary savings bank charter, and that its "object is a simple charity." Buckalew of Pennsylvania, one of the committee that considered and reported the bill, said that the only question was whether "we ought to establish such an institution outside of the District of Columbia," and Powell of Kentucky objected that the bill gave "a roving kind of a commission for these persons to establish a savings bank in any part of the United States. I think the bill is wholly unconstitutional. any right to establish a savings bank outside of the District of Columbia." An amendment was then adopted limiting the location of the bank to the District of Columbia, and the bill passed the Senate. The next day, March 3d, one day before the end of the session, Eliot of Massachusetts introduced in the House a bill which was supposed to be the one passed by the Senate. But on examination it was found that the Senate amendment had not been inserted in the bill. So the House added an amendment to the bill slightly different from the Senate amendment, though believed by Eliot to be identical.

Objection was made that the District of Columbia was not represented on the board of trustees, and Eliot met this objection by inserting the name of Chief Justice Salmon P. Chase. Thus amended, the bill passed the House. Since the bills as passed by the Senate and the House were not identical, a conference committee would under ordinary circumstances be necessary to harmonize them, but it seemed that no one noticed the slight differences. The next heard of the bill is when it was signed by the President on the same day, March 3d. The bill which was presented to the President for his approval was neither the bill passed by the Senate nor the one passed by the House, but the original bill introduced into the

Senate with the words "in the City of Washington, in the District of Columbia" inserted by some one in the body of the bill. The name of Salmon P. Chase was omitted. This was the bill that was published as law. In the hurry and confusion incident upon the close of the session the substitution was not noticed. This substitution of bills has never been accounted for; it may have been a mistake, or it may have been intentional. The only important difference was that the name of Chase was omitted.

The first section of the act named fifty prominent gentlemen as incorporators and trustees, with power to fill vacancies by election, at least ten votes being necessary to the election of a trustee. A successor might be elected to any trustee who neglected for six months to attend the meetings of the board. These meetings were to be held at least once a month. The trustees were to elect from their number a president and two vice presidents; and nine trustees, one of whom must be the president or a vice president, constituted a quorum. At least seven affirmative votes were acquired to authorize any investment, sale, or transfer of securities. The object of the corporation, as stated in the law, was to receive deposits from negroes and invest at least two-thirds of them in securities of the United States, one- third being held on deposit or otherwise as an "available fund" for current expenses. Not more than seven per cent. interest was to be allowed on deposits. The interest on deposits uncalled for within two years after the death of a depositor would be applied to the education of negroes, and the principal was to be so applied if not claimed within seven years. No one connected with the bank as trustee or official was to be allowed, directly or indirectly, to borrow the funds of the bank. None of the trustees, except the president and the vice presidents, was to receive any compensation whatever. The officials were to receive such salaries and give such bonds as might be fixed by the trustees. The books of the bank were at all times to be open to the inspection of the agents of Congress.

Such were the main provisions of the law as published. The act would seem to confine the business of the bank to the District of Columbia, and so Congress certainly intended. On the other hand, it is certain that the incorporators meant from the beginning to establish headquarters in New York City with branches in the various Southern States. No personal liability of the trustees was provided for, probably because it was recognized that their time was given as to a charity, and because of the high character of most of them. Besides, the law was specific as to of deposits—they must be invested in United States securities. As Congress could have the books inspected at will, no misuse of the funds seemed possible. the disposition to be made Headquarters were established in New York on April 4, 1865. Wm. A. Booth of New York was elected president, and J. W. Alvord corresponding secretary. The salary of the president was only $1,000, since it was understood that his duties were to be purely nominal. Alvord was to travel through the Southern States organizing branch banks and soliciting deposits. His work as inspector of Freedmen's Bureau Schools under General Howard would enable him to perform the more successfully his duties as bank missionary. Sperry and those who were endeavoring to perpetuate the military banks saw the superior advantages of Alvord's scheme and now joined forces with him, Sperry becoming a soliciting agent for the Freedmen's Savings Bank.

There was nothing in the charter that would sanction the establishment of branch banks outside the District of Columbia, but it is certain that Alvord's original plan involved the extension of the savings bank system into all negro districts, and the incorporators, paid no attention to,-perhaps they were ignorant of,— the will of Congress as expressed in the debates and the amendments, but proceeded to extend the system. As already stated, the New York office was opened on April 4, 1865, and on May 16th the first deposits were received. On June 8th the deposits amounted to $700.00. On June 3d Butler's military savings bank at Norfolk, Virginia, was absorbed with its $7,956.38 of unclaimed deposits of soldiers. The military bank established by General Saxton at Beaufort, South Carolina, became a branch bank on December 14, 1865, and turned over to the New York bank $170,000 of soldiers' deposits that were unclaimed. The New Orleans negro bank was not absorbed until January, 1866. A branch was established in Washington, D. C. on July 11, 1865, and then Alvord and Sperry went South to organize branches in each Southern State. Sperry secured permission from the War Department to accompany the colored troops of the army, and to be present at the pay tables to solicit deposits from the soldiers. He went with the army to the Mexican border and secured $120,000. Alvord's connection with the Freedmen's Bureau Educational Department was of decided advantage to him in his work for the bank. When he went South he carried with him the indorsement of General O. O. Howard, the Commissioner of the Bureau, and Howard's recommendation, which Alvord represented as an order, that negro soldiers should deposit their bounty money in the Freedmen's Bank. In many ways the Bureau was connected with the bank, and the connection was worked for all that it was worth. The negroes, as a rule, believed the bank to be a part of the bureau system. As inspector of Bureau Schools, Alvord traversed the South until 1870 in the interest of the bank. To meetings of negroes he explained its purpose and told of its advantages. He received numerous deposits from individuals and established branches in the larger towns. He, Sperry, and other agents scattered circulars broadcast among the negroes explaining the benefits of the bank, stating that Lincoln had favored the bank, and that General Howard considered it essential to the welfare of the ex-slaves. The negroes were given to understand that the bank was absolutely safe, being under the guarantee of Congress, and having the funds invested in United States securities, which were safe as long as the government should last, and that it was a benevolent scheme solely for the benefit of the blacks. The profits, they were told, would be returned to the depositors as interest, or would be expended for negro education.

George W. Balloch, later a trustee of the bank, then chief disbursing officer of the Freedmen's Bureau, gave material aid to the bank by allowing the offices of his agents throughout the South to be used rent-free by the branch banks; and often these agents acted as cashiers without charge. Nearly every bank official wore the uniform of the United States; the bureau offices and the branch banks were often in the same rooms; and the missionaries and agents of the bureau regularly solicited deposits. The plan of the bank was good enough, but the effect of its connection with the bureau was to make the depositors believe that they were dealing with the United States government, and there is no doubt that in order to increase the bank's business and extend the system this belief was intentionally fostered.

Success attended the efforts of the bank missionaries, and before the close of 1865 ten branches, including the military banks, had been established in the South at Beaufort, S. C., Huntsville, Ala., Louisville, Ky., Memphis, Tenn., Nashville, Tenn., Norfolk, Va., Richmond, Va., Vicksburg, Miss., Washington, D. C., and Wilmington, N. C. In 1866 ten more branches were organized, at Augusta, Ga., Baltimore, Md., Charleston, S. C., Jacksonville and Tallahassee, Fla., Mobile, Ala., Newberne, N. C., New York City, and Savannah, Ga. Owing to disturbing political influences among the negroes, no branch banks were organized in 1867, and in 1868 only three were established, at St. Louis, Mo., Raleigh, N. C., and Macon, Ga., and only one in 1869, at Chattanooga. By 1870 the negroes were getting out of politics to some extent, and in that year eight branches were founded, at Atlanta, Ga., Columbus, Miss., Lexington, Ky., Little Rock, Ark., Montgomery, Ala., Natchez, Miss., Philadelphia, Pa., and Shreveport, La. In 1871-1872 branches were organized at Columbia, Tenn., and Lynchburg, Va., making thirty-four branches in all, thirty-two of them being in the South. Headquarters remained in New York until March, 1868, when the principal office was removed to Washington and Alvord became president. The home of the bank was in a fine building erected especially for it, opposite the United States treasury. This building was later purchased by the government and used by the Court of Claims.

II. THE GOOD WORK OF THE BANK

In theory the bank system seemed to be perfect. As an Alabama Democratic Congressman said, "it was the very contrivance that was needed by these people [the negroes] above all others." From the principal office in New York or Washington the business of the whole system was controlled, and daily, weekly, and monthly reports were sent in by the branches. All deposits made at the branches, with the exception of small sums for current expenses, were sent to the central office to be invested in United States bonds. The cashiers and other officials were supposed to be men of the best character, chosen because of their interest in the welfare of the ex-slaves. Most of them were, at first, bureau or army officials, and several of them were ministers- missionaries sent down to help the blacks. Before the amendment of the charter in 1870, no loans could be made by the principal bank or by the branches, for by the law of 1865 all deposits must be invested in United States securities. After 1870, when Congress allowed loans on real estate, the branch banks in some cities were permitted larger privileges; but, as a rule, to the last, the branch banks simply gathered in the money and sent to Washington all that it did not pay out in drafts. An inspector travelled all the time among the branches examining the books and endeavoring to keep the accounts in good order.

In the branch banks and at Washington, after 1868, an efficient body of negro business men was being trained. There was a sentiment that, since the bank was for the benefit of the negroes, the latter should be its officers as much as possible, and about one-half the employees were colored. At nearly all of the branches, especially after 1870, when some of the branch banks were allowed to do a regular banking business, there was an advisory board, or board of directors, of responsible colored property holders. These men were very proud of the Freedmen's Bank and of their position in connection with it. They took a deep interest in all that pertained to the institution, advised in regard to loans and investments, and promoted in every way the habit of saving on the part of their people.

The negroes, believing that their deposits would be secure in these banks, which they understood were supported by the government, eagerly availed themselves of the opportunity to lay up small sums for the future. To each depositor a unique pass-book was given. In this book were printed simple rules governing deposits, a list of the branches of the bank, with names of the cashiers, and this statement:

"This is a benevolent institution. All profits go to the depositors, or to educational purposes for the freedmen and their descendants.

The whole institution is under the charter of Congress, and received the commendation and counsel of the President, Abraham Lincoln. One of the last official acts of his valued life was the signing of the bill which gave legal existence to this bank."

On one cover also was the following commendation from General Howard, which was to the negro sufficient proof of its connection with the Bureau:

"I consider the Freedmen's Saving and Trust Company to be greatly needed by the colored people, and have welcomed it as an auxiliary to the Freedmen's Bureau."-Maj. Gen. O. O. Howard.

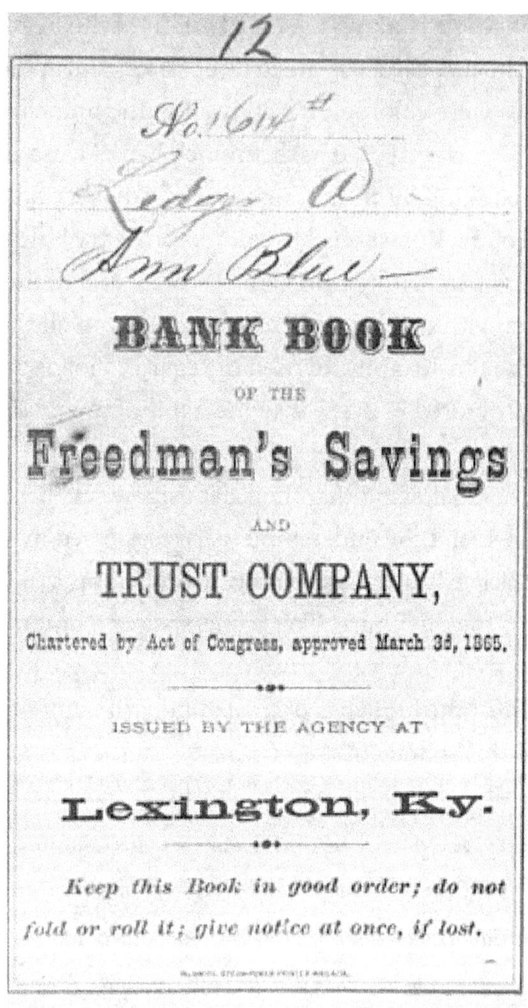

For the encouragement of the depositor a table was printed on the cover to show the possibilities of a small saving each day.

A man who saves ten cents a day for ten years, will have, if he puts it at interest at six per cent.

```
In 1 year  ...............................  $ 36.99
In 2 years  ..............................    76.20
In 3 years  ..............................   117.81
In 4 years  ..............................   161.94
In 5 years  ..............................   208.74
In 6 years  ..............................   258.42
In 7 years  ..............................   311.13
In 8 years  ..............................   367.03
In 9 years  ..............................   426.37
In 10 years ..............................   489.31
```

The rest of the cover was given up to pictures of Lincoln, Grant, Howard, and the United States flag, and some verses which the negroes believed were written by General Howard.

'Tis little by little the bee fills her cell ;
And little by little a man sinks a well ;
'Tis little by little a bird builds her nest ;
By littles a forest in verdure is drest.
'Tis little by little great volumes are made ;
By littles a mountain or levels are made ;
'Tis little by little an ocean is filled ;
And little by little a city we build ;
'Tis little by little an ant gets her store ;
Every little we add to a little makes more ;
Step by step we walk miles, and we sew stitch by stitch ;
Word by word we read books, cent by cent we grow rich.

On the passbook used in New York City was printed in English, French, and German this legend: "The Government of the United

States has made this bank perfectly safe." As a factor in negro education, there was nothing equal to that peculiar bank book with its useful covers, and the good effects of the bank system were observed almost at once. The negroes, who a few months before had been slaves, began to save money and put it into the bank. It became the fashion to have a bank account, no matter how small. Sums were received from five cents up, and on deposits of $1.00 and more interest was paid semi-annually at the rate of six per cent. Of course the deposits of a year were little larger than the drafts, but the money drawn out was often spent intelligently. The negro put money in the bank during the summer and fall to be used in the winter and spring, when supplies were scarce. Thrift was encouraged; many negroes saved money to purchase homes, or to purchase farm stock and implements. The drafts, it is said, nearly always went for useful purposes. Less money was spent for liquors and for the worthless finery so dear to the African heart. The negroes who kept bank accounts were less easily swindled by the multitude of sharpers who came to teach the blacks the ways of freemen. On January 1, 1866, six months after the bank had begun business, Alvord reported that it

"has gone into successful operation in nearly all the States south, and promises to do much to instruct and elevate the financial notions of the freedmen. The trustees and friends of the institution believe that the industry of these four millions furnishes a solid basis for its operations. Pauperism can be brought to a close; the freedmen made self-supporting and prosperous, paying for their educational and Christian institutions, and helping to bear the burdens of government by inducing habits of saving in what they earn. That which savings banks have done for the working men of the North it is presumed they are capable of doing for these laborers. I was privately and publicly told that the freed- men welcomed

the institution. They understand our explanations of its meaning, and the more intelligent see and appreciate fully its benefits. Calls were made upon me at all large towns for branches of the bank."

He stated several years later that "the banks are doing more for the people than the schools," which was doubtless quite true, since there were more depositors in the bank than there were children in the much over-rated Bureau schools, and the financial education given to the holder of the bank book was much more useful than the kind given to the children in the schools. Robert Somers, an Englishman who in the year 1870-1871 closely investigated economic conditions in the South, was favor- ably impressed with the good work that the bank was doing. He says:

"Go in any forenoon and the office is found full of negroes depositing little sums of money, drawing little sums, or remitting to distant parts of the country where they have relatives to support or debts to discharge. . . . [The literature of the Bank] contains an amount of general matter very suitable to the negroes and The Freedmen's Savings Bank. very desirable for them to read . . . the Freedmen's Savings and Trust Companies do for the negroes what our National Savings Banks do for the working classes of England, Scotland and Ireland . . . The negro begins to deposit usually with some special object in view. He wishes to buy a mule or a cow, or a house, or a piece of land, or a shop, or simply to provide a fund against death, sickness or accident, and pursues his object frequently until it has been accomplished."

Only those in the vicinity of the larger cities were directly affected by the bank, but the number of depositors reached within a few years the total of 72,000. About 3,000 of these had large deposits; and about 30,000 deposited sums of about $50 and under. The average total deposit during the life of the bank was $813, the average deposit in the bank at one time being about $50.

The following statistics will serve to illustrate the workings of the bank:

STATEMENT OF TWO ALABAMA BANKS TO MARCH 31, 1870.

	Huntsville Branch.	Mobile Branch.
Total deposits to March 31, 1870	$ 89,445.10	$539,534.33
Total number of depositors	500	3,260
Average amount deposited by each	17.89	165.60
Drawn out to March 31, 1870............	70,586.60	474,583.60
Balance to March 31, 1870	18,858.50	64,750.83
Average balance due to each depositor...	47.114	39.82
Spent for land (known).................	1,900.00	50,000.00
For dwelling houses	800.00	......
For seeds, teams, agricultural implements	5,000.00	15,000.00
For education, books, etc	1,200.00	......

STATEMENT OF THREE ALABAMA BANKS FOR THE MONTH OF AUGUST, 1872.

	Huntsville.	Mobile.	Montgomery.
Deposits for the month...	$ 7,343.50	$ 11,136.05	$ 8,522.90
Drafts for the month	10,127.61	18,645.62	8,679.60
Total deposits	416,617.72	1,039,097.05	238,106.08
Total drafts.............	364,382.51	933,424.30	213,861.71
Total due depositors......	52,235.21	105,672.75	24,244.37[1]

The business of the New York City branch to April, 1874, was as follows: Deposits, $3,559,298.02; drafts, $3,236,981.76. There were about 4,000 depositors in New York, of whom 3,000 were negroes.[1]

The Freedman's Bank Building, Washington, D. C.

The following table, compiled from the various reports of the bank and of the government, shows the entire business of the bank to 1874:

TOTAL BUSINESS OF THE FREEDMEN'S BANK.

Years ending with March.	Total Deposits.	Deposits each year.	Balance due Depositors.	Gain each year.
1866	$ 305,167.00	$ 305,167.00	$ 199,283.42	$ 199,283.42
1867	1,624,853.33	1,319,686.33	366,338.33	167,054.91
1868	3,582,378.36	1,957,535.03	638,299.00	271,960.67
1869	7,257,798.63	3,675,420.27	1,073,465.31	435,166.31
1870	12,605,781.95	5,347,983.32	1,657,006.75	583,541.44
1871	19,592,947.36	7,347,165.41	2,455.836.11	798,829.36
1872	31,260,499.97	11,281,313.06	3,684,739.97	1,227,927.67
1873	. . . .	. . . .	4,200,000.00	. . . .
1874	57,000,000.00	. . . .	3,299,201.00	. . . .

The interest paid on deposits amounted to the sums given in the following table:

INTEREST PAID BY FREEDMEN'S BANK :

To January 1, 1867,	$ 1,985.47
For 1867	9,521.60
For 1868, to November 1,	24,544.08
November 1, 1868 to November 1, 1869	43,896.98
" 1, 1869 " " 1, 1870	59,376.20
" 1, 1870 " March 1, 1871	20,840.32
March 1, 1871 to Jan. 1, 1873	122,215.17
Total	$262,379.82

The bank, it was believed, had a promising future, and the friends of the blacks relied upon it to assist the ex-slaves to economic freedom. The credit of the institution was rated A1 to June, 1874, a month before it closed its doors. The strongest branches were located at Augusta, Baltimore, Charleston, Louisville, Memphis, Mobile, Nashville, New York, Norfolk, Richmond, Savannah, Vicksburg, and Wilmington.

III. MISMANAGEMENT OF THE BANK

Notwithstanding the popularity of the institution, the rapid accumulation of deposits, and the good intentions of the founders and some of the later officials, there were grave weaknesses in the system, some existing almost from the beginning. The charter did not bind the trustees to any responsibility; branches were established that did not pay expenses; some of the officials were corrupt and others were inefficient; the accounts were badly kept and inspections were infrequent; many bad loans were made; the connection of the officials of the notorious District of Columbia government with the bank made people suspect corruption; the best class of the trustees neglected the bank and control fell into the hands of the District of Columbia clique; the rate of interest paid on deposits was too high; and there was a general shrinkage in real estate values after the bank had made heavy investments. All these influences operated to weaken the system. It will be of interest to examine some of these causes of weakness.

Of the 34 branches of the bank only about one half paid expenses, and not until 1872 was the entire institution making more than expenses. The organization was unwieldy, and the central administration was not efficient enough to control the branches. The establishment of branches necessitated the expenditure of funds, and about $170,000 was spent after the Freedmen's Bureau was withdrawn to purchase offices, etc., for the use of the branches. In Washington $260,000 was spent for a banking house. These expenses, added to the usual expenses of administration and heavy payments of interest on deposits, consumed the entire income from the United States securities in which deposits were invested. The branch banks suffered too from the hostility of the negro politician, who was unable to get his hands on the deposits. One of the negro trustees said that "every colored politician down South was the enemy of the bank." The State governments opposed the operation of the branch banks because they were not under local control; other banks were unfriendly to the objects and methods of the Freedmen's Bank. Many white men disliked the bank because they believed that it was connected with the Bureau, and all who disliked the negro disliked the negro bank. It was a race bank, as Fred Douglass said, and it aroused race opposition.

There was a persistent belief that the bank took part in Southern politics, and this belief came to be shared by the depositors. In 1872 a rumor that the funds of the institution were being used to elect Grant and to carry the local elections in North Carolina caused a heavy run on the deposits.

The accounts of the bank were never in good shape. This was due in part to the ignorance and inexperience of the negro clerks. It was difficult for the management to get rid of an inefficient negro employee. Alvord afterward stated that "the colored people seemed to think that they ought to be employed," and so thought the management. But too much pressure was brought to bear to get in and keep in as clerks and cashiers negroes who were not competent to do the work. The cashier at Jacksonville did not post his books for six months; other cashiers paid interest on total deposits, not on deposits in hand; few of them could ever make their books balance, and no pressure was put upon them from the central office. inspector employed was unable to get around to all the branches; several bad ones kept him busy and the rest were neglected bookkeeping in Washington was no better than elsewhere. One man did all the work and had to work fourteen hours a day to do it. This was too much for any man. For several years there was a discrepancy of more than $40,000 between the accounts of the branches and those of the principal office, and it could not be corrected. Several times entirely new sets of books were opened in the hope of leaving the past behind and keeping straight for the future. An examination of the books in later years showed that deposits were sometimes entered as drafts, and vice versa; a draft of $31.60 went down on the books at $3,160; $5,300 as $53.00, etc. One clerk testified that very seldom could the books be balanced at night—it would be from 5 cents to $5,000 one way or the other. When errors could not be found. "we always waited for something to turn up;" when the cash balanced, all went out to celebrate the event. The physical condition of the books was something fearful. A committee of experts reported that "we found leaves cut from the original ledger, leaves without number pasted together, balances not brought forward-original entries do not conform to the meaning of the transaction when carried to the ledger-credits posted as debits," etc.

The cashiers of the branch banks were not always men with the ability to say No to requests for favors made by influential men, and from the beginning there was a custom of allowing overdrafts. Until 1870 loans were forbidden, but this prohibition could be overcome by allowing overdrafts. In the end not a great deal of money was lost in this way, but it was quite difficult in many instances to get the money back. The negro officials were often overpersuaded by a certain strenuous kind of speculator such as Vandenburg, the District of Columbia public works contractor, who usually managed to make "Daddy" Wilson, the negro cashier in Washington, allow his overdrafts even when Wilson had positive instructions not to allow such favors to Vandenburg. After 1870 at the principal branches the cashiers were allowed to do some loan business. This was in order to overcome the many objections to the policy of the bank in gathering deposits all over the South to be loaned or used only in the District of Columbia. As soon as the authority was given to the cashiers to make loans, they were besieged by a dangerous class of borrowers, who would have received scant consideration at the ordinary bank. Often the law of 1870, requiring that loans be made only on property worth double the loan, was violated and the cashiers proceeded to make investments on their own responsibility. Some of them loaned funds on the worthless script issued by the carpet-bag State and local governments; others loaned on cotton; some even made loans on perishable crops. The Jacksonville branch put money on everything that offered, from saw-mills out in the woods to shadowy claims on property. Several branch banks, notably Beaufort and Jacksonville, endeavored to go into a regular banking business, and these with several others endeavored to act somewhat independently of the central office.

Not only was there incompetency and a disregard of laws and regulations and of business principles among the cashiers, but several of them were guilty of defrauding the institution or the depositors. Most of the incompetent officials, it seems, were blacks; most of the corrupt ones were white. There was a belief, often expressed after the failure of the bank, that when a white cashier had stolen funds and involved the accounts of a branch, a negro official would be put in his place to serve as a scapegoat. The white clergymen who were cashiers proved to be quite unable to withstand the temptations offered by the presence of the cash in the vaults. One of the trustees (Purvis) afterwards said: "The cashiers at most of the branches were a set of scoundrels and thieves-and made no bones about it-but they were all pious men, and some of them were ministers. The cashier at Jacksonville was a minister and today he has a large Sunday school; almost all of them are ministers." The cashier (Hamilton) at Lexington, Kentucky, a graduate of Oberlin, was also a preacher and a Sunday school superintendent. He did not steal from the bank but stole from the depositors, choosing those who seldom came about the bank and drawing out their money on forged checks. At Mobile the cashier, C. A. Woodward, appropriated to his own use $3,375 which, he stated, the Freedmen's Bureau owed to him. At Montgomery, Edwin Beecher, the cashier, made investments, contrary to regulations, of about $20,000 in securities that proved to be worthless, and for several years carried a shortage of $18,000 on his books. Reverend Philip D. Cory, cashier at Atlanta, tried to discourage negro depositors and secure white ones. He wanted a "white man's" bank. On this account the negroes were opposed to him, and the bank did not thrive. Finally, in 1874, he was removed, and a negro put in his place. covered that Cory had embezzled about $10,000 of the deposits, and had him prosecuted in the State courts of Georgia and sentenced to four years in prison-the only person connected with the Freedmen's Bank who was ever punished at all. Cory made a compromise: the prosecution was to allow him to be pardoned in order to accept an appointment as Indian agent out West. From the proceeds of this office he promised to repay what he had taken from the bank. Hamilton, the Lexington embezzler, also was allowed to accept an Indian agency.

The Beaufort branch was on a peculiar basis. From the beginning, when Saxton's military bank was absorbed into the Freedmen's Bank, the cashier, Scovel, had tried to run things to suit himself. He became almost independent of the central administration, and proceeded to do a regular banking business. He wanted to make a national bank out of his branch, and the trustees at Washington decided to allow him to do so. There was a great steal at Beaufort of at least $10,000, and bad investments amounting to many thousands more. At one time it was supposed that the loss would reach $100,000.

At the Washington branch "Daddy" Wilson, a negro, was cashier, and Boston, his son-in-law, was assistant cashier. Both lived in style far beyond their means, and repeatedly it was charged that they were using the funds of the depositors. But with one exception there are no instances of embezzlement proved against them. Most of the attacks on their management simply assumed that Wilson and Boston were the dupes of more cunning thieves. The following is an example of the way they were written up:

"Old Daddy Wilson stands about 5 feet 10 inches in his boots, is square built, solemn, the color of polished coal tar, and sports gold spectacles. . . . Brother Boston, young, airy, dressed in the height of fashion, and the color of Java coffee, moves lightly among . . the dingy and dilapidated customers. . . . Boston is fond of finery and fond of showing it. Finery and high sounding words are Boston's weakness. . Daddy Wilson got his wisdom in financial matters by keeping a little nick-nack shop on Fifteenth Street. Daddy Wilson and Brother Boston are mere figureheads kept here in dumb show by cunning fellows who work the machinery from behind the scenes and are filling their own pockets."

The case of fraud proved against the two was a small one but a very mean one. Boston had been "borrowing" small sums from an ignorant depositor named Watkins and giving no security, Watkins thinking that none was necessary. Also he had been checking out Watkins' money unknown to the latter, who could not read his passbook. Wilson, the cashier, allowed this and paid the money to Boston. In this way about $1,000 was stolen from Watkins before he discovered it. His losses were far greater than the losses of the average sufferer, but the experience was hardly more bitter. The following account from Watkins' deposition may be taken as typical of the feelings of thousands of ignorant negroes who lost money in the bank.

About a week after the bank closed I carried my passbook up there, and also my little boy's. My little boy had $60 in the bank, I think, and I had nine hundred odd. I wanted to find out how I stood. I saw Boston fifteen or sixteen times after the bank closed, and I waited and waited and waited, till at last I went to the bank to see about my book. I could not find Boston in, but I said to the clerk there, "Do you know how Watkins's account is?" He looked at the book and said, "Yes, you have 40 cents." I said, "Forty hells." He said, Yes." Said I, "What will I do?" Said he, "I don't know." I said I never had the money and asked him to tell me where I could find Boston. He told me where to find Boston, somewhere on "E" Street, below the Patent Office, and there I found Bos- ton. I went in and *commenced pulling off my coat to fight him right away. I said, "Boston, what is the meaning of this, that I have only 40 cents in the bank?" His face got white and said he, "Mr. Watkins, I drew it out." Hell," said I, " you drew it out and told me nothing of it?" "Well," said he, "I will fix that all right." The bank was to pay a dividend in two or three weeks' time, and he said,' 'I will pay you a dividend on the 15th of next month.' Said I, "Jesus Christ, I do not know what to do with you." The clerk at the bank showed me the checks on which the money was drawn, but, of course, I did not know one check from the other. I could not get anything out of Boston.*

I said, "Mr. Wilson, I don't want to get closed up in this concern. (This was before the bank closed.) A man in this town, unless he has money, is not worth more than a dog. I have worked hard, night and day, for this money, and so has my wife, and it should not be closed up in this way." He said, "You see that Treasury over there, don't you?" I said, "Yes." "Well," said he, "there is no more chance of this bank closing or bursting than there is of that Treasury." I said, "If that is so, it is all right." He said, "It is just prejudice that white people have got against us." I then made myself con- tented. My heart went down and I went to work. There the matter stood, and only 40 cents on my passbook to my credit. They did not rob my boy's book. When I was loaning money to Boston I supposed that it was all right as he was cashier of the bank. I supposed he owned it all himself. I did not know. [...] Question. I understood you to say that this money was the joint earnings of yourself and wife. Answer. Yes; she took in washing, and worked day and night, and I worked day and night, every day for the whole year. I have never been to a picnic or a ball since I have been in town.

The table below gives the list of branches where shortages were discovered by the inspector before the failure of the bank.

SHORTAGES AT THE BRANCH BANKS.

Branch.	Cashier.	Shortage.
Atlanta	Philip D. Cory	$ 8,000+
Beaufort	Scovel	100,000 ?
Mobile	C. A. Woodward	3,375
Newberne	Nelson	1,250
Wilmington	McCumber	3,000
Natchez	Jordan	1,125
Jacksonville	Coon	{ 100,000 ? 10,000+
Nashville	Cary	1,000
Vicksburg	Lee	11,000+
Lynchburg	Bronough	900
Lexington, Ky	Hamilton	5,000
Montgomery	Beecher	{ 29,000 ? 18,000+

It is not possible to ascertain from the records exactly how large the shortages were at Beaufort, Jacksonville, and Montgomery; in the table the smallest and largest estimates are given. There were shortages at other branches than those named above, but they were adjusted.

Another cause of weakness was the progressive deterioration of the character of the trustees. The original board was composed principally of men of the highest character, several of them noted for business ability, and as long as the central office was in New York the trustees attended meetings and kept the business going well. But after the removal to Washington many of the original body of trustees found it impossible to attend and through non-service the best members were gradually eliminated. The places on the board were somewhat difficult to fill, and it came about that most of those who were put in were incompetent persons elected simply to fill up the lists. They had little business capacity, no business connections, no property. The main qualification was to have some kind of a record as an abolitionist or as a friend of the freedmen. Too many of them took little interest in the bank.

The incapable ones were controlled by the few capables, who, after 1869-1870, were the District of Columbia members. These latter formed a kind of a "ring" for their mutual benefit. They were involved in other schemes that made their connection with the bank of great use to them. They were at once officials of the bank, and officers of the Bureau or of the army or of the government of the District of Columbia. Howard, Balloch, Alvord, and Smith were bureau officials and were connected with Howard University, and extensive borrowers from the bank; Cooke and Huntington were officials in another bank that put its bad loans off on the Freedmen's Bank; Cooke, Eaton, Huntington, Balloch, and Richards were officials of the notorious District government; Howard, Alvord, Eaton, Stickney, Kilbourn, Latta, Clephane, Huntington, Cooke, and Richards were connected with firms that borrowed large sums from the bank, notwithstanding the fact that officials were prohibited by law from using the funds of the bank, directly or indirectly. The trustees were under no penalties for the proper execution of their trust. They were not required to make any deposits in the bank. The law fixed as a quorum nine out of fifty trustees, and further required the affirmative vote of at least five on money matters. The trustees provided in the by-laws for a finance committee of five, of whom three should be a quorum. Thus three could and did habitually dispose of the financial business of the bank when the law required at least five. Often two trustees, or one, or even the actuary (cashier), negotiated important loans without reference to the trustees. Sometimes the actuary made a loan and then hunted up three members of the finance committee to sign the proper papers. Clephane testified that the actuary sometimes came to him and said, "I am going to count you present," when Clephane had not been at a finance meeting. As he said, "We left that [making loans] very much to the actuary to examine into. We were apt to take his representation of things." The honest and efficient trustees, like

Ketchum of New York and Stewart of Balti- more, were opposed to the management of the bank after it came to Washington, but were unable to reform it and resigned in disgust. At last when the rank and file of the trustees awoke to the fact that they were being used as dummies, then the sharpers who had been managing them resigned and left them to flounder about in their own confusion. Alvord, the president after 1868, was probably honest throughout, but he was weak and old and at one time was demented so that he had to be sent to a sanatorium. The finance committee managed him by refusing to allow him to vote on measures that came before them. He could only preside. The actuary, Eaton, and later Stickney, the nephew of Eaton, ran things as they pleased, and as the speculators on the board wanted them to do. The former possessed, as a token of the regard in which he was held by the speculators who borrowed money from the bank, a number of shares, which cost him nothing, in one of the various public works companies of the District.

The worst features of the bank management were exhibited in connection with the loans made under the amendment of 1870. After the removal of the central office to Washington, the control of the business fell into the hands of the District of Columbia members, who were directly or indirectly connected with various speculative enterprises then being conducted in Washington. The hoarded deposits of the Freedmen's Bank drew the attention of the speculators in Washington, and in 1870 an amendment to the charter was secured by the speculating element of the trustees. The amendment provided simply that one half of that portion of the deposits formerly invested in United States securities might be invested in notes and bonds secured by mort- gage on real estate of at least twice the value of the loan. It also provided that the bank might improve the real estate that it already held, provided that none of the principal of the deposits was used. This means that the bank was already holding property in violation of the original charter, which allowed no investments in real estate. The $260,000 spent in improving it and the $170,000 paid for property at branches was illegally taken from the principal of the deposits, for only in 1872 was the yearly income sufficient to pay interest on deposits. The amendment was secured through the efforts of one of the finance committee, W. S. Huntington, who belonged to the District of Columbia ring. The reasons given for the changes were: (1) that there was danger that the United States debt would be refunded at a lower rate of interest, and the bank could not then get a sufficient income from bonds; (2) that money was worth more than 5 per cent., and that unless the bank paid 6 per cent. or 7 per cent. interest on deposits the freedmen would place their funds elsewhere. Cooke of Ohio introduced the amendment in the House, where it passed without comment. In the Senate, Cameron of Pennsylvania strongly objected to the amendment on the ground that it would endanger the funds, which were in the hands of irresponsible persons, speculation and loss would certainly result, and the bank would be destroyed. The bank people stirred up the negroes to remonstrate with Cameron, and he ceased his objection, and the bill became law. Cameron's predictions were fulfilled within three years. Every cent that the bank could command was loaned as soon as possible to private individuals. The law requiring that the real estate be twice the value of the loan was never regarded. Kilbourne and Latta, borrowers from the bank and agents of a real estate combine, were appointed appraisers for the bank. Loans were made where there was no security at all, as on bills against the District government and on District securities issued without warrant of law. Vandenburg, a contractor, secured a loan of $30,000 without any security, except the verbal endorsement of A. R. Shepherd, the District "Boss." Vandenburg failed to pay, and Shepherd after delay made good the loan, but took occasion to remind Stickney, the actuary, that "if you do business in that kind of a loose way you are a damned fool." Jay Cooke & Co., the financiers, through their control of the finance committee of the Freedmen's Bank, were able to borrow at one time $500,000 of the freedmen's deposits, paying 5 per cent. interest, while the Freedmen's Bank was paying 6 per cent, to depositors. H. D. Cooke and W. S. Huntington, president and cashier respectively of the First National Bank of Washington, were trustees of the Freedmen's Bank and members of its finance committee. When Cooke's bank made a bad transaction, they used their position and influence to transfer the poor securities from Cooke's bank to the Freedmen's Bank. They also used the Freedmen's Bank as a dumping ground for the bad private claims of themselves and friends. Huntington lived in a house belonging to one R. P. Dodge, and in order to get his rent reduced negotiated for Dodge a $13,000 loan from his (First National) bank. This bank held Dodge's notes until they were due and then through Huntington's influence with the actuary, Eaton, they were transferred to the Freedmen's Bank. After Huntington died Dodge was asked to pay but objected on the ground that the money from the loan went to Huntington, not to himself. Of Huntington, Stickney, the actuary who succeeded Eaton, said, "if he wanted to have anything done, it was done." Trustees and finance committee could not check him.

The charter required a reserve of one third of the deposits as an "available fund" for immediate use. This was to be kept in the bank or on deposit. But after 1870 the actuary, counselled by the finance committee, began to use this fund for general banking purposes, and soon had the whole of it tied up in miscellaneous loans and investments of the worst character. No paper was so worthless that it would not pass at the Freed- men's Bank provided it had some trustee or friend of a trustee behind it. Loans were made on individual notes indorsed by trustees who had no deposits in the bank and no property in sight. Zalmon Richards, a trustee, had an accommodating custom of endorsing the notes of borrowers, and was finally ruined because of this practice. After the failure of the bank a committee of Congress was investigating, and Richards came before The following extract from his testimony will serve to illustrate his comfortable lack of any sense of responsibility and also his notions of business:

Mr. Richards: I know that judgment was taken against me as an indorser, and I am free to say that if the Lord ever puts money enough into my pocket I will pay it.

The Chairman [Senator Bruce]: The Lord will not do it for you. You must do it yourself in some way.

Mr. Richards: Well, the Lord may help me to do it. I have got a good deal of confidence in the Lord yet.

The Chairman: The Lord, Mr. Richards, doubtless is engaged in more profitable business than putting money in your pockets.

Richards did not know anything about the business of the bank or the requirements of its charter, yet he had been a prominent trustee. Sometimes no collateral of any kind was put up. Eaton, the first actuary, formed the habit of making loans and investments without consulting the finance committee. These he reported as "cash" or as "available."

It was often the case that, contrary to law, those who borrowed and those who negotiated the loans were identical persons. The trustees and the officials formed the companies that borrowed from the bank, or sold to it worthless securities. Cooke, Huntington, Clephane, Eaton, O. O. Howard, and Balloch were prominent among those who borrowed from the bank in which they were officials.

Balloch, a trustee and member of the finance committee, made a bad private loan in 1870, and in 1872 transferred his claim to the bank. Huntington borrowed $3,000 for one day and never repaid it. Eaton, the actuary, was given by Vandenburg one- half interest in a $100,000 sewer-pipe contract to reward him for his kindness in pushing loans for Vandenburg. Balloch borrowed $2,000 in 1872, giving as collateral $2,000 in United States five per cent. bonds. Later these bonds were removed and $1,800 in less valuable railroad bonds were substituted.

As examples to show the character of loans made after 1870 and to illustrate the business methods of the bank may be mentioned the loans made to Evan Lyons and to the Seneca Stone Company. Lyons owned real estate in Washington County, Maryland, and repeatedly applied for small loans. Four times was he refused by the finance committee, because it was suspected that his titles were not clear. Finally he secured a $34,000 loan, more than the property was worth. The facts that came out upon investigation were as follows: Lyons' land was covered with mortgages which he could not raise. His creditors wanted the money, so it was agreed that they should give up their first mortgages on the property, take second mortgages, and allow Lyons to secure a large loan from the Freedmen's Bank under a first mortgage. This was done; the creditors and Lyons divided the proceeds and left the bank with the land, on which it lost $25,000.

The Seneca Sandstone transaction was never fully cleared up, but the facts that were ascertained upon investigation were as follows: The Maryland Freestone, Mining and Manufacturing Company, commonly called the Seneca Sandstone Company, was a promising enterprise incorporated in 1867 with such men as General Grant, Secretary Seward, and Caleb Cushing as stock-holders. In 1868 Cooke and Huntington of the First National Bank, who were trustees of the Freedmen's Bank, got control, over-capitalized the stock, declared a stock dividend to the original incorporators, and issued a lot of first and second mortgage bonds, which were placed on sale, and speculation began. A loan of $51,000 was secured from the Freedmen's Bank in 1871, and $49,000 in second mortgage bonds and $20,000 in first mortgage bonds given as collateral. The second mortgage bonds were known to be worthless, and, the fact of the loan becoming public, attacks were made by newspapers upon the management. Thereupon Eaton the actuary went to Kilbourn and Evans, real estate brokers, and made an agreement with them and the Seneca Sand- stone Company to change the form of the loan and thus protect the bank from unfriendly attacks. The account of the Seneca Company was then closed, the loan being transferred on the books to Kilbourn and Evans, who gave their joint note, payable in six months, supported by good collateral. This seemed well, but at the same time a curious secret agreement was made with Kilbourn and Evans, securing them against loss. This agreement was signed for the finance committee, by Huntington (of the Seneca Company), Clephane, and Tuttle, and by Eaton, the actuary. It recited the list of the securities (including $75,000 in second mortgage Seneca bonds) purporting to have been deposited by Kilbourn and Evans, and stated that in case Kilbourn and Evans did not pay the note at maturity, their note and all collateral securities were to be returned to them except the $75,000 second mortgage Seneca bonds. It was understood that the transaction was not to make Kilbourn and Evans responsible in any way; they were simply allowing the bank to use their names as an accommodation. Two years later, in 1873, the note and securities were surrendered according to agreement and only the $75,000 in worthless second mortgage bonds were left to secure the bank against loss. The actuary early in 1874 closed the Kilbourn and Evans account and charged the Seneca Company with the $51,000 and accrued interest. The $20,000 first mortgage bonds held from the Seneca Company had disappeared in 1872 in a transaction in which Kidwell, president of the Seneca Company, purchased them for $20,580, but this money was never placed in the bank.

Such was the management that resulted in the ruin of the Freed-men's Bank. In 1873 the "available" fund was no longer available, the depositors had become alarmed, and three serious runs were made on the bank, taking out $1,800,000 in eighteen months. Business depression came, real estate declined in value, the bank could realize on few of its securities, and the bad loans could not be called in. Jay Cooke and Company and the First National Bank failed, and, in order to pass the crisis, the Freedmen's Bank had to sacrifice its best securities. As a result of the runs the bank was forced to require the depositors to give sixty days or more notice before drawing out deposits. This, though legal and provided for in the regulations, destroyed the confidence of the negroes, and few deposits were made during the latter part of 1873 and in 1874. Just as the deposits became large enough to pay the expenses of the bank the runs came. The Comptroller of the Currency reported in 1873 that there was serious mismanagement in the affairs of the bank, and in February, 1874, his report showed that the bank had been insolvent for a year.

When the bank began to show signs of failure the few trustees and the officials who had deposits drew them out, while at the same time the management tried to delude the negroes into putting more money in the bank and to evade investigation by Congress. During the runs the trustees neglected the affairs of the banks; only one of them-Purvis, a negro,—came to advise and assist the actuary, who during the runs had to act on his own responsibility. The clique of speculators resigned in good time and left affairs to the incompetents and the negroes. A faction of the trustees, dissatisfied with Alvord's mismanagement, determined to bring about a change by electing Fred Douglass to the presidency in the hope that he would restore confidence and reform abuses.

IV. THE ADMINISTRATION OF DOUGLASS AND THE COLLAPSE OF THE BANK

Douglass was elected president in March, 1874, and assumed office in April. He stated afterward that he accepted the presidency, not because he had any experience in banking, but because he thought that his influence with his race would strengthen the bank and enable it to weather the storm. Both Alvord, the outgoing president, and Stickney, the actuary, assured him that the bank was sound. Douglass knew nothing of the management of the bank, and the officials took care to keep him ignorant. He issued circulars assuring the blacks that the bank was safe. But his suspicions were aroused by the evident effort made by the actuary and others to keep him in ignorance of what was going on. He found that the correspondence was carried on in a cipher to which he was given no key. The report of the Comptroller of the Currency, which showed that the bank had liabilities of $3,338,896.15, with resources amounting to $3,121,010, a deficit of $217,886.15, finally convinced him that the bank was beyond redemption. He noticed also that the trustees and officials had withdrawn their deposits; that $10,000, borrowed from him in an emergency, was not repaid. So he turned to Congress for relief. Several months before this the reform element in the bank administration, headed by A. M. Sperry, the inspector, had tried to get Congress to investigate the affairs of the bank, but the trustees denied Sperry's allegations and succeeded in preventing any action by Congress.' to Senator Sherman, Chairman of the Senate Committee on Finance, and told him that the bank was insolvent and needed investigation by Congress. As he says; "I began to discredit the bank in the eyes of the Banking Committee of the Senate. . . I spent my time mostly in doing that sort of business." The trustees (some of whom had given information to Douglass to prove the unsoundness of the bank) and Stickney, the actuary, went before the Committee and denied that the bank was unsafe. Douglass, however, convinced the Committee and secured the passage of the Act of June 20, 1874, which in effect placed the old bank in liquidation and began a new one. The business of the past was to be separated from that of the future, loans were to be called in, non-paying branches closed, and all accounts of the old bank settled. The new bank was to invest one half of the deposits in United States securities and could make loans out of the remainder on real estate not only in the District of Columbia, but also in the vicinity of the branches. The rate of interest paid on deposits was limited to 5 per cent., and no loans of over $10,000 could be made to one person. The above provisions were to save appearances and to give the trustees an opportunity to get the bank out of its difficulties if it was possible to do so. But the real significance of the act was in the section which provided that, if the trustees thought it proper, they might nominate three commissioners to be appointed by the Secretary of the Treasury to close up the bank and its branches, collect its loans, realize on its investments, and pay the proceeds to the depositors.

After the passage of this act there was a faint pretense at reorganization. Douglass seems to have been somewhat optimistic, and issued a circular stating that the bank was now on a firm basis, that the $217,000 deficit, caused by non-paying branches, too high interest rate, "senseless" runs, hostility to the negro race and hence to the negro bank, and general hard times, could soon be diminished under careful management. He promised economy and prudence in future management, showed that new depositors were protected from old debts, while the best possible arrangements had been made for the old depositors. Hereafter, he stated, the constant drain of deposits to Washington from all over the country would cease, and investments would be made in the vicinity of the branches. The trustees tried to begin reformation by making Stickney, the actuary, give bond as required by law. He had held his position for two years and had never made bond. At first he was not asked to make bond, and later, when asked to do so, refused on the ground that the business of the bank was so involved that it was not safe for him to do so. Now when called before the trustees, who suspected him of crooked practices, he again refused to give bond, and as Purvis, one of the trustees, said: "Then Stickney commenced to cry. That was pretty good evidence of his guilt, for we were not in a prayer meeting."

After a few days it was decided to close the bank on June 29, 1874, and nominate commissioners to wind up its business. On June 30, 1874, the day after closing, we find that one Juan Boyle borrowed from Stickney on slender security $33,366.66.8 As near as can be ascertained there was due to depositors at the date of closing the sum of $2,993,790.68, on 61,144 accounts. In the bank was found only $400 in United States securities. The latest statement that can be obtained from the branches is that of January 24, 1874, which is given below. It will show approximately how the losses were distributed.

AMOUNT OF DEPOSITS AT THE BRANCHES, JANUARY 24, 1874.

Branches.	Deposits.	Branches.	Deposits.
Alexandria, Va.	$21,584	Natchez, Miss.	$22,195
Atlanta, Ga.	28,404	Nashville, Tenn.	78,525
Augusta, Ga.	96,882	New Berne, N. C.	40,621
Baltimore, Md.	303,947	New Orleans, La.	240,006
Beaufort, S. C.	55,592	New York, N. Y.	344,071
Charleston, S. C.	255,345	Norfolk, Va.	126,337
Columbus, Miss.	18,857	Philadelphia, Pa.	84,657
Columbia, Tenn.	19,823	Raleigh, N. C.	26,703
Huntsville, Ala.	35,963	Richmond, Va.	166,000
Jacksonville, Fla.	22,022	Savannah, Ga.	153,425
Lexington, Ky.	34,193	Shreveport, La.	30,312
Little Rock, Ark.	17,728	Saint Louis, Mo.	58,397
Louisville, Ky.	137,094	Tallahassee, Fla.	40,207
Lynchburg, Va.	19,967	Vicksburg, Miss.	104,348
Macon, Ga.	54,342	Washington, D. C.	384,789
Memphis, Tenn.	96,755	Wilmington, N. C.	45,223
Mobile, Ala.	95,144		
Montgomery, Ala.	29,743	Total	¹$3,299,201

Thus ended in failure a most promising plan to aid the negro race. The causes which led to this failure, as has been known, were various: bad business management; neglect of duty by the honest trustees; the failure of Congress to investigate in time; the general depression of business in 1873; hostility to the bank as a race institution and as a connection of the Freedmen's Bureau; dishonesty in the branches; and finally and fundamentally the corrupt use of its funds by the "ring" of District of Columbia trustees and officials. The bank had a splendid field and according to expert opinion could have survived all other bad influences had it not been for the lack of honesty on the part of those intrusted with its management at Washington. Like so many other enterprises in Washington and the South during that period it fell a prey to the general corruption that prevailed during Reconstruction.

V. THE WORK OF THE COMMISSIONERS

Douglass had wanted the commissioners who were to close up the bank to have no connection with the trustees; those who ruined the bank ought to have nothing to do with winding up its affairs, he said. But the act of June 20, 1874, allowed the trustees to nominate the commissioners, and forthwith three relatives of trustees were named-just what Douglass had feared. But the Secretary of the Treasury refused to appoint them, and other nominations were made: John A. J. Cresswell, formerly Postmaster General; R. H. T. Leipold, a Treasury accountant; and Robert Purvis, a Philadelphia negro, the father of Dr. Purvis, the negro trustee. These were then appointed by the Secretary of the Treasury. Leipold was chosen by the trustees because he was an expert accountant; Cresswell, "because he was a cabinet officer, the most practical Republican we ever had," and because he had a reputation for appointing negroes to office; Purvis was chosen because of his color, a negro being needed to represent the race.

Frederick Douglass, President of the Freedman's Savings Bank

On July 11, 1874, the commissioners made a bond and took charge. Cresswell and Purvis did practically nothing but sign the checks for dividends (which however was quite a task), and it was soon clear that they intended to do little work, but to leave all the business for Leipold to attend to. Cresswell seemed to think that his part was done by allowing the use of his name and his reputation as a friend of the blacks; and Purvis seemed to feel that his part was only to be a negro member on the board of commissioners. Leipold was an exceedingly unpleasant though very efficient person, and he was soon at loggerheads with the other commissioners because they would not work, and for other reasons. He was advised from the Treasury Department (neither Sherman nor Boutwell liked Cresswell), and he was very suspicious of crookedness among the trustees of the bank and wanted to prosecute some of them. Purvis, whose son was a trustee, stoutly defended them, and Cresswell advised against prosecution. Purvis wanted to employ negro lawyers, but Leipold would have none of them. When Leipold protested against doing all the work, Cresswell and Purvis proposed to pay him $500 a year each (the salary being $3,000 each), and for one year this was done. Purvis then objected and the payments stopped. To the last Purvis drew his salary for being a negro member and Cresswell drew his for being a friend of the negroes. Leipold was certainly not a friend of the negroes, and treated rudely all of them who had business with the bank. Purvis, who had all the American negro's dislike of foreigners, complained that Leipold was a low born, bad-mannered, foreign, fortune hunter, whose eccentricities almost amounted to craziness, but both Purvis and Cresswell testified that Leipold was very efficient. It was well-known that there were troubles among the commissioners and that only one was giving any service. All of them would have resigned, but they were informed by the Attorney General that only Congress could relieve them from their duties. Between 1875 and 1881 several bills were introduced into Congress to abolish the offices of these commissioners and turn the business over to one. Senator Sherman and Representatives Douglas of Virginia and Durham of Kentucky introduced such bills, but they were always defeated by the friends of Purvis and Cresswell, who were to be legislated out of office.

While the commissioners were wrangling, and the friends of the blacks were trying to induce Congress to settle the affairs of the bank, two Congressional investigations into the affairs of the institution were made-one in 1876 called the Douglas investigation, and one in 1880 by the Bruce committee. Both investigations were made at the instance of the Southern Democrats and the negro Republican members from the Southern States. The Northern Republicans and some of the Northern Democrats objected to any more time and trouble being wasted on the Freedmen's Bank. These two investigations laid bare the fraudulent methods and corrupt practices by which the bank had been ruined. The debate that followed the introduction of each measure aimed at settling the bank shows the members of Congress felt that they as a body were partly responsible for the failure of the bank. Bradford of Alabama declared that the government was to some extent responsible for the negro's faith in the bank, and maintained that Congress ought not to shirk its duty to the depositors. He said further, though, that the corrupt administration of the bank was only a phase of the general misgovernment all over the South after 1868, a logical outcome of the policy of the administration at Washington, and he showed that the bank officials were closely connected with the administration. Naturally this way of proving the responsibility of Congress did not appeal to the Republicans. When in 1875 Durham of Kentucky was trying to have a bill passed to relieve the depositors, he was opposed by Republicans such as Hawley of Connecticut, who objected, on the ground of "sympathy for the negro," to any measure that would legislate out of office Purvis, the negro commissioner. Durham answered him thus: "These 72,000 depositors. . . do not care very much about sympathy provided only they can get their money. They have been sympathized with by their friends until they have been literally robbed. These friends of the colored people have hugged them around the neck with one hand while they have stolen the money out of their pockets with the other." Senator Morrill said: "We certainly gave this institution of the Freedmen's Bank some sort of credit throughout the country" and are largely responsible. He thought the original trustees should have been prosecuted. Cameron of Pennsylvania contented himself with reminding the Senate that he had predicted the failure of the bank as a result of the amendment of 1870. Senator Sherman, who all along had tried to have Congress keep the bank straight, declared that "the original management of the Freedmen's Bank grossly and scandalously abused its trust; and all the powers conferred by Congress on that corporation were in my judgment abused." But until 1881 all the debate amounted to nothing but talk, and the commissioners were forced to proceed with their work.

The task of the commissioners was (1) to close up the branch banks and transfer all accounts to Washington; (2) to bring some order into the chaotic book-keeping of the institution; (3) to manage the property belonging to the bank; (4) to turn assets into cash; and (5) to pay dividends to the depositors as soon as possible. It was found that the negroes were so averse to seeing the branches closed that for several years it was necessary to keep agents at the old branches to explain the situation to the depositors and persuade them to send in their pass books. Far and wide the commissioners advertised for the pass books to be sent in, but the negroes for a while held them, their suspicions having been excited by that faction of the trustees who had opposed the closing of the bank, and by the speculators who wanted to buy up pass books for a small fraction of their value. To protect the depositors the commissioners ruled that no assignment of pass books would be allowed, and they began to flow in. When all the accounts of the branch banks that could be obtained were collected it was found impossible to get them into order. Pass books were found to be more correct than the ledgers, and by them the depositors were paid. Each loan had to be investigated to see how much had been paid and how much was due. Nothing could be collected without a lawsuit. Between 1874 and 1879 over three hundred cases were carried to court by commissioners. Often the lawyers' fees took the whole of the collections. Every obstacle was put in the way of the commissioners. The courts in the States and in the District of Columbia were easily prevailed upon to issue injunctions to prevent the sale of property for the bank. Property belonging to the branches was found to be almost worthless.

In order to prevent absolute sacrifice the commissioners were obliged to buy in all good property offered for sale, and this was held for years before it could be disposed of. The expenses of caring for the property took up most of the rents.

The Vicksburg Branch of the Freedman's Savings Bank

At first the trustees tried to control the policy of the commissioners. Cresswell and Purvis seem to have been on friendly terms with the trustees, but Leipold, inspired by the Treasury Department and by a natural distrust of the men who had assisted to bring on the ruin, refused to allow them to have anything to do with the winding up of the bank. He was intensely disliked by the negroes, who said that he "did not treat us politely, but would go on writing when we would speak to him." Colored attorneys were pressed upon Leipold to do his legal work. He wanted to do some of the work himself for the fees and remarked that he was "not here to make sacrifices for the colored race.'" When the depositors would worry him with questions he would say, "What are you pestering me for?" He told them that they had no business trusting such a bank-"Whoever knew of a Freedmen's Bank?... If I had not taken up this bank you would not have a dollar. We brought you out of slavery. You had nothing then and you need not think anything of these little losses." He was accused by his enemies of speculating in the property under his control and of trying to purchase claims. against the bank, but no proof was ever adduced, and there is little likelihood of his having done so. He did not like negroes, but he managed their accounts with honesty and efficiency.

As money was collected by the commissioners it was placed in the United States Treasury to await division among the depositors. Although large sums were kept in the Treasury no interest was allowed by Congress, nor could the commissioners invest the funds in interest-bearing United States securities. There were numerous preferred claims against the bank which had to be settled first, and this took all of the ready money in 1874. Then, as soon as there were enough funds, a dividend was declared, and the money distributed among the depositors. In this connection Purvis and Cresswell performed most of their work-at signing checks. A proposition to have the government depositories distribute the money was objected to, and the checks were written and sent through the mails. Under the commissioners three dividends were declared: 20 per cent. on November 1, 1875; 10 per cent. on March 20, 1878; and 10 per cent. on September 1, 1880. A 20 per cent. dividend amounted to $593,239.30.

When dividends were to be made the depositors were notified through the press, especially through the negro papers, from the negro pulpit, and by posters in the large cities. Every means of finding the depositors was taken, but many of them could never be found. After the average depositor found that he could not draw out his money when he wanted to, he decided that it was forever lost, and numbers went away from their old homes leaving no address. In 1881, after three dividends had been declared, it was found that of the 1875 dividend $39,248.24, due to 31,967 depositors, had not been claimed, an average of $1.20 each; of the 1878 dividend $30,927.26, due to 36,078 depositors, remained unclaimed, an average of 85 cents each; of the 1880 dividend $54,539.59 was not claimed, 40,000 depositors failing to appear. The average amounts due to and not claimed by the 40,000 depositors was $3.40. In other words, the small deposits were not claimed but were given up as lost, only the larger ones being called for. These small claims were barred by an act of Congress in 1881, but later all claims were again admitted.

VI. THE BUSINESS OF THE BANK UNDER THE COMPTROLLER OF THE CURRENCY

The excessive cost of the administration of the three commissioners, $355,994.77 to 1879; their lack of authority to dispose of property; their personal squabbles-all convinced Congress at last that a change was necessary, and in 1881 it abolished the board of commissioners and made the Comptroller of the Currency commissioner to wind up the bank. The funds collected by him were to be placed in the United States Treasury and were to draw interest. When dividends were declared he was to pay the depositors through United States depositories with government checks. He was given full authority to wind up the institution.

The Comptroller disposed at once of all property that could be sold and paid a dividend of 15 per cent. on June 1, 1882, and one of 7 per cent. on May 12, 1883, making 62 per cent. in all. To December 1, 1904, $1,727,398.80 had been repaid to depositors and $1,212,526.42 was still due. The government now has about $14,071.91 belonging to the bank, but it is not likely that this balance will increase.

When it was seen that the depositors had been defrauded, a widespread demand arose that the government reimburse them. From every Southern State, from all the cities where branches were located, from negro church congregations, from Southern State legislatures, Radical and Democratic-came memorials praying that Congress make good the loss. The petitions asserted that the government was responsible, because it had chartered the bank, had provided for Federal inspection, and had secured its funds by investment in United States bonds, and because the bank officials were usually government officials. All the advertising done by the bank had made it appear as an institution of the government, and the negroes had generally understood that they were giving their money to the government for safe keeping.

The Vault of the Freedman's Savings Bank in Vicksburg. Dual control was maintained by the two locks in the center of the steel door.

Frederick Douglass maintained that the government should make good the loss because it had allowed the bank to be considered a government institution, a part of the Freedmen's Bureau, and had through neglect of supervision allowed it to fail.

General Howard, trustee of the bank, formerly commissioner of the Freedmen's Bureau, who had allowed and encouraged the close connection of the bank and bureau, declared that the work of the bank was done under the guarantee of the United States, and that on that account the government should hold itself responsible.

General O. O. Howard

The several Comptrollers of the Treasury who after 1881 wound up the affairs of the bank repeatedly recommended legislation in favor of the depositors. Comptroller John J. Knox declared in 1882 that the United States government had "assumed a quasi responsibility" by its negligence in incorporating and failing to inspect the bank, as well as by allowing a close connection with the Bureau. He recommended that the losses be paid out of the "overflowing Treasury" of the United States. In 1884 and 1885, H. W. Cannon, the next Comptroller, renewed his predecessor's recommendations and said, "It seems impossible for these people to realize that they are to be deprived [of]... a portion of their earnings, which years ago they labored so hard to acquire and save. Thousands of them to this day believe that the dividends paid to them by the commissioners are but the interest on their deposits, and that sooner or later their original deposits will be returned to them. No explanation seems to convince them to the contrary, and calls are made daily both orally and in writing for their money.

W. L. Trenholm, Southern Democrat, Comptroller during Cleveland's first administration, renewed the recommendations for the relief of the negroes, and put their case more strongly than it had ever been stated before. And so it continued under Republican and Democrat until the 90's.

At various times the matter of compensating the depositors came before Congress. In 1875 a committee reported that the government was in no way responsible for the debts of the Freedmen's Bank. After the Bruce investigation in 1880 the question of assuming the losses of the depositors again came before Congress, and in 1883 John R. Lynch, a negro congressman from Mississippi, reported from the Committee on Education and Labor a bill to appropriate $969,000 to pay the losses of the depositors. The report stated that the government was not legally bound to reimburse the losses, but that "the circumstances that were connected with the inauguration and management of the bank were of such a character as to make the government morally and equitably responsible to its creditors, and it should, therefore, reimburse them for any losses they have sustained in its failure." A minority report by Money of Mississippi maintained that there was no warrant in law for paying such a claim, and that such a precedent would be extremely embarrassing to the government. President Cleveland, in his message of 1886, reviewed the history of the bank and declared that to assume the losses was "a plain duty which the government owes to the depositors, and that the latter should be paid by the government upon principles of equity and fairness."

In pursuance of the President's suggestion a bill was introduced in 1888 appropriating money to pay the losses of the depositors. It passed the Senate but failed in the House. Since then there has been no serious discussion of paying the depositors. Those who were in favor of paying the losses of the negroes in 1875 no longer urged it for various reasons; the depositors were dead, or scattered, and difficult to find, especially those who had most needed aid; if appropriations were to be made most claims would fall into the hands of speculators; and to most members of Congress it seemed a bad precedent to set, even if color of law could be found for it.

Note:

1. It is doubtful if, according to the charter, it was legal to receive deposits from whites. The act of incorporation specifically stated that the bank is for African depositors.

13

"Pap" Singleton, the Moses of the Colored Exodus

During an investigation of that movement of negroes from the South to Kansas in 1879-80, known as the "Colored Exodus," the writer of this sketch was impressed by the importance of the activity and influence of one man, an ignorant negro, who in himself seemed to embody the longings and the strivings of the bewildered negro race. His name was Benjamin Singleton, but on account of his advanced age and kindly disposition most people called him "Pap;" he himself later added and insisted upon the title, "The Moses of the Colored Exodus." He was born a slave in 1809 at Nashville, in middle Tennessee, and was by occupation a carpenter and cabinet maker. Evidently he was of a restless disposition, and probably his master considered him "trifling," for "Pap" asserted that although he was "sold a dozen times or more" to the Gulf States, yet he always ran away and came back to Tennessee. Finally he decided to strike for Canada and freedom, and after failing in three attempts he made his way over the "Underground Railway" to Ontario, opposite Detroit. Soon afterward he came back to Detroit where he worked, he says, until 1865 as a "scavenger," and also kept a "secret boarding- house for fugitive slaves."

Singleton was not of imposing appearance. From newspaper descriptions of him written during the 70's we learn that he was a slender man, below medium height, a light mulatto with long, wavy iron-gray hair, gray mustache, and thin chin whiskers. His square jaw showed strength of character; he had "full quick eyes and a general expression of honesty, courage, and modesty." He could not read. With all his later prominence Singleton remained frank, simple, and unspoiled.

"After freedom cried out," Pap was not content to remain in the North and soon went back to his old home in Tennessee to work at his trade. His experience in the North had opened his eyes to the economic weaknesses and dangers of his race, and soon he began to complain that the blacks were profiting little by freedom. They had personal liberty but no homes, and they were often hungry, he says, and were frequently cheated. He then began his "mission," as he called it, urging the blacks to save their earnings and buy homes and little plots of land as a first step toward achieving industrial independence. His later career showed that he had little confidence in political measures as a means of elevating the race and it was always difficult for political agitators to get indorsement from him. His ideas and plans were chiefly about industrial matters and much of the criticism he received from his race was like that later directed at Booker T. Washington. He declared in 1868 when he began his "mission" that his people were being exploited for the benefit of the carpetbaggers, whose promises were always broken:

After the war [he said] my race willingly slipped a noose over their necks and knuckled to a bigger boss than the old ex-one

Bimeby the fifteenth amendment came along and the carpetbaggers, and our poor people thought they was goin' to have Canaan right off. But I knowed better I said to 'em "Hy'ar you is a-potter'n' round in politics and tryin' to git in offices that aint fit, and you can't see that these white tramps from the North is simply usin' you for to line their pockets and when they git through they'll drop you and the rebels will come into power and then whar'll you be?"

For several years Singleton had but slight success in making converts to his plan of salvation for the blacks. But after the dream of "40 acres and a mule" had failed to materialize and after the negroes in Tennessee began to see that they were going to get few rewards from the politicians, they were willing to listen to other than political prophets, and Singleton at last found his opportunity. It was in 1869, he says, that he succeeded in inducing some negroes "to get it into their minds" that they ought to quit renting and farming on the credit system and endeavor to secure homes of their own. In order to direct their efforts he and others organized and incorporated at Nashville the Tennessee Real Estate and Homestead Association. The professed object of the organization was to assist Tennessee negroes to buy small tracts of farm land, or houses and lots in the towns to which so many negroes flocked after the war. All colored people were invited to join. Local societies were organized and incorporated under such names as the Edgefield Real Estate Association, in Davidson County, and these held frequent meetings in the negro churches and secret-society halls; committees were appointed by them to look out for land that was for sale, circulars of advice were scattered among the blacks, and speeches were made at the meetings by Singleton and others in regard to the economic situation of the negro race. Numbers of the whites favored the movement and gave assistance and encouragement to Singleton, while others opposed it. On the whole it was not successful in Tennessee. The real cause of failure was the inability of the negroes to purchase land at the high prices asked. The whites, hoping for better times, were still holding their lands at something like ante-bellum prices, notwithstanding the fact that the net income was yearly lessening. The only cheap lands were the worn-out lands, "where peas would not sprout."

The conviction grew upon Singleton that the negroes must be segregated from the whites. Whether they were friendly or unfriendly, he felt that they should be separated for the good of the blacks. In the South, after the failure to acquire land, the situation of the race was, he thought, precarious. He had no confidence in the new ruling class of whites that came after the carpetbaggers; they were not as friendly to the negroes as was the old master class which had been put out of politics after 1865; there was danger of helpless, hopeless serfdom. "Conditions might get better," said Pap, "a hundred years from now when all the present generation's dead and gone, but not afore, sir, not afore, an' what's agoin' to be a hundred years from now aint much account to us in this present o' de Lord." The only remedy, he decided, was for the blacks to quit the South and go to a new country where they would not have to compete with whites. "I had studied it all out," he said, "and it was clar as day to me. I dunno how it come to me; but I spec it was God's doin's. Any- how I knowed my people couldn't live thar The whites had the lands and the sense an' the blacks had nothin' but their freedom, an' it was jest like a dream to them."

Benjamin "Pap" Singleton

Singleton now turned his thoughts to. Kansas as the most promising place for the settlement of home-seeking blacks. There were several reasons for this choice. In the first place, the history of Kansas appealed powerfully to the negroes. Besides, railroad-building in Missouri, Arkansas, and Kansas had attracted numbers of Tennessee negroes as laborers and these sent back reports of the fine western lands open to settlement. Beginning with 1869 a few negroes went to Kansas each year to open small farms on the fertile prairies. In 1871, after finding that lands in Tennessee were too high priced for the blacks to purchase, Singleton's Real Estate and Homestead Association turned its attention to Kansas. An "exploring committee" was sent to "spy out" the land. A favorable report was made and a slight migration followed. In 1872 another committee sent to Kansas reported that negroes would do better to stay in Tennessee. Singleton then went himself to Kansas in 1873 as representative of the Tennessee Real Estate and Homestead Association, of which he was president. He was favorably impressed with the country and, returning to Nashville, he took three hundred blacks to the public lands in Cherokee County in the southeastern part of Kansas and there founded "Singleton Colony." Prospects seemed good and Singleton went back to Tennessee to get more emigrants. For this purpose the organization of the Tennessee Real Estate Association was continued.

From this time to 1879 Singleton was actively engaged in developing negro sentiment in Tennessee and Kentucky in favor of emigration or "exodus" to Kansas. The whites approved his policy, he says, aided him in various ways, told him that it "was better than politics," sat in his meetings, and in the Tennessee newspapers they published his notices and wrote up the movement for him. Every year with a few negroes he went to Kansas. Always upon his return he distributed circulars about "Sunny Kansas." He spent $600 for circulars, he says. All his life Singleton well understood the value of advertising. His literature was given to preachers going into the interior districts, to porters on the railroads, and to employees on the steamboats to be scattered among the negroes farther south. But not until 1876 was there much response to these efforts. In that year the local organizations in Tennessee were active, and

Singleton and Columbus Johnson, another shrewd Nashville negro, went to Kansas and looked up more good locations for settlements on the public lands. An arrangement was made by which Johnson was to stay in Topeka and from there direct the newly arriving blacks to the various colonies. A. D. DeFrantz, a Nashville barber, another lieutenant of Singleton's, assisted in working up the parties in Tennessee. Singleton had headquarters in Nashville, but traveled back and forth conducting immigrants to Topeka. The steamers from Nashville granted a special rate of $10 to Topeka.

There was more enthusiasm now at the meetings in Tennessee. At all of them Pap delivered addresses asking his people to stand together, to "consolidate the race," and to arouse them- selves to their duty to the race. Most of these gatherings were called "investigating meetings" — to investigate conditions in Tennessee and Kansas by listening to the reports of the officials who had been there. Now was the time to go, the leaders urged, or as Pap in highflown language said, "Place and time have met and kissed each other. The leaders of this migration saw to it that a certain selection of the emigrants was made. None who were entirely without means were advised to go; "no political negroes" were wanted, for "they would want to pilfer and rob the cents before they got to the dollars;" "it was the muscle of the arm, the men that worked that we wanted;" it was "root hog or die." One of the circulars entitled, News from Kansas, declared that there was "abundant room for all good citizens, but no room for loafers in Kansas."

For educated negroes, Singleton had a profound and bitter contempt, perhaps because they generally opposed his movement. Most of the negroes in the North who were well situated wanted no more of their race to come; they feared that a negro migration to the North would make uncertain the position of those already there. For obvious reasons the negro politicians opposed it. Singleton asked his people not to believe in those who would keep the blacks in the South for selfish reasons.

The colored race [he said] is ignorant and altogether too simple, and invests too much confidence in Professor Tom Cat, or some of the imported slippery chaps from Washington, Oberlin, Chicago, or scores of places whence are sent intriguing reverends, deputy doorkeepers, military darkeys or teachers, to go often around the corrals and see that not an appearance of a hole exists through which the captives within can escape or even see through.

The "exodus" songs possess considerable interest and afford an insight into the feelings of the black people. At the meetings held to stimulate interest in the "exodus," as Singleton called it, it was the custom to sing songs composed for such occasions. Pamphlet copies of these, poorly printed by negro printers, were sold by Singleton at ten cents each. The money received helped to pay expenses. One of these songs was called "The Land That Gives Birth to Freedom." Some of the verses were as follows:

1. We have held meetings to ourselves to see if we can't plan some way to live.

{Repeat.)

Chorus — Marching along, yes, we are marching along, To Kansas City we are bound.

{Repeat.)

2. We have Mr. Singleton for our president. He will go on before us and lead us through.

{Repeat.)

4. For Tennessee is a hard slavery state, and we find no friends in that country.

{Repeat.)

6. We want peaceful homes and quiet firesides; no one to disturb us or turn us out.

{Repeat.)

As soon as a party was enrolled Singleton would advertise that on a certain date the "Tennessee Real Estate and Homestead Association" would leave "for the Southwest in pursuit of homes." At the meetings before departure and at the start another "exodus" song was sung. This was called "Extending Our Voices to Heaven." Some lines were:

1. We are on our rapid march to Kansas, the land that gives birth to freedom. May God Almighty bless you all. Chorus — Farewell, dear friends, farewell.

2. Many dear mothers are sleeping in the tomb of clay, have spent all their days in slavery in old Tennessee.

4. It seems to me that the year of jubilee has come; surely this is the time that is spoken of in history.

These songs indicate clearly the feelings of the negroes who were going on the new "Exodus from the land of Egypt." An- other song sung on the way and after arrival, was altogether hopeful:

In the midst of earth's dominion

Christ has promised us a kingdom

Not left to other nations

And we've surely gained the day.

Three colonies were founded by Singleton, Johnson, and De-Frantz, and to these most of the negroes who went to Kansas in 1876-78 were conducted. Dunlap Colony was in the Neosho Valley in Morris and Lyon counties ; Singleton Colony in Cherokee County in the southeastern corner of the state, and Nicodemus Colony in the northwestern part of the state in Graham County. Singleton Colony, already referred to as having been settled in 1874, was soonest in good condition. Here, by 1878 the negroes had paid for 1,000 acres of land, good cabins had been erected, cows and pigs were common, and shade trees and fruit trees were growing. 15 The climate here was better suited to the negro than that of the other colonies. Dunlap Colony, also founded in 1874, grew slowly and was in good condition in 1878. In that year there were at Dunlap 200 negro families, two churches and a school, and the settlers had purchased 7,500 acres of government land. In all the colonies the negroes took up homesteads on government land or bought railroad and university lands on long credit at low prices.

Nicodemus, the third colony and later the largest, was in less prosperous condition in 1878. Prominent Topeka negroes were promoting this colony, and in 1877 it was being "boomed" as a negro paradise. It was, the promoters claimed, "the largest colored colony in the United States." A town company was incorporated and a fee of five dollars entitled one to membership in the company and to a town lot. Churches were to be built by the company, and no saloons were tolerated. The promoters invited "our colored friends to come and join us in this beautiful Promised Land." But a migration of negroes reached Nicodemus in the fall of 1877 too late to make crops that year, and in consequence there was considerable suffering during the following winter. Most of the early settlers of Nicodemus were from Kentucky. They had a song all their own called "Nicodemus." The allusion is obscure, though it may be said that some ignorant negroes believed that the biblical character (Nicodemus) was "Nigger Demus," that is, a negro. The first verse and the chorus were:

Nicodemus was a slave of African birth,
And was bought for a bag full of gold.
He was reckoned a part of the salt of the earth,
But he died years ago, very old.
Chorus — Good time coming, good time coming,
Long, long time on the way;
Run and tell Elijah to hurry up Pomp
To meet us under the cottonwood tree,
In the Great Solomon Valley,
At the first break of day.

The year 1878 marks the close of the second period of Single-ton's activity as a "Moses of the negro race." By the end of the year he had brought to Kansas, so he claimed, 7,432 negroes. 20 Nearly all of these were doing fairly well — certainly as well as could have been expected during a period of readjustment, and better than they would have done in Tennessee, because they worked harder and were more frugal. In addition to the colonies named above, there were many negroes about the larger towns ; "Tennessee Town," the negro suburb of Topeka, was growing ; a few had settled in Crawford County in southeastern Kansas, just above Cherokee; and numbers had stopped on the way, at Kansas City, St. Louis, and other Missouri towns.

In the early spring of 1879 began what the entire country soon knew as the "negro exodus" from the Egypt of the south- ern states to the Kansas Canaan. The remote but fundamental mental causes of the movement lay in the disturbed conditions in the South — social, economic, and political. The credit and crop-lien system which had been substituted for the slave-labor system had worked badly; the "40 acres and a mule" delusion, the Freedmen's Bank failure, and educational disappointments had discouraged the race; the negro-republican governments in the South had all fallen, and now the blacks declared that legal protection was often denied them ; the failure within ten years of all the plans for the immediate elevation of the blacks to the position of the whites had left the entire race restless and anxious for a change. The circulars sent out by Singleton had penetrated into all parts of the black South, and far and wide had spread exaggerated reports of his work. Speculators in western lands, agents for railroads and steamboat companies that were anxious for passenger traffic, negro preachers and white and black politicians, now out of jobs, took advantage of the uneasy feeling and stirred up the blacks of the far South to go to "Sunny Kansas."

As a result there began in February, 1879, a heavy migration from the black districts bordering on the Mississippi River, which continued, with some interruptions, for two years. It was a surprise to the white South and even more of a surprise to Kansas. Pap Singleton, perhaps the immediate cause of the exodus, was for a while lost sight of in the excitement that arose in Kansas when the first boatloads of unexpected negroes arrived. The exodus from the lower South overshadowed the smaller one from Tennessee and Kentucky. However, Pap worked on as usual, carrying people from Tennessee to Dunlap, Nicodemus, and Singleton colonies. Circulars were sent among the Mississippi and Louisiana "exodusters" to herald the virtues of the several negro colonies. The name of Singleton is attached to all of them and he always signs himself as "Father of the Exodus," or "Moses of the Colored Exodus."

Not all of the negroes from Mississippi, Arkansas, and Louisiana went directly to Kansas. Many of them stopped in St. Louis and waited to hear about conditions in Kansas before going farther. Others stopped because their funds gave out. But the whites and blacks of St. Louis were anxious to speed the "exodusters" on their way, and formed several aid societies to assist them to go farther west. One of these, "The Colored Men's Land Association of St. Louis," sent Singleton and DeFrantz as "land inspectors" to search out other suitable places for the settlement of "exodusters" in the western states. All the colonizing societies had Singleton on their lists of officials, as president, "founder," or "father of the exodus." His fame had a cash value to them.

Most of the immigrants were destitute, and the whites of Kansas were forced to organize the "Kansas Freedmen's Relief Association" in order to save some of the needy blacks from starvation. Pap was now brought forward by them as an authority on exodus conditions, and for several years he was considered the leading negro of Kansas. At first he was inclined to glory in the movement as a result of his efforts and to say little about causes. However, the "exodus" soon became an issue in Kansas and national politics, and Singleton found that the past treatment of the negroes in the South rather than his own ideas of their future in the Northwest was what northern people, especially the radicals, wanted to know about. So for the first time he raises the familiar "southern outrage" issue, and describes the South as a horrible place where murder, outrage, theft, etc., were common crimes by whites against the negroes. The Southern people were, he said, like "a muddy-faced bellowing bull," and "Democratic threats were as thunder in a colored man's ear," and in consequence the negroes were "exodusting." However, he never went into particulars, and always preferred to talk about "consolidating the race" in a new country.

Singleton's activity sometimes embarrassed the relief association. He published frequent appeals in Kansas and eastern news- papers asking that aid be sent to the Kansas Freedmen's Relief Association, not only for the relief of the refugees in Kansas, but also for the purpose of assisting more negroes from Egypt to Canaan. But the whites of Kansas wanted no more; the Demo- crats were accusing the Republicans of stirring up the migration for political purposes, that is, to lessen the southern representation in Congress and to make Kansas safely Republican ; and the relief association was try- ing to close up its work. Hence the numerous appeals for assistance signed by Singleton, DeFrantz, and other negroes, were embarrass- ing, because it seemed that they were acting under authority. The association on the contrary was doing all in its power to check the migration. The "exodus" was not well supported by public opinion in Kansas even among the blacks. The whites and resident blacks of Kansas helped the "exodusters" much, but they wanted no more of them ; the laboring-class of whites threatened violence if more negroes should come.

This larger "exodus," like Singleton's original one, met opposition from the leading negroes like Fred Douglass, Pinchback, and Bruce, who objected to any scheme of moving masses of negroes into the North. Against these race leaders Singleton spoke with considerable feeling. "They had good luck," he said, "and now are listening to false prophets; they have boosted up and got their heads a whirlin', and now they think they must judge things from where they stand, when the fact is the possum is lower down the tree — down nigh to the roots;" they either "saw darkly" or were playing into the hands of the southern planters who feared a scarcity of labor. To those who objected that negroes without means should not come to Kansas he replied that "it is because they are poor that they want to get away. If they had plenty they wouldn't want to come. It's to better their condition that they are thinking of. That's what white men go to new countries for, isn't it? Who was the homestead law made for if it was not for poor men?"

However, Pap was finally made to see that popular opinion in Kansas was not in favor of encouraging further migration of "paupers," and through the influence of the whites he was brought to the point where he used his influence to discourage the exodus movement. But unwillingly did he come to this. In May, 1879, he had denounced in advance a meeting of the National Negro Convention soon to be held at Nashville for the purpose of considering the causes of the exodus and the condition of the blacks. He feared that the negroes like Douglass and Pinchback would control the convention and try to keep the blacks in the South. He wanted the Kansas Negro Convention, which was to be held about the same time, to inform southern negroes about Kansas and assist them to get there. Soon, however, in order to relieve and reassure Kansas, he planned to divert the immigration to the states farther west, but only a few went to Nebraska and Colorado. His next plan, suggested by the whites, was to turn the migration to the states north of the

Ohio. He visited Illinois and Indiana to investigate conditions, but received little encouragement. He then began to play upon the fear of the whites in those states about a possible "exodus," declaring that the "exodus was working," but that if the North would force the South to treat the negroes well, let them vote, sell land to them, etc., they would stay in the South.

The migration began to decrease in the summer of 1879 and Singleton busied himself in looking after the negroes in the colonies, and in the relief work. About 200 Tennessee negroes went to his colonies in 1879, besides those from the lower South. When the exodus began afresh in the spring of 1880, the Kansas newspapers very willingly published statements from Singleton advising prospective "exodusters" either to stay at home or to scatter out into other northern states, for, as all maintained, Kansas had her share, there was no employment for more, and no more aid could be given to them. The southern newspapers gave wide circulation to this advice, for the planters wanted to keep the negro labor, and soon the exodus was checked. After this, Singleton moderated his activity as an organizer of immigration to the North and West. The scattering of circulars was stopped and he now always advised that none come north unless with enough money to last one year.

In 1880 we hear Singleton and others complaining that certain funds raised by the relief societies for the needy "exodusters" had been turned over to a negro school. This, they protested, was not right; the money should be divided among those for whom it was raised — the "exodusters" — and not given to a school. Singleton cared little for schools and disliked educated negroes, for, as a matter of fact, the educated blacks then best known to the race had not been good examples of the benefits of education.

Singleton was called before the exodus committee of the U. S. Senate in 1880 and in his testimony explained at length his plans and methods. After describing the "real estate" companies, his

Kansas colonies, and his method of advertising, he spoke of the causes of the movement which, in his opinion, were mainly social and economic : the negro was helpless in the South, which was "all out of joint;" the only way "to bring the South to her senses" was for the negroes to leave in large numbers, and thus force a reorganization of industry and a bettering of the condition of the laborers who remained in the South. He scored a point on the Democratic majority of the committee when he pointed out the fact that they had selected their witnesses from a class of negroes who were prosperous and who knew little of the conditions surrounding the average black. As to himself, he declared "the blood of a white man runs through my veins" — hence he could understand both races. "I am the father of the exodus .... the whole cause of the Kansas migration," he boasted and looked upon the attempt of the Democrats to place responsibility for the movement upon Kansas Republicans as a scheme to defraud him of due credit.

When in the fall of 1880 Singleton went to Illinois and Indiana he had a double mission: to see if there was room for "exodusters," and to deliver Republican speeches in favor of Garfield. As to the first he received no encouragement, but he delivered several speeches on conditions in the South and notified Illinois and Indiana that unless conditions were bettered and a Republican president elected a great migration across the Ohio might be expected. In November after the Republican victory, Singleton declared that to him was due the credit for making Indiana safe for Garfield. He explained it by saying that after he learned that the Democrats feared colonization of negroes by the Republicans, he had gone to their leaders and told them that "unless they allowed the state to go Republican he would import 250,000 negroes into the state." They were so impressed, he says, that several thousand failed to vote, and thus the state was saved to the Republicans. In spite of the vivid imagination shown by these incidents, they indicate that Pap had learned that neither

Republican nor Democrat in the North would welcome an exodus of negroes.

After the exodus ceased the negroes who had come to Kansas felt that they needed race organization and a settled policy in order to enable them to do their best. Almost at once they had become of importance as voters and as laborers. So in January, 1881, Singleton called and presided over a colored convention in Topeka, which considered means of bettering the condition of the race. A result of this meeting was the organization on March 4, 1881, in "Tennessee Town," Topeka, of the "Colored United Links," Singleton being the "founder and president." The objects were to "consolidate the race as a band of brethren," and to "harmonize together," to keep the race out of labor disputes, to care for the sick and the destitute, and to provide for training the children in trades from which they were now excluded by the jealousy of the white laborers. "In unity there is strength," and "United we stand, divided we fall" were the favorite mottoes on the circulars sent out to advertise the "United Links." Local orders of the "Links" were formed in each Kansas town that had a negro population, and for several years an annual convention was held at Topeka. The first convention in 1881 showed a body of fairly prosperous negroes. At the conventions the opening song was always "John Brown's Body."

For various reasons some of the negroes, especially the ex-politicians from Louisiana and Mississippi, were dissatisfied with the "lily white" policy of the white Republicans, and their rest-lessness invited an attempt by the "Greenbackers" to capture the organization of the "Links." Singleton himself began to talk as an "independent," and declared that the Kansas Democrats had treated the negroes as well as the Republicans had. The "Links" and the "Greenbackers" had meetings on the same day at Topeka, and had a joint barbecue, but no fusion was effected. However for several years the Republicans were not certain of the entire negro vote. The

"Links" flourished for some years and in 1887 Pap declared that the body had done much good in uniting the race and that the "hand of the Lord must of been upon him" when he organized that society.

The "exodusters" soon met opposition in labor matters. The migration caused a lowering of wages and the poorer whites became incensed against the blacks in the parts of the state where the "exodusters" were more numerous. One of the professed objects of the "United Links" was to avoid trouble by trying to regulate wages. The negroes were willing to work for less than white laborers, and on this account white employers and white laborers were divided in their opinion as to what the negroes should do. The latter were inclined to take the advice of the employers. There was complaint that negro youths were not admitted to the trades.

The matters that came up in the public meetings of the negroes showed that social and political agitators were attempting to use the race to further their own ends. Some rather noisy ones complained that the whites of Kansas kept them apart, treated them as a separate people, refused to accommodate them in hotels, etc. About the earliest and loudest complaint was that of J. M. Langston, who was refused admission to an ice-cream parlor in 1881. This was disappointing conduct from the white people of Kansas, the state of John Brown. The Mississippi and Louisiana ex-politicians, of whom there were many, began to talk about a proper division of offices. The Kansas whites were willing that the blacks should vote, but nominated none of them for office. The blacks were divided on the question as to whether an organization should be maintained for the purpose of bar- gaining with the Democratic and Republican parties for the disposal of the negro vote. Singleton cared little about these questions except as indicating the attitude of the whites toward his race. However, though a Republican always, he favored bargaining with both political parties, not so much for office, but to secure consideration for the race.

Under such circumstances, more and more did Kansas prove disappointing to "the father of the exodus." Too many of those who came insisted on staying about the towns and living as they had lived in the South; lands and homes were as far off as ever; competition with the whites was keener than in the South; the whites were distinctly business-like in their treatment of the blacks, and some were unfriendly; little sentiment was allowed to interfere in relations between races, and most threatening of all, thousands of European immigrants were coming every year to the prairie lands of Kansas and thus decreasing the opportunities of the blacks.

So Singleton looked about for another "Promised Land." Remembering Canada as a haven for runaway slaves, he suggested an exodus to that place. The British government, he believed, would assist the blacks. It was objected that Canada was too cold. He then suggested Liberia, began to preach a new exodus, and in September, 1883, issued an address to the blacks of the South declaring that since they had refused to come to Kansas in sufficient numbers to accomplish good results, the best that they could now do was to go to Canada under the protection of the British government or go to Liberia where they could have a government of their own. He advised them to leave the South at once, and said that in North Carolina, South Carolina, and Georgia 27,000 blacks had enrolled and were ready to go. There was no hope he thought, for political and economic independence in the South, and conditions were but little better in the North.

Some person who objected to Canada and also to Liberia proposed Cyprus as a substitute and wrote a long description of it for a St. Louis newspaper. He stated that England no doubt would willingly grant the negroes permission to settle there. Singleton had not the slightest idea as to where and what Cyprus was but eagerly accepted the suggestion and for about two years tried to work up a migration to that place. He was, in his dis- appointed old age, more credulous and visionary. Finally he started to Cyprus to investigate and went as far as St. Louis where he stopped, probably because of lack of funds.

Pap was now about seventy-five years old and somewhat feeble, but he kept up his "mission." He could with difficulty speak above a hoarse whisper and was accompanied by a smooth- tongued preacher, who did most of the talking and drew his income from the results of Singleton's popularity. Singleton declared that the blacks were unable to compete with the whites, and must make "a fresh start where the color line is not too rigid;" there was no hope for final success in America, for here "there can't be no trans-mogrification of the races;" foreigners had many advantages over negroes and were welcomed; but not even by his friends was the negro wanted, and foreign immigration "would shortly prove the uprooting of our race."

After the Cyprus disappointment Singleton was again attracted by the Liberian or Ethiopian movement which was being agitated in the lower South by Bishop Turner and other southern negroes. In furtherance of this movement in January, 1885, Singleton orga-nized the "United Transatlantic Society" for the "great and grand purpose of migration to Africa." All over the South the negroes were thinking of "Ethiopia" as a refuge that might soon be needed. The election of Cleveland in 1884 had caused uneasy feelings among the southern blacks, in spite of the fact that he had sent personal messages to them to assure them that slavery was not to be re-established. Some waves of this uneasiness reached the Kansas negroes and many of them enrolled in the United Transatlantic So-ciety. According to the official papers of the society the movement was the result of the conviction that the relations between whites and blacks would continue to be unsatisfactory and that negroes could not expect to reach "perfect manhood" in America; for it was clear that ex-slaves would never be accorded important positions in political or social life, and that fewer and fewer opportunities would be open to them. The negro could not accept such a condition; therefore, the only solution was "a national existence" apart from the whites. The society evidently intended to deal with foreign powers, for in the constitution there is a curious clause providing that "No persons shall hold any communications with any foreign power .... without the authority of this organization .... and the Father of this organization, Benjamin (alias) Pap Singleton, if he be alive and sane."

Singleton in his addresses and proclamations as "father" of the United Transatlantic Society, went to the root of the trouble. The negroes must be a separate "nation," he said; in no other way can they survive. They had been able to secure no stronghold in America, for after emancipation "we were turned loose like so many cattle with nothing to live on," and all efforts at economic independence had failed. Now the "scum of foreign powers emigrate to America and put their feet on our necks;" and they could live and work where a negro would starve. This was shown by conditions in Kansas, he said, where "three thousand women and children once fully engaged in washing and ironing are now forced into idleness and hundreds of them into base prostitution through the steam laundries and Chinamen;" the races were bound to be separate from the cradle to the grave, and "prejudice will follow you to the days of your offspring twenty generations ahead of this." For these reasons he advocated colonization in Africa, though he acknowledged that the average "exoduster" who had stayed in Kansas was doing fairly well. The United Transatlantic Society had considerable strength for several years; it held regular meetings and always passed resolutions in favor of negro "national existence" in Liberia, but it sent out no organized body of emigrants. Possibly individuals from Kansas joined the parties from the South that went, but they were few. For better or for worse the movement for a "national existence" failed.

The last years of Pap's life were not spent in obscurity as might have been expected. He was ignorant, he had no property, no home, no family, and it was suspected that smart rascals made use of him in his old age to get money from the generous blacks. But he himself was always popular with both races. In all the mass of material relating to Pap and his schemes there is no hint that he was not just what he professed to be; no doubt is manifested of his honesty and sincerity. Wherever he went the negroes welcomed him as the "father of the exodus." All his savings he spent on his schemes, and by 1881, in his seventy- third year, he was in want. So he proceeded to announce through the Topeka newspapers that he would accept donations if sent to a certain warehouse. The Topeka Commonwealth indorsed his character and motives; and the donations received kept him from want for a time.

A year later the blacks at Topeka planned a birthday party for the old man. The celebration was to be held in a park and five cents admission fee charged. Pap at once announced that all who desired to assist him entertain his friends on his birth- day might send donations — "anything in the way of eatables," he said, "will be kindly received." He invited the higher government officials at Washington to attend his party, and some of them sent polite regrets which he had printed in the local news- papers. He made out a programme and put the Kansas notables — governor, mayors, preachers — down for speeches. They did not come, but the party was a success. One hundred guns were fired at sunrise and a hundred more at sunset; "John Brown's Body" was sung, everybody had a good time, and Pap made $50 clear. The next year a barbecue on his birthday netted him $274.25. In 1884 the negroes of St. Louis gave him a celebration, and so it was until he died at Topeka in 1892 at the age of eighty-three. At all of his celebrations Singleton gloried in his title of "father (or Moses) of the exodus," and as the years passed his achievements were greatly magnified by himself and others. For instance, the St. Louis and Topeka newspapers in the late 8o's declared that Singleton brought 82,000 negroes out of the South; this was about ten times the actual number.

It is usually asserted that the "exodus" failed. But did it really fail? Most of the negroes were discouraged and returned to the South. The weak ones who remained in Kansas went to the wall, the stronger ones who remained did well, as negroes usually do when in small numbers surrounded by whites and incited by white example, competition, and public opinion to exertions not known in the "black belt." Kansas, too, was on a business basis; the "black belt" was not so and could not be; the industrious negro in the "black belt" would be "eaten up" by visiting friends and relations, while in Kansas he might hope to enjoy more of the fruits of his labor. The negroes certainly had to work harder in Kansas, but that was what they needed, and some succeeded because they had to work who would have been loafers in Mississippi. Then, too, on the race question a radical state became moderate; the change, if correctly illustrated by newspaper comment, was ludicrously sudden. Could Singleton and others have succeeded in bringing a large portion of the blacks to the North and thus have somewhat equalized conditions and nationalized the negro problem, it might have had some far-reaching good effects, political, social, and economic; it certainly would have relieved the "southern situation." Meanwhile, one fact was again proven by the Kansas experiment — individual negroes could succeed under severe conditions, even though the mass might fail.

14

The Servant Problem in a Black Belt Village

Auburn is a small college town in the Black Belt of Alabama, twenty-five miles from Tuskegee. The total population in 1890 was 1440; in 1900 it was 1447, of whom nearly 1000 are negroes. There are, roughly speaking, four classes of white families in the town: (1) the families of college professors, teachers, and preachers; (2) the families of merchants, real estate owners, well-to-do farmers, and of those who have moved in from the country to educate their children; (3) a large number of families who are more or less dependent for a livelihood upon taking boarders during the college session when there are about four hundred students in town; (4) several families of poorer people who rent land or have small farms near town, or clerk in stores, or do carpenter work. These last employ no negro servants, and are their own masters; while the first three classes are absolutely dependent upon the African for all servant's work.

The black population may be classified into (1) those who are industrious and fairly prosperous, who own their own homes or are able to rent good houses, who have regular occupations and who, as a rule, do not go out to service (2) those who live by doing day work, cooking, nursing, washing, hauling, cutting wood, mowing lawns, working gardens, and other odd jobs; (3) those who do nothing at all until forced to work by hunger or cold; and (4) those who live on the outskirts of the town and work the greater part of the time on the farms near by, but who, in the summer and winter, may condescend to work as servants in town.

There are no white servants and few white day laborers. The town is dependent upon the negroes for all out-door manual labor and for all house work not done by the white housekeepers. There are, perhaps, a dozen trifling young white fellows from fourteen to twenty years of age who as a daily duty occupy the chairs and benches at the street corners. Like the lilies of the field they toil not, neither do they spin; their mothers do both for them. But as a rule the young white people leave the town as soon as they are grown, and find occupation elsewhere. Here, as in other Black Belt towns, the white population increases but slowly; the young people find no inducements to stay.

A few of the negro men work all of the time, probably half of them work half the time, and the others only once in a long while when they are compelled to do so by hunger and want. The industrious ones are porters in the stores, drivers of drays, wood cutters, visiting gardeners, and common laborers. At least half of the negro men and boys have no regular occupations, and earnestly desire none. In the summer the majority of them do not work at all; in the fall and winter and early spring they are more industrious. At all times the demand for labor is greater than the supply. The negro men spend much of their time in loafing around their homes where they are supported by the work of their wives, mothers or sweethearts, or hanging around the negro stores up town waiting for some darkey with a quarter who may buy a watermelon or a bag of crackers and a tin of meat and "set up the crowd." They wear the old clothes given them by the college students and the citizens; wait on the former for tips; carry notes for dimes and bring trunks from the station for quarters; and for small sums carry water to and look after the uniforms for the various college athletic teams. Burglaries are quite common. The woodcutters and the majority of the gardeners are old men who are not physically- able to do heavy work. An old man will, if permitted, spend a month on a cord of wood, coming in once or twice a week in time to get a meal after an hour's work. They get fifty cents a cord for cutting light pine into stove wood, and have several cords for different families on hand at one time. Nothing is said about meals, but they usually get them. The old chaps are great at courting the cooks. I watched an old fellow last summer who spread out his work on a cord of wood over a month and during the time had eight meals. He also made a conquest of the old colored woman who was doing the cooking.

The gardeners who attend to the flowers, vegetables, fruit trees, and lawns, are extremely trying to the mistress of a household. When a negro goes regularly (one or two days in a week) to a place to work, it becomes known as "his place," and if discharged, no amount of persuasion will induce another "to take his place." Trim Drake was a gardener who had borrowed a dollar in advance on his wages, and being so much ahead and sure of all the work elsewhere that the state of his health would permit, did not return to "his place" for fear that the dollar would be deducted from his wages. Other negroes would not work in "Trim's place," for "to take his place" would have been a cardinal sin. Many, however, will promise to come and never appear. In this case there were six promises. Some agree in good faith to come, and being afterwards informed of the crime they are about to commit, they stay away; others promise to come simply to avoid giving a reason for not coming, or perhaps, out of politeness, and to give a fleeting pleasure to the would-be employer who hopes to get some work done. They are very willing to give that kind of pleasure. It is a kind of genuine politeness, a desire to be agreeable, for the average negro man is still polite, much more so than the negro woman. A negro's agreements to work are like a Spaniard's gift of a thing admired — not to be taken seriously.

But at last two negroes were found who did not know that Trim had a mortgage on this place and who agreed to cut the long grass and weeds that were growing up during his absence. Each worked half a day and did not return, having been informed that they were working in "Trim's place." Meanwhile, Trim (when an attempt was made to get him to release "his place") sent, as his excuse for not appearing, that he had the rheumatism — an old chestnut. I saw him several times during the summer working elsewhere. For three months the lawn was neglected, the grass and weeds choked out the vegetables and flowers and smothered the young fruit trees. Finally an old man was found who did not recognize the usual code of labor ethics. He did all he could, but his son who wanted employment also now refused to do the heavy work, which his father could not do, because it was his father's "place." One lady who possessed a lawn and garden on which no darkey had a claim, found herself unable to get a negro in the usual way to do some needed work. She went up town, along the Black Side of the street and asked a crowd of negroes in front of a negro store if any of them wanted the work, which would bring fifty cents and two meals a day. She counted twenty-two idle negro men sitting in front of the store on boxes, barrels, on the ground, and on the porch. None of them had any regular occupation, or any visible means of support; but not one of them would do the work. And this was not in the bountiful summer time either; it was in the hungry spring.

Some of the gardeners have little failings. One will carry off the seed given him to plant and will say that you have given him bad advice as to planting and that they did not come up. Another will take away more vegetables than his employer thinks he ought, and, in reply to his or her expostulations, will declare that "de moles et em." Other handy little things will disappear. One man cut a lot of long grass, which was given him to make a mattress. Before he raked it up there was a large coil of wire lying on the ground near by, but when the grass had been raked into a pile the wire was no longer to be seen, for it was carried away in the middle of the grass. These are not isolated cases, but each is only *e pluribus unum*.

The negro women who take in washing and ironing do a thriving business during nine months of the year when the college students are in town, and during the summer they manage to get along fairly well. Their charges are twenty-five cents a week or $1.00 a month for individuals, and $1.00 to $1.50 a week for families. Some are experts and do high grade work; others are the worst kind of makeshifts. One has to guard against the lazy washerwoman who, to save trouble and labor, uses "powders" (some strong preparation to make washing easy) sold in the negro stores to "eat out the dirt," which also " eats " holes in the clothes. Some washerwomen have a trouble- some habit of wearing for several days certain garments sent out in the wash. Between Monday, when they come for the clothes, and Saturday, when they return them, several days' wear can be had. Again, they will forget to return a garment and wear it to church the next Sunday. Sometimes they report garments as lost, which after a few weeks' dilapidation and some slight alteration, they do not mind wearing in the owner's presence. The best washerwomen earn from $15.00 to $40.00 a month in the busy season. Many a one of them supports herself and a husband or lover and several children who live in idleness. These last may do as much as to go for and to return the clothes, but the husband of a good washerwoman seldom works.

The younger women and half grown girls often go out by the day as nurses. They get a small wage of $2.00 to $5.00 a month, three meals a day, and perquisites in the way of old clothes, shoes and hats. A nurse has nothing to do but look after the baby once in a while for about twelve hours a day. There are objections to the Auburn nurse-girl. She is sure, in- stead of going around by the sidewalks, to take the short cuts and pull the baby, bumping in its carriage, over the stiles to the great danger of its peace of mind and wholeness of body. On hilly sidewalks she likes to experiment with the carriage, turning it loose and running to catch it. Sometimes she fails to overtake it and the baby goes into the ditch. Fond of the sun herself, though she likes to carry an umbrella — to save her complexion perhaps — she is sure to forget that the white baby does not thrive in the Southern summer sun, and leaves the umbrella of the carriage down, perhaps even going off and leaving the baby in the carriage in the broiling sun. The nurses take the little fellows to their own homes, which, to say the least, is not a good practice and may be dangerous to health. They have been known to give Jimson weed seed to obstreperous babies in order to quiet them; Jimson weed is poisonous. They will go to sleep on the back verandah and let the infants roll down the steps. They like to combine pleasure with duty, and I have seen at one time, three empty little carriages near a public building into which the nurses had taken the children, in order to flirt with a couple of young bucks in the janitor's dark and stuffy basement room. In the street near the negro stores may often be seen a baby in a carriage alone or in charge of a little bit of a negro, while the nurse is in the back of the store talking with the young negro men. The nurses will sit with the children in the grass on the college campus or on the lawns quite unconcerned by the presence of "red bugs" until the babies' little bodies are covered with the insects, and the next day the mothers wonder why the children scream so and physic them for colic. Red bugs do not trouble the nurses.

In a way, the nurse girls are faithful to their little white charges, and probably like them much better than they do their own small brothers and sisters. I have often heard negro nurses express preference for white children. They are affectionate, even too much so. A negro does not really know how to kiss, but the Auburn nurse tries sometimes to kiss the baby, as she sees the whites do, and this, in Auburn, I am sure, is unhygienic. It is as about as much trouble to look after a nurse as to look after a baby.

But the crowning glory of the servant world of Auburn is the combination negro cook and housegirl. She probably lives a mile from where she works and does not want to live nearer, nearly all the negroes preferring to live close together on the edge of the town. The cooks are usually late enough in coming in the morning to make the housekeeper feel uncomfortable about breakfast. All cooks do not, by any means, have the same amount of work to do. Some cook three meals a day for the average family of five or six. Boarding house cooks have more to do and have an assistant. Others cook for a small family and also do or pretend to do the work of a housemaid; some cook two meals a day — breakfast and dinner — and leave the family to shift for themselves for supper. One family will keep the cook busy nearly all day ; another will have very little for her to do. Yet there will not be much if any difference in the rate of wages paid. The cooks themselves do not seem to think that any grievance lies here. No cook will stay all day where she works; she must go home after dinner as well as after supper. Those who have several hours spare time each day do not, as a rule, work at anything else during this time; they claim to be too tired and to need rest, though I have never seen nor heard of a negro servant who was overworked. The negro servant in an up town New York boarding house who gets four times the pay does at least twice as much work as the average good Auburn house servant does and does it better, because she must ; she has no choice but to do so. Efficient work is demanded by the housekeeper, and the negro must do as good work as the white servant or lose her place. And to lose a place is a much more serious affair in the North than in the South.

The rate of pay of the Alabama cook is the result of history and experience. During slavery the wage of a slave, man or woman, was as much as or more than the wage of an unskilled white. As a laborer the slave could be made more efficient than the unskilled white, and only the best of them were hired. In 1865 and 1866, that precious institution, the Freedmen's Bureau, ordered that the rate of wages for the free negroes should be the same as the old slave wages, that is, from $8.00 to $12.00 a month for women, and from $12.00 to $20.00 for men. The white people, the former owners of the negroes, had already begun to experiment with something like the old rate of wages, only rather lower because the grade of work was lower. In spite of the fact that the Bureau made it a criminal offence not to pay the full rate, it was done only a short time. The negroes could no longer be made to work when they were disinclined, and they were now much less efficient workers. Petty pilfering was universal in a country where locks had never been used and inventories seldom taken. To hire a negro house-servant meant to lose something by her light-fingeredness, and, in con-sequence, the rate of pay began to decline. A certain amount had to be deducted, so to speak, from the cash wages in order to offset what the servant appropriated. The rate of wages for men in the fields remained about the same ; but the pay of the women house servants fell rapidly, for the latter had better opportunities than the men to "take things." Always along with the cash paid went certain privileges, such as free house, fuel, water, garden plot, pasture for a pig or calf, etc. This was and still is true principally of the country districts, but there are many privileges given to the negro in small villages like Auburn. And there are also many perquisites belonging to the house- servant, such as old clothes, left over food, fruit — all this be- sides what the woman may "take" semi-secretly. Under such circumstances, the decline in the rate of wages was rapid, and for many years negro cooks in the country and in the villages have been paid from $4.00 to $5.00 a month in cash, with the tacit understanding by both mistress and servant that the latter is going to supplement her wages by carrying away various articles of food and perhaps other small things that attract her fancy. This is not in the bond, nothing is said of it, but seldom does the mistress remonstrate with or in any way punish the servant for "totin' off" what the latter considers her informal wages. However, the practice is underhand, as the cook carries away her spoils more or less secretly, and the housekeeper never knows what the woman has in the bucket or basket which always hangs on her arm when she goes home. The mistress can only endeavor so to manage that unreasonable quantities may not be "toted off." Thus the matter stands, — a kind of underhand commutation of wages. The money paid is about half the value of the servant's work, which, with the dishonest (from a Caucasian point of view) addition to her wages, is sufficient to make the whole equivalent to $8.00 to $12.00 a month. On a strictly business basis, this would be the pay of a first-class cook. This nominal rate is a hardship to the few servants who are too honest and too self-respecting to supplement their pay in the usual way.

I know of one cook who was paid $4.00 a month. She had three young children whom she fed on what she carried from the "big house." Her house rent was given her, also her firewood and water. For twelve months she did not draw a cent of money but banked it with her employer. Besides, at odd hours she did some extra work for extra pay. She sent one of her boys to school in the winter, and at the end of the year she drew her money, amounting to $50.00, and "decided to rest." For an entire year she rested, visiting among her friends, with whom she was popular as long as her money lasted. When it was all gone, she again went to work. Another woman who was paid $4.00 a month for light house work a few hours each day, and who was not able to carry off much, saved, after paying $1.00 a month house rent and supporting three small children whom she fed on cornbread as it was cheap, over $50.00 in three years. These were exceptional cases ; most negro cooks, or their male dependents, spend the wages as soon as received, or before.[1]

It is to carry home the spoils that the genius of the kitchen must visit her family twice a day. As long as only a moderate quantity is carried away the housekeeper makes no complaint. It is considered a matter of course; and though the custom is deplored, there is no likelihood that it will soon be broken up. A woman who tries to stop it in her home gets the reputation among the servants of being a mean, stingy person, and the result is that she finds it hard to get a cook.

The contents of the basket "toted off" are varied, but are nearly always food supplies for the hungry family at home. The mistress of the household is supposed to stay out of the kitchen while the mysteries of cooking are going on, nor must she inquire too closely into culinary affairs, for the presiding genius of the cook stove resents visits of inspection as a kind of espionage to which a self-respecting servant cannot submit. A few house- keepers keep up the old practice of carrying the keys and giving out the materials for each meal. This affords much less opportunity for pickings and stealings, and is frowned upon by the servant world, for then the colored family in the suburbs gets only what is left over from meals. But in such cases the white family is likely to find the waffles and battercakes run short at breakfast, and a part of the roast will disappear, the chicken will have only one wing, and the beaten biscuits will be fewer. If the next day one catches a whiff of a cake baking that does not appear on the table, it is best not to ask questions. A new cook is not easily secured.

A common way of securing a supply is for the cook to go to the next door neighbor and, in the name of her mistress, borrow coffee, flour, sugar, meat, etc., which she carries to her own home. She will also take from her employer and say that the neighbors borrowed the missing things. An elaborate system of stealing by borrowing may go on for months before being discovered. A cook addicted to the borrowing habit can give her employer the reputation of being a "dead head," and I have known families who lived near together tell sad experiences of the borrowing exploits of one another, and all the time it was only the cooks.

The better the borrowing and taking succeeds the easier the lot of the idle ones at home, — the children, the husband, the friends, and the dog. Seldom are the younger women found supporting their parents. The old negroes who are not able to work are, for the most part, pensioners on the bounty of the whites. One old woman who was grown when "freedom cried out," succeeded in getting a place to cook where a better servant had been coaxed away, though the old woman was not a very good cook. A few days earlier her daughter had hired to the minister's wife, but, when the mother began to work where the pickings were good, the daughter "decided to rest" the remainder of the summer, the old woman's sister also made her a long visit, and the minister's wife cooked for herself.

The old negroes are the best and most willing servants, but they are few in numbers. They do not approve of the course of "dese hyeh young niggers." A few of the younger generation stay in one place long enough to get some training and become good servants. The intelligent black girl who thus learns to do her work well will take pride in it and is in much demand, but the ordinary shiftless sister in black will not stay long enough in one place for the training "to take." Yet there are several negro women in town who are intelligent, industrious, capable and honest, and these get from $9.00 to $15.00 a month with board. They have offers of much more work than they can possibly do, but even these seldom work in one place longer than a few months.

One can never tell what day the cook may decide to leave. A good servant may stay for years and at a day's notice "decide to rest," as she calls it. This past summer nearly every woman in town who has a cook was shivering with fear lest she would "quit." The older housekeepers who have known the negro from slavery days are the best managers of the black help. The younger ones do not understand them so well, are less patient with their shortcomings, expect more, and get less. The Northern woman is apt to arrive with new notions of handling the negro servants. She sometimes thinks that the natives do not know how to manage, that the wages are too low, and that the servants are not treated as free American citizens should be. If she attempts to make a reform she is likely soon to be doing her own work, for the Northern newcomer usually demands efficiency and Caucasian honesty of the negro, makes little allowance for racial shortcomings, and tries to apply white standards to black conduct. The result is an abiding disgust on the part of the reformer, and her unpopularity among the negroes, until finally she ends by becoming a philosophical and perhaps an extreme Southerner on the negro problem. But some people from the North cannot, from the first, endure the shiftless negroes, and dispense with their services as much as possible.

The average servant, though she takes her loot in an underhand way, does not consider the practice dishonest unless she is caught. There is an old feeling, dating back to the days of the Freedmen's Bureau and the carpetbag missionaries and orators, that, taking from a white person is not stealing. The negro race was then taught a lesson that was easily learned and has never been forgotten, that the property in the South was produced by negro labor and that therefore by right much of it should belong to the blacks. Politicians, teachers, and preachers told them this story and advocated and predicted confiscation. For many years the negroes expected the division, and to-day there are some who still are waiting for it. To some extent it still is a doctrine based on the authority of the preacher that to take enough to keep from want is not stealing and is not wrong. This is comforting doctrine and in practice lends itself to liberal interpretation. In theological language this practice is known as "spilin de Gypshuns," and too many believe it.

Amusing things happen on account of despoiling the Egyptians. One instance: There was a wedding in colored society. The mother and some of the friends of the bride worked for three prominent families, members of which were invited to and were present at the wedding. There was quite a display of wedding presents, several of which the employers recognized as having disappeared from their own homes within the past year.

Generally the house servants are not so bad about taking things beyond the ordinary as are their friends and back door callers. Where there is much visiting the callers have to be closely watched, and it is worth much to a boarding house keeper not to have a back gate. Early one morning, I counted seven negro men and boys in the backyard of a boarding house waiting for "hand-outs." It is the custom for a friend to drop in to escort the cook home at night, and the escort must be entertained with meat and drink.

There is no calling in a policeman when things are stolen. The laws are probably too severe, and no one wants to send a negro to jail for trifling thefts. If the laws could be strictly enforced a majority of the blacks would come to grief. In a case of aggravated theft, the first step is to recover the stolen articles if possible, then the offending party may be informally fined or have his or her pay docked, or, if a boy, may be soundly thrashed, though seldom discharged, — a species of compounding of felony. It is one of the curiosities of human nature, the implicit faith the members of a family sometimes have in their own servants who have been long with them and to whom they have become attached. They will not believe that their servants will take valuable things from them, but, at the same time, they are skeptical in regard to the honesty of the servants of the neighbors. And so it is with each family.

When a house servant is discharged for any reason other women, like the men under similar circumstances, will refuse to work in "her place." Until the aggrieved cook expresses her willingness for some one to fill "her place," it is likely to remain vacant unless the poorest of servants are taken, — those who hold to no code of labor ethics.

During the summer when green corn, melons, berries, fruit, revivals and baptizings are plentiful, there is a general disposition among the darkies to refrain from working. To cook in a hot kitchen is "too hot for us," they say, as well as for the white women. It is taken as a personal insult by some to be asked to work during the summer, and they consider it an imposition to be requested to work at something the white woman does not want to do. When revivals and baptizings are the order of the day the cook must be handled tenderly. She must be allowed to give the family cold suppers, or leave them to shift for them- selves. She is greatly interested in those who are "comin' thu" at the meeting, and often stays out until two o'clock in the morning at a religious debauch. The next day she comes late and is unfit for work, and much of her time is spent hanging over the back fence talking to other negroes about the progress of the meeting. Cheap excursions and circuses also appeal to the African who has or can borrow the price of a ticket; then work must wait.

There are numerous white women's clubs in the town, but no housekeepers' club where the condition of domestic affairs and means of bettering it might be discussed. Such things have been tried; the women met and talked over matters and agreed to start a reform towards strictly business methods. But the good resolves came to nothing. The boarding house keeper, often a widow, who has no income except from taking boarders, and who must pay rent and market bills, clothe and educate her children, and exist during the summer when there are no boarders, is a slave to the negro servant. She is afraid to exact good service. If she needs a servant and no other appears she will have to hire the one who has just been discharged by some more independent housekeeper.

It is a sad fact that a good cook or a nurse who has been carefully trained by a good housekeeper may receive sub rosa inducements from some one who envies her neighbor's good fortune, and thus the servant is allured away before the unfortunate employer knows anything about it. It is not considered proper to make an underhand offer of a new place to a negro servant, because the latter never uses that offer as a means of se- curing higher wages and better privileges, but if she likes the offer she accepts at once, often giving her former employer no notice whatever. Needless to say, she who secures her neighbors' good servants in this way is not popular in the housekeeping community.

There are some women who keep servants when they are not financially able and when they have no real need for them. They hire a poor class of blacks and pay them even lower wages, from $2.00 to $3.00 a month. The quality of the service secured may be imagined. . There are a very few women who have the reputation of not being exactly honest with the negro in the matter of wages. When pay day comes, forgotten delinquencies are remembered and deductions made, or the servant may be charged with things which she thought had been given her. Sometimes the reputation is un- deserved, as when the servant wants her pay in small amounts, — from ten cents to a dollar at a time — whenever he or she needs a little money, and at the end of the month is surprised that little or nothing is due. Others ask for "orders" on the store, and when reckoning day comes cannot understand why those paper notes are counted against them. In some instances wages have been extinguished by putting off on the servant, who is perfectly willing at the time, useless articles of clothing, shoes and finery. The old clothes habit is still strong, though not so strong as it once was. A few years ago it was an interesting sight to see in the negro church parades on Gay street the familiar costumes of Auburn's white dames and damsels now displayed by the colored sisters.

The servants have something like an organization, or at least, a better understanding than have their white employers. As already stated, usually the negroes will not work where one of their number has been discharged. A cook may quit of her own accord and pass the word among her friends and the place will be filled, but, according to etiquette, the servant must quit of her own free will and march out with colors flying and all the honors of war. One colored woman, discharged for general worthlessness by a reckless housekeeper, reported that she was only taking a rest; and for six weeks the mistress of the house paid the penalty of her indiscretion by doing her own work.

An incipient strike is going on nearly all the time except in the winter when food is scarce among the negroes, — not for higher wages, strange to say, until recently, — but for greater privileges and less work. Each servant holds up the conduct of the woman next door as an example to her mistress. "Mrs. Jones does not have her cook to cook supper," or, "she hires extra help, and you must do the same for me." During the past few years, however, the servants, feeling, probably, that the state of affairs is somewhat impossible, have been talking of an organized strike, or a general "quitten," as they call it Why? no one seems to know exactly. As yet they have not succeeded in accomplishing anything except to make themselves more discontented. At present, the general state of the servant mind has resulted in a club or society, the members of which pay regular dues. As soon as the finances are in a good condition they propose to go on a regular strike, in order to show their employers how dependent they are upon them, and to secure higher wages. They do not propose any reform in the "toting" habit. The programme will be for all- to hire out at the beginning of the college session, when there are several hundred students in town, work for one day (no rate of pay being stated), and then make a demand for a general rate of wages of $12.00 a month instead of $4.00 and $5.00 as now paid. If the demand is refused a strike is to be declared. Whether all are to strike or only those who do not succeed in their demands, the negroes themselves do not clearly understand. Some say one thing, some say another. If a cook should weaken and work for less than the pay demanded, she is to be taken out by her sister servants and beaten with many stripes "until she is nearly dead." The movement can succeed only partially, if at all. The organization and plans are defective ; the average negro has little talent in such things, and cannot understand them. The old negroes and the best of the younger ones will not join heartily in the movement. The rate of pay demanded is too high unless the house- keeper can protect herself against pilfering or privileges, and this would require almost a reorganization of the Southern social system. The country darkies will come in and take the places of some of the strikers. In short, though the situation at present is almost as far removed as possible from a business basis, the plan proposed by the strikers will not better it. But finally, the servants will secure higher wages because of the demand for them in the cities and in the cotton fields where they are better paid. Then the employer will be forced to demand better work, will cut off privileges and donations, and will stop "toting" and pilfering. This will be better for all concerned. In one small village that I know of, the servants began to ask for higher wages. The housekeepers were more independent and, as they did not consider the quality of the work worth the wages demanded, no effort was made to keep the servants. The latter gradually went into the fields where their pay was better. Now the servants are better paid and better work is done, but there are fewer servants.

Tuskegee is only twenty-five miles away, but few Auburn negroes go there to school, and not many of them know anything about it. Those who have heard of the school are prejudiced against it, because, they say, the students have to work too hard, (a serious objection to a school), and because some years ago a couple of young Auburn negroes died after returning from Tuskegee. They caught their death there, it was said, but that was not correct.

Some of the unskilled but industrious black women are deciding that they can make more money by working on the farms, and by chopping and hoeing cotton and corn in the spring and picking cotton in the fall. The old " freedom " prejudice of the women against working in the fields is dying out, and a number of women work on the farm in the spring and fall and go out as house servants in the summer and especially in the winter. It is an amusing sight to see how a corn field negro fattens after securing a job in the kitchen. The poorer class of women have a hard time when shifting for themselves and lose their summer plumpness by Christmas, but when one of these again has regular meals, again the fattening process takes place.

The emigration of blacks from Auburn is about equal to the increase by birth. They go to the cities, for more amusement is found there. The men usually go to Birmingham as miners, and the women go as servants to Birmingham and Memphis. In the cities they get higher wages and do much more work, but the Auburn servant will not do in Auburn even for city wages the amount of work required in the city. Yet Auburn servants are in demand in Birmingham and other neighboring cities, and Au- burn people who think that the servant problem is a perplexing one hear from their Birmingham sisters that Auburn cooks are "angels from Heaven" when compared with the native Birmingham blacks.

A negro servant in a New York house once told me that she liked Southern people better than "Yankees," because they were kinder and more patient and indulgent, but that she preferred to work for "Yankees," for, she said, "Southern people just assumes that you is dishonest." Her objection is largely correct and is a serious one, but, the Southern assumption is also about correct, and there seems to be no immediate remedy in either case.

Note:

1. This paper was written in 1903. There is at present a tendency to- ward higher wages for the better servants. The migration to the cities and to the cotton fields has lessened the supply of would-be cooks, and some house-keepers are beginning to declare their independence of the African. The better servants can get better wages; the poorer ones find it harder to get employment. The pay in the cities, compared with the pay in the North, is very high considering the quality and quantity of the work performed. But over the greater part of rural Alabama, with which I am somewhat familiar, the wages mentioned are about the average. The same is true also of parts of Mississippi, Georgia, Florida, and South Carolina where I have been. An agricultural colony from the North will pay more and make the negro work for it or get out; he or she usually gets out. The merely nominal wage paid is, allowing for " taking, toting and privileges," all that the work performed would be worth in any market, but, of course, there is nothing of business principles about the present arrangement; it seems to be about the best com- promise possible now; the students from such schools as Tuskegee may help to put things on a less absurd basis. At present the Southern white women are worried almost beyond endurance by the intolerable conditions, and many who have seen the work of

white servants would infinitely prefer them were it possible to get them. It does not help matters that Northerners and Westerners so often congratulate Southerners on having a plentiful supply of willing servants. Of course there are some Southern people so ignorant that they think the negroes are the best servants in the world; others prefer not to have white servants about them, believing that a white person should be above personal service.

15

The Formation of the Union League in Alabama

The Union League movement began in the North in 1862 when the outlook for the Northern cause was gloomy. The moderate policy of the Washington government had alienated the extremists; the Confederate successes in the field and Democratic successes in the elections ; the active opposition of the "Copperheads" to the war policy of the administration; the rise of the secret order of the Knights of the Golden Circle in the West opposed to further continuance of the war; the strong Southern sympathies of the higher classes of society; the formation of societies for the dissemination of Democratic and Southern literature ; the low ebb of loyalty to the government in the North especially in the cities; all these causes resulted in the formation of Union Leagues throughout the North. This movement began among those associated in the work of the United States Sanitary Commission . These people were important neither as politicians nor as warriors, and had sufficient leisure to observe the threatening state of society about them. "Loyalty must be organized, consolidated and made effective," they declared. The movement first took effective form in Philadelphia in the fall of 1862, and in December of that year the Union League of Philadelphia was organized. The members were pledged to uncompromising and unconditional loyalty to the Union, the complete subordination of political ideas thereto, and the repudiation of any belief in states' rights. The New York (Union League) Club followed the example of the Philadelphia League early in 1863, and adopted, word for word, its declaration of principles. Boston, Brooklyn, Chicago, Baltimore, and other cities, followed suit, and soon Leagues were formed in every part of the North. These Leagues were modeled after the Philadelphia plan, and were connected by a loose bond of federation. The "Loyal National League" of New York, an independent organization with thirty branches, was absorbed by the League. These Leagues were social as well as political in their aims. The "Loyal Publication Society" of New York came under the control of the League, and was used to disseminate the proper kind of political literature. As the Federal armies went South, the Union League spread among the disaffected element of the Southern people. Much interest was taken in the negro and negro troops were enlisted through its efforts. Teachers were sent South in the wake of the armies to teach the negroes, and to use their influence in securing negro enlistments. In this and in similar work the League acted in cooperation with the Freedmen's Aid Society, the Department of Negro Affairs and later with the Freedmen's Bureau.

With the close of the war the Leagues did not cease to take an active interest in things political. It was one of the earliest bodies to declare for negro suffrage and white disfranchisement, and this declaration was repeatedly made during the three years following the war. Its agents were always in the lobbies of Congress clamoring for radical measures. The reconstruction policy of Congress was heartily endorsed and the President condemned.

Part of the work of the League was to distribute campaign literature, and most of the violent pamphlets on reconstruction questions will be found to have the Union League imprint. The New York League alone circulated about 70,000 publications, while the Philadelphia Union League far surpassed this record, circulating 4,500,000 political pamphlets within eight years.

The literature printed consisted largely of accounts of "Southern Atrocities." The conclusions of Charles Schurz's report on the condition of the South justified the publication and dissemination of such choice yarns as this: A preacher in Bladon (Springs), Alabama, said that the woods in Choctaw County stunk with dead negroes. Some were hanged to trees and left to rot; others were burned alive.

Southern "Unionists" who went North were entertained by the Union League, and their expenses paid. In 1866 the Philadelphia Convention of Southern "Unionists" was captured by the League, carried to New York and entertained at the expense of the latter. In 1867 several of the Leagues sent delegates to Virginia to reconcile the two warring factions of Radicals. The formation of the Union League among the Southern "Unionists" was extended throughout the South within a few months of the close of the war, but a "discreet secrecy" was maintained. It was easy for all the disaffected whites, especially those who had been connected with the Peace Society, to join the Union League, which soon included Peace Society men, "loyalists, " deserters and many anti-administration Confederates. The most respectable element consisted of a few old Whigs who had an intense hatred of the Democrats and who wanted to crush them by any means. In this stage the League was strongest in the white counties of the hill and mountain country.

The League was continued several years after the war as a kind of Radical Bureau in the Republican party to control the negro vote in the South. Its headquarters were in New York, and it was represented in each state by "state members." John Keffer was "state member" for Alabama.

It is quite likely that such Leagues as that in New York and Philadelphia, after the first year or two of reconstruction, rather grew away from the strictly political "Union League of America" and became more and more social clubs. The spiritual relationship was close, however, and in political belief they were one. The eminently respectable members of the Union Leagues of Philadelphia and New York, had little in common with the Southern Leagues except radicalism.

Horace Greeley was attacked by the League because he had signed the bond of Jefferson Davis. He, in turn, attacked the League in stinging articles in the *Tribune.*

Even before the end of the war the Federal officials had organized the Union League in Huntsville, Athens, Florence and other places in Northern Alabama. It was understood to be a very respectable order in the North, and General Burke, and later General Crawford, with other Federal officers and a few of the so-called " Union" men of North Alabama, formed Lodges of what was called the Union or Loyal League. At first but few native whites were members, as the native "Unionist" was not exactly the kind of a person the Federal Union Leaguers cared to associate with more than was necessary. With the close of hostilities and the establishment of army posts over the state, the League grew rapidly. The civilians who followed the army, the Bureau agents, the missionaries, and the Northern school teachers were gradually admitted. The native "Unionists" came in as the bars were lowered, and with them that element of the population which during the war, especially in the white counties, had become hostile to the Confederate administration. The disaffected politicians saw in the organizations an instrument which might be used against the politicians of the central counties who seemed likely to remain in control of affairs. At this time there were no negro members, but it has been estimated that in 1865, 40 per cent. of the white voting population in North Alabama joined the Union League, and that for a year or more there was an average of half a dozen Lodges in each county north of the Black Belt. Later, the local chapters were called Councils. There was a State Grand Council with headquarters at Montgomery, and a Grand National Council with headquarters in New York. The Union League of America was the proper designation for the entire organization .

The White Union Leaguers were few in the Black Belt counties and even in the white counties of Southeast Alabama where one would expect to find them. In Southern Alabama it was disgraceful for a person to have any connection with the Union League, and if a man was a member he kept it secret. To this day no one will admit that he belonged to that organization. So far as the native members were concerned, they cared little about the original purposes of the order, but hoped to make it the nucleus of a political organization, and the Northern civilian membership, the Bureau agents, preachers and teachers and other adventurers, soon began to see the possibilities of the organization.

From the very beginning the preachers, teachers and Bureau agents had been accustomed to gather the negroes around them at times for advice and to make speeches to them. Not a few of them expected confiscation, or some such procedure, and wanted a share in the division of the spoils. Some began to talk of political power for the negro. For various purposes, good and bad, the negroes were, by the end of 1865, largely organized by their would-be leaders, who as controllers of rations, religion and schools, had great influence over them. was but a slight change to convert these informal gatherings into Lodges, or Councils of the Union League. The early organization of the League was not considered Republican and political so much as a purely mercenary organization for the reception of future plunder from confiscation or governmental appropriation.

After the refusal of Congress to recognize the restoration as effected by the President, the guardians of the negro in the state began to lay their plans for the future . Negro Councils were organized, and negroes were even admitted to some of the white Councils which were under control of the Northerners. The Bureau gathering of Colonel John B. Callis of Huntsville, was transformed into a League. Such men as the Rev. Lakin, Colonel Callis, D. H. Bingham, all men of questionable character from the North, went about organizing the negroes during 1866 and 1867. The Bureau agents were the directors of the work, and in the immediate vicinity of the Bureau offices they themselves organized the Councils. To distant plantations and to country districts agents were sent to gather in the embryo citizen. In every community in the state where there was a sufficient number of negroes the League was organized sooner or later.

In North Alabama, the work was done before the spring of 1867; in the Black Belt and in South Alabama it was not until the end of 1867 that the last negroes were gathered into the fold.

The effect on the white membership of the admission of negroes was remarkable. With the beginning of the manipulation of the negro by his Northern friends, the native whites began to desert the order, and when negroes were admitted for the avowed purpose of agitating for political rights and for political organization afterwards, the native whites left in crowds. Where there were many blacks, as in Talladega, nearly all of the whites left the order. Where the blacks were not numerous and had not been organized more of the whites remained, but there was a general exodus in the hill counties.

Professor Miller estimates that 5 per cent. of the white voters in Talladega county and 25 per cent. of those in Cleburne county, where there were few negroes, remained in the order for several years, The same proportion would be nearly correct for the other counties of North Alabama. Where there were few or no negroes, as in Winston and Walker counties, the white membership held out better, for in those counties there was no fear of negro domination, and if the negro voted he would be controlled by the native white population no matter

what was his politics; and what the negro would do in the black counties, the white Leaguers in the hill counties cared but little. The character of the whites left in the League was extremely shady. The native element has been called "low down, trifling white men" and the alien element " itinerant, irresponsible, worthless white men from the North." Such was the opinion of the native white people, and the later history of the Leaguers has not improved their reputation. The sprinkling of whites served to furnish leaders for the ignorant blacks. In the black counties there were practically no white members in the rank and file . The alien element was probably more able than the native white, and had gained more completely the confidence of the negroes, and soon had complete control over them whenever they were in large numbers. The Bureau agents saw that the Freedmen's Bureau could not survive much longer, and they were especially active in looking out for soft places to fall. With the assistance of the negro they had hoped to pass into high offices in the state and county governments.

One thing about the League that attracted the negro was the mysterious secrecy of the meetings, the weird initiation ceremony that made him feel shivery good from his head to his heels, the im-posing ritual and the songs. I have been informed that the ritual was not used in the North; it was probably adopted for the particular benefit of the African. The would-be Leaguer was told in the beginning of the initiation that the emblems of the order were the altar, the Bible, the Declaration of Independence, the Constitution of the United States, the flag of the union, censer, sword, gavel, ballot box, sickle, shuttle, anvil and other emblems of industry. He was told that the objects of the order were to preserve liberty, perpetuate the union, maintain the laws and the constitution, to secure the ascendancy of American institutions, to protect, defend and strengthen all loyal men and members of the Union League of America in all rights of person and property, to demand the elevation of labor, to aid in the education of laboring men, and to teach the duties of American citizenship. This was fine sounding and impressive, and at this point the negro was always willing to take an oath of secrecy, after which he was asked to swear with a solemn oath to support the principles of the Declaration of Independence, pledge himself to resist all attempts to overthrow the United States, and to strive for the maintenance of liberty, elevation of labor, education of all people in the duties of citizenship, to practice friendship and charity to all of the order, and to support for election or appointment to office only such men as were supporters of these principles and measures.

Then the Council sang "Hail Columbia" and "The Star Spangled Banner," after which an official harangued the candidate, saying that though the designs of traitors had been thwarted, there were yet to be secured legislative triumphs with complete ascendancy of the true principles of popular government, equal liberty, elevation and education, and the overthrow at the ballot box of the old oligarchy of political leaders.

Prayer by the Chaplain then followed, the room was darkened, the "fire of liberty" lighted, the members joined hands in a circle around the candidate who was made to place one hand on the flag and, with the other raised, swear again to support the government, to elect true Union men to office, etc. Then placing his hand on a Bible for the third time he swore to keep his oath, and repeated after the President "the Freedman's Pledge": "To defend and perpetuate freedom and union, I pledge my life, my fortune and my sacred honor. So help me God!" Another song was sung, the President charged the members in a long speech concerning the principles of the order, and the marshal instructed the members in the signs. To pass one's self as a Leaguer, the "Four L's" were given: (1) With right hand raised to heaven, thumb and third finger touching ends over palm, pronounce "Liberty"; (2) Bring the hand down over the shoulder and say "Lincoln"; (3) Drop the hand open at the side and say "Loyal"; (4) Catch the thumb in the vest or in the waistband and pronounce "League".

This ceremony of initiation was the most effective means of impressing the negro, and of controlling him through his love and fear of the secret, mysterious, and midnight mummery. An oath taken in daylight would be forgotten before the next day; not so , an oath taken in the dead of night under such impressive circumstances. After passing through the ordeal, the negro usually remained faithful.

In each populous precinct there was at first one Council of the League. In each town or city there were two Councils, one for the whites and another, with white officers, for the blacks. The Councils met once a week, sometimes oftener, and nearly always at night, in the negro churches or schoolhouses. Guards, armed with rifles and shotguns, were stationed about the place of meeting in order to keep away intruders, and to prevent unauthorized persons from coming within forty yards. Members of some councils made it a practice to attend the meetings armed as if for battle. In these meetings the negroes met to hear speeches by the would- be states-men of the new regime. Much inflammatory advice was given them by the white speakers; they were drilled into the belief that they and the Southern whites were natural enemies, and passion, strife and prejudice were excited in order to solidify the negro race against the white, and thus prevent political control by the latter. Many of the negroes still had strong hopes of confiscation and division of property, and in this they were encouraged by the white leaders. Prof. L. D. Miller was told by respectable white men, who joined the order before the negroes were admitted and who left when they became members, that the negroes were taught in these meetings that the only way to have peace and plenty, to get " the forty acres and a mule, " would be to kill some of the leading whites in each community as a warning to others. The League in Tuscumbia received advice from Memphis to use the torch, that the blacks were at war with the white race. The advice was taken. Three men were to go in front of the council as an advance guard, three were to follow with coal oil and fire, and others were to guard the rear. The plan was to burn the whole town, but first one negro and then another insisted on having some white man's house spared because " he is a good man'. The result was that no residences were burned, and they compromised by agreeing to burn the Female Academy. Three of the leaders were lynched. The general belief of the whites was that the objects of the order were to secure political power, to bring about on a large scale the confiscation of the property of Con-federates, and while waiting for this to annex all kinds of portable property. Chicken houses, pig pens, vegetable gardens and orchards were invariably visited by members of the League when returning from the midnight conclaves. This evil became so serious and so general that many believed it to be one of the principles of the order. Everything of value had to be locked up for safe keeping.

As soon as possible after the war each negro had supplied himself with a gun and a dog as a badge of freedom. As a usual thing he carried them to the League meetings and nothing was more natural than that the negroes should begin drilling at night. Armed squads would march in military formation to the place of assemblage, there be drilled , and after the close of the meeting, would march along the roads shouting, firing off their guns, making great boasts and threats against persons whom they disliked . If the home of such a person happened to be on the roadside, the negroes usually made a practice of stopping in front of the house and treating the inmates to unlimited abuse, firing off their guns in order to awaken them. Later military parades in the day time were much favored. Several hundred negroes would march up and down the roads and streets , and amuse themselves by boasts, threats, and abuse of whites, and by shoving whites off the sidewalks or out of the road. But on the whole, there was very little actual violence done the whites; very much less than might have been expected. That such was the case was due, not to any sensible teachings of the leaders, but to the fundamental good nature of the blacks, who were generally content with being impudent.

The relations between the races, with exceptional cases continued to be somewhat friendly for several years. In the communities where the League was established the relations were soonest strained. For awhile in some localities, before the advent of the League, the negroes looked to their old masters for guidance and advice, and the latter for the good of both races, were most eager to retain a moral control over the blacks. Barbecues and picnics were arranged by the whites for the blacks, speeches were made, good advice given and all promised to go well. Sometimes the negroes themselves would arrange the festival and invite prominent whites to be present, for whom a separate table attended by the best waiters would be reserved; and after dinner there would be speaking by both whites and blacks. With the organization of the League, the negroes grew more reserved and finally unfriendly and hostile to the whites. The League alone, however, was not responsible for the change. The preaching and teaching missionaries were at work. On the other hand, among the lower classes of whites an unfriendly feeling quickly sprang to oppose the feeling of the blacks.

When the campaign grew exciting, the discipline of the League was used to prevent the negroes from attending democratic meetings, or hearing democratic speakers. The League leaders even went further and forbade the attendance of the blacks at Radical political meetings where the speakers were not endorsed by the League. Almost invariably the scalawag hated the Leaguer, black or white, and often the League proscribed them as political teachers. Judge Humphrey was threatened with political death unless he joined the League. This he refused to do as most whites did where there were many negroes. All Republicans in good standing had to join the League. Judge (later Governor) D. P. Lewis was a member for a short while, but he soon became disgusted and published a denunciation of the League. Nick Davis and J. C. Bradley, both scalawags, were forbidden by the League to speak in the court house at Huntsville because they were not Leaguers. At a Republican mass-meeting a white Republican wanted to make a speech. The negroes voted that he should not be allowed to speak because he was opposed to the Loyal League. He was treated to much abuse and threats of violence . He then went to another place to speak but was followed by the crowd which refused to allow him to say anything. The League was the machine of the Radical party, and all candidates had to be governed by its edicts. Candidates were usually nominated in its meetings.

Every negro was *ex colore* a member of or under the control of the League. In the opinion of the League, white Democrats were bad enough, but black Democrats were not to be tolerated. The first rule of the Leaguers was that all blacks must support the Radical program. It was possible in some cases for a negro to refrain from taking an active part in political affairs. He might even fail to vote . But it was martyrdom for a black to be a Democrat- that is, try to follow his old master in politics. The negroes often liked the white Democrats, but life was made miserable for the black Democrat. The whites, in many cases, were forced to advise their faithful blacks to vote the Radical ticket that they might escape mistreatment. There were numbers of negroes as late as 1868 who were inclined to vote with the whites, and to bring them into line all the forces of the League were brought to bear. They were proscribed in negro society; expelled from negro churches; the women would not "prashay" (appreciate) a black Democrat. The negro man who had Democratic inclinations was sure to find that the League was bringing influence to bear upon his dusky sweetheart or wife to cause him to see the error of his ways, and persistent adherence to the white party would result in the loss of her. The women were converted to Radicalism long before the men, and almost invariably used their influence strongly for the purposes of the League. If moral suasion failed to cause the delinquent to see the light, other methods were used. Threats were common from the first and often sufficed, and fines were levied by the League on recalcitrant members. In case of the more stubborn, a beating wrought a change of heart. A sound whipping was usually effective. The offending darkey was "bucked and gagged, " and the thrashing administered, the sufferer being afraid to complain of the way he was treated . There were many cases of aggravated assault and a few cases of murder. By such methods the League succeeded in keeping under its control almost the entire negro population.

The discipline of the League over its active members was stringent. They were sworn to obey the orders of the officials. A negro near Clayton disobeyed the "Cap'en" of the Loyal League and was tied up by the thumbs; and another for a similar offense was "bucked" and whipped. A candidate having been nominated by the League it was made the duty of every member to support him actively. Failure to do so resulted in a fine or other more severe punishment, and members that had been expelled were still under the control of the League.

The effects of the teachings of the League orators were soon seen in the increasing insolence and defiant attitude of some of the blacks, in the greater number of stealings, small and large, in the boasts, demands, and threats made by the more violent members of the order. Most of them, however, behaved remarkably well under the circumstances, but the few unbearable ones were so much more in evidence that the suffering whites were disposed to class all blacks together as unbearable. Some of the methods of the Loyal League were similar to those of the later Ku Klux Klan. Anonymous warnings were sent to the obnoxious individuals, houses were burned, notices were pasted at night in public places and on the doors of persons who had incurred the hostility of the League.

In Bullock county, near Perote, a Council of the League was organized under the direction of a negro emissary who proceeded to assume the government of the community. A list of crimes and punishments was adopted, a court erected with various officials established , and during the night all negroes, who opposed them, were arrested. The black sheriff and his deputy were arrested by the civil authorities. The negroes then organized for resistance, flocked into Union Springs, the county seat, and threatened to exterminate the whites and take possession of the county. Their agents visited the plantations and forced the laborers to join them by showing orders purporting to be from General Swayne giving them the authority to kill all who resisted them. Swayne sent out detachments and arrested fifteen of the ring leaders, and the Perote government collapsed.

When the League was first organized in the Black Belt, and before native whites were excluded from membership, numbers of whites joined the League upon invitation in order to ascertain its objects, to see if mischief were intended toward the whites, and to control, if possible, the negroes in the organization. Most of these became disgusted and withdrew, or were expelled on account of their politics. In Marengo County several white Democrats joined the League at McKinley in order to keep down the excitement aroused by other Leaguers, to counteract the evil influences of alien emissaries, and to protect the women of the community where but few men were left after the war. These men succeeded in controlling the negroes, and in preventing the discussion of politics in the meeting. The League was made simply a club where the negroes met to receive advice, which was that they should attend strictly to their own affairs and vote without reference to any secret organization . Finally they were advised to withdraw from the order.

For two years, 1867-1869, the League was the machine in the Radical party, and its leaders formed the "ring" that controlled party action. Nominations for office were made by the local and state Councils. It is said that there were stormy times in the Councils when there were more carpet-baggers than there were offices to be filled. The defeated candidate was apt to run as an independent, and in order to be elected would sell himself to the whites. This practice resulted in a weakening of the influence of the League, as the members were sworn to support the League nominee, and the negroes believed that the terrible penalties would be inflicted upon the political traitor. The officers would go among the negroes and show their commissions which they pretended were orders from General Swayne or General Grant for the negroes to vote for them. A political catechism of questions and answers meant to teach loyalty to the Radical party was prepared in Washington and sent out among the Councils to be used in the instruction of negro voters.

After it was seen that existing political institutions were about to be overturned, the white Councils and, to a certain extent, the negro Councils became simply associations of those training for leadership in the new party soon to be formed in the state by act of Congress. The few whites who were in control did not care to admit many new white members as there might be too many to share in the division of the spoils. Hence we find that terms of admission were made more stringent, and, especially after the passage of the Reconstruction Acts in March, 1867, many applicants were rejected. The alien element was in control of the League. The scalawags had no love for the negro, nor the negro for them. Consequently, they were not able to associate together in League meetings and in political work. The result was that where the blacks were numerous the largest plums fell to the carpetbaggers. The negro leaders, -politicians, preachers and teachers-trained in the League, acted as subordinates to the white leaders in controlling the black population , and they were sent on to drum up the country negroes when elections drew near. They were also given minor positions, when offices were more plentiful than carpet-baggers. Altogether they received but few offices, which fact was later a cause of serious complaint.

The largest white membership of the League was in 1865-1866 and after that date it constantly decreased. The native Radicals did not belong to the League except in the remote white counties. The largest negro membership was in 1867 and 1868. Only the Councils in the towns remained active after the election of 1868, for after the discipline of 1867 and 1868, it was not necessary to look so closely after the plantation negro, and he became a kind of visiting member of the Council in the town. The League as an organization gradually died out by 1869 except in the largest towns. Many of them were simply transformed into political clubs loosely organized under local political leaders. The Ku Klux Klan undoubtedly had much to do with breaking up the League as an organization. The League was largely the cause of the Ku Klux movement, because it created the conditions which made such a movement necessary. In 1870 the Radical leaders missed the support formerly given by the League, and an urgent appeal was sent out all over the state from League headquarters in New York by John Keffer and others advocating the reestablishment of Union Leagues to assist in carrying the elections of 1870.

The leaders of the Union League were such men as Lakin, Callis, Spencer, Bingham, Norris, Keffer, Nealy and Strobach, all aliens of shady character. Nearly all of them were elected to office by the support of the League. After the order was broken up the carpetbaggers found it harder to get office.

However, before its dissolution, the League had served its purpose. It had completely alienated the races politically and made it possible for the outsiders to control the negro. It enabled the negroes to vote as Radicals for several years where without it they either would not have voted at all or they would have voted as Democrats along with their former masters. The League was necessary to the existence of the Radical party in Alabama. No ordinary political organization could have welded the blacks into a solid party. The Freedmen's Bureau, which had much influence over the negroes for demoralization, was too weak in numbers to control effectually the negroes in politics . The League finally absorbed the personnelle of the Bureau and inherited all its prestige.[1]

Note:

1. In the Ku Klux Report, Alabama Testimony, will be found many details concerning the workings of the League. The Conservative and sometimes the Radical witnesses, in Alabama and in all the other Southern states, uniformly assert that the Ku Klux movement was caused by the workings of the Union League.

16

The Ku Klux Testimony Relating to Alabama

In 1869-70 the Radical leaders began to observe signs in the Southern States that indicated the growing strength of the Democratic party. The Fifteenth Amendment was added to the Constitution by the forced ratifications of Virginia, Texas, Mississippi and Georgia. President Grant sent in a message to Congress announcing the ratification as "the most important event that has occurred since the nation came into life." Congress responded to the hint in the message by passing the first of the Enforcement Acts. For two years this measure had been impending, and the excuse now for making it a law was that the Ku Klux organizations would prevent the blacks from voting in the fall of 1870. This act was approved on May 31, 1870; a supplementary Enforcement Act was passed on February 28, 1871; and on April 20, 1 87 1, the last of the series, the notorious "Ku Klux" Act, was passed into law.

The effect of these Enforcement Acts was to take over to the Central Government all the powers of the State governments relating to suffrage and elections.

The acts were said to be for the purpose of enforcing the XlVth and XVth Amendments.

The laws were ostensibly but not really aimed at the Ku Klux movement. The Ku Klux organizations had disbanded before 1870. The South was more peaceful than it had been in 1868 and 1869, but was more Democratic. The real purpose was to prevent the newly reconstructed Southern States from being carried by the Democrats in the elections of 1870 and 1872. It was especially important that those States be held in the Republican ranks until after the presidential election in 1872. To justify this "Force" legislation, and to obtain material for use in the next year's campaign, Congress appointed a committee to investigate the condition of affairs in the Southern States. This committee was organized on April 20, 1871, the date of the approval of the Ku Klux Act.

The members of the sub-committee that took testimony in Alabama were: Senators Pratt and Rice, and Messrs. Blair, Beck and Buckley, of the House. Blair and Beck, the Democratic members, were never present together. So the sub-committee consisted of three Republicans and one Democrat. C. W. Buckley was a carpet-bag Representative from Alabama, a former Bureau reverend, who worked hard to convict the white people of the State.

The sub-committee held sessions in Huntsville, October 6-14; Montgomery, October 17-20; Demopolis, October 23-28; Livingston, October 30 to November 3; and in Columbus, Miss., for West Alabama, November 11. All these places were in Black counties. Sessions were held only at easily accessible places, and where scalawag, carpet-bag and negro witnesses could easily be secured. Testimony was also taken by the committee in Washington from June to August, 1871.

It is generally believed that the examination of witnesses by the Ku Klux Committee of Congress was a very one-sided affair, and that the testimony is practically without value for the historian, on account of the immense proportion of hear- say reports and manufactured tales embraced in it. Of course there is much that is worthless because untrue, and much that may be true but cannot be regarded because of the character of the witnesses whose statements are unsupported. But, nevertheless, the 2,008 pages of testimony taken in Alabama are a mine of information concerning the social, religious, educational, political, legal, administrative, agricultural and financial conditions in Alabama from 1865 to 1871. The report itself, of 632 pages, contains much that is not in the testimony, especially as regards railroad and cotton frauds, taxation and the public debt, and much of this information can be secured nowhere else.

The minority members of the sub-committee which took testimony in Alabama, General Frank P. Blair and later Mr. Beck, of New York, had summoned before the committee at Washington, and before the sub-committee in Alabama, the most prominent men of the State — men who, on account of their positions, were intimately acquainted with the condition of affairs in the State. General Blair took care that the examination covered everything that had occurred since the war. The Republican members often protested against the evidence that Blair proposed to introduce, and ruled it out. He took exceptions, and sometimes the committee at Washington ad- mitted it; sometimes he smuggled it in any way, by means of cross questioning, or else he incorporated it into the minority report. On the other hand, the Republican members of the sub-committee seem to have felt that the object of the investigation was only to get a lot of campaign stories for the use of the Radical party in the coming elections. They summoned a sorry class of witnesses, a large proportion of whom were ignorant negroes who could only tell what they had heard or had feared. The best of the

Radicals were not summoned unless by the Democrats. In several instances the Democrats caused to be summoned the prominent scalawags and carpet- baggers, who usually gave testimony damaging to the Radical cause.

An examination of the testimony shows that sixty-four Democrats and Conservatives were called before the committee and sub-committee. Of these, fifty-seven were Southern men, five were Northern men residing in the State, and two were negroes. The Democrats testified at great length, often twenty to fifty pages. Blair and Beck tried to bring out everything concerning the character of carpet-bag rule.

Thirty-four scalawags, fifteen carpet-baggers and forty-one negro Radicals came before the committee and sub-committee. Some of these were summoned by Blair or Beck, and a number of them disappointed the Republican members of the committee by giving good Democratic testimony. The Radicals could only repeat, with variations, the story of the Eutaw riot, the Patona affair, the Huntsville parade, etc. Of the prominent carpet-baggers and scalawags whose testimony was anti- Democratic, most were men of unsavory character.

The testimony of the higher Federal officials was mostly in favor of the Democratic contention.

The negro testimony, however worthless it may appear at first sight, becomes as clear as day to one who, knowing the negro mind, remembers the influences then operating upon it. From this class of testimony one gets valuable hints and suggestions. The character of the white scalawag and carpet-bag testimony is more complex, but if one has the history of the witness, the testimony usually becomes clear. In many instances the testimony gives a short history of the witness.

The material collected by the Ku Klux Committee and other committees that investigated affairs in the South after the war, can be used with profit only by one who will go to the biographical books and learn the social and political his- tory of each person who testified. When the personal history of the important witness is known, many things become plain. Unless this is known, one cannot safely accept or reject any specific testimony. To one who works in Alabama reconstruction. Brewer's *Alabama,* Garrett's *Reminiscences,* the *Memorial Record,* old newspaper files and the memories of old citizens are indispensable. There is in the first volume of the Alabama Testimony a delightfully partisan index of seventy-five pages. In it the summary of Democratic testimony shows up almost as Radical as the worst on the other side. It is meant only to bring out the violence in the testimony. According to it, one would think all those killed or mistreated were Radicals. The same man frequently figures in three situations, as shot, outraged and killed. General Clanton's testimony of thirty pages gets a summary of four inches, which tells nothing; that of Wager, a Bureau agent, gets as much as twelve pages, which tell something; and that of Minnis, a scalawag, twice as much.

There is very little to be found in the testimony that relates directly to the Ku Klux Klan and similar organizations. Had the sessions of the sub-committee been held in the white counties of North and Southwest Alabama, where the Klans had flourished, probably they might have found out something about the organization. But the minority members were determined to expose the actual condition of affairs in the State from 1865 to 1 87 1. No matter how much the Radicals might discover concerning unlawful organizations, the Democrats stood ready with an immense deal of facts concerning Radical misgovernment to show cause why such organizations should arise. Consequently the three volumes of testimony relating to Alabama are by no means pro- Radical except in the attitude of the majority of the examiners.

Below is given a table of alleged Ku Klux outrages, compiled from the testimony taken. The Ku Klux report classifies all violence under the four heads: Killing, Shooting, Outrage, Whipping. The same case frequently figures in two or more classes. Practically every case of violence, whether political or not, is brought into the testimony. The period covered is from 1865 to 1871. Radical outrages as well as Democratic are listed in the report as Ku Klux outrages. In a number of cases Radical outrages are made to appear as Democratic, Many of the cases are simply hearsay. It is not likely that many instances of outrage escaped notice; for 'every case of actual outrage was proven by many witnesses. Every violent death of man, woman or child, white or black. Democratic or Radical, occurring between 1865 and 1871 appears in the list as a Ku Klux outrage. Evidently careful search had been made, and the witnesses had informed them- selves about every actual deed of violence. There were sixty four counties in the state and in only twenty-nine of them were there alleged instances of Ku Klux outrage:

TABLE OF ALLEGED OUTRAGES COMPILED FROM THE KU KLUX TESTIMONY

17

Introduction to Lester and Wilson's "Ku Klux Klan: Its Origin, Growth, and Disbandment"

Twenty-one years ago there was privately printed in Nashville, Tennessee, a little book by J. C. Lester and D. L. Wilson, that purported to be an account, from inside information, of the great secret order of Reconstruction days, known to the public as Ku Klux Klan. It attracted little notice then; and since that time it has not been given the attention it deserved as a historical document. At the time of writing, sectional feeling was still inflamed; the Northern people were not ready to hear anything favorable about the Ku Klux Klan, which they considered a band of outlaws and murderers ; and the Southern people were not desirous of being reminded of the dreadful Reconstruction period. Many of the members of the Klan who had been hunted for their lives, and who were still technically out-lawed, were unwilling to make known their connection with the order and some even considered their oaths still binding'. But since the book was printed, the Prescripts or Constitutions of the order have come to light, and the ex-members are now generally willing to tell all they know about the organization. As yet, no other member has written an account of the Klan, though several have been projected, and Lester and Wilson's History seems likely to remain the only one written altogether from inside sources.

The authors, Capt. John C. Lester and Rev. D. L. Wilson, were in 1884, when the booklet was written, residents in Pulaski, Tennessee, where the first Den of the Klan was founded. 'Major Lester was one of the six original members of the Pulaski Den or Circle. He made a fine record as a soldier in the Civil War in the Third Tennessee (Confederate)' Infantry, and afterwards became a lawyer and an official in the Methodist Church, and was a member of the Tennessee legislature at the time of writing the book. Rev. D. L. Wilson, who put the account into its present form, was born in 1849, in Augusta County, Virginia. He went to school to Jed Hotchkiss and was graduated as valedictorian of his class from Washington and Lee University, in 1873, and a year later from the Union Theological Seminary, near Hampden-Sidney, Virginia. From 1874 to 1880 he was pastor of a Presbyterian church at Broadway, Virginia, and from 1880 to 1902 he served a church in Pulaski, Tennessee. He died in 1902 after a six months' residence in Bristol, Tennessee, as pastor of the First Presbyterian Church. He was not a member of the Klan, but was acquainted with the founders and with many other former members, and had access to all the records of the order that had not been destroyed. In addition to information received from other members, Wilson was assisted by Captain Lester, who furnished most of the facts used, revised the manuscript and the book was printed with both names on the title page.

As a general account of the Ku Klux movement Lester and Wilson's History leaves something to be desired. It is colored too much by conditions in Tennessee, No knowledge is shown of other organizations similar to Ku Klux Klan, when in fact there were several other very important ones, such as the White Brotherhood, the White League, the Pale Faces, the Constitutional Union Guards, and one, the Knights of the White Camelia, that was larger than the Klan and covered a wider territory. Then, too, in an attempt to make a moderate statement , that would be generally accepted, the authors failed to portray clearly the chaotic social, economic and political conditions that caused the rise of such orders, and in endeavoring to condemn the acts of violence committed under cloak of the order they went too far in the direction of apologetic explanation. Consequently, the causes seem somewhat trivial and the results not very important' It would seem from their account that after a partial success, the movement failed in its attempt to regulate society, and degenerated into general disorder. This is a superficial conclusion and is not concurred in by the survivors of the period and those who understand the conditions of that time. The remnants of such a secret, illegal order were certain to degenerate finally into violence, but before it reached this stage it had accomplished much good in reducing to order the social chaos.

In view of the fact that the Lester and Wilson account does not mention names it will be of interest to examine the personnel of the original Pulaski Circle, out of which the Klan developed. There were six young men in the party that first began to meet in the fall and winter of 1865: (1) Captain John Chester, of whom something has been said. (2) Major James Richard Crowe, now of Sheffield, Alabama, who was a native of Pulaski and was educated at Waterbury Academy and Giles College. When the Civil War began he was studying law in Marion, Alabama, and enlisted at once in the Marion Rifles, Company "G," Fourth Alabama Infantry, Later he was transferred to the 35th Tennessee Infantry. He was in the battles of Manassas, Fort Donelson, Shiloh, Shelton's Hill, White Farm, Richmond, Perrysville, and others of less importance. Three times he was severely wounded and twice discharged for disability. He was captured with Sam Davis and both were tried as spies; Crowe was acquitted and Davis was hanged. He has held high rank in the Masonic order and has been an official in the Cumberland Presbyterian Church, (3) John Kennedy, the only survivor of the original six except Major Crowe. He was a soldier in the 3rd Tennessee Infantry during the Civil War, is a Presbyterian, and an honored citizen of Lawrenceburg, Tennessee. (4) Calvin Jones, son of Judge Thomas M. Jones, was a lawyer, and a member of the Episcopal Church. He was Adjutant of the 32nd Tennessee Infantry during the Civil War. (5) Richard R. Reed was a lawyer, a Presbyterian, and during the war had served in the 3rd Tennessee Infantry. (6) Frank O. McCord was editor of the Pulaski Citizen, a Methodist, and had been a private soldier in the Confederate service. Two others came in at the second or third meeting — Capt. J. L. Pearcy, later of Nashville, now of Washington, D. C, and James McCallum. The founders were all of Scotch-Irish descent and most of them were Presbyterians.

In regard to the founding of the Pulaski Circle, Major J. R. Crowe says : "Frank O. McCord was elected Grand Cyclops, and James R. Crowe, Grand Turk. A committee composed of Richard R. Reed and Calvin Jones' was appointed to select a name for the organization. The Greek for circle was chosen. We called it Kuklos, which was changed to Ku Klux afterward when the name was proposed to the Circle. John Kennedy suggested that we add another K, and the order was then called Ku Klux Klan. . . .

"The mysterious lights seen floating about the ruins presented a weird and uncanny appearance and filled the superstitious with dread of the place; so we were never disturbed, and it only required a quaint garb and a few mysterious sounds to convince the uninitiated that we were spirits from the other world. We were quick to catch on to this idea and we governed ourselves accordingly. During our parades or appearances in public the darkies either hid out or remained close in their houses. The origin of the order had no political significance. It was at first purely social and for our amusement. It proved a great blessing to the entire South and did what the State and Federal officials could not do — it brought order out of chaos and peace and happiness to our beloved South. . . . The order was careful in the admission of members and I have never known of a betrayal of the secrets of the order. I am proud to say that I never knew of one single act done by the genuine Ku Klux Klan that I am ashamed of or do not now endorse."

Major Crowe and other members repeatedly mention the fact that the membership of the Klan was largely of Scotch- Irish descent. This was bound to be the case since in the territory covered by the Klan proper the great majority of the Scotch-Irish of the South were settled. The Ku Klux Klan extended from Virginia to Mississippi through the white county section — the Piedmont and mountain region. It seldom extended into the Black Belt, though it was founded on its borders. There another similar order — the Knights of the White Camelia— held sway. In the Piedmont region before the spread of the Klan, there were numerous secret protective societies among the whites, and these were later absorbed into the Klan. The Klan led a more strenuous existence than the Black Belt orders. In most of its territory, social conditions were worse than in the black counties. It is a mistake to consider that in 1865-1870, the whites in the densest black districts were in the place of greatest danger. There the blacks were usually the best behaved; there the whites were never divided and never lost their grip on society; there the negro still respected the white people as beings almost superhuman. But race relations were worse in the white districts where there was a lower class of whites, some of whom mistreated the negro and others encouraged him to violence. Here the negro had never had the great respect for all whites that the Black Belt negro had, and here the whites were somewhat divided among themselves. During the war the "tories," so called, or those who claimed to be Union sympathizers and the Confederates, alternately mistreated one another, and the close of the war brought no peace to such communities. To this region escaped the outlaws, deserters, etc., of both armies during the war, and here the wreckage of war was worst. Such was the nature of the country where the Klan flourished. It was a kind of ex-Con- federate protest against the doings of the "tories," Unionists and outlaws, and the negroes banded in the Union League. For several years neither the Federal Government nor the State Government gave protection to the ex-Confederates of this region, and naturally secret associations were formed for self-defense. This method of self-defense is as old as history.[1]

The members of Ku Klux Klan are nowadays inclined to consider that their order comprehended all that took shape in resistance to the Africanization of society and government during the Reconstruction period. As one ex-member said : "Nearly all prominent men — ex-Confederates — in all the Southern states were connected in some way with the Klan." This is true only indirectly. Nearly all white men, it may be said, took part in the movement now called' the "Ku Klux Movement" But more of them belonged to other organizations than were members of the Klan. The Klan had the most striking name and it was later applied to the whole movement. The more prominent politicians, it is said, had no direct connection with any such orders. Such connections would have embarrassed and hampered them in their work, but most of them were in full sympathy with the objects of the Ku Klux movement, and profited by its successes. Many of the genuine Unionists later joined in the movement, and there were some few negro members, I have been told. Some prominent men were honorary members, so to speak, of the order. They sympathized with its objects, and gave advice and encouragement, but were not initiated and did not take active part. General John B. Gordon, of Georgia, and General W. J. Hardee, of Alabama, were such members. The active members were, as a rule, young men. In this respect the Klan differed from the order of White Camelia, which discouraged the initiation of very young men.

Some well-known members of the Klan were General John C. Brown, of Pulaski, Tennessee; Captain John W. Morton, now Secretary of State of Tennessee; Ryland Randolph, of Tuscaloosa, Alabama, editor of the Independent Monitor, the official organ of the Klan in Alabama; General N. B. Forrest and General George W. Gordon, of Memphis, Tennessee; Generals John B. Gordon, A. H. Colquitt, G. T. Anderson and A. R. Lawton, of Georgia; General W. J. Hardee, of Alabama; Colonel Joseph Fussell, of Columbia, Tennessee. General Albert Pike, who stood high in the Masonic order, was the chief judicial officer of the Klan.

General Forrest heard of the order after it began to spread, and after investigation consented to become its head as Grand Wizard. He was initiated by Captain John W, Morton, who had formerly been his chief of artillery. Under him the order, which was becoming de- moralized, was reorganized. As soon as it had done its work he disbanded it. An enterprising newspaper reporter interviewed General Forrest, in 1868, on the subject of Ku Klux Klan and extracted much information;' but when before the Ku Klux Committee of Congress, in 1871, the General would make only general statements and he evaded some of the interrogatories. To the committee he appeared to be wonderfully familiar with the principles of the order, but very ignorant as to details. The average member of Congress, ignorant of Southern conditions, did not understand that the members of the order considered themselves bound by the supreme oath of the Klan and that other oaths, if in conflict with it, were not binding. That is, the ex-Confederates under the command of Forrest, Grand Wizard of the Invisible Empire, were obeying the first law of nature and were bound to reveal nothing to injure the cause, just as when Confederates under Forrest, Lieutenant-General of the Confederate Army, they were -bound not to reveal military information to the hostile forces. The government, in their view, had not only failed to protect them, but was being used to oppress them. Consequently they were disregarding its claim to obedience.

Now that General Forrest's connection with the Klan is known it is amusing to read the testimony he gave before the Ku Klux Committee of Congress in 1871. Though evading questions aimed to elicit definite information, yet he was willing to speak of the general conditions that caused the development of the organization in Tennessee, He stated that it was meant as a defensive organization among the Southern whites to offset the work of the Union League, which had organized, armed and drilled the negroes, and had committed numerous outrages on the whites; to protect ex-Confederates from extermination by Brownlow's "loyal" militia; to prevent the burning by negroes of gins, mills, dwellings, and villages, which was becoming common; to protect white women from criminal negro men; in short to make life and property safe and keep the South from becoming a second San Domingo. He stated that about the time the order arose he was getting as many as fifty letters a day from his old soldiers who were suffering under the disordered conditions that followed the war, whose friends and relatives were being murdered, whose wives and daughters were being insulted, etc. They wanted advice and assistance from him. Not being able to write himself, on account of a wounded shoulder, he kept a secretary busy answering such letters. Most of the defensive bodies, Forrest stated, had no names and had no connection with one another. He admitted that he had belonged to the Pale Faces, and that he fully approved of the objects of the Klan. A copy of the original Prescript was shown to him and he was able to say that he had never seen it before. In his day, the Revised and Amended Prescript was used, which was never dis- covered by any investigating committee. He maintained that the order was careful in admitting new members, only sober, mature, discreet gentlemen being allowed to join. At one time, Forrest estimated, so a newspaper reporter stated, that the Klan had 40,000 members in Tennessee and 550,000 in the entire South. This estimate was probably not exaggerated if the entire membership of all the orders similar to the Klan be counted in. For- rest refused to give the names of members. It is likely, from several bits of evidence, that he had much to do with consolidating the order, giving it a military organization, and making its work effective. General John B. Gordon, the most prominent military man, next to Forrest, who was connected with the Klan, gave a clear account of the conditions in Georgia that led to the organization of the defensive societies of whites.^ In Georgia the state of affairs where General Gordon lived was in some respects unlike conditions in Tennessee. In Tennessee the whites were somewhat divided among themselves and there were not so many blacks. In Georgia, according to Gordon, the principal danger was from blacks, incited to hostility and violence by alien whites of low character. The latter organized the negroes into armed Union Leagues, taught them that the whites were hostile to all their rights, and that the lands of the whites were to be, or ought to be, divided among the blacks. Under such influences the negroes who had not made trouble began to show signs of restlessness; some of them banded together to plunder the whites, and serious crimes became frequent, especially that of rape, and men were afraid to leave their families in order to attend to their business. The whites feared a general insurrection of the blacks, and as Gordon stated, "if the sort of teachings given [to the negroes] in, Georgia had been carried out to its logical results the negroes would have slaughtered whole neighborhoods." That they did not do so, was, in his opinion, due to the forbearance and self- control of the whites, and to the natural kindness and good disposition of the negroes and their remembrance of former pleasant relations with the whites. There was no great danger, as one can see to-day, of the negro uprisings, but the whites thought then that there was. The religious frenzy of the blacks during the year after the war also alarmed the whites. The black troops stationed in Georgia were frequently guilty of gross outrages against white citizens and were a constant incitement to violence on the part of their fellow blacks. The carpetbag government pardoned and turned loose upon society the worst criminals. There was no law for several years. The whites were subject to arbitrary arrest and trials by drumhead courts-martial; military prisoners were badly mistreated. In general, society and government were in a condition of anarchy; the white race was disorganized, and the blacks organized, but not for good purposes. "

General Gordon spoke of another matter often mentioned by the best class of ex-Confederate soldiers: the Southern soldier believed that the "Appomattox Program" had not been carried out At Appomattox the magnanimity of General Grant and the victorious soldiers had impressed very favorably the defeated Confederates. The latter believed that if Grant and the soldiers who had defeated them had been allowed to settle matters, there would have been no more trouble. Instead, the politicians had taken charge and had stirred up endless strife. No effort at conciliation had been made;

and the magnanimity of Grant gave way to the vindictive policies of politicians.[2]

The whites believed that the "understanding of Appomattox" had been violated and that they had been deliberately humiliated by the Washington government.

Such were some of the influences, in General Gordon's opinion, that caused the spread of the Klan in Georgia. He says that he heartily approved the objects of the order, that it was purely for self- protection, an organization for police purposes, a peace police, which kept the peace, prevented riots, and restrained the passionate whites as well as the violent blacks. Its membership was, he said, of the best citizens, mostly ex-Confederates, led by the instinct of self-preservation to band together. It was secret because the leaders were sure that the sympathy of the Federal Government would be against them and would consider a public organization a fresh rebellion. It took no part in politics and died out when the whites were able to obtain protection from the police and the courts.

These were the explanations of men who were high in the order but who never attended a meeting and were never in actual contact with its workings. Private members — Ghouls they were called — could have told more thrilling stories. But deficient as the accounts of Gordon and Forrest are in detail they supplement the history of Lester and Wilson in explaining the causes that lay at the bottom of the secret revolution generally called the Klux Movement .

As to the the success or failure of the movement, Lester and Wilson, condemning the violence that naturally resulted from the movement, cause the impression that the main result was disorder. Such was not the case, nor was it the intention of the writers to create such an impression. The important work of the Klan was accomplished in regaining for the whites control over the social order and in putting them in a fair, way to regain political control. In some States this occurred sooner than in others., When the order accomplished its work it passed away. It was formally disbanded before the evil results of carpet bag governments could be seen. When it went out of existence in 1869, there had been few outrages, but its name and prestige lived after it and served to hide the evil deeds of all sorts and conditions of outlaws. But these could be crushed by the government, State or federal. In a wider and truer sense the phrase "Ku Klux Movement" means the attitude of Southern whites toward the various measures of Reconstruction lasting from 1865 until 1876, and, in some respects, almost to the present day.

Notes:

1. Examples in European history are the Carbonari of Italy, the Tugenbund and the Vehngericht of Germany, the Klephts of Greece, Young Italy, the Nihilists of Russia, the Masonic order in most Catholic countries during the first half of the Nineteenth Century, Beati Paoli of Sicily, the Illuminati, etc. The "Confriries" of Medieval France were similar illegal societies formed "pour defendre les innocentes et reprimer les violences iniques." — Lavisse et Rambaud, Histoire General, Vol 2, p. 466.

2. General Clanton, of Alabama, complained that the Southern people had passed "out of the hands of warriors into the hands of squaws." General Edmund W. Pettus, now U. S. Senator from Alabama, said that the entire Reconstruction was in violation of the understanding made at the surrender of the Confederate armies. The Confederate soldier surrendered with arms in hand and in return a certain contract was made in his parole according to which, as long as he was law- abiding, he was not to be disturbed. This contract had been violated. The government of the United States had made a promise to men with arms in their hands and had violated this promise by passing the Reconstruction measures, which amounted to punishment of individuals for alleged crime without trial by law. See Ku Klux Report, Alabama Testimony, pp. 224, 377, 383.

18

Re-Organization of the Industrial System in Alabama After the Civil War

ANTE-BELLUM SYSTEM

The cotton-planter of the South, the master of many negro slaves, organized what was probably the most efficient plantation labor system the world ever saw. Each plantation was an industrial community almost independent of the outside world, with a most minute division of labor, each servant being assigned a task suited to his or her strength and training. Nothing but the most skilled management could save a planter from ruin, for though the labor was efficient, it was the most costly ever known. The value of an overseer was judged by the general condition, health, appearance, and manners of the slaves; the amount of work done with the least punishment; the condition of stock, buildings, and plantation; and the size of the crops. All supplies were raised on the plantation — corn, bacon, beef, and other food-stuffs; farm implements and harness were made and repaired by the skilled negroes in rainy weather when no outdoor work could be done; clothes were cut out in the " big house " and made by the negro women under the direction of the mistress. There was much need for skilled labor, and this was done by the blacks. Work was often done by tasks, and industrious negroes were able to complete their daily allotment and have three or four hours a day to work in their own gardens and "patches." They often earned money at odd jobs, and the church records show that they contributed regularly. Negro children were trained in the arts of industry and in sobriety by elderly negroes of good judgment and firm character, usually women. Children too young to work were cared for by a competent mammy in the plantation nursery, while their parents were in the fields.[1]

In the Black Belt there was little hiring of extra labor and less renting of land. Except on the borders, nearly all whites were of the planting class. Their greater wealth had enabled them to outbid the average farmer and secure all the rich lands of the black prairies, canebrake, and river bottoms. The small farmer who secured a foothold in the Black Belt would find himself in a situation not altogether pleasant, and, selling out to the nearest planter, would go to poorer counties in the hills or pine woods, where land was cheaper, and where most of the people were white.

In the Black Belt cotton was largely a surplus money crop, and once the labor was paid for, the planter was a very rich man. In the white counties of the cotton states about the same crops were raised as in the Black Belt, but the land was less fertile and the methods of cultivation were less skillful. In the richer parts of these white counties there was something of the plantation system with some negro labor. But slavery gradually drove white labor to the hills and mountains, and to the sand and pine barrens. No matter how poor a white man was, he was excessively independent in spirit and wanted to work only his own farm. This will account for the lack of renters and hired white laborers in black or in white districts, and also for the fact that the less fertile land was taken up by the whites who desired to be their own employers. Land was cheap, and any man could purchase it.[2]

There was some renting of land in white counties, and the form it took was that now known as " third and fourth." It was then called " shares." There was little or no tenancy " on halves " or "standing rent." But the average farmer worked his own land, often with the help of from three to ten slaves.

On the borders of the Black Belt in Alabama was a peculiar class, called "squatters." They settled down, with or without permission, on lots of poor and waste land, built cabins, cleared " patches," and made a precarious living by their little crops, and by working for wages as carpenters, blacksmiths, etc. Some bought the small lots of land on long-time payments and never paid for them, but simply stayed where they were. On the borders of the Black Belt in the busy season were found numbers of white hired men working alongside negro slaves; for there was no prejudice against manual labor; that is, no more than anywhere else in the world.[3]

BREAKUP OF THE OLD SYSTEM

As soon as the war was over, the first concern of the returning soldiers was to obtain food to relieve present wants and to secure supplies to last until a crop could be made. In the white counties of the state the situation was much worse than in the Black Belt. The soil of the white counties was less fertile; the people were not wealthy before the war, and during the war they suffered from the depredations of the enemy and from the operation of the tax-in-kind which bore heavily upon them when they had nothing to spare. The white men went to the war, and there were only women, children, and old men to work the fields. The heaviest losses among the Alabama Confederate troops were from the ranks of the white-county soldiers. In all of these counties there was destitution after the first year of the war, and after 1862 from one-fourth to one-half of the soldiers' families received aid from the state. The bountiful Black Belt furnished enough for all. At the close of hostilities the condition of the people in the poorer counties was pitiable. Stock, fences, barns, and in many cases dwellings had disappeared; the fields were grown up in weeds ; and no supplies of any kind were available. How many of the people managed to> live was a mystery. Some walked twenty miles to get food, and there were cases of starvation. No seed of any kind and no farm implements were to be had. The best work of the Freedmen's Bureau was done in relieving these white people from. want until they could make a crop.

The Black Belt was the richest, as well as the least exposed, section of the state, and fared well until the end of the war. The laborers were negro slaves, and these worked as well in war time as in peace. Immense food crops were made in 1863 and 1864, and there was no suffering among whites or blacks. Until 1865 there was no loss from Federal invasion, but with the spring of 1865 misfortunes came. Four large armies marched through the central portions of the state, burning, destroying, confiscating. In June, 1865, the Black Belt was in almost as bad condition as the white counties. All buildings in the track of the armies had disappeared; the stores of provisions were confiscated; gin- houses and mills were burned; cattle, horses, and mules were carried away; and nothing much was left except the negroes and the rich land. The returning planter, like the farmer, found his agricultural implements worn out and broken, and in all the land there was no money to purchase the necessaries of life. But in the portions of the black counties untouched by the armies there were supplies sufficient to last the people for a few months. A few- fortunate individuals had cotton, which was now bringing a fabulous price, and it was the high price received for these few bales not confiscated by the government that saved the Black Belt from suffering as did the other counties.

Neither master nor slave knew exactly how to begin anew, and for a while things simply drifted. Now that the question of slavery was settled, many of the former masters felt a great relief from responsibility, though for their former slaves they felt a pro- found pity. The majority of them had no faith in free negro labor, yet all were willing to give it a trial, and a few of the more strenuous ones said that the energy and strength of the white man that had made the savage negro an efficient laborer could make the free negro work fairly well ; and if the free negro would work, they were willing to admit that the change might be beneficial to both races.

During the spring, summer, and fall of 1865 the masters came straggling home, and were met by friendly servants who gave them cordial welcome. Each one at once called his slaves and told them that they were free; that they might stay with him and work for wages, or that they might find other homes. Except in the vicinity of the towns and army posts, the negroes usually chose to stay and work; and in the rural districts affairs were little changed for several months after the surrender. There the surrender hardly caused a ripple on the surface of society. Life and work went on as before. The staid negro coachmen sat upon their boxes on Sunday as of old; the field hands went regularly about their appointed tasks. Labor was cheerful, and the negroes went singing to the fields. "The negro knew no Appomattox. The revolution sat lightly, save in the presence of vacant seats at home and silent graves in the churchyard, in the memorials of destructive raids, in the wonder on the faces of a people once free, now ruled, where ruled at all, by a bureau agent." Here it was that the master-race believed that, after all, freedom might be well. In other sections, where the negro was more exposed to outside influences, the whites were not hopeful. The common opinion was that with free negro labor cotton could not be cultivated with success. The northerner thought that it was a crop made by forced labor, and that no freeman would willingly perform such labor; the southerner believed that the negro would neglect the crop too much when not under strict supervision. Yet later years have shown that free white labor is most successful in the cultivation of cotton because of the care now expended on farms in the white counties; while cotton is the only crop that the free negro has cultivated with any degree of success, because some kind of a crop can be made on the fertile soils of the Black Belt by the most careless cultivation.

At first no one knew just how to work the free negro. Innumerable plans were formed, and many were tried. The old patriarchal relations were preserved as far as possible. Truman, who made a long stay in Alabama, reported that in most cases there was a genuine attachment between masters and negroes; that the masters were the best friends the negroes had; and that, though they regarded the blacks with much commiseration, they were inclined to encourage them to collect around the big house on the old slavery terms, giving food, clothes, quarters, medical attendance, and some pay. At that time no one could understand the freedom of the negro. As one old master expressed it, he saw no "free negroes" until the fall of 1865, when the bureau began to influence the blacks. But with the extension of the bureau and the spread of army posts, the negroes, who for a while had been taking freedom on faith, now determined to enjoy the reality. Crops that had been planted in the spring were neglected in the summer and fall, while the darky moved away from his slave quarters, changed his name, probably deserted his family, joined a new church and attended many revivals, bought a gun and acquired a dog, and went hunting and fishing to his heart's content. The house servants and the artisans, who were the best and most intelligent of the negroes, began to go to the towns. Many were attracted by the reports of confiscation and division of property, and stopped working. Negro women, desiring to be as white ladies, refused to work in the fields, to cook, wash, or to perform other menial duties. It was years before this "freedom" prejudice of the negro women against domestic service died out. The precarious support offered by the bureau attracted many negroes to town and made agricultural labor unreliable. The negro would work one or two days in the week, go to town two days, and wander about the rest of the time. Under such conditions there was no hope of continuing the old patriarchal system, and new plans, modeled on what they had heard of free labor, were tried by the planters. In the white counties the ex-soldiers went to work as before the war, but they had come home from the army too' late to plant full crops, and few had supplies enough to last until the crops should be gathered. In the white counties the negroes were so few as to escape the serious attention of the bureau, and consequently they worked fairly well at what they could get to do.[4]

THE FREEDMEN'S BUREAU SYSTEM

The first work of the bureau was to break up the labor system that had been partially constructed, and to endeavor to establish a new system based on the northern free-labor system and the old slave-hiring system, with the addition of a good deal of pure theory. The bureau was to act as a labor clearing-house; it was to have entire control of labor; contracts must be written in accordance with the regulations of the bureau, and must be registered by the agent, who charged large fees. Unskilled labor was classified into three grades, and men and women were to be paid $10, $8, and $6 per month, according to the grade, and half- grown children $6. 13 In addition, they were to have food, full quarters, clothing, medical attendance, and schooling for their children. The working-day was ten hours from April to October, and nine hours from November to March. The task system, as well as the overseer, was forbidden, and the "share" system was discouraged. Wages were secured by a lien on crops or land, and this was prior to any other lien. Breach of contract was tried by bureau agent, bureau court, provost-marshal, or military com- mission. No contract for a longer time than six months was approved. The chain-gang hard labor system of punishment of convicts was abolished. Where the laborer received no supplies his pay was fixed at the rate of wages paid for able-bodied slaves before the war. If a negro was found working under a verbal contract, his employer was arrested or warned to conform to regulations. Planters were continually in trouble with the bureau agent, who summoned them before him on the slightest pretexts. The lien on the crop prevented the moving or sale of the crop, unless the negro consented; yet the planter had to sell before he could pay wages.[5]

The result of these regulations was to destroy industry where an alien bureau agent was stationed, unless the agent was purchasable; for the planters could not afford to have their land worked on such terms. In some of the counties, where the native magistrates served as bureau agents, no attention was paid to the rules of the bureau, and the people floundered along trying to develop a workable basis of existence. In the districts infested by the bureau agents the negroes had fantastic notions of what freedom meant. On one plantation they demanded that the plantation bell be no longer rung to summon the hands to and from work, because it was too much like slavery. In various places they refused to work, and congregated about the bureau offices, awaiting the expected division of property, when they would get the "forty acres and one old gray mule." When wages were paid, they believed that each should receive the same amount, whether his labor had been good or bad, and whether the laborer was present or absent, sick or well. In one instance a planter was paying his men in corn according to the time each had worked. The negroes objected and got an order from the bureau agent that the division should be made equally. The planter read the order (which the negro could not read), and at once ordered the division as before. The negroes, thinking the bureau had ordered it, were satisfied. In the cane- brake region the agents were afraid of the great planters, and did not interfere with the negroes except to organize them into Union Leagues; but elsewhere in the Black Belt the planter could not afford to hire negroes on the terms fixed by the bureau.

NORTHERN AND FOREIGN IMMIGRATION

With the breakup of the slave system the planter found himself with much more land than he knew what to do with. He could get no reliable labor, he had no cash capital, and in many cases he offered his best lands for sale for low prices. The planters wanted to attract northern and foreign immigration and capital into the country; the cotton-planter sought for a northern partner who could furnish the capital. Owing to the almost religious regard of the negro for his northern deliverers, many white landholders thought that northern men, especially discharged soldiers, might be able to control negro labor better than southern men. General Swayne, the head of the bureau in the state, said that the negroes had more confidence in a " blue coat " than in a native, and that among the larger planters northern men, as partners or overseers, were in great demand.

For a short time after the close of the war northern men in considerable numbers planned to go into' the business of cotton-raising. DeBow gives a description of the would-be cotton- planters who came from the North to show the southern people how to raise cotton with free negro labor. They had notebooks and guide-books full of close and exact tables of costs and profits, and from them figured out vast returns. They acknowledged that the negro might not work for the southern man, but they were sure that he would work for them. They were self-confident, and would listen to no advice from experienced planters, whom they laughed at as old fogies, but from their notebooks and tables they gave one another much information about the new machinery useful in cotton culture, about rules for cultivation, how to control labor, etc. They estimated that each laborer's family would make $1,000 clear gain each year. DeBow would not say that they were wrong, but he said he thought they should hasten a little more slowly. Northern energy and capital flowed in; plantations were bought and the various industries of plantation life started; and mills and factories were established. Because of the paralyzed condition of industry, the southern people welcomed these signs of prosperity, but they were very skeptical of their final success. The northern settler had confidence in the negro, and gave him unlimited credit or supplies; consequently, in a few years, he was financially ruined and had to turn his attention to politics and to exploiting the negro in that field in order to make a living. Both as employer and as manager the northern man failed to control negro labor. He expected the negro to be the equal of the Yankee white. The negroes themselves were disgusted with northern employers. Truman reported, after an experience of one season, that "it is the almost universal testimony of the negroes themselves, who have been under the super- vision of both classes — and I have talked with many with a view to this point — that they prefer to labor for a southern employer."[6]

Northern capital came in after the war, but northern labor did not, though the planters offered every inducement. Land was offered to white purchasers at ridiculously low rates, but the northern white laborer did not come. He was afraid of the South with its planters and negroes. The poorer classes of native whites, however, profited by the low prices and secured a foothold on the better lands. So general was the unbelief in the value of the free negro as a laborer, especially in the bureau districts, and so signally had all inducements failed to bring native white laborers from the North, that determined efforts were made to obtain white labor from abroad. Immigration societies were formed, with officers in the state and headquarters in the northern cities. These societies undertook to send south laboring people in families — especially German — at so much per head. The planter turned with hope to white labor, of the superiority of which he had so long been hearing, and he wished very much to give it a trial. The advertisements in the newspapers read much like the old slave advertisements: so many head of healthy, industrious Germans of good character delivered f. o. b., New York, at so much per head. One of the white labor agencies in Alabama undertook to furnish "immigrants of any nativity and in any quantity "to take the place of negroes. Children were priced at the rate of $50 a year; women, $100; men, $150; they themselves providing board and clothes. One of every six Germans was warranted to speak English. Most of these agencies were great frauds, and only wanted an advance payment on a carload of Germans who did not exist. In a few instances some laborers were actually shipped in; but they at once demanded an advance of pay, and then deserted. Like the bounty jumpers, they played the game time and time again. The influence of the radical northern press was also used to discourage emigration to the South; consequently white immigration into the state did not amount to anything, and the Black Belt received no help from the North or from abroad, and had to fall back upon the free negro.

In the white counties there had been no hope or desire for alien immigration. The people and the country were so desperately poor that the stranger would never think of settling there. Many of the whites in moderate circumstances living near the Black Belt took advantage of the low price of rich lands and acquired small farms in the prairies, but there was no influx of white labor to the Black Belt from the white counties. Nearly every man, woman, and child in the white districts had to go to work to earn a living. Many persons — lawyers, public men, teachers, ministers, physicians, merchants, overseers, managers, and even women — who had never before worked in the fields or at manual occupations, were now forced to do so because of loss of property, or because they could not live by their former occupations.[7]

While the number of white laborers had increased somewhat, negro labor had decreased. Several thousand negro men had gone with the armies; many of the most intelligent had drifted to town to earn a precarious living at their trades; great numbers congregated in the towns where bureau supplies were doled out ; and in the vicinity of the larger towns there was a general disposition among the blacks to crown into the outskirts of the towns, where the sanitary arrangements were bad and where thousands died. The rural negro had a promising outlook, for at any time he could get more work than he could do; the city negro found work scarce even when he wanted it. Several attempts were made by the negroes in 1865 and 1866 to work farms and plantations on the co-operative system — that is, to club work — but with no success. They were not accustomed to independent labor; their faculty for organization had not been sufficiently developed ; and the dishonesty of their leading men sometimes caused failures of the schemes.

In the summer of 1865 the Monroe County Agricultural Association was formed to regulate labor and to protect the interests of both employer and laborer. It was the duty of the executive committee to look after the welfare of the freedmen, to see that contracts were carried out and the freedmen protected in them, and, in cases of dispute, to act as arbitrator. The members of the association pledged themselves to see that the freedman received his wages, and to aid him in case his employer refused to pay his wages. They were also to see that the freedman fulfilled his contract, unless there was good reason why he should not. Homes and the necessaries of life were to be provided by the association for the aged and helpless negroes, of whom there were several on every plantation. The planters declared themselves in favor of schools for the negro children, and a committee was appointed to devise a plan for their education. Every planter in Monroe County belonged to the association. An organization in Conecuh County adopted, word for word, the constitution of the Monroe County association. In Clarke and Wilcox Counties similar organizations were formed, and in all counties where negro labor was the main dependence some such plans were devised. But it is noticeable that in those counties where the planters first undertook to reorganize the labor system there were no regular agents of the Freedmen's Bureau and no garrison.[8]

The average negro, quite naturally, had little or no sense of the obligation of contracts. He would leave a growing crop at the most critical period and move into another county, or, working his own crop "on shares," would leave it in the grass and go to work for someone else in order to get small change for tobacco, snuff, and whisky. After three years of experience with such conduct, a meeting of citizens at Summerfield, Dallas County, decided that laborers ought to be impressed with the necessity of complying with contracts. They agreed that no laborers discharged for failure to keep contracts would be hired again by other employers. They declared it to be the duty of the whites to act in perfect good faith in their relations with freedmen, to respect and uphold their rights, and to promote good feeling.

DEVELOPMENT OF THE SHARE SYSTEM

At first the planters had demanded a system of contracts, thinking that by law they might hold the negro to their terms. But the bureau contracts were one-sided, and the planters could not afford to enter into them. General Swayne early reported a general breakdown of the contract system, though he told the planters that in case of dispute, where no contract was signed, he would exact payment for the negro at the highest rates. The "share " system was discouraged, but where there were no bureau agents it was developing. And so bad was the wage system that even in the bureau districts share-hiring was done. The object of share-renting was to cause the laborer to take an interest in his crop and to relieve the planter of disputes about lost time, etc. Some of the negroes also decided that the share system was the proper one. On a plantation near Selma the negroes demanded shares, threatening to leave in case of refusal. General Hardee, who was living near, proposed a plan for a verbal contract: wages should be one- fourth of all crops; meat and bread to be furnished to the laborer and his share of the crop to be paid to him in kind, or the net proceeds in cash; the planter to furnish land, teams, wagons, implements, and seed to the laborer, who, in addition, had all the slavery privileges of free wood, water and pasturage, garden lot and " truck patch," teams to use on Sundays and for going to town. The absolute right of management was reserved to the planter. It was understood that this was no copartnership, but that the negro was hired for a share of the crop; consequently he had no right to interfere in the management.

On another plantation, where a share system similar to Hardee's was in operation, the planter divided the workers into squads of four men each. To each squad he assigned one hundred acres of cotton and corn, in the proportion of five acres of cotton to three of corn, and forty acres of cotton for the women and children of the four families. The squads were united to pick the cotton, because they worked better in gangs. Wage-laborers had to be kept to look after fences and ditches, and perform odd jobs. A frequent source of trouble was the custom of allowing the negro, as part of his pay, several acres of " outside crop " to be worked on certain days of the week, as Fridays and Saturdays. The planter was supposed to settle disputes among the negroes, give them advice on every subject except politics and religion, pay their fines or get them out of jail when arrested, and some- times to thrash the recalcitrant.

Several kinds of share systems were finally evolved from the industrial chaos. They were much the same in black as in white districts, and the usual designations were: "on halves," "third and fourth," and "standing rent." The tenant " on halves " received one-half the crop, did all the work, and furnished his own pro- visions. The planter furnished land, houses to live in, seed, plows, hoes, teams, wagons, ginned the cotton, paid for half the fertilizer, and went security for the negro for a year's credit at the supply store in town, or else furnished the supplies himself and charged

them against the negro's share of the crop. The "third and fourth "
plan varied according to locality and time, and depended upon
what the tenant furnished. Sometimes the planter furnished everything, while the negro gave only his labor and received one- fourth
of the crop; again, the planter furnished all except provisions and
labor, and gave the negro one-third of the crop. In such cases
"third and fourth " was a lower grade of tenancy than "on halves."
Later it developed to a higher grade. The tenant furnished teams
and farming implements, and the planter the rest, in which case
the planter received a third of the cotton and a fourth of the corn
raised. "Standing rent " was the highest form of tenancy, and only
responsible persons, white or black, could rent under that system.
It called for a fixed or "standing " rent for each acre or farm, to be
paid in money or in cotton. The unit of value in cotton was a five-
hundred-pound bale of middling grade on October 1. Cotton rent
practically amounted to a money rent, since price and grade had to
be guaranteed. Tenants who had farm stock, farming implements
and supplies, or good credit would nearly always cultivate for
"standing rent." The planter exercised a controlling direction over
the labor and cultivation of a crop worked "on halves;" he exercised
less direction over " third and fourth " tenants, and was supposed
to exercise no control over tenants who paid "standing rent." In all
cases the planter furnished a dwelling-house free of rent, wood and
water (paid for digging wells), and pasture for the pigs and cows of
the tenants. In all cases the renter had a plot of ground of from one
to three acres, rent-free, for a vegetable garden and " truck patch."
Here could be raised water-melons, sugar cane, potatoes, sorghum,
cabbages, and other vegetables. Every tenant could keep a few pigs
and a cow, chickens, turkeys, and guineas, and especially dogs, and
could hunt in all the woods around and fish in all the waters. "On
halves " was considered the safest form of tenancy for both planter
and tenant, for the latter was only an average man. This method

allowed the superior direction of the planter. Many negroes worked for wages; the less intelligent and the unreliable could find no other way to work; and some of the best of them preferred to work for wages paid at the end of each week or month. Wage-laborers worked under the immediate oversight of the farmer or tenant who hired them. They received $8 to $12 a month, and were "found," that is, given their rations. In the white counties the negro hired man was often fed in the farmer's kitchen. The laborer, if hired by the year, had a house, vegetable garden, "truck patch," chickens, a pig perhaps, and always a dog, and he could hunt and fish any- where in the vicinity. Sometimes he was "found; " sometimes he "found " himself. When he was "found," the allowance for a week was three and a half pounds of bacon, a peck of meal, half a gallon of sirup, and a plug of tobacco ; his garden patch furnished vegetables. This allowance could be varied and commuted. The system worked out in the few years immediately following the war and has lasted almost without change. In the negro districts the large plantations have not been broken up into small farms, the census statistics to the contrary notwithstanding. The negro tenant or laborer had too many privileges for his own good and for the good of the planter. The negro should have been paid more money or a larger proportion of the crop, and given fewer privileges. He needed more control and supervision, and the result of giving him a vegetable garden, a "truck patch," a pasture, and the right of hunting and fishing was that the negro took less interest in the crop. The farming system was never brought to a real business basis.[9]

CREDIT OR SUPPLY SYSTEM

The universal lack of capital after the war forced an extension of the old ante-bellum credit or supply system. The merchant, who was also a cotton-buyer, advanced money or supplies until the crop was gathered. Before the war his security was both crop and slaves; after the war the crop was the principal security, for land was a drug on the market. Consequently, the crop was more important to the creditor. Cotton was the only good cash crop, and the high prices encouraged all to raise it. It was to the interest of the merchant, even when prices were low, to insist upon his debtors raising cotton to the exclusion of food crops, as much of his money was made by selling food supplies to them. Before the war only the planter had much credit, and even then a successful one did not make use of the system, but after the war all classes of cotton-raisers had to have advances of supplies. The credit or crop-lien system was good to put an ambitious farmer on the way to independence, but it was no incentive to the shiftless. Cotton became the universal crop under the credit system, and even when the farmer became independent he seldom planted less of his staple crop or raised supplies at home.[10]

WHITE FARMERS AND NEGRO FARMERS

At the end of the war everything was in favor of the negro cotton-raiser, and everything except the high price of cotton was against the white farmer in the poorer counties. The soil had been used most destructively in the white districts, and it had to be built up before cotton could be raised successfully. The high price of cotton caused the white farmer who had formerly had only small cotton patches to plant large fields, and for several years the negro was hardly a competitor to be considered. The building of railroads through the mineral regions afforded transportation for crops and fertilizers — an advantage that before this time had been enjoyed only by the Black Belt — and improved methods gradually supplanted the wasteful frontier system of cultivation. The gradual increase of the cotton production after 1869 was due entirely to white labor in the white counties, the black counties never again reaching their former production, though the population of those counties doubled. Governor Lindsay said in 1871 that the white people of north Alabama, where but little had been produced before the war, were becoming prosperous by raising cotton, and at the same time raising supplies that the planter on the rich lands with negro labor had to buy from the West. This prosperity, he thought, had done more than anything else to put an end to Ku Klux disturbances. Somers reported in 1871 that the cotton crop in the Tennessee valley was made by white labor, not by black. As long as there was plenty of cheap, poor land to be had, the poor but independent white would not work the rich land belonging to someone else ; and, before and long after the war, there was plenty of practically free land. Therefore the tendency of the whites was to remain on the less fertile land. Dr. E. A. Smith in the Alabama Geological Survey of 1881-82, and the Report on Cotton Production in Alabama (1884), shows the relation between race and cotton production, and race location with respect to fertility of soil: (1) On the most fertile lands the laboring population was black; the farmers were shiftless, and no fertilizers were used ; the credit evil was worse; the yield per acre was less than on the poorest soils cultivated by whites. (2) Where the races were about equal the best system was found; the soils were medium; the farms were small, but well cultivated, and fertilizers were used. (3) On the poorest soils only whites were found; these by industry and use of fertilizers could produce about as much as the blacks on the rich soils. [11]

The average product of the Black Belt is lower than the lowest in the poorest white counties. Only the best of soil, as in Clarke, Monroe, and Wilcox Counties, is able to overcome the bad labor system and produce an average equal to that made by the whites in Winston, the poorest county in the state. In white counties where the average product per acre falls below the average for the surrounding region the fact is explained by the presence of blacks, segregated on the best soils, keeping down the average production. For example, Madison County in 1880 had a majority of blacks, and the average production of cotton per acre was 0.28 bales, as compared with 0.32 for the Tennessee valley, of which Madison was the richest county; in Talladega, the most fertile county of the Coosa valley, the average production per acre was 0.32, as compared with 0.40 for the rest of the valley ; in Autauga, where the blacks outnumbered the whites two to one, the average fell below that of the country around, though the soil was the best in the region. The average product of the rich prairie cultivated by the blacks is 0.27 bale per acre ; the average product in the poor mineral region cultivated by whites was 0.26 to 0.28; in the short-leaf-pine region the whites outnumber the blacks two to one, and the average production of 0.34, while in the gravelly hill region, where the blacks are twice as numerous as the whites, the production is 0.30, the soil in the two sections being about equal. In general, the fertility of the soil being equal, the production varies inversely as the proportion of colored population to white. Density of colored population is a sure sign of fertile soil; predominance of whites, a sign of medium or poor soil. Outside of the Black Belt white owners cultivate small farms, looking closely after them. The negro seldom owns the land he cultivates, and is more efficient when working under direction on the small farm in the white county. In the Black Belt nearly all land is capable of cultivation, but in the white counties a large percentage is rocky, in hills, forests, mountains, etc. But many soils in south- east and north Alabama, formerly considered unproductive, have been brought under cultivation by the use of commercial fertilizers, hauled, in many cases, from twenty to a hundred miles. Fertilizers have not yet come into general use in the Black Belt. In the negro districts are still found horse-power gins and old wooden cotton compresses; in the white counties, steam and water power and the latest machinery. In the white counties it has always been a general custom to raise a part of the supplies on the farm; in the Black Belt this has not been done since the war.

Though many of the white farmers remained under the crop-lien bondage, there was a steady gain toward independence on the part of the more industrious and economical. But not until toward the close of the century did emancipation come for many of the struggling white farmers.

WHITES IN OTHER INDUSTRIES

In other directions the whites did better. They opened the mines of north Alabama, cut the timber of south Alabama, built the railroads and factories, and to some extent engaged in commerce. Market gardening is now a common occupation. Negro labor in factories failed. It was the negro rather than slavery that prevented, and still prevents, the establishment of manufactures. The development of manufactures in recent years has benefited principally the poor people of the white counties. "For this mill people is not drawn from foreign immigrants nor from distant states, but it is drawn from the native- born white population, the poor whites, that belated hill-folk from the ridges and hollows and caves of the silent hills. The negro artisan is giving way to the white ; even in the towns of the Black Belt the occupations once securely held by the negro are passing into the hands of the whites. [12]

In the white counties during Reconstruction the relations between the races became more strained than in the Black Belt. One of the manifestations of the Ku Klux movement in the white counties was the driving away of negro tenants from the more fertile districts by the poorer classes of whites who wanted these lands. For years immigration was discouraged by the northern press. Aliens were afraid to come to the "benighted and savage South." But in the eighties the railroad companies began to induce Germans to settle on their lands in the poorest of the white counties. Later there was a slow movement from the Northwest. As a rule, where the northerner and the German settle the wilder- ness blossoms and the negro leaves.

After plowing their hilltops until the soil was exhausted, the whites, even before the war, decided that only by clearing the swamps in the poorer districts could they get land worth cultivating. This required much labor and money. After the war, with the increase of transportation facilities, fertilizers came into use, the swamps were deserted, and the farmers went back to the uplands.

DECADENCE OF THE BLACK BELT

The patriarchal system failed in the Black Belt, the bureau system of contracts and prescribed wages failed, the planters' own wage system failed, and finally all settled down to the share system. In this there was some encouragement to effort on the part of the laborer; and in case of failure of the crop he bore a share of the loss. After a few years' experience the negroes were ready to go back to the wage system, and labor conventions were held demanding a return to that system. But whatever system was adopted, the work of the negro was unsatisfactory. The skilled laborer left the plantation, and the new generation knew nothing of the arts of industry. Labor became migratory, and the negro farmer wanted to change his location every year. Regular work was a thing of the past. In two or three days of a week a negro could work enough to live, and the remainder of the time he rested from his labors, often leaving much cotton in the field to rot. He went to the field when it suited him to go, gazed frequently at the sun to see if it was time to stop for meals, went often to the spring for water, and spent much time adjusting his plow or knocking the dirt and pebbles from his shoes. The negro women refused to work in the fields, and yet did nothing to better the home life; the style of living was "from hand to mouth." Extra money went for whisky, snuff, tobacco, and finery, while the standard of living was not raised. The laborer would always stop work to go to a circus, election, political meeting, revival, or camp-meeting. A great desolation seemed to have passed over the Black Belt country.[13]

The value of the wage-laborer is shown by the following table of wages:

Year	Men	Women	Youths over 14
1860	$138	$ 89	$66
1865–66	150–200	100–150	75–100
1867	117	71	52
1868	87	50	40

In the interior of the state the negroes worked better during and after Reconstruction than where they were exposed to the ministrations of the various kinds of carpet-baggers. In the Tennessee valley, where the negroes had taken a prominent part in politics, and had not only seen much of the war, but had also in considerable numbers enlisted in the Federal army, cotton- raising almost ceased for several years. The only crops made were made by whites.

In Sumter County, where the black population was dense, it was in 1870 almost impossible to secure labor, and those who wished to work went to the railways. A description of a "model negro farm" in 1874 was as follows: The farmer purchased an old mule on credit and rented land on shares, or for so many bales of cotton ; any old tools were used; corn, bacon, and other supplies were bought on credit and a lien given on crop; a month late, corn and cotton were planted on soil not well broken up; the negro would not pay for "no guano" to put on other people's land; by turns the farmer planted, fished, plowed, hunted, hoed, and frolicked, or went to "meeting." At the end of the year he sold his cotton, paid part of his rent and some of his debt, returned the mule to his owner, and sang:

Nigger work hard all de year;

White man tote de money.

If the negro made anything, his fellows were likely to steal it. Somers said: " There can be no doubt that the negroes first steal one another's share of the crop, and next the planter's by way of general redress." Crop-stealing was usually done at night. Stolen cotton, corn, pork, etc., was carried to the low doggeries kept on the outskirts of the plantation by low white men, and there exchanged for bad whisky, tobacco, and cheap stuff of various kinds. These doggeries were called "dead falls," and their proprietors often became rich. So serious did the theft of crops become that the legislature passed a " sunset " law making it a penal offense to purchase farm produce after nightfall. Poultry, hogs, corn, mules, and horses were stolen when left in the open. During the decade from 1868 to 1878 it was estimated by several grand juries which investigated the matter that the cotton and corn stolen from the open fields amounted to more than one- fifth of the crops produced.

The negroes deteriorated much in personal appearance and dress; immorality increased; religion nearly died out; consumption and other diseases attacked the childish people who would not care for themselves; foeticide was common; negro children died in swarms when very young; there was a tendency to return to the barbarous customs of their African forefathers; witchcraft and hoodoo were practiced, and in some cases human sacrifices made.

Emancipation destroyed the agricultural supremacy of the Black Belt. The uncertain returns from the plantations caused an exodus of planters and their families to the cities, and many well-kept plantations were divided into one- and two-house farms for negro tenants who let everything go to ruin. The negro tenant system was much more ruinous than the worst of the slavery system, and none of the plantations again reached their former state of productiveness. Ditches filled up, fences down, large stretches of fertile fields growing up in weeds and bushes, cabins tumbling in, and negro quarters deserted, corn choked by grass and weeds, cotton not half as good as under slavery — these were the reports from travelers in the Black Belt toward the close of Reconstruction. Other plantations were leased to managers who also kept plantation stores, whence the negroes were furnished with supplies. The manager has succeeded the planter; the great supply houses in the cities own numerous plantations. The money-lenders — often Jews — came into possession of many plantations. By the crop lien and blanket mortgage the negro became an industrial serf. The "big house" fell into decay. For these and other reasons, the former masters, who were the best friends of the negro, left the Black Belt, and the black steadily declined. The unaided negro has steadily grown worse; but Tuskegee, Normal, Calhoun, and similar bodies are endeavoring to assist the negro of the black counties to become an efficient member of society. In the success of such efforts lies the only hope of the negro, and also of the white of the Black Belt, if the negro is to remain.[14]

Notes:

1. The accounts of the wild and idle negro children of the rice and tobacco districts are not true of those in the Cotton Belt. The smallest tot could do a little in a cotton field.

2. See J. W. DuBose, in *Birmingham Age-Herald*, March 31 and April 7, 1901 ; R. H. Edmonds, " The Cotton Crop of To-Day ," *Review of Reviews*, September, 1903 ; Ingle, *Southern Sidelights*, p. 271 ; address of President Thach, of the Alabama Polytechnic Institute, before the American Economic Association, New Orleans, December 29, 1903 ; Tillinghast, *Negro in Africa and America*, pp. 126, 143; Mallard, *Plantation Life before Emancipation*; Washington, *Up from Slavery*, and *The Future of the American Negro,* passim. The immense cost of the slave labor is seen when the value of the slaves is compared with the value of the lands cultivated by their labor. In 1859 the cash value of the lands in Alabama was $175,824,622, and that of the slaves was $215,540,000. The larger portion of this land had not a negro on it and was cultivated exclusively by whites. (See the Census of i860.) The effect of the loss of slaves on the welfare of a planter is shown in the case of William L. Yancey. His slaves were accidentally poisoned and died. The loss ruined him, and he was forced to sell his plantation and practice law. A farmer in a white county employing white labor would have been injured only temporarily by such a loss of labor.

3. The tenant furnished labor, supplies, and teams, and gave to the landlord a fourth of the cotton and a third of the corn produced. There was usually good feeling between the whites and blacks at work together, but the negroes at heart scorned the poor whites, and had to be closely watched to keep them from insulting or abusing them. The negro had little respect for the man who owned no slaves, or who owned but few and worked with them in the fields. To protect the slaves against outsiders was one reason why

discipline was strict, supervision close, passes required, etc. When both white and black were allowed to go at will over the plantation and community, trouble was sure to result from the impudent behavior of the negro to "white trash," and the consequent retaliation of the latter. The whites often came to the master and wanted him to whip his best slaves for impudence to them. The master, to pre- vent this, regulated the liberty of the slave by passes, etc., and the whites, especially strangers, were expected not to trespass on a plantation where slaves were. The so-called "prejudice" against manual labor is perhaps due largely to abolitionist theories and arguments, which have been partially accepted since the war by some southerners who think it due to the old system to show its lofty attitude toward the common things of life. But the negro had, and still has, a certain contempt for a white who works as he does. And it has always been a custom of mankind — white, yellow, or black — to avoid manual labor if there is anything else to do.

4. Colonel Saunders, a noted slaveholder in one of the white counties in north Alabama, established a patriarchal protectorate over his former slaves. He built a church for them, and organized a monthly court, presided over by himself, in which the old negro men tried delinquents. It is said that the findings of this court were often ludicrous in the extreme, but order was preserved and for a long while there was no resort to the bureau. (See Saunders, *Early Settlers*, p. 31.) Many similar protectorates were established in the remote districts, but the policy of the bureau was to break them up.

5. While General Howard was in Mobile, some of the planters asked him to bind to them for a term of years their former slaves, in case the latter were willing. Howard was, of course, horrified at such a proposal. The so-called "black laws" passed by the legislature in 1865-66 were scarcely heard of by the people who hired negroes, and were never in force.

6. Many of the carpet-bag statesmen were northern men who had failed at cotton-planting or as overseers.

7. Note: The greatest evil of slavery was its tendency to drive the whites who were in moderate circumstances away from the richer lands of the prairie and canebrake, leaving that section to the few slaveholders and the immense number of slaves. Emancipation thus left on the finest lands of the state a shiftless laboring population, which still retains possession. Now, as in slavery times, the white prefers not to work as a field hand in the Black Belt when he can get more independent work elsewhere. And, besides, he does not wish to live among the negroes. Negro slavery kept whites from settling on the fertile lands; the negro keeps whites from taking possession now. - A number of young women of Montgomery, who were once wealthy, worked in the printing-office of the *Advertiser*. One of them was a daughter of a former president of the United States. Many women became teachers, displacing men who then went to the fields. Disabled soldiers generally tried teaching. - There seems to be a belief that emancipation had a good effect in driving to work a certain " gentleman-of-leisure " class that had been supported by the work of slaves and had scorned labor. (See W. B. Tillett in the *Century*, Vol. XI, p. 769.) It is a mistake to regard the slaveholding, planting class as in any degree idle, unless from the point of view of the negro or the ignorant white who believed that any man who did not work with his hands was a gentleman of leisure. The Alabama planter was, and had to be, a man of great energy, good judgment, and diligence. It was a belief that a man who could not successfully manage a plantation or other business should not be intrusted with an official position. One of the most serious objections made by the cotton planters to Jefferson Davis as president was that he had

failed to manage his plantation with success. (See also Somers, *Southern States*, p. 127.)

8. Trowbridge, *The South,* p. 431; reports of General Swayne, December 26, 1865, and January, 1866, in House Executive Document, No. 70, Thirty-ninth Congress, First Session. General Swayne strongly approved the objects of these societies. He said there was not, and never had been, any question of the right of the negro to hold property. Free negroes had held property before the war. The Creoles of Mobile had all the rights of citizens by the treaty of cession of west Florida.

9. Somers, an English traveler, thought that the economic relations of planter and negro were startling, and anywhere else would be absurd. The tenant, he said, was sure of a support and did not much care if the crop failed. Even his taxes, when he condescended to pay any, were paid by his master. For all work outside of his crop he had to be paid, and often he went away and worked for someone else for cash. And his privileges were innumerable. " The soul is often crushed out of labor by penury and oppression. Here a soul cannot begin to be infused into it through the sheer excess of privilege and license with which it is surrounded." — *Southern States since the War,* pp. 128, 129. - My father's tenants, white and black, rented on all systems. The negroes usually began as wage-laborers or as tenants " on halves," for they had no supplies when they came. Then the more industrious and thrifty would save and rent farms for " third and fourth " or for " standing rent." The whites usually attained the highest grade of tenancy, and the average white man would save enough of his earnings to purchase a team, wagon, buggy, farm implements, and a year's supply, and then spend all else, though some would save enough to buy land of their own in cheaper districts, or to support themselves for a year or two while opening up a homestead in the pine woods.

The negro, as a rule, rented " on halves," for he spent all his earnings and required supervision. The average negro stays only a year
or two at one place before he longs for change and removes to
another farm. About Christmas time, or just before, the negroes
and many of the whites begin to move to new homes.

10. In the census each person cultivating a crop is counted as a
farmer and the land he cultivates as a farm. Thus a plantation
might be represented in the census statistics by from five to
twenty-five farms.

11. Note: Any stick is good enough to beat slavery with, so it is
usually stated that slavery was responsible for the wasteful methods
of cultivation that prevailed in the South before the war. That can
be true only indirectly, for the soil always received the worst treatment in the white counties. Like frontiersmen everywhere, the
Alabama white farmers found it easier to clear new land or to
move west than to fertilize worn-out soils. The lack of transportation facilities in the white districts made it impossible to bring in
commercial fertilizers or to transport the crops when made. If
there had not been a negro in the state, the frontier methods would
have prevailed, as they still do among the farmers in some parts of
the West. On the other hand, the rich lands worked by slave labor
were kept in good condition. Under free negro labor they are in
the worst' possible condition. Experience, necessity, the disappear-
ance of free land, and the increase of transportation facilities have
caused the white-county farmer to employ better methods and to
keep up and increase the fertility of his land by using fertilizers. - It
was nearly forty years before the entire cotton crop of the state was
again as large as in 1859. - *Southern Magazine*, January, 1874; *Ku
Klux Report*, Alabama testimony (Lindsay), pp. 206, 207; Somers,
Southern States, p. 117. In i860 it was estimated that of the whole
cotton crop 10 to 12 per cent, was produced by white labor; in

1876 the proportion of whites to blacks in the cotton fields was 30 to 51; in 1883 white labor produced 44 per cent, of the cotton crop; in 1884, 48 per cent. ; in 1885, 50 per cent.; in 1893, 70 per cent. And this was done by the whites on inferior lands. (See W. B. Tillett in *Century*, Vol. XI, p. 771; Hammond, *The Cotton Industry*, pp. 129, 130, 182.) - DeBow estimated that the entire acreage of the cotton crop was as follows: 1836, 2,000,000 acres; 1840, 4,500,000; 1850, 5,000,000; i860, 6,968,- 000. The commissioner of agriculture in 1876 estimated that the acreage in i860 was 13,000,000. Taking this estimate, which, while probably too large, is more nearly correct, only 4 per cent, of the arable land was planted in cotton — the staple crop. (Hammond, *The Cotton Industry*, p. 74.)

12. See also Kelsey, Negro Farmer — a valuable monograph on present conditions in the Black Belt. A pamphlet on cotton published by the Manufacturers' Record shows that conditions in Mississippi are similar. - So poor were the people after the war that, even though the worth of the mineral and timber lands was well known, there was no native capital to develop them, and the lion's share went to outsiders, who bought the lands at tax and mortgage sales during and after the carpet-bag regime. - Slavery or negroes prevented the establishment of manufactures by crowding out a white population capable of carrying on manufactures. The census shows that in 1860 the white districts had a fair proportion of manufactures for a state less than forty years old.

13. Note: The figures for 1860 are based on the hire of an able-bodied negro. The statistics of 1867 are taken from tables of wages prescribed by the Freedmen's Bureau; those for 1867 and 1868 show the decline caused by the worthlessness of the negro laborer. Yet the demand for labor was greater than the supply. In 1860 clothing and rations were also given; in 1866-68, rations and no

clothing. In 1866-68 the currency was inflated, and the wages for 1868 were really much lower. (Hammond, *The Cotton Industry*, p. 124; *Montgomery Mail*, May 16, 1865; *Freedmen's Bureau Reports*, 1865-70.) - "A convention held in Montgomery in 1873 recommended that the share system be abolished and a contract-wage system be inaugurated; wages should be secured by a lien on the employer's crop; separate contracts should be made with each laborer, and the " squad " system abolished. In this way the laborer would not be responsible for bad crops. To aid the laborers, Congress was asked to pass the Sumner Civil Rights Bill providing for the recognition of certain social rights for negroes, to exempt homesteads from taxation, and to increase the tax on property held by speculators. And the President was asked to supply bread and meat to the negro farmers. (*Annual Cyclopadia*, 1873, p. 19; *Tuscaloosa Blade*, November 20, 1873.)

14. Note: The prosperity of a number of large Hebrew commercial houses in Alabama is said to date from the corner groceries of the seventies.- A northern traveler in the Alabama Black Belt in recent years says : " The white population is rapidly on the decrease and the negro population on the increase There are hundreds of the ' old mansion houses ' going to decay, the glass broken in the windows, the doors off the hinges, the siding long unused to paint, the columns of the verandas rotting away, and the bramble thickets encroaching to the very doors. The people have sold their land for what little they could get, and moved to the cities and towns, that they may educate their children and escape the intolerable conditions surrounding them at their old beloved homes These friends have largely gone from the negro's life, and he is left alone in the wilderness," held down by crop liens and mortgages given to the alien. Land rent is half its value; the tenant must purchase from the creditor's store, and raise cotton to pay for what he has already

eaten and worn. (C. C. Smith, *Colonization of Negroes in Central Alabama*, published by the Christian Woman's Board of Missions, Indianapolis, Ind.) - See also Edmonds in Review of Reviews, September, 1900 ; Dillingham in Yale Review, Vol. V, p. 190; Stone, *The Negro in the Yazoo Mississippi Delta*; Dowd in *Gunton's Magazine*, September, 1902 ; Census of 1900, Vol. VI, Part 2, pp. 406-16; *Harper's Monthly*, January, 1874; Grady, ibid., 1881 ; Kelsey, *The Negro Farmer*; Hammond, The Cotton Industry. Another solution to the problem is often suggested, viz., the crowding out of the blacks from the Black Belt by the whites — especially northerners and Germans — who want to cultivate the Black Belt lands, who settle in colonies, and who have no place for the negro in their plans of industrial society. The Black Belt landlords are becoming weary of negro labor and are disposed to make special inducements to get whites to settle in the Black Belt. In Louisiana Italians have on many sugar and cotton plantations replaced negroes. Georgia and Alabama, in order to make the negro work, have recently passed stringent vagrancy laws. There is a general demand for foreigners who will work on the farms and planta-tions. *The Manufacturers' Record* during recent years has published much information in regard to industrial conditions in the southern states ; its articles on immigration are especially inter-esting.

19

The American Negro Academy

This review was first published in the *Southern History Association Publications, IX, in 1905*.

Since its organization in 1897 the *American Negro Academy* of Washington, D. C. , has issued ten numbers of its *Occasional Papers*, as follows: 1. A Review of Hoffman's Race Traits and Tendencies of the American Negro, by Kelly Miller; 2. The Conservation of Races, by W. E. Burghardt DuBois ; 3. Civilization the Primal Need of the Race, and The Attitude of the American Mind toward the Negro Intellect, by Alexander Crummell; 4. A Comparative Study of the Negro Problems, by Charles C. Cook; 5 . How the Black St. Domingo Legion Saved the Patriot Army in the Siege of Savannah, 1779, by T. G. Steward 6. The Disfranchisement of the Negro, by John L. Love; 7. Right on the Scaffold, or the Martyrs of 1822, by Archibald H. Grimke; 8. The Educated Negro and His Mission, by W. S. Scarborough; 9. The Early Negro

Convention Movement, by John W. Cromwell; 10. The Defects of the Negro Church, by Orishatukeh Faduma.

The *Occasional Papers* are of value to all who are interested in the peculiar race problems of America. The writers represent, generally, that large class of educated negroes who hold that Booker T. Washington's gospel of work is not sufficient for the needs of the race. In these essays are set forth the negro's view of race problems as distinguished from the white man's view. Most well read whites are familiar with the doctrines of Tuskegee and Hampton, but it is necessary also to be informed by the other side. The writers in these monographs have no practical suggestions to offer, no expedient compromises to make, but demand theoretical and exact justice for the negro race, but what that justice may be is not clearly defined.

The general characteristics of the series may be noted as follows: (1) When slavery or anything connected with it is mentioned we hear the clank of chains and the cutting swish of the lash; the slaves, we infer, hate the whites with a consuming hatred, and the cruel masters endeavor to crush out the human feelings of the black; attempts at insurrections in which white women and children are to be massacred by wholesale are glorified. (2) There is not the slightest sign of an ability to understand why white people North and South usually consider that Reconstruction was a failure; there is the usual argument of the ballot as a protection, of the public school system being founded in Reconstruction, and of the Rights of Man. Consequently, the later disfranchising movement is believed to be only one manifestation of the peculiar meanness of the Southern people who are believed to be hostile to all that is good for the negro. (3) There is a marked tendency to minimize race distinctions, to treat color as a superficial matter, about equivalent to the difference between a Frenchman and a German. Consequently the white man's belief that there are fundamental differences between the races seems to be rejected. (4) In regard to negro education, it is contended that what is good for the white is good for the black, and hence there should not be one kind of training for the white and another for the black. The real meaning of the work of Armstrong and Washington is not understood. (5) The mental attitude of the whites in America is believed to be hostile to manifestations of intellect by negroes. There is undoubtedly much ignorance regarding negro ability especially as displayed in business enterprise, but no negro who poses as a leader ought to complain of the recognition received. Many a prominent negro would be considered merely ordinary as a white man.

Generally speaking the writers read lessons of hope from the past history of other races; they reject the doctrines of the modern sociologists; and foretell the final ruin of any people or nation that subjects other races. Platitudes and generalities are as common in these papers as in accounts by white men on the same subject. There is a marked self-conscious feeling, which is quite natural. It is manifested for instance in the use of " Mr." by certain of the writers, where a white man would never think of using it in speaking of the white race. There is much display of half assimilated learning and of a wide, but biased acquaintance, with history. The feeling displayed is in but few cases what is considered characteristic of the negro race; it is rather what white men under similar conditions would feel. The writers, trained in the learning of the white race and perhaps mixed in blood, have ceased to be "negroes" of the "negro problem" as usually understood and, in almost all respects save color and prospects, have become "white men," and are hence hardly representative of the black race. This is one of the saddest aspects of the "problem,"-it is really a new "problem. "

To the historian the most interesting papers are Numbers 5, 7, 9 and 10. The one that shows the best race pride and race respect is that of Professor DuBois. The most practical paper is that on the Negro Church presumably written by a native of Africa. They are all valuable to show what the educated, theoretical, negro or mulatto thinks of the negro race and its difficulties. We do not get the impression that these men are doing as much practical work for the negro race as are Washington and Councill. And we shall probably still believe that the better teachings and the saner feeling and the more practical suggestions are found in "Up From Slavery."

20

Review of The Negro and the Nation, by George S. Merriam

Originally published in the December, 1906 **Political Science Quarterly.**

The Negro and the Nation: A History of American Slavery and En-franchisement. By GEORGE S. MERRIAM. New York, Henry Holt & Co., 1906.—436 pp.

This book at once suggests comparison with John C. Reed's *The Brothers' War*, published last year. Both deal with the same subject, the negro influence in American history, and in both the treatment is calm and philosophical, as befits books written by men of wide reading and experience. It must be said that the earlier work is more original, and that it suggests a more judicial temper in its author. Mr. Reed kept his attention fixed upon the negro, while

Mr. Merriam allows politics to hide the colored brother most of the time. Reed treats a hackneyed subject in a new way, exhibiting new facts; Merriam follows old and well-trodden paths to familiar conclusions. Most of his book is devoted to the political history of the controversy over the negro, and this is narrated from the ethical point of view. Though the history in this part of the book is fairly accurate, no real contribution is made to knowledge nor is the philosophy sound and convincing. To the author pro-slavery and anti-slavery are almost the only important forces in our early history; most else seems to hinge upon these. He sees only pro-slavery forces in ante-bellum territorial expansion. In the Kansas troubles the administration side was certainly weak enough, but here it gets no sort of justice. He overlooks the fact, moreover, that the anti-slavery spirit in the South and West was less due to moral convictions than to social and economic instincts.

After showing that the North and South were politically, socially and economically unlike, he declares that secession could not be because the United States was a "nation." His political theories throughout are those of 1861-65. Secession he pronounces "anarchy," seeing only the superficial aspects of the situation and not the social and industrial forces supporting the movement. To the Southerner it was a desperate measure taken mainly to prevent social anarchy. Time has shown, of course, that the South was mistaken; that after all, in spite of war and reconstruction, the Southerner has about all that he seceded and fought for, viz., the relations between the races described by A. H. Stephens in the much misunderstood "corner-stone" speech. In assuming that Stephens's "corner stone" has been knocked out, Mr. Merriam manifests his lack of acquaintance with the practical present aspects of his subject.

On Reconstruction his views are somewhat contradictory. He condemns the radical policy, analyzes at length the shortcomings of the scalawags and carpet-baggers, and then intimates that the minority of leaderless whites might have controlled affairs, had they seen fit to make the effort, by controlling the negroes. This they certainly tried hard to do in several states, but the attempt was defeated by the radicals. Its success was clearly impossible so long as the radicals remained in power. On the "black laws," which he considers iniquitous, he follows Blaine rather than Burgess, although he cites the latter. Evidently he has read none of these laws nor any of the corresponding laws for the whites. It seems also that he is unacquainted with the substitutes of later days. For the facts about Reconstruction Mr. Merriam accepts the testimony of the radical side and rejects that of the other side, even clearing the Ames government in Mississippi on the statements of two carpet-baggers. Following such authorities he naturally finds that most of the deviltry of Reconstruction was on the side of the whites, and that for this there was no justification. He here holds a brief for the reconstructionists. He does not understand why there should have been any fear of " negro domination " after 1876. He shows no knowledge of the manner in which the negroes have been manipulated since that eventful year. In describing the new disfranchising constitutions the objectionable temporary clauses are dealt with as permanent. In short, the entire account of political conditions in the South is superficial and shows a lack of exact information.

The best part of the book will be found in the numerous character sketches of prominent leaders in the nineteenth-century sectional controversies. Of these sketches there are about twenty—from Webster, Clay and Calhoun to Garrison and John Brown. The author's estimates are fair and judicial, in most cases sympathetic, never partisan. Mr. Merriam can understand and describe men much better than the principles they advocate.

The negro in this book is a vague sort of a person, whose main business is to cause a political situation. To "Slavery as it Was " fourteen pages are given—a curious mixture of Harriet Beecher

Stowe, Kemble, Smedes, Olmstead, etc. To Mr. Merriam slavery was sinful and bad for all; freedom therefore must be the opposite. If he will only read the census volumes, he will find that the average free negro has not been as efficient as the average slave. He can learn the same thing by talking to a Black Belt planter or by going over the accounts of a plantation. It is true that the Southern white usually knows little of the upper thousandth of progressive blacks; Mr. Merriam knows only of these, and generalizes accordingly. There is little evidence of any practical knowledge of the various race problems; to Mr. Merriam there are none. Slavery is the scapegoat, and to it and to the failure of the South to hold proper views about it most complications are due. The author's views appear to be those of a man who has read much and seen little of the things about which he reads and writes. Like objections may be made to his conception of the Southern social system. Here again is the old story: aristocracy and poor whites were distinct classes in the ante-bellum system ; the latter was under control of the former, and was "led into revolution," etc. Reasoning from conditions found in Boston or New Haven he finds no cause for the race separation insisted upon in the South. More and more, he says, do the cultured representatives of both races mingle socially in the North, and he informs the South that its position in regard to social separation of the races must be modified. That there are any, real difficulties in the way, any fundamental questions of race, he does not admit.

As to the general tone of the book, it may be said that while the views set forth are those of a generation ago, merely somewhat moderated in their form of statement, yet the author's judgments and expressions of opinion are remarkably free from partisan feeling. It cannot be said that he is sympathetic, for he does not understand; but the kindly intention is always evident, although at times its manifestations are irritatingly patronizing. Considering that the author so seriously endeavors to give an impartial treatment, to maintain a fair attitude, one regrets that he did not see fit to base his work upon a thorough investigation of the subject. For in these days of many books on the race problem, a writer must first be fair-minded in order to write of Southern blacks and whites, and next he ought to be a negro or a Southern white, or one who has at least seen something of these people and their ways. Interest in a problem does not qualify a person to write about it.

21

Review of The Negro Church, W. E. B. DuBois, ed.

Originally published in the December, 1904 **Political Science Quarterly.**

The Negro Church. A Social Study. Made under the direction of Atlanta University by the Atlanta Conference. Edited by W. E. BURGHARDT Du Bois. Atlanta University Press, 1903. — 212 pp.

In this compilation of forty sections are comprehended short accounts of primitive negro religion arid the negro church, a summary statement of missionary work among the negroes in slavery, sketches of noted preachers, church statistics and details regarding the various denominations, studies of local churches-, and criticisms of the character of negro preachers and negro religion of the present. The reports and statistics are from various sources; the historical sketches are by the editor. The local studies, by different persons, are of great value and throw much light upon the condition of the negro church at present. Inquiries made by the conference among negro laymen and Southern whites make it clear that a large proportion of the negro ministers are unfit to be moral leaders — debts, women and drink being the chief stumbling blocks. In many localities the lay pillars of the church are of lax morals. . Young men in the church are few. Divisions in churches and secessions are frequent, especially in the Baptist church. The statistics are drawn principally from the census of 1890, but in some cases have been brought down to date.

The historical sketches by the editor are interesting but a little onesided; the census of 1890 has a fuller and more impartial history of each denomination. The conversion of the negroes to Christianity seems of less importance to the editor than the restrictions upon halfsavage negro congregations. The sketch of early efforts at conversion is principally a summary of the restrictive colonial legislation designed by the whites to crush the pagan practices of the Africans and to regulate the negro preacher, who was then usually the leader in all race troubles. Negro conversion really became general about the end of the eighteenth century, when "the Rights of Man" were believed in, and after the rigid discipline of slavery had partially crushed out heathenism, thus preparing the negro for conversion to Christianity by the enthusiastic Methodists and Baptists, who were then beginning their marvellous expansion. But Mr. Du Bois does not think that the negro needed to be prepared to receive Christianity. His theories and opinions are interesting, especially since they are the exact opposite of those held by the Southern whites. His thesis is that the negro was better off in Africa than in American slavery and that the blacks cannot remain in the same churches with the whites. He maintains: (i) that the negro church is the sole surviving social institution from Africa, that it was heathen but is now Christian, that the African priest, with his vast power, survived in the Christian negro preacher; (2) that slavery destroyed the African family and definite and long-formed political, social and religious habits, that the African polygamous family was a powerful institution, greatly superior to the slave family; (3) that the blacks must have churches separate from the whites because the latter do not, and have never, admitted the negro to a proper participation in church government. The historian of slavery will, on the other hand, assert (i) that slavery forcibly destroyed African superstition and voodoo worship and substituted the Christian religion, that the negro church is a borrowed institution; (2) that there was no family life worthy of the name in Africa and that the negro family, such as it is, was forcibly created in slavery; (3) that the blacks in the white churches served a period of necessary probation, being on exactly the same footing that white children were.

In some way, by 1865 there had come to be hundreds of thousands of negro Christians. Most of these were in Southern white churches, whose work receives scant notice. The fact is overlooked that the most fruitful missionary work among the negroes was done by the Southern churches after 1845 when the Methodist and Baptist denominations in the South drew away from the Northern churches! They were then free to work among the slaves without fear of being suspected as abolitionist agents. Of the separation of the negroes from the white churches Mr. DuBois says little except to bear out his theory that the races cannot get along together in the same church. Of the methods employed by religious carpetbaggers from 1865 to 1870 to force all negroes to leave the Southern white churches, he makes no mention. In reality it was equivalent to martyrdom for a negro to remain faithful to his master's church. The persecution of the Colored Methodist Episcopal Church, consisting of the negroes who tried to remain with the whites, but who yet for their safety had to be organized separately, shows the kind of pressure brought to bear by aliens and by blacks under their control in order to draw the race line in the churches.

Mr. Du Bois's theories and opinions may be correct; they are certainly worthy of attention; but they are not well supported by any known facts, nor by the mass of valuable material here collected by himself and his fellow workers. Indeed the effect of the intermingling of facts and theories in this monograph is somewhat confusing and
contradictory.

22

Review of The Aftermath of Slavery by William Sinclair

Originally published in the June, 1906 **Political Science Quarterly.**

The Aftermath of Slavery. A Study of the Condition and Environment of the American Negro. By WILLIAM A. SINCLAIR. With an introduction by THOMAS WENTWORTH HIGGINSON. Boston, Small, Maynard & Co., 1905.—xiii, 358 pp.

The quality of this book may be appreciated when it is known that the late Edward Atkinson expressed his approval of it, and that Col. T. W. Higginson wrote the introduction; while still more light is thrown upon its general character by the latter's inability to accept some of the extreme positions taken by the author. The volume has but one chapter that justifies the title—chapter viii, on the " Rise and Achievements of the Negro Race, " a valuable summary. The other chapters are almost wholly made up of arguments in favor of political and social privileges for the blacks and of assertions of the extreme moral and political depravity of the Southern whites.

A summary of the main theses of the author will be of use to an understanding of the position of the constantly increasing class of negro agitators: (i) As to slavery, he believes that all the evils of the present "reign of terror and blood " "have their roots in the essential barbarism of the slave system" which was "as black as moral turpitude could make it. " (2) The so-called " Black Codes' of 1865-1866 were the "most barbarous series of laws ever written by a civilized people." (3) There was really no such thing as Reconstruction, as it is generally understood—the Radicals treated the South with a "gracious magnanimity and generosity" and "a lasting and incalculable debt of gratitude" is due to the negroes, carpetbaggers and scalawags for the "orderly governments" and other benefits given by them. (4) "While the white vote of the South has been inimical to the great interests of the country, these have been saved by the colored vote," which " was cast strictly in accordance with good sense, the dictates of humanity, the highest welfare of the republic." . . . "The negro vote saved the country from the follies and crimes of free silver, free trade and free riot," and " it is therefore not too much to say that the glory and the power of the republic . . , may be traced to the effective use of the negro as a soldier and as a voter." (5) " Negro domination " is not and has never been possible. (6) The Southern public school system was founded upon and preserved by the negro vote. (7) The Southern whites are determined to bring about practical reenslavement and many thousand negroes have been slain in the " war against negro suffrage." (8) Negro leaders to be honored and emulated were Nash, Smalls, Pinchback, Cardoza, Elliott, Rainey and Ransier—and so on.

To the student of social problems the book is of great value, not as a repository of facts, for the facts in it are badly warped, but simply as a "human document " which illustrates the feelings and attitude of a large class of those educated negroes, living principally in the Northern and Border states, who, in numbers, probably are to Washington and Councill and their kind as 50 to 1, who oppose what is called the "Washington idea" , who think that the negro's salvation must be in voting with, traveling with, going to school and the theater and dining with whites, who forget the wishes and needs of the masses of the race. These men are not those who make sacrifices for their race, who make things come to pass as do Washington and Councill, who make up the National Negro Business Men's League. As voicing the sentiments, then, of the class of influential negro radicals the book has a distinct value.

23

Review of Problems of the Present South, by Edgar Murphy

Originally published in the March, 1905 **Political Science Quarterly.**

Problems of the Present South. A Discussion of certain of the Educational, Industrial, and Political Issues of the Southern States. By EDGAR GARDNER MURPHY. New York, The Macmillan Co., 1904.—x, 335 pp.

The purpose of the volume under review is, the author states, "to discuss the rise of genuine democracy in the South" — a statement which places him among those persons who hold to the theory that ante-bellum Southern politics were essentially aristocratic or oligarchic, even as concerned the whites. The history of the "hill billy" influence in his own state, Alabama, accords ill with this theory.

413

The discussion of the unifying influence — social and political — of the Civil war and Reconstruction upon the whites is clear and convincing. There is much insistence upon the fact that the "common man" has arrived since the Civil war.

The papers on education in the South are illuminating. The writer holds to the Southern view on all social questions, including the separation of the races in schools. He shows that, in spite of all discouragements, great progress has been made in the education of both races. The education of the negro has been undertaken in good faith by the overburdened Southerners, who are nevertheless lectured occasionally by ignorant Northerners for neglecting the blacks. The often misunderstood "Ogden movement" is proven to be a distinctly Southern movement with an ornamental fringe of Northern financiers. Mr. Murphy makes some sharp and pertinent remarks about Northern criticism of things Southern.

The educational statistics given are like nearly all the statistics of the new educational crusaders—true, but not the whole truth. Why continually harp upon the fact that the school term is only 76 or 78 days, when it is well known that the schools, even the negro schools, are held for a longer period? The 76-day term is that paid for by the state. The most hopeful sign about Southern education is that practically all whites and many blacks willingly contribute by tuition fees to make the school term last six to eight months. The states have not, until recently, given liberally for education; but the people have carried on the schools nevertheless. Mr. Murphy ought to mention the fact.

The negro problem is well handled. The evils of slavery are not emphasized to the neglect of its good. The attitude of the slave holder to the negro in slavery, and later in freedom, is fairly explained. The race problem is to be solved, however, by the joint efforts of the new negro and the new white man, neither of whom understands or cares much for the other. The author dismisses almost without discussion the question of future economic friction between the races. Lynching is denounced — as bad for the white. The tendency of all negroes to shield the black criminal is, we are told, giving way to a disposition to let the law deal with him. Social equality is a dogma not to be discussed, he says; the South has settled that for all time.

In politics, the Reconstruction policies are severely criticised, and recent disfranchisement is defended on the ground of expediency. Mr. Murphy discloses his lack of practical experience in politics by saying, almost hysterically, that for twenty years there has been no danger of negro domination in Southern politics under any circumstances. He thinks that the attitude of the whites makes the negro vote solid. In his own state within recent years there have been instances of negro domination. The Democrats went over in a body to the Populists to prevent it. For twenty-five years the negro voters stood ready, under their few white leaders, to take advantage of any division among the whites. That is why they were disfranchised.

The wonderful industrial growth of the South is proved by reliable statistics. Mr. Murphy has the art of making statistics interesting. Unlike most recent writers, he goes back to ante-bellum days to find the beginnings of Southern manufacturing. The Civil war destroyed many promising Southern industries. The child-labor evil in Southern factories is blamed upon New England capitalists who have mills in the South and who use their influence to defeat restrictive legislation. But is it not somewhat childish to call upon the conscience of New England to frown upon her capitalists and thus relieve the Southern children? Why cannot Southern public opinion be brought to bear upon the Georgia and Alabama lawmakers who were controlled by the New England mill owners?

All in all the book is a good one — packed with useful information concerning the South both past and present. It is written in an admirable spirit, in rather rhetorical language, by a Southern

Episcopal minister whose very calling and station place him on the "outside" of the real life of the mass of the people. For Mr. Murphy, like so many of the best men, is not and has never been on the "inside" in regard to the crude social and political conditions in the South. He speaks for the old ruling, responsible element, the slave holders and their spiritual descendants; for the leaders of to-day, not for the followers. The followers in the South have more than once forced the leaders to "about face."

24

Review of The Domestic Slave Trade of the Southern States, by Winfield Collins

Originally published in the September, 1906 **Political Science Quarterly.**

The Domestic Slave Trade of the Southern States. By WINFIELD H. COLLINS. New York, Broadway Publishing Co., 1904.—154 PP

In seven short chapters the author of the monograph under review discusses the following topics: the foreign slave trade of America; the development and extent of the domestic slave trade; the kidnapping of free negroes; the breeding of negroes for sale, and the state laws relating to the domestic slave trade. The book is based mainly upon the accounts of anti-slavery travelers and the material collected by the *Liberator* relating to the slave trade. The value of much of this material is extremely doubtful, but Mr. Collins seems to have been aware of this, and his judgment has saved him from the absurdities usually committed by those, who endeavor to write from such sources. Sometimes the statistics' given are conflicting, and no attempt is made to explain the variations. The census statistics, however, are used to. good effect. There are numerous typographical errors, and often names of authors and books are given incorrectly.

The causes of the development of the domestic slave trade are clearly set forth. These were the abolition of the foreign slave trade, expansion to the West, the growth of the cotton industry and the industrial decay of the border slave states. Before 1820 the trade was of slight extent. Between 1820 and 1830 the selling states were Virginia, Maryland, Delaware, North Carolina, Kentucky and the District of Columbia. During the next ten years South Carolina and Missouri were added to the list of selling states. ' Slavery was thus pursuing its natural and inevitable course toward extinction in the border states. It is a fact worth noting that nearly all the slave states before the thirties and forties had stringent laws against the importation of slaves for sale. These laws were repealed by the buying states as the cotton plant spread over the South and abolition agitation over the North, but several of the slave states had prohibitive laws until the last.

The discussion of the extent of the slave trade is of particular interest. After a study of the census statistics the author comes to the conclusion that between 1820 and 1860, 735,000 slaves were carried to the lower South from the border states, and of these 296,000 were sold, the remainder being carried by immigrating owners. The decade 1820-1840 was the period of greatest trade, the sales averaging 10,600 per year. A noticeable fact is the great difference between the price of slaves in the border states and in the lower South. Any slave trader could soon make a fortune.

Mr. Collins disposes of the tradition about the breeding of slaves in the border states for sale to the South. In the first place it would not pay—a good five-year-old horse was worth as much as an eighteen year-old negro and cost less per year to keep up. Secondly, had the selling states been breeding for sale, the census should show a larger proportion of children to adults in these states (since the slaves sold were usually adults) than in the buying states. The census shows the reverse is true. The fact is only a part of the surplus increase was sold South. The planter in the border states had more slaves than he knew what to do with—he was often eaten out of house and home by them. There was no profitable work for them to do. John Randolph predicted that the time would come when the "masters would run away from the slaves and be advertised by them in the public papers." Several important points, in this connection, are left undeveloped; but on the whole, the discussion of the economic and social hindrances to the breeding of slaves for the market is quite satisfactory.

25

Review of The Political History of Virginia During the Reconstruction by Hamilton Eckenrode

Originally published in the March, 1905 **Political Science Quarterly.**

The Political History of Virginia during the Reconstruction. By HAMILTON JAMES ECKENRODE. Johns Hopkins University Studies in Historical and Political Science, series xxii, nos. 6, 7, 8. Baltimore, The Johns Hopkins University Press, 1904.—128 pp.

This latest monograph on the period of Reconstruction traces the steps by which Virginia was brought back into the Union. Beginning with the revolt of Virginia's western counties in 1861, the author briefly describes the erection of the "reorganized government of Virginia" under Pierpont, its career in western Virginia and at Alexandria, the formation of the new state of West Virginia, and the situation at the close of the war. Succeeding chapters outline the political activities in Virginia under the plans of Johnson and of Congress, the political influence of the Freedmen's Bureau and the Union League, the convention of 1868, and the restoration of the state in 1870.

The position of Virginia in 1865 was in some respects unlike that of other southern states. No provisional government was set up. According to the logic of the situation, Virginia should have been restored when Pierpont moved to Richmond; but Pierpont's government was not sufficiently radical to suit Congress. With few exceptions it was made up originally of northern men; but the latter were overwhelmed by the native whites, as a result of the amnesty proclamation of May 29, 1865, and the nature of the provisional government changed. It fell into the hands of moderates, while its former radical supporters now became more radical, hostile to the state government and friendly toward negro suffrage, which alone would return them to power.

Clearly and concisely the author describes the political development from 1865 to 1870: the gradual formation of two parties, the one radical, based on the support of the blacks, the other conservative, and opposed to the political equality of the blacks; the division in the Republican ranks between extreme radicals and moderates; the attempt and failure of the old Whigs to influence the negroes; the reaction against the radical program and the fusion of the conservatives and the moderates of both parties, resulting in the restoration of the state. There is no account of the social and economic aspects of the Reconstruction: only its superficial political features are described. Some statements
and conclusions of the author are worthy of note. He shows that

the Republican party in the state was opposed to negro suffrage as long as it seemed possible to disfranchise the mass of the whites. He answers the wearisome question, why the respectable whites did not try to control the negro voters instead of leaving them to unscrupulous aliens, by showing that a serious attempt was made to do this, and that it was repulsed with scorn by the blacks, who at the very beginning had fallen under outside control. It was generally believed that the former owners would control the blacks; but the latter were rendered suspicious and independent of the whites by the Freedmen's Bureau, while the Union League united them in a strong political organization and taught them to hate and fear the whites.

The radical leaders succeeded so well that to the convention of 1868, composed of 95 delegates, a solid negro vote sent 72 delegates, pledged to radical policies. Of these, 24 were negroes, 13 were native whites, and the rest were carpet-baggers. Though the negro failed to secure social-equality legislation, the constitution contained sweeping provisions for disfranchisement of whites. The radical nature of this instrument, the lack of funds, the proximity of the state to Washington, which rendered misgovernment too visible, and the fact that the vote of Virginia was not needed to elect the president, caused the authorities to defer the vote on the constitution until a more favorable time, and the worst provisions were then voted down. But there was carpet-bag government in 1868 and 1869 under the provisional regime, Congress having decreed that all officials must take the " iron-clad test oath." Of course few decent people could take it.

On some matters the author's theories and opinions may be criticised. If party distinctions had faded out in Virginia in 1865, then Virginia was unlike other southern states. Too much importance is ascribed to the effect on Congress of the state legislation affecting freedmen. The views accepted are those of Mr. Blaine and others who were searching for excuses for the course of Congress. Congress had decided to reject the president's plan before the so-called " black laws" were passed. They served later as convenient excuses for what had been done. The laws, with few exceptions, were timely and sensible, and in substance had long been and still are on the statute books of most of the states of the Union. It is also a mistake to attribute any great importance to the adverse testimony of the Virginia witnesses who came before the Committee on Reconstruction. The committee was in quest of testimony to support a course already decided upon, and the witnesses were carefully selected with that end in view. Again, the author is wrong in ascribing to the northern people generally an enthusiasm for the rights of man and an acceptance of the doctrine of the social and political equality of the races. Reconstruction was only partially due to humanitarian motives; it was for the most part cold-blooded, practical politics. Moreover, in view of the state of politics at that time, it was not necessary to criticise Virginia for refusing to ratify the Fourteenth Amendment. To have done so would have added another humiliation. Further, popular education is a partial success in Virginia, not because of, but in spite of, the reconstructionists. As to the results of Reconstruction, the author accepts the apologetic view that it secured the negro's personal freedom, his economic independence, and his right to vote and to educate his children. Exactly how this was done we are not told. It is not correct to look upon the recent disfranchisement movement as entirely opposed to the political rights of the negro; it is more correct to say that in the new constitutions the whites for the first time freely admit the right of the capable black men, distinguishing these from the unfit, and thus recognize negro suffrage.

On the whole, Mr. Eckenrode has produced a good account of politics in Virginia during Reconstruction; but in interpreting the facts he is too much influenced by the memoir writers and the apologists.

26

Review of History of the United States from the Compromise of 1850, by James Ford Rhodes

Originally published in the September, 1906 **Political Science Quarterly.**

History of the United States from the Compromise of 1850. By JAMES FORD RHODES, LL.D., Litt. D. Vol. V, 1864-1866. New York, The Macmillan Company, 1904.

In the last appeal of the Confederate Congress to the southern people to rally against the invader is the significant, though somewhat ludicrous, sentence : "Failure [to maintain independence] will compel us to drink the cup of humiliation even to the bitter dregs of having the history of our struggle written by New England historians." And surely in the forty years that have elapsed since that appeal the worst fears of the Confederates in regard to biased history-writing have been realized. However, in the volumes of Mr. Rhodes there are few statements of fact or expressions of opinion to which the southerners of that day or of this would object. The fifth volume, which has recently appeared and which covers the period of the most bitter memories, is no exception to the general rule. The first three chapters are devoted to Sherman's campaigns in Georgia and Carolina, ending with the surrender of Johnson, the disastrous Tennessee expedition of Hood, the Hampton Roads conference, the last campaign of Grant, and the surrender of Lee, a discussion of numbers and losses of the combatants, and a statement of the beginnings of Reconstruction under Lincoln. Other chapters relate to the treatment of prisoners of war, life in the North and in the South during the conflict, and finally the process of Reconstruction is traced down to the fall elections of 1866.

In his account of Sherman's march through Georgia and South Carolina, Mr. Rhodes makes it plain that he has no sympathy with the later northern policy of making the war cruel toward non combatants, but, nevertheless, he lets Sherman off very lightly, and some of the more serious aspects of the destruction wrought by him are not touched upon. A few lines tell of the destruction of Atlanta, and no mention is made of the expulsion of its population. The facts in regard to the wholesale pillage and destruction by Sherman's army are clearly set forth, but seemingly without a realization of the hideous suffering thereby caused among the helpless non-combatant population. Rather is it Sherman's view of " a vast holiday frolic" that is accepted. Too much credit is given to the various commanders for their good intentions as expressed in general orders, which were cheerfully neglected by the soldiers, and when blame must be given it is placed upon "bummers" and "stragglers." It will be news to those who lived in the line of march that mistreatment of women and murder were almost unknown. A more exhaustive examination of local southern authorities would have furnished some necessary supplementary facts. And likewise, in regard to the burning of Columbia, no one will care to criticise Mr. Rhodes's impartial attitude toward the question, but here again his habit of preferring to develop his account mainly from northern sources results in a cumulation of facts that do not seem to justify his conclusions. In other words, the author's conclusions are more unbiased than is warranted by the evidence presented. Again it is sometimes difficult to ascertain just how the author wants his reader to accept a certain set of facts and what conclusion is to be drawn. This is often caused by his inserting a quotation where an evaluation of his own is to be expected. But when it comes to such characters as Butler and Kilpatrick, there is no doubt as to the author's estimate.

In discussing the peace movement in 1864-1865 resulting in the Hampton Roads conference, Mr. Rhodes seems to get glimpses of the fact that the southerners were not fighting altogether for the privilege of owning negroes. It is not fair at this late day to intimate, as the author does, that Davis was stubborn and selfish in continuing the war to the end. In this course he was supported by all really responsible persons, most of whom, however, foresaw defeat—and here is a fact for historians to explain though it is very clear to most southern people. Davis is said to have "misconstrued sadly" Lincoln's procedure by considering the emancipation proclamation to be an incitement to slave insurrection. In this Davis only represented the general southern opinion and also a considerable northern opinion, and with all respect to Mr. Rhodes and the Lincoln legend, may it not be said that on January 1, 1863, the welfare of the southern whites was not under consideration at Washington? The opinion expressed that Grant in his final operations outgeneraled Lee is open to criticism. Conditions were too unequal for comparison. Almost any of us could have caught Lee in 1865. If Grant was a better general than Lee he proved it before the final campaign. The author accepts the estimates of Colonel Livermore as to the numbers enlisted in the Federal and Confederate armies. The exact number of enlistments in the Federal army is known; the number of enlistments in the Confederate army is not known. But by using the census, the War Records, and the enrollment laws Livermore arrives at an estimate of the Confederate forces, as being two-thirds those of the Federals when both are reduced to a three-year basis. But there are serious objections to Livermore's method, (i) Even with the Federal enlistments there is no evidence as to the number of different individuals who. made up the entire number of enlistments; many individuals enlisted more than once; hundreds of organizations were in service only a few months. (2) Likewise, in the Confederate army the number of enlistments and the number of individuals who bore arms have very slight relation to one another. On account of the multiplication of enlistments, the varying lengths of terms of service and the lack of records, there is not sufficient evidence on which to base a reduction to three years' service. In no two southern states were conditions similar; a rule that will hold for one state fails in another. (3) Livermore's estimates assume the reliability of the southern governors' estimates, the perfection of the conscript service, the possibility of getting out for service the men called for by the census, the enforcement of reserve and militia laws,, the uniform size of regiments, and other" theoretical possibilities. But it is notorious that the southern governors, like some northern governors, exaggerated the size of the quotas from their respective states, always counting an enlistment as a man (and some enlisted five times); the conscript laws were useful to cause people to volunteer, but otherwise were regarded only in the breaking; the laws regarding recruitment and formation of new regiments were not obeyed, eighteen regiments in Alabama alone being formed in violation of the conscript laws; the regiments in Virginia were larger than in the West, and in neither army was there uniformity; and the reserve and militia existed only on paper. As late as 1865 the Confederate authorities hopefully scanned the census columns after the method of Livermore, but they were unable to get the men the census said should be available. The estimates are based on evidence that will give the theoretically possible numbers; they should be modified by an examination of the material in each state, which will show the practical difficulties in the way of getting out the full military strength. It is quite likely that estimates of the northern forces should be modified in the same way, to get at the number of real soldiers. The proportion of actual fighting men is probably about correct as Livermore gives it. The present reviewer has made a careful investigation of the local records of two southern states and is convinced that the theoretical statistics must be cut down by about one-third. A bit of negative testimony is the fact that the local orators on Confederate Memorial Days in their wildest estimates of the troops furnished by their respective states do not surpass Livermore's figures. Livermore's estimates are prettily worked out; but the reasoning reminds one of that ante-bellum mathematical military prophecy based on Bible texts and entitled Armageddon.

As to the treatment of prisoners of war Mr. Rhodes's verdict is that there was " no deliberate intention on either side to maltreat prisoners," and that the North has no reason to reproach the South. He accepts the statistics of General Ainsworth in regard to the numbers of prisoners and deaths on each side. The causes and extent of suffering in southern prisons are discussed with good temper and fairness, but it is not quite so clear why prisoners suffered so much in the North. On the whole, from the evidence adduced by Mr. Rhodes, we may conclude that the Confederates, considering their difficulties, exerted greater efforts to care for prisoners. The case of six hundred Confederate prisoners exposed on Morris Island, S. C, to the fire of their own comrades is not mentioned. We should like to know more about the reasons for the execution of Wirz.

In the chapters on life in the North and in the South is given the first well-rounded treatment of social and economic conditions among the people at home during the years of strife. For the South the work has been partially done before; not so much for the North. In the South, the author concludes, the press was freer than in the North; there was less interference by the government with individual liberty, less political persecution and fewer political arrests. In the South, too, popular opinion sustained the government more unanimously, and the officials did not enjoy the use of despotic power as did Seward and Stanton, who were not so, well supported by public opinion as the southern leaders. The North was " a dictatorship " and the South " a grand, socialized state," is the comment of Mr. Rhodes, based, perhaps, as to the South, too much upon the evidence of official documents. These latter also lead him to infer that the Confederate administration in the states, especially the conscript service, was efficient, when in reality it was from beginning to end miserably inefficient. Public opinion, however, took to a certain extent the place of a strong central administration. Most men of ability went into the army, and the civil service suffered. Yet, as the author says, the Confederate Congress showed much political capacity and was not as subservient to Davis as is usually believed; the departments were well conducted, and the state governors were of fair ability. In comparing the northern and southern leaders well balanced character sketches illustrate the prominent traits of great opponents: Lincoln and Davis, Stanton, Benjamin, Campbell, Grant and Sherman, and the Reconstruction leaders Stevens, Fessenden and Trumbull.

The treatment of Reconstruction is confined principally to the Washington side of it. Some points of interest freshly brought out may be mentioned : the bitter sermons from northern pulpits after

Lincoln's murder; the feeling of relief felt by radicals when Johnson came to the presidency with violent threats; the idea of the blacks about freedom; and the plans of the radicals for the blacks. Mr. Rhodes inclines to the view that Lincoln could have carried through a moderate reconstruction but that Johnson on account of untactful conduct was mainly responsible for turning matters over to the radicals. There is a good but too short account of conditions in the South; a more detailed account of the " Black Laws " which are so much in controversy would have been useful. The behavior of Johnson in the campaign of 1866 is treated without mercy. Nothing is said of Stanton's manipulation in the affair of the New Orleans riot, and Sheridan's account is accepted. Not all will agree that the Fourteenth Amendment was " magnanimous " or that Stephens and Lee should be enfranchised while Davis was proscribed.

In summing up it may be said that the history of Mr. Rhodes, while as fair and judicial as any American can now make it, is distinctly from the northern standpoint; that there is the intent, usually successful, to treat the other side with fairness, though a sympathetic treatment of both sides is naturally impossible at present; that in examining evidence the author confines himself closely to that in favor of the northern contention. Mr. Rhodes is not misled by the partisan nature of the evidence examined ; yet it is not always clear that his treatment of material leads one up to the liberal and unbiased conclusions usually arrived at. In other words, his judgments on matters of controversy are as a rule more favorable to the southerners than the presentment of facts seems to warrant. If the southern view of the various controversies were more plainly set forth against the northern view, then the reader would have the satisfaction of following the author to his conclusions. As it is, there are those who will think the author too moderate in some respects. As a whole, the book is far superior in liberality to anything that has yet been written and the average southern sympathizer will probably be better pleased with it than the average northern man. It is to be hoped that the fine spirit and admirable temper shown in this work will have definite results in correcting the bias of the average school histories, the most potent agencies for perpetuating sectional misunderstandings.

27

Review of A History of the United States Since the Civil War, by Ellis Oberholtzer

Originally published in the October, 1927 **American Historical Review.**

A History of the United States Since the Civil War, by ELLIS PAXTON OBERHOLTZER. Vol. III (New York: MacMillan, 1926. Pp. x-529.)

Mr. Oberholtzer's lively third volume covers the years 1872 - 1878 and through eight chapters deals in characteristic fashion with the rise of opposition to the administration President Grant, culminating in the bizarre Greeley campaign, the decline and fall carpetbagger in the South, the continuance of evil conditions in national affairs under the domination of the surviving radical leaders, the Hayes-Tilden campaign, and the beginnings of the Hayes administration. Somewhat from the main account, an informing chapter on the West tells the story of the expansion of the cattlemen, the gold-hunters, and the farmers and the fate of the Indians hemmed in by the whites and starved under the guardianship of the Indian Bureau. The lonely last chapter is not a record of badness but changes to the pleasanter subjects of letters and art.

The author, as is his custom, makes much use of newspapers, pamphlets, public documents, biographical material, political party pronouncements, and the manuscript collections in the Library of Congress. Deliberately or otherwise he avoids following the path opened by Dunning and Rhodes but he examines the same problems from different angles. As a result there is an appearance of superficiality in this account as compared with those of the writers mentioned. There is little moralizing, there are no ponderous judgements as in Rhodes and little keen characterization as in Dunning. And project that not enough attention is devoted to the constructive economic and social forces in American life were preparing the way for a more genuine reconstruction. For the most part this volume is a long record of bad government and corruption in all parts of the country, of conditions brought about by the rather complete breakdown of administration under an honest but naïve and politically incompetent chief executive. It is a clear and vivid account of the strong fight made by able radical leaders to continue against Rising opposition the Congressional domination of the national government which began in 1866 the gradually decreasing scrupulousness this leadership.

The outstanding features of the book are the exposures of "Grantism", the descriptions of the Greeley fiasco, the account of the efforts of Hayes to bring about reform within his party, and the portraits, some of them slightly dim and in the rogues gallery, of the major and minor personages in public life. Mr. Oberholtzer shows that the disorder in public life was to not only to the upheaval following the Civil War but also to the fact that the president was but a simple honest soldier, ignorant of politics, uncritically loyal to his curious friends and to his needy relatives, and possessed of an inferiority- complex which made him intolerant of the proper sort of advisors and associates. With a pathetic admiration of business success or its appearance he was easily swayed by the attention and flattery of rich men and their representatives but had an instinctive aversion to leaders of the type of Schurz or Bristow. In time he came to be almost inaccessible except to the representatives of the corrupt forces in government and politics.

But while Mr. Oberholtzer, easily and with some evident pleasure in the job, shows that Grant was unfit to be President, no less enthusiastically does he prove that Greeley was even less fit. The campaign Of 1872 offered a sorry choice to American voters.

Turning to Hayes, Oberholtzer, opening another window, lets a cleaner breeze blow through the muck of public life. Coming in when national disgrace had reached its lowest depths, Hayes worked slowly along some lines, more rapidly in other ways, in effecting constructive reforms, and, though compromising in smaller things, break with half his party in order to carry out the "understanding of 1876". It is an amazing picture to us in this volume, when idealism and sentimentality, honesty and patriotism are harnessed for so long to the chariot of realism, selfishness, and corruption.

Although is exhibited of sounder political thinking and acting, which however is only by slow degrees effective, the evaluation of other strong forces of economic and social convalescence and progress plainly lies outside the plan of the volume. This account of the dreary closing years of the ten-year period of 'reconstruction", when the best of statesmanship was demanded and only low partisanship was available, would leave the reader with a disagreeable taste did not Mr. Oberholtzer oblige with a pleasant draught at the end when he briefly sketches the state of art and letters, of colleges and universities, of great newspapers and monthly magazines. These are better indications of the true American spirit than are the Indian Bureau, the District of Columbia ring, and the work of the Joint Committee on Reconstruction.

28

Review of Reconstruction in North Carolina by J. G. Hamilton

Originally published in the July, 1907 **American Historical Review.**

Reconstruction in North Carolina. By J. G. DE ROULHAC HAM-
ILTON. (Raleigh, N. C.: Edwards and Broughton. 1906.)

This work under review is the latest published result of those investigations in the field of Reconstruction history which were begun some years ago under the direction of Professor Dunning of Columbia University. If carried to completion Dr. Hamilton's promises to be one of the most useful of those studies. In North Carolina as in other Southern states the Reconstruction can be explained only after an examination of ante-bellum and Civil War conditions, so in this work Dr. Hamilton has first given a summary of political conditions before 1865, with special reference to the development of the secession movement and to the rise of a peace party during the war. The second chapter is devoted to an account of the two attempts at reconstruction during the war—one by natives from within, the other an attempt by President Lincoln to set up the Stanley government. Social and economic conditions at the close of the war are also described in order to complete the background of the Reconstruction. The remainder of the book is devoted to a detailed history of the " Johnson "government, its overthrow by Congress, and the inauguration of the new regime under the Reconstruction Acts. The volume closes with the second coming into power of Governor W. W. Holden in 1868, leaving for later treatment the working out in North Carolina of the congressional plan of Reconstruction.

In making this study the author has evidently exhausted the material relating to his subject. He has used not only the stock sources, but it seems that he has made an examination of practically all of the newspapers of the state, and of the manuscript archives of the state—a source that none of those who have previously worked in the Reconstruction field have been able to explore. To the reviewer it appears that the use of these sources has been careful and the interpretation judicious. The material has been digested and condensed in order to avoid overloading the text with details. A more extended use of the correspondence in the better Northern newspapers would have given sidelights upon conditions in North Carolina that could not be had from local newspapers.

A work of this kind must, of course, go again over ground already partially explored by previous workers on similar subjects. The marked originality of Dr. Hamilton's treatment consists in its being an account of affairs in North Carolina, a state of the Upper South which had its own peculiar problems, distinct from those of the Lower South which have been already described. In North

Carolina the problem of the negro, for instance, was far from being as grave as in the Lower South. This allows other factors to become more important and makes possible a marked political division of the whites before, during, and after the war. Dr. Hamilton does his best work in his treatment of the shifting of political parties and leaders during the decade before 1868. A similar work must be performed for each other reconstructed state before a clear understanding of Reconstruction and of present politics can be had.

Some points are worthy of special mention: the author emphasizes the continuing influences of the ante-bellum rivalry of the Whig and Democrat: the curious fact is clearly brought out that some of the radical secessionist leaders not only soon wanted peace, but later strongly opposed negro suffrage and finally became leaders of the negro party – W. W. Holden of North Carolina and F. J. Moses of South Carolina are types; the conservatives, largely Whigs, effected secession at the last, fought the war, formed the "Johnson" governments, and later organized the Democratic party – so that in North Carolina even more than in other Southern states the present Democratic party rests on a Whig foundation.

In criticism of the work little can be said. The influence of secret societies in forming the negro party was, as the author says, important, yet this point is not developed; in discussing the number of North Carolina troops in the Confederate army (p.35) the total enrollment is given, not the number of individuals; and since there was such a close relation between the number of negroes in a community and the politics of the whites in that locality, it would have been well if the author had shown more clearly the differences between the black and the white counties, especially since the geographic, social, and political sectionalism of North Carolina was more complicated than that in other Southern states. However, it is possible that in the second volume these matters are to be dealt with, and the neglect of them in this volume does not prevent it from being the most useful treatment of state politics during this period.

29

Review of The Influence of Reconstruction on Education in the South by Edgar Wallace Knight

Originally published in the March, 1915 **Mississippi Valley Historical Review.**

The Influence of Reconstruction on Education in the South. By Edgar Wallace Knight, (New York: Teachers College, Columbia University, 1913.)

We are told by one school of historians that public education in the southern states was inaugurated by the locally much despised carpetbag and Negro governments of the reconstruction period; by others we are assured that the reconstruction school policies accomplished no permanent results except bad ones. Which view is correct? Is either wholly correct? Mr. Knight, the author of this book, undertakes to answer these questions for North Carolina and South Carolina, which are taken as typical southern states.

In order to arrive at a proper estimate of the educational system of reconstruction the author makes a comparative study of ante-bellum and post-bellum conditions in each state. In North Carolina, in spite of the sparseness and poverty of the population, there was a steady development of a public school system, with public opinion more and more strongly favoring it until, according to the testimony in 1869 of the carpetbag superintendent of education, "North Carolina had a creditable system of common schools at the outbreak of the Civil War." There were then 2,834 tax supported schools in 79 counties in which were enrolled 108,938 children out of a total of 186,174 children of school age.

The system was strong enough to last through the Civil War. The school term was longer in 1860 than it was again before 1900 and the salaries paid were better than those of reconstruction. The authors of the reconstruction system of education in North Carolina were, as in other states, anxious to use the schools for the purpose of inculcating their peculiar principles into the young confederates and the freedmen. This attitude, though translated into action in but few instances, was the principal cause of the practical failure of the carpetbag educational system in North Carolina. The question of mixed schools was wrangled over but never settled; the work of the freedmen's bureau schools (1865-1867) for Negroes had caused hostility to Negro education; the character of the carpetbag school officials was not always above criticism; there was such a waste of public funds by the party in power that communities feared to vote taxes for schools - these were the conditions that hindered the development of the schools. In general the reconstruction system in North Carolina was much inferior to that of earlier days. In 1870 only about one-fourth of the white children and one-half of the blacks were in school and in 1874 about one-third of the whites and one-fourth of the blacks. Teachers were paid less, the terms were shorter, and the schools were less efficient. The constitutional and legal provisions for education were about the same as before the war, except that blacks were admitted to the schools. After the adoption of a new constitution in 1879 there was progress.

In South Carolina early conditions were different. There was statutory but not constitutional provision for "free" schools from 1811 onward, but the ante-bellum system was ruined by the custom of giving preference in the schools to poor children and thus fixing the character of the schools as "pauper" institutions. In 1814 there were 225 public schools and in 1860 only 1,270. Much money had been spent with but slight results. Undoubtedly the worst hindrance to the development of public schools in the South before the war was this "pauper," "charity," "beneficiary" notion which spread out over the South from Virginia and South Carolina to check the sounder views of the North Carolinians.

The carpetbag system in South Carolina was based upon adequate legislation but the school authorities were corrupt and intolerant. They proceeded upon the principle that the children of both races should mingle in the schools, and thus the whites were driven out. South Carolina College was opened to Negroes and soon was forced to close its doors to all. Other higher schools met the same fate. Appropriations though large did not reach the schools but stopped in the pockets of some of the "statesmen." In 1872 nearly all schools were closed. The reconstruction schools of South Carolina were worse than those of antebellum days, poor as those were.

Appended to this detailed account of North Carolina and South Carolina are notes and statistics relating to the school systems of the other southern states, showing that each had an organized system before 1860. In each state the laws were somewhat expanded after the war and provision made for Negroes. There was much corruption among officials and irritation of the races. There was a general increase of salaries and of officials but the schools everywhere received less money than before 1860. The schools were in general distinctly inferior to the old schools and in many places purposely made unacceptable to the whites. There was in consequence a rapid development of private schools, which in recent days have somewhat hindered the development of public schools. There is reason to believe that a school system under the control of the native whites after 1867 would have made more progress.

In this book Mr. Knight has written an interesting and valuable introduction to a study which he or another must complete -a thorough working out of the educational aspects of the reconstruction. This and other books on the subject are based too much upon statutes, constitutions, and official documents. Not enough attention is given to the actual working out of the reconstruction plan over the southern states, to the use of the schools as a political instrument, to the reaction of this upon politics, to the effect upon popular opinion in regard to public education and particularly in regard to Negro education. It is this aspect of reconstruction as much as the political revolution that made the "Solid South."

30

<hr>

Review of American Civilization and the Negro. The Afro-American in Relation to National Progress, by C. V. Roman

Originally published in the March, 1917 **Mississippi Valley Historical Review.**

American Civilization and the Negro. The Afro-American Relation to National Progress, by C. V. Roman. (Philadelphia: F. A. Davis Co., 1917).

The aim of this book, so the author says, is "to show that humanity is one in vices and virtues as well as blood; that the laws of evolution apply equally to all; that there are no lethal diseases peculiar to the American negro; that there are no vices peculiar to the African; that there are no cardinal virtues peculiar to the European; that we are *all* sinners and have come short of the glories of civilization." In order to prove this rather comprehensive thesis the writer draws his evidence from the pages of history and from results of many scientific investigations. Quite naturally he rests heavily upon medical science for much of his support, but throughout the work there is evidence of his wide familiarity with the field of history and sociology. Dr. Roman's convictions are strong but are stated in moderate language and his exposition is always good tempered, a rare quality in a book which deals with the race question. He everywhere shows an understanding and an appreciation of the attitude of the liberal whites and wastes but little time upon the radical views of such as Vardaman and Dixon.

The book opens with an application of biological tests to the race problem. There is next a comparative study of the morals of black and white with illustrations drawn from history which are quite effective. In other chapters he deals with racial fusion, the variations of types in the negro race, and the effect of American slavery upon the negro. The latter part of the work is given to discussions of the negro as a freeman, his relations with the whites, the material and intellectual progress of the race, and the influence of the American environment. Some interesting appendices and a glossary of technical terms close the work.

Civilization is an evolution, the author says, and he never gets far away from this principle. The white race has developed from lower stages; the negro can do and is doing likewise. "Science knows no innately superior race;" the morals of the negro of recent times are much like the morals of the whites in earlier stages of civilization, and the neg-roes are improving as fast as the whites did. Dr. Roman invites comparison with the serfs of Russia who have evidently made slower progress than the negroes who were emancipated about the same time. Among the propositions advanced by the author, accompanied by more or less adequate proofs, the following are interesting: slavery ended be cause of economic failure - not because of moral influences; the negro is the only colored race that can get along with the white man; there is no adequate reason for believing that skull dimensions and facial angles mean anything, nor can it be proved that essential differences are due to the mingling of blood; there is no such thing as a typical American negro, for there is as much variation in the black race as among the whites.

The author is a firm believer in the necessity of race pride and individual self-respect. " The negro ashamed of his blood is a nuisance; neither God nor man has yet found any use for a man ashamed of his race." Consequently he thinks that harm was done by those enthusiastic post-bellum missionaries who almost persuaded many negroes that they were, for all practical purposes, white. " The white man is right when he insists that a black man cannot be a white man, but wrong when he insists that *all* men are white. The Negro who does not accept the first proposition is a fool; but the Negro who accepts the second is both a fool and a menace." It is evident that the author has no respect for race fusion as a solution of the race problem.

There is in this work very little of the conventional belaboring of slavery and glorification of the reconstruction. Exception, however, may be taken to the statement that in the gulf states it was cheaper to work a slave to death than to treat him decently and to the credit given to the educational system of reconstruction. Emancipation succeeded, he says, "because it was accepted in good faith by the slave holders" but "enfranchisement and reconstruction [failed because] they were not accepted in good faith and were never fairly tried."

A proper solution of the problem will result finally, Dr. Roman believes, in a racial comity, a bi-racial democracy. There will be no con fusion of the "rights of life with privilege of place." The negro will work with, not against, the white man and he will expect the latter not to fear him, but to be just and sympathetic, to concede to him the right to stay on the earth, " to cease parading universal human failures as peculiar negro vices," and to aid him in his evolution toward the standards already achieved by the whites.

31

Review of History of Public School Education in Alabama and The History of Public School Education in Arkansas, by Stephen B. Weeks

Originally published in the June, 1916 **Mississippi Valley Historical Review.**

The History of Public School Education in Alabama and *The History of Public School Education in Arkansas* by Stephen B. Weeks. (Washington: Government Printing Office, 1915 and 1912).

With these monographs on education in the southern states the United States bureau of education begins the publication of a new series. The commissioner of education states that as a result of the rapid development of education in the southern states the need has been felt for historical accounts which will deal with the origin and growth of the public school system in each commonwealth, the attitude of the people and their leaders toward public education, the administration of state, local, and federal grants and funds, the methods of public school organization, etc. It is planned that the series shall deal principally with the development of elementary and secondary school work with only slight reference to the history of higher schools, which was fairly well covered by the series of monographs written under the supervision of Mr. Herbert B. Adams, of Johns Hopkins university and published some years ago by the bureau of education. The task of working up the new histories has been as-signed to Mr. Stephen Beauregard Weeks of the bureau of education.

In nature and scope the books on Alabama and Arkansas are very much alike. The author first discusses the composition of the population in each state and follows this with a description of ante-bellum school systems, public and private, with some account of the administration of the public lands and public funds, state and federal, which were available for school use; next he discusses the effects of war and reconstruction upon the public schools of each state; and finally, the development and organization of the schools of today.

The author 's studies of the populations of Alabama and Arkansas lead him to the conclusion that each state has possessed a homogenous population drawn from all over the eastern south, with some contributions from the northern states. This homogeneity of population resulted in a rather uniform attitude towards public education which the author describes as the English attitude, but modified by the influence of Princeton university, which sent out so many early educators, and by social and economic conditions within the southern states. Before the civil war he finds that the public school system developed very slowly more slowly in Arkansas than in Alabama. This was due to the following causes: the sparse population; the rather general belief that education was for those who could pay and that free education was but a charity for the indigent; the tendency for the schools to seek church support and control; and the development of strong private schools conducted as a source of income. But nevertheless a public school system controlled by state and local authorities did manage to develop in Alabama before the civil war and there was a beginning of such a system in Arkansas. Education, while not free, was not costly. Public funds were frequently used to subsidize private and denominational institutions and the land was filled with pine log colleges with powers of granting the highest degree.

The civil war and its results ruined the private schools, which either went out of existence or turned themselves into public schools and asked for state aid. Then, too, the problem of educating both races had to be settled and during reconstruction the public school field was the battleground of clashing ideals and policies. From the middle of the seventies to the end of the nineteenth century the history of public school education is a record of slow but sure development. But soon after the beginning of the new century there began a much more rapid progress. Probably the most remarkable thing about the century of educational history of these states, is the shiftless administration by state authorities of the public school funds obtained from federal land grants, such as the "seminary" grants, the "sixteenth section" grants, and in Arkansas, the "saline" land grants. It is probable that public education would have developed more rapidly without the a-id of these large grants. They were valuable gifts made to a population which did not know how to use them. In this respect the history of Arkansas and Alabama is probably paralleled by the history of nearly every other western state.

To the social historian these monographs will be of considerable value for they contain, in easily available form, much information which is now scattered throughout numberless reports and statute books.

32

Review of The Education of the Negro Prior to 1861, by C. G. Woodson

Originally published in the March, 1916 **Mississippi Valley Historical Review.**

The Education of the Negro Prior to 1861, by C. G. Woodson, (New York: G. P. Putnam's Sons, 1915.)

The author of this book exhibits what is coming to be a common phenomenon in historical writing, a combination of modern scientific method with the bias of ancient prejudice. Thinking of slavery makes him angry; and in his anxiety to get a shot at the hateful institution, he falls into a morass of contradictions. The value of the work, however, is not greatly injured by this, for the bias and the flag-waving are confined mainly to sweeping general statements, while the facts discovered are stated fairly and accurately.

The scope of the work is sufficiently comprehensive and the author covers his field well. His aim is to trace the development of education among the negroes from their appearance in America to 1861. He first gives a useful and comprehensive history of the education of the negro during the colonial period, followed by an adequate estimate of the influence of religion and of the "rights of man" philosophy upon negro education. Next come studies of the reactionary influences introduced by the industrial revolution, of the development of cotton production, and of the rise of abolition agitation; and finally a comparison of conditions-North and South.

The triumph of natural feeling over facts is shown in the following quotations: After the industrial revolution the "rich planters not only thought it unwise to educate men thus destined to live on a plane with beasts but considered it more profitable to work a slave to death during seven years and buy another in his stead than to teach and humanize him with a view to increasing his efficiency" (p. 8). "Reduced thus to the plane of beasts, where they remained for generations, negroes developed bad traits which, since their emancipation, have been removed only with great difficulty" (p. 12). "To prevent the slaves from co- operating to rise against their masters, they were often taught to mistreat and malign one another to keep alive a feeling of hatred. The bad traits of the American Negroes resulted then not from an instinct common to the natives of Africa, but from the institutions of the South and from the actual teachings of the slaves to be low and depraved that they might never develop sufficient strength to become a powerful element in society" (p. 200). And as a very proper conclusion we have this hoary proposition: "It was the liberated negroes themselves who during the Reconstruction gave the Southern States their first effective system of public schools" (p. 17).

But frequently there is conflict between feeling and carefully cultivated fairness as to facts which results in contradictory conclusions, such as: The masters did not want their slaves educated because they would then be less easily controlled; they wanted them educated because they were then more valuable and more firmly attached to the master; legislation against the teaching of negroes was designed to reduce them to the level of beasts; this legislation was aimed mainly at trouble-making outsiders, and there was much "winking at the teaching of negroes in defiance of the law and a better day for their education brightened in certain parts of the South about the middle of the nineteenth century." Probably these contradictions result from too frequent attempts to generalize, interpret, and explain laws, statistics, and tendencies of unlike situations and widely separated times.

There are good discussions of the reasons given by the whites for the education of negro slaves: first, it was done for the purpose of making it possible to christianize them; next, under the influence of revolutionary doctrines, they were to be "fitted for citizenship," but later, it was rather to prepare them for colonization abroad; during the reactionary period it was believed that religious instruction only should be given; while a little later it was argued that education increased the value and attachment of the slave.

Much of the incidental discussion is of interest and also of value. It is evident, for example, that until late the views of North and South were on this matter much the same. A large migration of negroes from the South to a northern community always dampened there the ardor of the latter for the education of the negro. Only gradually was the op- position in the North relaxed enough to admit the negroes to public schools. In some places where there was an aristocratic prejudice against public schools, negro parents were found who strongly objected to being forced to send their children to the democratic free schools; they preferred the more aristocratic pay school. North as well as South, it was. the lower industrial class of whites who objected to negro education; and in the North all attempts at industrial training failed because of this opposition.

Most of the work relates to the education of free negroes or of slaves who were later emancipated because only for free negroes are statistics available. But there a-re interesting accounts of how individual slaves secured education. Some were taught by master, mistress, or their children; some by their white fathers; some in schools; and some secretly by one another; a few by the churches which needed negro preachers, or by masters who needed them in business. The many instances mentioned show that it was not difficult for the house slaves to get the beginnings of an education.

It is not difficult to form an estimate of the number of literate free negroes. In 1850 about 345,000 free negroes were reported literate, and in 1860 about 400,000. But during the same period the number of negroes in the South regularly attending school decreased; there were 4,354 in school in 1850 and ten years later there were only 3,651. The tendency was for the educated southern negro to migrate to the North; this was especially true during the period 1850-1860. The author thinks that as late as 1840 there were more educated blacks in the South than in the North.

As to the literate slaves it is impossible to secure definite, statistics. Woodson comes to the conclusion that about ten per cent of all negro adults were able to read. Other authorities have suggested that fifteen to sixteen per cent had some little learning. Therefore the slaves who could read numbered between one per cent and six per cent, not a very definite conclusion. It is certain only that at the end of the civil war there was quite a number of negroes with more or less education even in the South, and probably a larger number in the North. A comprehensive bibliography is appended to the work, and there is throughout evidence that Mr. Woodson has made extensive research. In spite of the defects mentioned above it will never be necessary for any one to do this work again.

33

Indicting a Section

Originally published in the July, 1925 **The Nation.**

The Southern Oligarchy: An Appeal on Behalf of the Silent Masses of Our Country Against the Despotic Rule of the Few. By William H. Skaggs. The Devin-Adair Company.

Mr. Skaggs brings a terrific indictment against his native South. It is ruled by an unenlightened oligarchy; the people are partisan and prejudiced and easily scared by the bugbear of Negro domination; the voters seldom vote; illiteracy makes the people victims of designing demagogues; the South is the land of lynch law, the Ku Klux Klan, and the chain-gang, of hookworm, child labor, and political corruption; it has the most appalling record of crime in the world and "may be called the nursery of crimes in America"; it is economically backward and financially dependent and has a less creditable debt-paying record than Haiti; it even failed in its duty during the World War – in short, it is a menace to the nation.

Now, who is responsible? The oligarchy, or, in other words, the Democratic Party of the South, which because of the failure of re-construction has been "able to perpetuate its power by misleading the people and appealing to sectional prejudice and racial animosities." For the past forty years it has misruled the South, and at times, notably during the Wilson Administration, it has controlled the nation. And "during the Wilson Administration this provincial oligarchy was a greater menace to democratic institutions than the slave oligarchy was under the Buchanan Administration."

Though much of the book is padding a part of it is valuable, notably the discussions of the dormant ballot, the fee system, the chain-gang, and education, and the comparison of wealth and tax-paying in eleven Southern States and eleven Northern States. Yet every discussion is colored by the author's desire to ascribe social and economic shortcomings to political causes for which the Democrats are responsible. Then, too, he relies too much upon quotations of opinion from other writers and from newspapers which he has not assimilated into a coherent account. In places we have only a scrap-book collection of testimony for the prosecution, with the charge not clearly stated. Though Mr. Skaggs may know of serious defects in Southern life and character, he has not shown them up clearly enough. He is not strong in history, economics, or politics, and is therefore a poor interpreter of conditions which he sees but does not fully understand. He is too anxious to tar and feather the Democratic lawyer-politicians. For example, they were guilty of the "gross and stupendous frauds of the Wilson Administration"; the scalawags were the "antecedents of the leading spoilsmen under the Wilson regime"; the greater the hookworm infection the larger the Democratic vote, and so on.

The author was evidently a part of that about which he writes. His book reflects, it would seem, the state of mind of one whose political views trace back from the Republicanism of today through the "Jeffersonian Democracy" and the Populism of the nineties to the conservative democracy of the eighties, perhaps even to Whig connections. If Mr. Skaggs had written of his own experiences and observations the result must have been more interesting and valuable. In the role of an interpreter he is not successful.